TAKING LAND

TAKING LAND

Compulsory Purchase
and Regulation
in Asian-Pacific Countries

EDITED BY
Tsuyoshi Kotaka
AND
David L. Callies

University of Hawai'i Press
Honolulu

Library of Congress Cataloging-in-Publication Data

Taking land : compulsory purchase and regulation in Asian-Pacific countries /
edited by Tsuyoshi Kotaka and David L. Callies.
     p. cm.
  Includes bibliographical references and index.
  ISBN 0–8248–2519–5 (alk. paper)
  1. Eminent domain—Asia.   2. Land use—Law and legislation—Pacific
Area.   3. Eminent domain—Pacific Area.   4. Land use—Law and legislation—Asia.   I. Kotaka, Tsuyoshi.   II. Callies, David L.

KNC 648.T35 2002
343.5′0252—dc21

                             2001046285

University of Hawai'i Press books are printed on acid-free paper and meet the
guidelines of permanence and durability of the Council on Library Resources.

Designed by Bookcomp, Inc.

Printed by The Maple-Vail Book Manufacturing Group

CONTENTS

ACKNOWLEDGMENTS

A comparative study of any subject of necessity depends upon two factors: institutional and financial support, and research and writing. We were blessed from the start with plenty of both. First and foremost, this study would have been impossible without the generous support and encouragement of Osaka's Hanshin Expressway Compensation Center (and in particular Mr. Yoji Shimizu and Mr. Kiyoshi Chubachi), which provided not only generous funding for the project, but also sent representatives on virtually all of the half dozen or so field trips during which the editors and selected scholars conferred with government, academic, and private-sector experts and visited sites. It was Professor Kotaka who persuaded the Center of the usefulness of such a study, which proceeded on the basis of confidence in him and the quality of the study team he could and did assemble. We are both also most grateful for the support of our respective home academic institutions: Meijo University's Faculty of Law and its Dean Shinoda, and the University of Hawai'i's William S. Richardson School of Law and its Dean, Dr. Lawrence A. Foster.

We are equally indebted to our chapter authors, who labored for over a year, researching, writing, and rewriting chapters about often diverse compulsory purchase and land use practices in order to fit the Procrustean Bed of an outline with which we provided them, cutting here and stretching there, so the body of their careful work would fit within the parameters of the comparative study: Dr. Murray J. Raff, Australia; Prof. Zhan Xian Bin, China; Dr. Anton Cooray, Hong Kong; Prof. Tsuyoshi Kotaka, Japan; Prof. Won Woo Suh, Korea; Prof. Grace Xavier, Malaysia; Prof. Glenys Godlovitch, New Zealand; William J. M. Ricquier, Esq., Singapore; Prof. Li-Fu Chen, Taiwan; Prof. Eathipol Srisawaluck, Thailand; and Prof. David L. Callies, United States. Their good-natured response to our redrafting suggestions and their timeliness in submitting their drafts kept this work remarkably close to its original schedule, to the surprise and delight of its editors. We are also indebted to Ms. Heidi Guth, a 2002 graduate of the William S. Richardson School of Law, who labored through all of her second year and part of her third year in law school on this project as our research and editorial assistant. Her previous editorial and writing background saved us both a lot of time and effort in the initial stages of the project and in the tedious proof-reading at its end.

We would also like to thank Professor A. Dan Tarlock, codirector of the environmental law program at Chicago-Kent Law School and coeditor of the *Land Use and Environmental Law Review*, and Professor Eric Damian Kelly, FAICP, past president of the American Planning Association and former dean of the urban planning school, Ball State University, for their review, suggestions and comment upon earlier drafts of our book. It is, as a result, much improved for their wise counsel. Finally, many thanks to Mr. William Hamilton, director, and Ann Ludeman, managing editor, of the University of Hawai'i Press for their unstinting support and guidance throughout this project, and David and Maria denBoer of Bookcomp, Inc., for their superb copy editing, adherence to deadlines, and overall professionalism, all of which made for a better—and more timely—book than the editors could possibly have produced if left to their own devices.

Tsuyoshi Kotaka
David Callies
January 2002

TAKING LAND

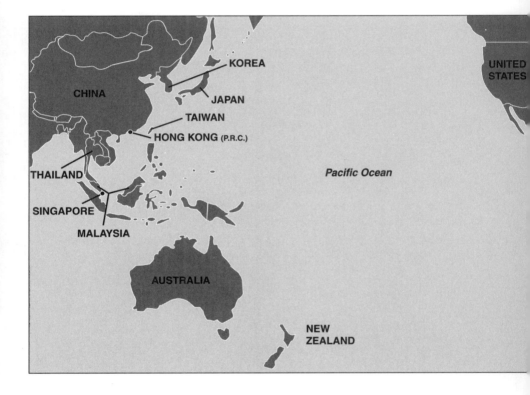

Introduction

Tsuyoshi Kotaka and David L. Callies

The government use of compulsory purchase and land use control powers appears to be rising worldwide as competition for usable and livable space increases. The need for large and relatively undeveloped space for agriculture and conservation purposes often competes with the need for shelter and the commercial and industrial facilities accompanying such development for employment, product production and distribution, and other largely urban uses. The free market does not always—some would say often—result in a logical and equitable distribution of land uses and attendant public facilities necessary to serve the use of land. One function of government is therefore to regulate the use of private land for the health, safety, and welfare of its citizens, and to help provide roads, water, sanitation, schools, parks, airports. Accomplishing the former—regulation—is generally done in accordance with some form or level of plan. Accomplishing the latter often requires the exercise of compulsory purchase powers, providing public land or interests in land in order to construct such public facilities or infrastructure.

The Asia-Pacific region and its rapid urbanization has generated a need for both land use control and use of compulsory purchase powers. The same rapid urbanization and the need for accompanying public facilities has generated areawide interest in the mechanics (rather than the theory) of compulsory purchase and related land use control mechanisms. While there are certain commonalities among the eleven countries that form the basis of our comparative study, there are differences as well, some of them (such as the ratio of public and private land ownership) fundamental. The purpose of our study is to summarize the principal compulsory purchase and land use control systems in the eleven countries that make up the basis of our comparative study, and to attempt to draw some parallels and note some differences among them. However, any comparative study of law and administrative practice is bound to be somewhat general if truly comparative. This study is no exception.

Major Themes

LAND USE CONTROL

Virtually every country studied has some mechanism for the control of private land use, particularly those uses most often associated with urbanization: residential, commercial, industrial, and institutional uses of land. These mechanisms range from the relatively detailed to the relatively broad-brush. What follows is a summary of the major themes that emerge from examining each Asia-Pacific country's concepts of land use and planning.

Ownership of Land

There is some private ownership of land or rights in land in most of the countries studied. In countries like the United States, most developable land, and virtually all land in urban areas, is privately owned. Much the same is true in New Zealand and Australia. However, in a significant number of countries—Malaysia, China, Hong Kong, and Singapore— the state owns virtually all of the land, although in Hong Kong and its administrative region, it is theoretically possible for a citizen to acquire the equivalent of a fee simple interest in government land through adverse possession over a sixty-year period. There is no record of anyone having ever done so, however. This has considerable implications for the regulation of land use. In those states where the state owns most of the land, private development takes place almost exclusively on leased land with the government as lessor. The lease provides an added—sometimes the principal—method of control through lease covenants, often of a sophisticated nature, as in Hong Kong. Indeed, in China the government retains the power to unilaterally modify the terms of the lease, and in Hong Kong, a lessee's increased use of leased land requires the payment of a premium to the government-lessor.

Statutory Framework

The majority of the countries studied provide for land use controls through a national statute that either imposes a minimum level of land use control or sets out a framework for regional and local control, or both. Indeed, only the United States appears to be virtually silent on national land use policy respecting the private use of land, although virtually every state has an enabling act that permits local land use controls through zoning. This, of course, may be due principally to the federal nature of the United States, where most powers of an internal nature reside with the states rather than with the national government, coupled with the country's comparatively large landmass (only China and Australia are comparable in this sense) and historic distrust of land use control in all but urban areas. Japan is a typical example of a country with national legislation that both sets policy and provides minimum standards. Most urban areas are required to undertake a minimum level of land use control. Each is further required to use roughly the same dozen use zones in regulating land use. Most, like Taiwan, further require consistency, more or less top-down, among national, regional, and local land use regulatory schemes, with the national setting broad policy and the local implementing it at the construction and development levels.

Plans and Planning

Virtually every country integrates some sort of land use planning into the control of land use and development. Some, like Japan and Thailand, have national plans. Others, like the United States, have mainly local plans, where there is often only the most rudimentary of plans even at the local level. Others, like Australia, exercise the planning function at the state or regional level. Most countries require conformance with the appropriate level of plan document, and further require the compliance of the next governmental tier down with the plan. Thus, Taiwan's three-tiered planning system begins with the national, flows to the regional, and then to the local, with the higher tier guiding the lower one.

Zoning

In a majority of the countries studied, the implementation of land use controls comes at the local level, through some sort of zoning. Korea, Japan, Taiwan, and Hong Kong make it clear that such zoning must conform to the applicable—usually local—plan or planning document. The same is true with respect to most U.S. states through either court decision or zoning enabling act, although conformance with plans, if any, is often more honored in the breach. Typically, such zoning divides the jurisdiction of a local government into various residential, commercial/business, and industrial zones, sometimes with open space, agricultural, and institutional zones as well. The uses permitted in each zone are found in a local (sometimes guided by national, as in Japan) zoning ordinance, resolution, or rule, together with a process, if any, for changing the zones upon petition of the landowner/lessee/user of a parcel within a particular zone. In some of the countries studied—such as Japan and Korea—the national government imposes a standard set of zoning districts on all local governments. In others—like the United States—the choice of districts remains within the discretion of local governments, which may choose not to zone at all.

Building Regulations

A surprising number of countries—Japan, Korea, Taiwan—regulate buildings as well as land use by means of a national statute. In others—such as the United States—building codes are the most localized of land development controls.

Courts and Common Law

The United States appears to be alone in its reliance on vast numbers of cases in the shaping of the land use regulatory framework, although a few also appear in Australia, Singapore, and Hong Kong. This may be due largely to the common law traditions in these countries, together with the history of private rights to develop land, whether through leasehold or fee simple ownership.

"Regulatory Taking"

In the United States, since 1922 at least, a town planning or land use regulation that goes "too far" may be treated by courts the same as a physical taking or compulsory purchase. Usually to be so treated, the landowner must have been deprived by regulations of all economically beneficial use of the subject parcel of land. Similar "regulatory taking" theories appear in Japan and Korea. In Japan, where a town planning zone designation "takes" all future use and requires cessation of existing uses, the landowner is entitled to compensation. In Korea, a designation that prevents all construction similarly requires landowner compensation.

Indigenous Peoples

The accommodation of indigenous peoples, their rights and traditional practices, often clashes with town planning and land use regulatory schemes that are directed primarily at land development issues. In particular, Australia and New Zealand are dealing with this emerging land use issue.

Colonial Heritage

The land use planning schemes of many countries are rooted in colonial practices imported from outside the country. This sometimes results in an overlay of outside influence over traditional notions of property, particularly if the basic real property law of the country remains rooted in its precolonial history. Australia, New Zealand, Singapore, Korea, and the United States are examples of countries dealing with some of these issues.

Common Problems

Principal among the problems that commonly arise under the various land use planning and control systems is enforcement. The pace of development has been swift in many Asian countries and violation of planning policy and regulation is common, particularly in Thailand and Taiwan. Often there is a concomitant loss of open space and agricultural land to more urban forms of development, as reported in Korea and Thailand. On the surface, there appear to be less enforcement problems in Singapore, Japan, and the United States. Australia has two methods of enforcement: its municipal councils criminally prosecute breaches, and any person can bring a civil case against another. There is also a problem with meaningful public participation in the process reported in Taiwan and Thailand.

EMINENT DOMAIN

Every country in the study claims the right of government to take or reclaim private property. Without such a right, public works of any kind would be extremely difficult to undertake. There is virtually no private landowner defense to such a governmental exercise of compulsory purchase or reclamation, absent some clear evidence of bad faith. The only remedy, as appears below, is compensation, and even this is not necessarily guaranteed. What follows are some general themes that emerged from the study.

Source of Authority

While generally held to be a natural attribute of sovereignty, virtually every country provides some written authority for exercising its compulsory purchase powers, generally phrased as some sort of limitation on that power. The majority of countries provide such articulation/limitation in a constitution, as in the United States, Japan, Taiwan, Malaysia, and Thailand. Australia's federal constitution provides limitations only for federal exercises of the power, and state constitutions are by and large silent. Neither China's nor Singapore's constitution contains compensation provisions, but both countries allow for compensation through individual legislative acts. This makes protection tenuous, however, because those laws can be changed or eliminated at any time, leaving land occupiers no protection from the governments' landholding policies because no clear constitutional protection exists. The process for exercising compulsory purchase powers, however, is almost universally a matter of national or, where relevant, state statutory law.

Public Purpose and the Extent of Power

One would expect the extent of the power of compulsory purchase to depend upon the particular country's view of private rights in land: the more private rights are recognized, the weaker the power of compulsory purchase. Our study does not necessarily validate this presumption. Either by common law (United States) or by statute and practice (Malaysia, China, Australia, Singapore, Korea), most of the countries make broad statements of public purpose as justification for the exercise of compulsory purchase powers. China, and especially Hong Kong, however, where there is virtually no fee simple private ownership of land, have limitations on the power of eminent domain. China limits the taking of interests in land from collectives. Hong Kong sets out specific purposes for which leaseholds may be appropriated, although these are sufficiently broad and numerous that they probably provide very little protection against such compulsory acquisition by government. China views such compulsory purchase as "reacquisition," and Hong Kong calls it "resumption." Australia, on the other hand, finds a need to force citizens to be socially and environmentally responsible, without an even balance being struck with a constitutional protection of private property. The Australian High Court has not decided what is required of the citizen who is sacrificing property for the benefit of the wider community via a particular government program, and to what compensation that citizen is entitled.

Compensation

Virtually every country provides some measure of compensation to the private owner of rights in property for the interests taken by compulsory purchase. Many—as in the United States, Japan, Australia (limited to federal acquisitions), Korea, and Malaysia—require such compensation in their respective constitutions. Others, such as Singapore, provide for it by statute. However, the level and circumstances of compensation vary widely. China and Australia provide compensation largely for raw land value only. Moreover, China provides for compensation on a legislative, case-by-case basis. Thus, for example, one province provided compensation of five or six times the value of the average output for three years for compulsorily taken agricultural land. Many of the countries studied provide for resettlement costs (China, the United States, New Zealand, and Singapore), although the method varies widely. Some of China's provinces, for example, provide for the cost of relocation plus up to one month's lost wages for displaced workers. Others provide little or no compensation in particular circumstances (Singapore, China, Australia), although Australia provides increased compensation up to an additional 10 percent of market value for "solatium": "intangible and non-pecuniary disadvantage resulting from the acquisition."[1] A very few provide for compensation for a so-called regulatory taking as, for example, when a governmental regulation prevents virtually all economically beneficial use of a parcel of land. (See previous discussion under "Regulatory Taking.")

Japan is also one of the few countries to use the idea of "land readjustment," whereby the state returns to the landowner a stake in the "combined project" for which the landowner's land was compulsorily taken. Malaysia and Thailand are considering the concept of exchanging government land for newly appropriated land. Thailand's problems with its backlog of appropriated land and its inefficient methods of appropriating that land may be answered by Japan's system or by that of Taiwan, which appropriates extra land for a project to give to the original home owners in an "offset" manner.

Due Process

Most countries articulate a need for some minimum process that guarantees certain procedural rights to the landowner. Several of the countries set out a broad right of due process in their respective constitutions (the United States, Malaysia, Taiwan, Korea, and Singapore), although in at least one country—Singapore—the courts rendered such a process unnecessary. Some countries require negotiation between landowner and government to precede some or all exercises of eminent domain (the United States, Thailand, and Singapore), and most countries provide for negotiation at some stage of the process. Virtually every country requires notice to the occupier/owner of the land (or interests therein) to be acquired.

Most countries also provide a process for appealing—if not the declaration of public purpose, then at least the process or the compensation award. Most also require at least one public hearing. Some countries provide a specific tribunal for appeals purposes (Hong Kong, New Zealand, and Singapore). Others grant extensive compulsory powers to a "super-agency" that does the bulk of the government "condemnations," as in Singapore and its powerful Urban Redevelopment Authority.

Country Summaries

AUSTRALIA

Australia began planning municipalities in the late 1800s to provide its citizens with residential areas unaffected by industrial smoke or other nuisances. Since the 1920s, many planning schemes began to focus more on environmental conservation and historic preservation. These planning schemes map what is permitted, what requires permission, and what is prohibited in all sections of cities, states, and territories. Murray J. Raff focuses on Victoria, Australia's most urbanized state. He explains that once a state creates its general planning scheme, that scheme is separated into state and local sections. If a municipality wants to vary the scheme based on its unique environmental, cultural heritage, or natural disaster concerns, it must create its own overlays to the plan or condition its planning permits. Rezoning and permission for certain projects in discretionary land use zones require public notice in all cases and environmental impact assessments for major developments. Major planning concerns taken into account at this point include such things as public amenity, pollution protection, environmental conservation, and heritage preservation. An appeals process exists for parties dissatisfied with initial decisions, be they developers or members of the public impacted by proposed development.

The appeals process for compulsory land acquisition is less regimented. The federal constitution requires compensation for land takings, but who gets that compensation and why remains debatable. A recent High Court decision (*Newcrest Mining Ltd. v. Commonwealth of Australia*) found that, for example, a mining company can be compensated for the loss of income for being unable to use cyanide leaching in a fragile environment, but Aborigines cannot obtain compensation from the government for taking that same land for preservation.

While the Australian constitution limits federal land acquisition and requires some compensation, the state constitutions do not. In Australia, Raff explains, state governments view compulsory acquisition as taking back land previously held privately before the grant of a freehold tenure to private citizens. Compensation is therefore generally limited to the owner's market value of the land and loss of its then use, with damages from nearby public projects or changes in the planning scheme only obtainable through nuisance litigation or other torts. Compensation for regulatory "expropriation" is generally unavailable, although the High Court seems to be leaning toward such compensation for total loss of economic use. The government can use private land for "public good" with little difficulty. Public good can include infrastructures such as roads, electrical supply, sewage, and telecommunications, as well as public health, safety, and environmental protection. Takings for these goals can include physical use and loss of title as well as changes in the planning scheme that alter the uses available to a landowner. The public responsibility of the landowner means expropriation may not have occurred.

Raff argues that a balance should be struck between constitutional protection of a private property and the government's need to force citizens to be socially and environmentally responsible. He writes that the High Court must decide what is required of the citizen who is sacrificing property for the benefit of the wider community through a particular government program, and to what compensation that citizen is entitled. The citizen may have a responsibility to society, but that society also has a responsibility to him or her.

CHINA

The Chinese constitution has no system for compensation for compulsory land acquisition. Zhan Xian Bin writes that because the state officially owns all land, and only allows collectives, businesses, and individuals to use it, the government can reclaim its land at any time. China uses specific legislative acts, not the constitution, to calculate damages paid to land users for resettlement and for such individual national projects as building hydroelectric dams or maintaining flood control. While Zhan appears to approve of policy deciding compensation, because laws can be changed and improved, he writes that he is concerned that those laws could be eliminated, leaving the people no protection from the government's land whims because no clear constitutional protection exists.

There are nevertheless some limits to what land government can seize.

For example, land taken from farming collectives, or state-owned land that is having its use changed, must be used for national economic, infrastructure, defense, or social service projects, all of which are defined by the federal government. Also, state land bureaus must approve any government use of, and construction on, the land. The failure of either condition results in the failure of land appropriation.

The government grants payment for resettlement costs and for probable or real loss of use, not for how the land might have been used or for emotional loss. The organization that will use the expropriated land actually pays the compensation. If the present land users must be moved before expropriation, the new users must relocate the old. If the original land users move themselves, the new users must compensate them. Compensation takes the form of cash, bank deposits, or direct replacement of buildings and/or crops. That compensation must be used according to a plan prepared by the original land user and approved by the expropriating organization, with strict disciplinary measures for failure to comply.

Each region sets its rules for compensation use and its standards of compensation for resettlement. Calculation of compensation for land is very specific, and is determined by the use of the land before its expropriation, and by a multiple of the average amount earned by that land over a set number of years. If the land had been used by the state for offices, armed forces, or nonprofit organizations, the state would pay for the material costs of the demolished buildings on the land. If the land is to be used for "special" circumstances, such as for water supply or hydroelectric power plants, different calculations would be used, based on the specific legislation for those land uses. Calculations for the loss of residences are based on the material costs of the buildings, and compensation includes residences in the new location, either via rent money or providing the residence itself.

If land compensation and resettlement payments according to the government equations still fail to put people back at their original level, restitution follows. The national government decides all of the values, and national policy dictates what use of the land is most appropriate and by whom. Zhan argues that this is appropriate because the government owns all the land for the people, and any use of that land is also a use for the people.

China's land use planning appears to revolve around whether land is designated urban, suburban, rural, or mountain. All cities are owned by the state, while collectives (local forms of administrative rule) own the suburban and rural areas unless designated as state-owned. Collectives also own residential districts and mountain reserves. Because the government owns all of China's land, and dictates how that land will be used, the government resolves any land disputes, not the courts. Thus, the government decides the land use and allows citizens the right to fulfill that use.

HONG KONG

Hong Kong is the ultimate landlord, writes Anton Cooray. Hong Kong's government, as landlord and planner for the territory, controls every element of land use through planning ordinances, lease conditions, and building ordinances. While the People's Republic of China officially owns all the land, Hong Kong manages the property according to its long-term plans for density, location, and manner of development. Hong Kong has three population density zones that are maintained through the building regulations and lease conditions, which are created when leases are renewed, modified, or newly granted. These leases, however, are site-specific. Therefore, zoning changes can only be implemented piecemeal and sometimes slowly, because most leases are for seventy-five years.

The building ordinances also follow the zoning plans and are site-specific. These ordinances are for safety and to maintain congruity in an area. The Buildings Ordinance ensures that a building maintains the appearance of a neighborhood, and implements the density controls of the site's zone, as set out in the Town Planning Ordinance. The Building Authority has no control over any change of a building's use but changes to its structure.

Two types of nonstatutory plans and two types of statutory plans set the stage for development in Hong Kong. The nonstatutory plans set out standards and guidelines on such topics as the environment and residential densities, and create medium- and long-term planning strategies for Hong Kong's five subregions. These broad plans provide the platform for the more local statutory development plans. The Town Planning Ordinance allows the planning board to permit certain uses within zone-based development plans beyond those specified uses as of right.

The board reviews contested decisions made by one of the board's two planning committees. Any further review goes to the Town Planning Appeal Board, whose decision is final, unless a judicial review is approved. Like the original plans, these decisions do not include public input or hearings; they are matters only for the developer and the appropriate committee. Permission comes after consideration of a detailed master layout plan and with conditions, such as that permission will lapse unless the project begins within three years. For violations of a development plan, the director of planning has three methods of enforcement: issuing a notice requiring the development be made to conform, the development be stopped, or the land be reinstated to its original use. Not all development goes before the planning committees, however. If the land is not part of a statutory development plan, the developer must only meet the requirements of the applicable building ordinances and lease conditions.

The government rarely exercises compulsory acquisition. It does, however, occasionally reclaim leased land before the lease expires, for breach of lease (no compensation), or for public purpose (with compensation) often including that option in the lease. The Lands Resumption Ordinance also allows takings if the property has become a health hazard, is needed for national defense, or is needed for any other "public purpose." At least one month's public notice is required, and during that time either the land's owner or an interest holder may agree to a voluntary sale. With such an agreement, the resumption procedure ends, and the transaction becomes a sale. Otherwise, the land still reverts to the government at the end of the notice period. Within twenty-eight days, the government must begin the compensation procedure. Compensation is paid on the value of the land (determined by the amount of time left on the lease), the value of any legally built construction on the property, and the costs of disrupting the owners' and the neighbors' livelihoods. These amounts, which usually relate to the amount expected if the property were offered on the open market, can be appealed to the Lands Tribunal, but the "resumption" itself cannot. The land user can also appeal compensation amounts for takings of easements or parts of his or her land for roads, railways, and airport height restrictions, as well as partial takings through changed ordinances. Compensation for property affected by conservation areas or by changes in land value because of new zoning is rare, however. Thus, although the Basic Law of Hong Kong requires compensation only at market value, the author notes that the government has learned that to speed up the acquisition of land, it should pay higher compensation than legally required.

JAPAN

Japan has a multitiered system of land planning, from the national to the municipal, based on public safety and even distribution of industry and residential zones, while preserving set percentages of historic and natural areas. The national plan includes such considerations as use of natural resources, protection from natural disasters, locations and sizes of urban and suburban areas, industry locales, and projections of electrical needs for metropolitan areas. Tsuyoshi Kotaka writes that because of the rise of land values in Japan, the country enacted the Land Fundamental Law in 1989, declaring, through policy objectives, the country's vision of organized development while preserving public welfare on multiple levels.

Public welfare also controls the expropriation of private land, which is limited by the constitution. Most land expropriation includes a negotiation among the project initiator, the landowner, and any other concerned parties, even when it is the type of project listed under the Land Expropriation Law. If the project planner thinks negotiation will be difficult, he or she can ask for "recognition" of the project by the Minister of Land, Infrastructure, and Transport, who then sets the extent of land needed, how it will impact the public and the environment, the exact list of interested parties, and how much compensation the owner deserves. The recognition process may require less diplomacy, but it is time-consuming and "bureaucratic." The project initiator, the landowner, and any interested parties also must sign the record of land and articles.

National guidelines decide the compensation required by Japan's constitution for the public taking of both private and public property. Complete physical loss of private property receives full economic compensation, via market value, but nothing for potential economic, subjective, emotional, historical, or cultural value. If any party is dissatisfied with the appropriation of the land or the amount offered in compensation, that person may request an investigation by the minister of construction or file a lawsuit. If a public facility is appropriated, the project initiator must replace it elsewhere, not just pay replacement value. For example, a recent decision by the Sapporo District Court held illegal the government's taking process for the construction of a dam owing to the failure to adequately consider the cultural interests of indigenous Ainu property owners.

Some regulations also lower the value of property by limiting its uses. For example, a regulation that limits the use or lowers the value of a parcel to prevent disasters does not require compensation because such a regulation has more value in public safety and welfare. Seen as forms of public welfare, zoning and regulations for public works, maintenance, and safety also do not require just compensation. If the regulation is to protect historical, natural, or cultural sites, however, that kind of regulatory taking requires compensation. Compensation is paid for the value of the lost use of the land if an actual loss in property can be proved. The Land Expropriation Law was amended in 2001.

KOREA

The South Korean constitution guarantees the property rights of all citizens, including just compensation for compulsory acquisition. Won Woo Suh explains that strict land use planning acts, such as the Urban Planning Act (UPA) and the Building Act, limit constitutional rights of property ownership, particularly concerning construction. If these restrictions require specific sacrifices of owners, beyond accepted zoning prohibitions, the government may owe compensation, but that is rare. Suh writes that with Korea's small landmass, general limitations on construction are widely accepted.

Orderly urban growth controls most Korean planning decisions, with both safety and aesthetics playing a role. For Korea's system of specific use areas, planners consider the shape and quality of the land to find its best purpose, and then prevent any contradictory uses. After dividing the land into urban and nonurban areas, the government further divides the land into four nonintegrated categories: residential, commercial, industrial, and green.

Suh finds this system to be outdated, and argues that urban and nonurban zones should be integrated for better equality of land value. Each urban area has zoning restrictions on the types, sizes, and locations of buildings and their functions. The regulations governing land use in each area determine the respective landowners' rights. A landowner will not be compensated for lack of ability to use his or her land in a manner that the regulations prohibit.

The "zone system" determines those development regulations. Zoning attempts to evenly spread population, services, and facilities—including agriculture, parks, and green belts—through four zones: Urbanization Control, Detailed Planning, Metropolitan Planning, and Development Restriction (green belt). Once determined, the UPA provides the specific regulations for the zones. Administrative actions that change one's land designation may be considered a taking that requires compensation.

Whether such restrictions should be compensated is being debated now, because only a "restriction of private property for public necessity" warrants compensation under the constitution. Interpretations of that phrase vary. If, for example, one owns property that is later rezoned, scholars believe that the owner makes a special sacrifice and is owed compensation, while the government views a rezoning as the constant creation of the expected social boundaries and limitations of landowner- ship, which do not require compensation. Under consideration now is the request of people living in the Development Restricted Zone (DRZ) (2.2 percent of the national population) for compensation through elim- ination of the zone because of the low economic value of their property and an arguable lack of "public necessity" of that type of zone. Another debate revolves around how much compensation for rezoning is needed. According to the Constitutional Court, compensation for rezoning by designation of a DRZ is based on the immediate change of value, not on projected earnings on the land as it was zoned before. The value dif- ferential is substantial, especially because the court found compensation necessary only for a building site.

Another difference is that between the compensation given to those who accept the government's offer through consultation and those who adjudicate. When the government wants to physically appropriate pri- vate land, the agency involved must both publicly and directly notify local authorities, the landowner, the project contractor, and other con- cerned parties. Upon surveying the land and structures, an offer is made to the owner. Usually the offer is much lower than that which could be obtained through adjudication by a land commission. This is an added concern because the number of acquisitions rose from ninety-six in 1980 to 2,010 in 1991, due in part to strong economic development and a resultant increased number of public projects. The landowners can agree through consultation with the government or appeal the land's appro- priation, its proposed use, the length of that use, and the amount of compensation, unless the property is needed for temporary emergency public safety requirements after natural disasters or other major accidents. The latter type of land appropriation cannot exceed six months.

MALAYSIA

While the Malaysian constitution protects a person's right to own prop- erty, that right is not absolute, according to Grace Xavier. All land is vested in the state, and the state allows citizens to own the land subject to the state's needs. In this regard, only the state is empowered to dispose of state land. The government can impose categories of land use on land's title, make conditions and restrictions on interest in the land, and reacquire any land ostensibly needed for the country's economic development, public need, or recreational purposes. The government determines the land use (agricultural, building, or industrial) when someone buys or leases the land, assuring that the use conforms to long-term development plans. The use is documented on the register document of title. Aside from allowing the owner to make a living from and enjoy her or his land, only lawful use and reasonable enjoyment is permitted.

For the taking of private land, the Land Acquisition Act of 1960 requires due process for government appropriation. Government appropriation is considered valid for any public or recreational purpose, or to improve the economic status of Malaysia, all of which are hard to disprove. However, the landowner is entitled to a hearing during which the owner may object to the amount of the award or attempt to show mala fides on the part of the state. The government rarely loses these cases, but occasionally faces difficulties with the initial application process to acquire the land. The specific government agency must prove that the purpose of the compulsory land taking is in the public interest or for the economic development of the state, and that the taking is feasible. A new amendment to the Land Acquisition Act of 1991, however, implies that whether or not the government uses the appropriated land as proposed, the appropriation will remain valid. Only if the appropriation is not completed within two years of being "gazetted" (officially advertised) will a legal technicality nullify the acquisition proceeding and return ownership of the parcel to the private landowner.

Compensation for government appropriations is based on the owner's present and future possible uses (if they are not too remote) for the land in existing planning zones. Prices on similar tracts of land in the area help determine the amount of compensation, and compensation is available only for buildings on the land that meet regulation codes. No law regulates the specifics of compensation amount, but the guiding principle is to put the claimant back into an economic position equivalent to that before the land was taken. The First Schedule of the Act explains compensation computation by finding the market value of the land; any value increase or decrease because of the anticipated, new use; and what elements are to be ignored. The landowner or other interested party can contest the award amount, but only if the amount exceeds RM 15,000 and only before accepting the money or within a certain time limit. The burden is on the owner to prove that the amount offered is inadequate. A judge and two land assessors hear the case, and their judgment is final.

The method of compensation in Malaysia may be changing. Instead of paying the landowner for appropriated property, the government is considering a system of land exchange within the same area. This method may increase the landowner's sense of participation, but it has yet to be implemented.

Xavier questions where the rights of the landowner begin and the rights of the citizen as "nation builder" end. Most anything can be seen to be prescriptive of national economic improvement, which is all that legislation requires of a land acquisition, but the constitution states a right to private property. Xavier argues that the latter is more important.

NEW ZEALAND

A requiring authority—through direct negotiations between the government and the owner, statutes, compulsory requirements for public works, or an Environment Court order—may appropriate land in New Zealand. The defining legislative acts follow the principles of sustainable management and regulate takings and compensation for public works. If a requiring authority needs the land for a public works or utility, the land can be "designated." This means that once the requiring authority proves its need and the legality of a land taking, through a public notice and hearing process, the then-designated land can be taken despite objections, so long as its planned use legally fits the area's development plans. Glenys Godlovitch writes that the irrelevance of the landowner's consent and level of compensation makes land acquisition less complicated. The designated land must be acquired for its stated purpose within five years, or the designation lapses. Any interested person can seek a "resource consent" from someone in control of the land. The resource consent lasts only two years.

New Zealand does not consider compulsory land acquisition as an infringement on property rights, but more as a need to provide adequate compensation. Compensation entails economic replacement for the land on the basis of fair market value and planned use, as well as resettlement costs together with a small amount for loss of enjoyment. The government also pays compensation to affected holders of future estates, neighbors, and tenants. Objections about the proposed taking go before the Environment Court, but the court does not decide compensation amounts.

If the Environment Court reverses compulsory acquisition, barring appeals to the High Court, the land must be offered for resale to its original owner, if practicable. Otherwise, the land may be offered for sale to adjoining landowners or to the public. By default, it also could be labeled "Crown land," something the indigenous Maori continue to fight.

SINGAPORE

William Ricquier is proud of Singapore's strict planning and resultant aesthetic and functional properties. Singapore's State Lands Act regulates all state land in the nation, and sets out four methods of alienating land from the state to private owners. Two of these methods (the estate in perpetuity and the lease) are subject to state conditions and covenants, and the leases cannot exceed ninety-nine years. The government can change the conditions and covenants at any time, and the land grantee or lessee is bound by the changes, with or without notice. One method, the fee simple, does not include these conditions, but it is very rare for the state to alienate land in fee simple. The other method, the temporary occupation license, is governed by the State Lands Rules.

The Planning Act defines all legal rules of planning in Singapore. The Planning Act includes the "Master Plan," which is reviewed every five years. It is the framework for zoning under which the Urban Redevelopment Authority (URA) and private developers work. Public works and urban planning authorities can submit proposals for changing their area's master plan at any time. The Planning Act also contains development and subdivision plans. A landowner cannot subdivide or develop his or her property in any way that changes the outer appearance of buildings or land without getting permission from the authorities, who look to the master plan. Permission for any changes also requires a development charge, which is a percentage of the estimated appreciation in the land's value after the development is complete. Noncompliance at any level is a criminal offense.

One way that Singapore has been able to retain control over its growth is through the compulsory purchase of land, Ricquier writes. As of 1975, the state owned about 65 percent of the nation's land, compared to 49 percent in 1969, and the trend toward increasing state ownership seems to be continuing. Much of the planning work of the past thirty years has been accomplished by the URA, which is responsible for accumulating land, planning future growth and resettlement of those whose land the government takes, preserving history, and maintaining property acquired for future plans. The URA may also declare an area to be an urban development area, thus setting in motion the government's acquisition of the area within three years. Other public agencies can also appropriate private land if they can prove the land is needed for their functions, such as for roads and other public infrastructure or facilities. While the Land Acquisition Act requires the government to first attempt private negotiation for land, the courts have ruled that negotiation is too much of a burden. To speed along acquisitions, the government often resorts to compulsory purchase.

Singapore amended its constitution to eliminate a guarantee of adequate compensation for all compulsorily taken property. Now, the Land Acquisition Act governs compensation. This compensation includes the property's present market value, damage to land still owned by the private party, resettlement expenses for home or business, and title fees. The Land Acquisition Act provides that property to be taken requires public notice and printing in a gazette. Such "gazetting" is considered sufficient evidence that the property is required by the government. The printing in the gazette also sets the date of acquisition by the government. When the need for the property is particularly urgent, the government can take the land prior to public notice, if the notice is published within a week of taking possession. Only "interested parties" (does not include tenants) can apply for compensation, which has no set procedure for allocation or amount. If a party disagrees with the amount offered, that person must object immediately or lose the chance of an appeal. The Appeals Board decides on the amount or existence of the payment, or, if the amount is accepted, the collector takes possession of the property upon payment.

Ricquier writes that while the regularity and ease of compulsory purchase are beneficial, the level of compensation has been a cause for concern. In accordance with the formula set out in the Land Acquisition Act, the date on which the property is acquired determines the rate at which the property will be assessed. The market value is based on retrospective values and the lowest of possible uses, either that for which the landowner used the land or that for which the government plans to use it. Improvements made to the land two years prior to government acquisition are not taken into account, nor, among eight other factors, are the urgency of its acquisition or the injury caused to the landowner by the land's taking.

TAIWAN

Taiwan's three-tiered planning begins with the national, flows to the regional, and then moves to the local, with the higher tier guiding the lower one. The national plan sets the policies for the country and standardizes the ideas for regional plans, which focus on development and natural resource preservation. The national plan, unlike the regional plans, lacks legal stature. The local plans split between regulating land use within urban and nonurban areas. The urban area is divided into several zones to which use and development must conform, or the landowner will be subjected to fines and orders to remove, change, or stop using the building or land. Every five years, the governmental authority reviews the zones: residential, commercial, industrial, agricultural, conservation, administration, culture and education, scenic, and specified-use zones. However, despite the enforcement mechanisms for these zoning controls, Li-Fu Chen writes that land use violations are evident everywhere, due apparently to the nonbinding status of the national plan, and the lack of serious enforcement efforts by the responsible government authority.

The public has little chance to comment on any of the processes of land use planning. Aside from a thirty-day comment period on creating urban land use zones, landowners have no opportunity to present their opinions. For example, if land is zoned nonurban, landowners can neither complain nor seek compensation. Instead, the landowners must donate their land and money to the government to establish the nondevelopable land for environmental protection.

While Taiwan's constitution provides for property rights, it says nothing about expropriation. The Land Expropriation Act of 2000 fills that gap with the requirements and methods of compulsory acquisition. Such takings are grouped into general land, political, and zoning expropriations. General land takings are for specific public needs, such as national defense, infrastructure, environmental protection, government facilities, public education, and "others." The only qualification for these public needs, according to Li-Fu Chen, is that government or a government-assigned entity must operate them. Political land expropriation enables the state to ban private ownership of certain land, like that within a certain distance from the coast, or that which is beyond the maximum amount allowed to one owner. (This is in the law, but has never been practiced.) Lastly, government can acquire land in a specified zone, in whole or in part, for planned development or improvements.

The purpose for acquisition is almost always approved, with little to no public comment. Unless the land is needed for an emergency, defense, transportation, water conservation, sanitation, or protection of the environment, the agency must first attempt to negotiate directly with the landowner. Only if negotiations fail will the land be expropriated. Once public announcement of the appropriation is made, the landowner can make no changes to the land for thirty days. The negotiation can include relocation of any improvements found on the land and reimbursement for improvements that cannot be moved. Price is determined by the latest official land price set by the local government together with replacement costs for any improvements. The government land prices relied upon for compensation often are below market prices; in fact, public officials can be punished criminally for offering more than the official prices. Indeed, the Land Expropriation Act does not require market rates, and the government rates are set every July 1. Within fifteen days after the expiration of the announcement, the promoter of the new development must pay the compensation. If payment is not made, the appropriation is invalidated, unless the lack of payment is because the landowner refuses to accept the payment, in which case the money will be deposited anyway, and the compensation will still be treated as received. Objections by neighbors and the landowner as to the appropriation or the compensation amount will be heard and are allowed on appeal.

In the case of zone appropriation, maps must be filed for approval with the Ministry of the Interior, and affected landowners can comment within thirty days. If landowners prefer, they can apply for a percentage of offset land instead of full cash for compensation. Available offset land is defined by whatever is left over after the development is complete, and should be at least 40 percent of the appropriated land. After the offset land has been allocated, the rest of the unused land is designated for such public facilities as roads, parks, and schools. Any remaining land can be sold.

Li-Fu Chen finds that while so many types of legal land acquisition may make public undertakings simple, Taiwan relies heavily on the process without consistently protecting the right to private property. For example, in 1997, Taiwan expropriated 2,275 hectacres, and in 1999, the government expropriated 5,893 hectacres. Proving need is easy for the state, and constitutional protection has become secondary at best. Other national acts uphold the constitution, but are seemingly ignored. When the federal government is looking for land to appropriate, landowners, local government agencies, and other affected landowners get little to no chance to speak. As a result, until recently, almost all land appropriation applications have been approved. Li-Fu Chen suggests making the Land Law more specific so that the government must prove serious need for land takings, and creating more opportunities for negotiation between the government and landowners so that expropriation is not the only and easiest answer.

THAILAND

Thailand has divided its land use planning into multiple levels, beginning with a five-year national economic and social development plan. The National Economic and Social Development Plan determines the national framework by providing guidelines for land use planning at the regional, provincial, and district levels, as well as for town plans. Therefore, all of the regional, provincial, district, and town plans are to some extent consistent with one another. Thailand's rapidly expanding population undermines its series of specific planning laws, especially conservation ones, which are not strictly enforced. While the Town Planning Act of 1975 was to control urban land use through zoning, it has not been effective even though it has been amended twice, writes Eathipol Srisawaluck. People buying agriculturally zoned land have converted it to nonagricultural uses to make it more profitable, with no repercussions. Agricultural land takes precedence over forests, urban centers continue to grow, and the pressures for land increase.

The 1997 constitution of Thailand includes rights to private property and to compensation for conditional land acquisition. The constitution gives the government the right to compulsory acquisition, but only if a specific law allows acquisition for a specific use. Acquisition must be for the public good, and compensation must be fair and paid within a reasonable period of time.

Several specific laws allow for the acquisition of property. The Immovable Property Acquisition Act of 1987 allows the state to expropriate real estate property, and other legislation specifically allows for acquisition of property for such things as airports, railways, highways, and industry. Agencies follow a series of steps toward acquisition, from requesting that the property be donated, to negotiation for sale, to issuing a royal decree or announcing the Immovable Property Act to cover that specific piece of property. Compensation then entails the government's valuation of the land and its assets, damage to properties, demolition costs of any immovable properties, labor and material costs, inconvenience, and a computation of the value of the land prior to acquisition versus prospective value. Negotiation ensues, with appeals available.

Because of rising competition for land, negotiations often break down, which can cause endless delays, because the executing agency can only take over the property when the compensation has been completely paid. Srisawaluck takes issue with the lack of efficiency of the appropriation process, citing public protests, obstructions to government projects, and lack of compensation equations. The lack of formulaic methods also means that many experience long delays in receiving their compensation, making landowners less likely to cooperate and extending the appeals process. Because it takes so long to acquire the amount of needed land, public works projects often take twenty years to complete, letting some appropriated land lie unused the entire time. Thailand, like Malaysia, is considering trying the concept of land readjustment, as done in Japan, but whether that will help the efficiency problem and land utilization backlog remains to be seen. Srisawaluck recommends a ceiling for the amount of private landholdings, or increased taxes that would discourage large private ownership and make for more equitable and efficient land management.

UNITED STATES

Land use controls in the United States are generally exercised at the local government level. David Callies writes that the most effective of these controls is zoning, which is used by local governments to divide regions into use districts. Statutes permit local governments to divide their jurisdictions into zones with permitted uses and restrictions. Another local land use method that has gained popularity is the subdivision process, which requires an area of land to be completely platted and those plats to be approved before lots can be sold to individuals, who will develop their lot according to the approved plat. Subdivisions must include plans for their own infrastructures and public facilities, as well as dedicating open spaces and public buildings, thus managing local growth and expenditures. In the same vein, developers must often pay impact fees to the community that provides the subdivision with such public facilities as sewers and roads, both on- and off-site, but only if the improvements are required because of the subdivision. Building (prospective) and housing (retroactive) codes list minimum standards for the health, safety, and welfare of the public.

Some states have reclaimed their land use control through regional or statewide zoning and planning. Often this is to protect a resource and to control developments that impact an entire region. Also, the federal government has overriding statutes and implementing regulations for clean air and water, for managing coastal zones, and for protecting known flood

zones. Regulations that leave a landowner without economically beneficial use require compensation as if the land were compulsorily purchased.
Regulations that deprive a landowner of some, but not all economic
use, *may* require compensation, depending upon such factors as the
investment-backed expectations of the landowner and the character of
the governmental action.

As with land use controls, local, state, and federal governments all
have the power to acquire land by compulsory purchase. The United
States constitution limits this ability, however, by requiring that such a
taking must be for a public use, and the private owner must be justly compensated. Compensation is generally calculated for the value of the land
and its present improvements (or the loss of value, depending upon the
kind of taking involved) at the time of the confiscation, with no consideration given to the future worth of the property after its confiscated use.
Various local government authorities have the right to condemn private
land for such things as housing, airports, convention centers, and other
public purpose projects. Public utility corporations may also acquire land
through compulsory purchase because of their quasi-public functions. To
allow for taking immediate possession and use of a condemned property,
quick-take provisions often require the condemner to pay a deposit of
sorts with the court, which then orders surrender of the property.

A non-negotiable condemnation action usually begins with an agency
filing a complaint in court. The complaint must include the government's
plans for the land and a specific mapping of it. The court summons all
interested parties to decide on a fair price and to verify that the government will use the land as claimed.

Most federal agencies try to negotiate with landowners during the
process of compulsory purchase. The property is appraised, with the
owner able to comment on various values that may not be readily apparent. The sales records of comparable properties are checked; replacement
costs, loss of business, and the fate of tenants are all considered in the
compensation process. Often not considered are such things as business
goodwill, loss of future business, frustration of plans, and costs of removing buildings or fixtures, unless specifically provided in the statute. Once
an offer is made, the owner can agree, or condemnation proceedings may
begin in court.

Not only must the landowner be fairly compensated for the highest
and best use of the land, but he or she must also be given "due process":
fair notice of the government's intent to acquire the property and a day
in court if he or she so desires. In California, for example, if a landowner

can prove that the particular agency does not possess appropriate compulsory purchase power, that the proposed use will not be public, that the property will be used for a different purpose, that the property will not be used within a set amount of time, that the property is not subject to compulsory purchase for that purpose, or any other ground provided by law, the landowner can keep her or his land. The government must also be careful not to take more land than it needs, and to avoid so publicizing its eventual condemnation that it lowers the value of the to-be-condemned land. Sometimes the government can prove the necessity for excess condemnation, but if it ever abandons the use for which the land was initially condemned, statutes often require that property to be resold to the original condemnee.

Note

1. See Australia Land Acquisition and Compensation Act, §44.

Chapter 1

Planning Law and Compulsory Acquisition in Australia

MURRAY J. RAFF

The Australian continent was settled as a group of six colonies of the British Empire, commencing with New South Wales in 1788. Tasmania, Victoria, Queensland, South Australia, and Western Australia followed.[1] These colonies federated to form the Commonwealth of Australia in 1901,[2] and in 1942 Australia gained unquestioned sovereignty to legislate over her own affairs regardless of British law.[3] Through this colonial history Australia acquired a common law system in the English style. Accordingly, the basic background juristic principles are to be found in statements about the law that judges have made when deciding cases in the past. In addition to the former colonies, which are now states within the federation, Australia has two semiautonomous federal territories: the Australian Capital Territory, where the national capital city, Canberra, is located; and the Northern Territory.[4]

With respect to broader issues in resource management, such as mining, forestry, and heritage protection, the Commonwealth government has played a significant role over the past fifty years through exercise of its specific constitutional powers over such issues as trade and commerce with other countries,[5] external affairs, and corporations.[6] However, constitutional authority over land use planning in this federal system of government has generally been asserted by the state governments, joined in later times in this role by the territories. Local municipal government has played a very significant role in the day-to-day operation of the state and territory land use planning systems, with respect to development and implementation of individual planning schemes, as well as the grant of

---

Senior Lecturer, Law School, Victoria University.

planning permission in accordance with them. Thus, if one set out to describe land use planning in Australia exhaustively, one would have to consider complex legislative structures in each of the nine Australian jurisdictions. From a broader perspective, however, the various land use planning systems in Australia were inspired by similar historical movements and have more in common than in contrast. I shall therefore concentrate on the land use planning system in the state of Victoria, which is Australia's most industrialized and closely settled area, and deal with the other jurisdictions by cross-reference.

Land use planning is an institutionalization of forethought, a precautionary approach to dealing with the problems of the present while creating favorable conditions for the future, with established procedures for ascertaining future environmental impacts and drawing this information into the decision-making process. This orientation to the future that we observe in planning is viewed uncomfortably, however, from the viewpoint of conventional judicial decision making in the common law tradition, which is primarily concerned with the identification of relationships and liabilities in a past situation or event—the ramifications of which have ceased for legal purposes—and then quantifying any damage for the purpose of compensation. This backward-facing, or historically oriented, approach of the conventional judicial style is deeply embedded in a common law system, in which the applicable principles of law are molded from past court decisions. Even in fast-moving fields like planning law and environmental law, with their many connections to rapidly expanding scientific and engineering fields, the patchwork of distant historical sources from which the common law judge formulates the applicable law is still drawn from times when the human ability to destroy the environment was not so powerful and the need to find effective legal protection for the future was not so urgent.

For these methodological reasons the derivation of legal norms for the present from the ancient principles of the English common law hinders the implementation of "ecologically sustainable development" (ESD) principles in land use planning. One basic principle attributed to English property law is that one is fundamentally entitled to do whatever one likes with what one owns.[7] In the Australian common law systems, the provisions of land use planning law are interpreted to conform with basic principles of common law unless a departure has clearly been intended. Therefore, if there is any ambiguity in the law, or the planning scheme, the property owner has the benefit of the doubt. This might sound fine in abstract, but one of the great skills of a lawyer, at least in the common law tradition, is to construe legislation so far as possible in the interests of his or her client, so rendering law merely ambiguous is generally no great challenge. When this occurs, the common law presumption that one may do whatever one wishes with one's land without social responsibility takes over, and even the best forward-thinking land use plans can be "unpicked" case by case. A study of Melbourne's past planning schemes in comparison with aerial photographs has shown that this case-by-case unpicking of the plans in favor of commercially profitable low-density urban development, consuming prime fertile agricultural land and supplanting other green belt uses, has severely frustrated the realization of land use plans for Melbourne's outer suburbs and programs to consolidate urban density.[8] I have argued that there is legal material in the history of the common law from which a principle of social and environmental responsibility could be developed to contextualize the rights of property owners within the actual environmental capacity of the land in question.[9] Further, specifically with respect to land, a concept of property with immanent responsibilities was introduced with the Torrens land title registration system, which was inspired by the system operating in Hamburg in the 1840s,[10] when it superseded common law deeds conveyancing.

Also forming part of the common law background to land use planning are two fields of property law that were developed mainly through court decisions in the nineteenth century. These are the principles of restrictive covenants, which are private agreements between landowners that restrict the uses to which relevant land may be put; and the law of easements, which are rights over areas of private land granted by the owner of it to the benefit of other land for purposes such as gaining access with vehicles, pipes, or cables.[11] With land title registration systems now in place with respect to private landownership all over Australia, it is generally necessary for the existence of covenants and easements to be noted on the certificate of title of the land burdened by it. In Victoria we have legislation[12] that subjects private restrictive covenants and easements to land use planning schemes, allowing these obligations to be released through an amendment of the relevant planning scheme. However, anyone who legally benefits from such obligations effectively has a veto power over public changes to them.

The Land Use Planning System and Planning Schemes

The dynamic relationship between international developments and domestic planning law is often overlooked. Past experience in Victoria has suggested that local planning solutions to local environmental problems often lead to corresponding international measures. International measures both reinforce and are implemented by a local land use planning system that facilitates public input in its decision making. This is not surprising, when we recall that many of the principles in the *Stockholm Declaration*[13] directed at the increasingly obvious and hazardous degradation of the environment, and the rapid depletion of the world's resources, contrary to the interests of future generations,[14] were to be implemented through planning. The emphasis on planning is most obvious in Principles 13, 14, and 15. For example, Principle 14 provides that "rational planning constitutes an essential tool for reconciling any conflict between the needs of development and the need to protect and improve the environment."

The strong confidence among the nations of the world that environmental problems could be averted through planning was clear. This proved insufficient, and perhaps naive, but the rapid expansion of environmental law in the ensuing period did not signal the abandonment of forward planning. Rather, it saw the development of additional measures and new institutions of forward thinking for the preservation and restoration of environmental qualities that were not necessarily envisaged at Stockholm. Thus, the importance of planning was again confirmed at the World Summit held in Rio de Janeiro in 1992. In contrast to the more abstract statements of the *Stockholm Declaration,* the *Rio Declaration,*[15] particularly *Agenda 21,* provided more detailed goals and strategies for development. The extensive details of *Agenda 21* embraced issues in planning[16] that ranged from environmentally appropriate transport systems to the participation of indigenous people in the planning process.

The most important theme of the *Rio Declaration* and *Agenda 21* was the confirmation and expansion of the concept of "sustainable development," development satisfying the needs of the present without prejudicing the ability of future generations to satisfy their own needs, which had been developed in the *Brundtland Report.*[17] In Australia, a concept of ESD was adopted in an accord between all of the states and the federal government.[18] It set out the following principles, which are implicit in the concept of ESD:

- intergenerational equity—development must not claim finite resources in a way that is unfair to future generations;
- precautionary principle—when faced with uncertainty about the

effects that a development will have on the environment, decision makers should be cautious, at least until they have reliable information with which to make a realistic assessment of the risks;[19]

- biological diversity and ecological integrity—the number of diverse species in the world must be maintained, and an ecological approach is required to preserve them in their habitats; and
- environmentally sensitive methods of valuation and costing are to be adopted.

Environmental impact assessment—the public study of the anticipated environmental impacts of a project undertaken before a decision is made to proceed with it—is regarded internationally as a key procedure to ensure the achievement of ESD in practice.[20]

All of these principles and approaches are relevant to land use planning. In Victoria, planning schemes are made pursuant to powers in the Planning and Environment Act of 1987.[21] The emergence of this legislation illustrates the dynamic relationship between international developments and domestic planning law referred to above.

Powers to designate land use restrictions for identified areas of urban land were first granted to local municipal councils in Victoria in the 1920s. As in other parts of Australia, this initiative was largely inspired by the British Garden City Movement and the Town and Country Planning Movement that followed it. The most important and most consistently held aim of the nineteenth-century pioneers of public town planning was to plan for an improved urban environment, by spatially defining areas where the advantages of city life could be enjoyed without the urban disadvantages of interferences such as smoke.[22] The underlying objective was thus public health and an aesthetic contentedness, and ultimately a "safety of property" that was broadly conceived.[23] A parallel intention was to guarantee minimum land parcel sizes and building standards, which private restrictive covenants had failed to achieve. Almost a decade passed before the Supreme Court of Victoria recognized the value of land use planning and the number of successful challenges to municipal plans decreased. In the 1940s and 1950s, a Modernist phase saw the centralization of land use planning and the perception of it as a technocratic exercise for experts. The views of private citizens, and even municipal councils, were almost excluded from the system. A period of planning oriented to "development steering" ensued in the 1960s and 1970s.

In 1987, the Planning and Environment Act passed into law, heralding a phase of community planning that recognized a stronger role for citizens' engagement in planning their common civic future. Anticipating developments that would take place at the international level five years later, the objectives of planning set out in section 4 of the Act relate to the concept of sustainable development. They include:

- protection of natural and man-made resources and the maintenance of ecological processes and genetic diversity;
- conservation and enhancement of buildings, areas, and other places of scientific, aesthetic, architectural, or historical interest or other cultural value;
- balancing the present and future interests of all Victorians; and
- ensuring that the effects of projects on the environment are considered.

The Structure of Australian Land Use Planning Systems

To start at the simplest level, planning schemes in Australia generally comprise

1. a set of maps of the relevant locality, with different areas of land (zones) designated by symbols for different purposes; and
2. a text or "ordinance" that links the symbolic designators on the maps with detailed prescriptions about activities and developments that may or may not be pursued on land parcels in the respective zones, as well as broader statements of policy.

The prescriptions of relevant activities and developments are generally grouped into:

- "as of right uses," which may be undertaken on the land without permission, and any conditions to which compliance might be required in doing so;
- "discretionary uses" for which planning permission must be obtained, and the conditions that may be imposed on that permission; and
- "prohibited uses," which may not be pursued in any circumstances.[24]

Beyond this basic regulatory mechanism, the planning schemes found in the Australian states and territories are presented in various formats and under various names. In the ACT, the Territory Plan and the National Capital Plan coexist. In the Northern Territory, there are land use control plans (also known as town plans) and interim development control orders. In New South Wales, there is a hierarchy of development control plans, local environmental plans, regional environmental plans, and a state environmental planning policy.[25] In Queensland, local municipal councils make planning schemes, while the state government develops state planning policy.[26] In South Australia, there is a central planning strategy and development plans. In Tasmania, there are planning schemes operating under state policies, such as the sustainable development policy. In Western Australia, there are town planning schemes that apply to local municipal areas, regional planning schemes, and a state planning strategy.

It may be observed that most jurisdictions include in their planning schemes a formal policy or strategy document. This document generally guides the interpretation of the planning scheme, the amendment of the planning scheme, and the exercise of planning discretions inherent in the system—such as whether to grant a planning permit—at first instance and on appeal.

In Victoria[27] we have a planning scheme for each municipal district. Each scheme is divided into state and local sections. These sections are further subdivided into:

- State Planning Policy Framework
- Local Planning Policy Framework, comprised of Municipal Strategic Statements and Local Planning Policies
- an array of standard planning zone classifications and their provisions
- overlays

ZONES

Following legislation in 1996,[28] a standard "tool set" of centrally drafted zone classifications and their applicable planning provisions, as well as state policies and provisions, has been available from which individual planning schemes may be constructed. These are called the Victoria Planning Provisions (VPPs). A planning authority, generally a municipal council, may select from the standard provisions but may not modify them. For example, there are five possible residential zones: Residential 1, Residential 2, Low-Density Residential, Mixed Use, and Township.

A standard set of land use prescriptions accompanies each of these classifications. In a Residential 1 zone, for example, an existing building on land may be used "as of right" as a dwelling without conditions. It could be used to provide "bed and breakfast" accommodations, but this is subject to conditions—no more than five people may be so accommodated, for example. With respect to "discretionary uses" on the same land, a planning permit could be sought for a convenience shop, but it must not have a floor area greater than 80 square meters. On the same land, nightclubs are prohibited. Although one may *use* a residential building on Residential 1 land as a dwelling "as of right," permission is required to *develop* the land by construction of a new dwelling, or extension of an existing one, on a land parcel of less than 300 square meters. This reflects a distinction frequently made for a range of purposes in Australian planning law between *use* and *development.*

Local municipal councils have the authority to use or not to use such standard zones in their municipalities, consistent with state planning policy. The main idea behind this standardization is that the same economic activity should be subject to the same planning constraints in all the municipalities of the state. Formerly, the sensitivity of unique environments could be dealt with in land use zones tailored for them. Such variations on the standard "tool set" must now be accomplished through conditions placed on planning permits, or through the use of overlays.

Overlays

These is a further set of standard form designations of land. They generally represent information about some natural quality or inherent characteristic of the land or buildings on it, and thus may apply in addition to zoning. The standard overlays available in the category of "Environment and Landscape" include Environmental Significance, Vegetation Protection, and Significant Landscape. Others apply to Heritage, Airport Environs, Land Subject to Inundation, and so forth. Specific development controls apply to land identified in this way.

Making and Amending Planning Schemes ("Rezoning")

The procedures for making and amending land use planning schemes in Victoria are set out in the Planning and Environment Act of 1987 (Vic).

The usual procedure requires that notice of the proposal be given to other government agencies and to members of the public who are affected by it. If there is significant disagreement, a panel is assembled to hear submissions from interested parties, to consider the proposal, and to report to the planning authority that is proposing the change. At the local level the "planning authority" is usually the relevant municipal council. The environmental effects of proposed amendments must be considered.[29] With respect to major projects, an environmental impact assessment might be undertaken to gather scientific data on the likely environmental impacts that might be caused or facilitated by the proposed change. The resulting assessment would be considered by the panel, and the conclusions would be incorporated into the panel's report. If the relevant land is being rezoned for a more sensitive use, the Environment Protection Authority must be notified with a view to assessment in respect to possible industrial contamination. A limited avenue of appeal to the Victorian Civil and Administrative Tribunal (VCAT)[30] is available if the procedures for amending a planning scheme are not correctly followed or an error of law is made.

PLANNING PERMISSION

With respect to those discretionary land uses for which permission must be obtained, there are procedures that the authority responsible for implementation of the planning scheme must follow when deciding whether a permit should be granted with respect to a proposed land use. At the local level, the "responsible authority" is usually the relevant municipal council. In the usual case, notice of an application for a planning permit must be given to neighboring landowners and others who are materially affected. They must be allowed the opportunity to object to the proposal and to make submissions about it. Also, a number of government agencies, such as the Environment Protection Authority, have been designated as "referral authorities," and they must be consulted with respect to applications for planning permission, where relevant.

The decision whether to grant permission is made in the light of wide-ranging considerations. In Victoria, the objectives of planning set out in section 4 of the Planning and Environment Act must be taken into consideration. Significant environmental effects of a project must be considered at this point,[31] and with respect to major projects, this can lead to an environmental impact assessment being conducted. Social and economic effects, governmental policies, demographic changes, and many other considerations are considered relevant. The decision maker may also consider the provisions of an amendment to the relevant planning scheme that is still in the process of being made but which has not yet taken legal effect. If an amendment comes into effect in the course of deciding the application, then the decision must be made to accord with the amended planning scheme.

Among the wide range of planning considerations relevant to the decision, a number are acknowledged by planning appeal tribunals around Australia as having particular importance, regardless of the specific legislation under which the decision is being made. Some examples of such issues with environmental importance are:

- Amenity—detriment to the "amenity" of the neighborhood is an important planning consideration. The concept of amenity embraces the features, benefits, or advantages of the local environment that people currently enjoy. There is a planning principle that, so far as possible, the amenity of an area should be improved by any change, or at least there should be no detraction from it. A detraction from amenity requires substantial justification.
- Protection from Pollution—potential pollution from a new development is highly relevant. State Environment Protection Policies[32] and other health and environmental standards, such as recommended buffer areas between inconsistent land uses, should not be departed from.[33]
- Conservation of Nature and Habitat—where a development might remove the habitat and thus the existence of a rare or endangered species, planning permission might be refused. In the case of *Department of Conservation and Natural Resources v. Robson,*[34] the Administrative Appeals Tribunal (AAT) refused to approve a planning permit for the removal of native vegetation on private land that formed part of the habitat of a very rare bird, the helmeted honey eater. This bird is protected under nature conservation legislation,[35] which is difficult to enforce without governmental assistance. Such assistance is not generally forthcoming because the government might become liable under that legislation to pay compensation to the private landowner. The land use planning system has thus become an important aspect of nature conservation. This reflects the *World Charter for Nature,* Principle 7, which states:

In the planning and implementation of social and economic development activities, due account shall be taken of the fact that the conservation of nature is an integral part of those activities.[36]

- Preservation of Heritage—decisions made in heritage disputes under former planning legislation[37] tended to diminish the cultural importance of historical buildings and other features.[38] As noted above, the conservation and enhancement of places of cultural value are now objectives of planning in Victoria. More recent decisions are thus concerned about the authenticity and sensitivity of developments in the vicinity of heritage areas.[39] Even when a valuable building has not been included in a Heritage Overlay, VCAT has considered state and local policies, and scrutinized the value of the new development against loss of the building.[40]

Consideration of such issues does not always lead to refusal of permission. More often, the decision maker will impose conditions on the planning permit that seek to reduce the impact of the proposal in the relevant respect.

PLANNING APPEALS

The merits of a decision to grant planning permission may be appealed to the Victorian Civil and Administrative Tribunal (VCAT).[41] This opportunity extends to a person who has applied for a planning permit and been refused, or who is dissatisfied with a condition that has been placed on the permit. Generally, a person who has made an objection against an application for a permit may also appeal to VCAT if the permit is granted.[42] Any person who is affected by the permit granted, but who did not object to the application in the first place, may apply to VCAT for leave to appeal if the responsible authority received at least one written objection to the permit from some other person. VCAT, and the AAT before it, have been relatively flexible about granting leave to appeal in that situation.

The Tribunal remakes de novo the planning decision appealed against. That is, it reconsiders all of the evidence and the discretionary considerations that the original decision maker took into account, as well as new evidence and issues. VCAT is not required to conduct proceedings in a formal judicial manner as a court would, but it is bound by the rules of natural justice.[43] If an error of law is made by VCAT, there is an avenue of appeal on the point of law to the Supreme Court of Victoria.

ENFORCEMENT OF PLANNING SCHEMES

The authority responsible for administration of a relevant planning scheme, which in practice is usually the municipal council, has the task of enforcing it when someone uses land in a manner that breaches the planning scheme. This can be done in the Magistrates Court, which is the lowest court in Victoria, through criminal prosecution for breach of the Planning and Environment Act. This approach has some disadvantages. The breach must be proved to criminal standards—"beyond reasonable doubt"—and magistrates generally are not well versed in environmental and planning law, often seeing the issue as minor in comparison to the crimes and family welfare issues that more often pass before them. The other approach is to seek an Enforcement Order in VCAT. Anyone may seek such an order against a person who is breaching a planning scheme or the conditions in a planning permit. This need be proved only to the civil standard—"on the balance of probabilities." If the defendant continues to act in defiance of an Enforcement Order, an injunction may be obtained. Breach of a VCAT Enforcement Order is also a serious criminal offense that may be prosecuted in the Magistrates Court, simply by proving the existence of the Enforcement Order and the facts that show that the defendant breached it. VCAT may also cancel or amend a planning permit; for example, where false information was provided in support of the original application, or notice of the application was not given to all who were entitled to receive it, or there has been a material change of circumstances or failure to comply with conditions in the permit.

Current Issues in Land Use Planning

From a juristic point of view, the most interesting contemporary planning law issue is the challenge of integrating ecological considerations into decision making. From the 1920s, land use planning has been concerned with environmental issues, originally emerging to ensure the spatial separation of industrial and residential areas in order to reduce interference from smoke and other nuisances. More recently, conservation and other environmental measures have been implemented in Victoria through planning schemes. Even standards of building quality can be incorporated into a planning scheme.[44] Planning has thus emerged as an important tool for implementation of strategic programs and policies, or strategic planning. For example, the policy of reducing greenhouse gas emissions could be advanced by measures implemented through land use planning, such as setting energy-efficiency standards for buildings to reduce consumption of energy that produces the gases,[45] and locating new developments near energy-efficient public transport. The facility of planning law to play a coordinating or integrating role in the implementation of other environmental laws and policies has also been widely recognized. This movement is supported by international instruments such as the *Stockholm* and *Rio Declarations*. Administrative implementation of this expanding role is greatly assisted by the rapid development of computer Geographic Information Systems (GIS), which can record and compare planning and environmental information of a scientific nature as well as land title information and governmental administrative information about matters ranging from animal disease quarantine areas to land tax indebtedness. Wide availability of this information to private citizens assists them in enforcing environmental and planning law themselves. This is facilitated by the opportunities to object to planning scheme amendments and applications for planning permission, wide access to the planning appeal system, and the ability to enforce planning schemes.

It is a simple but fundamental feature of the structure of Australian planning law that the "land parcel" is the basis for organizing the regulatory information. This is highly compatible with land title registration systems, thus introducing a high level of Western administrative rationality to decisions about land use, which in other cultures are often made differently. It remains a serious methodological question whether this "science of land administration," which is extremely powerful when electronic GIS databases are employed, should be permitted to run the process through centralized technocracy, or whether it can be constrained to its role as a highly efficient method of recording, on a spatial basis, the decisions reached about vital cultural and economic issues through traditional processes. If the latter course can be maintained, with technical expertise taking an advisory role, the comprehensive power of this regulatory method and its technologies is ideally suited to reintegrating ecological considerations, which stem from the character of the land itself, back into its administration and management, and determining who is responsible for the maintenance of its environmental qualities.

At this point of determining responsibility for the maintenance of environmental qualities, the planning system still strikes the challenge of the common law powers of the private landowner, and the ensuing problem of environmental measures in planning schemes being interpreted narrowly, or subjected to rights of compensation. This is illustrated by the need to preserve indigenous vegetation, and the habitat it provides for wildlife, situated on private land.[46]

Related to all of these issues is the ever-present question of access to the planning process. Since 1993, efforts have been made in Victoria to reduce public rights of objection and appeal in the planning system. The practical effect of this has been to reduce opportunities to advocate environmental issues in the process, mainly in the area of urban heritage.

Compensation

According to British constitutional principles inherited by Australia, parliament has sovereignty to make laws for the compulsory acquisition of private property without payment of compensation. This astonishing situation is qualified by two factors. First, as a matter of principle, the courts interpret legislation to have the least detrimental impact on proprietary rights possible unless this is required by express words or necessary intendment.[47] Second, a written constitution may limit the power of compulsory acquisition, and that has been done in section 51(xxxi) of the Australian constitution.[48] However, the state constitutions are not limited in this way.[49] It would nevertheless be politically unacceptable for a state government simply to take a citizen's land title, and there are limited rights to compensation in state legislation.[50]

These rights to compensation are, however, generally restricted to situations where a tangible area of land is being acquired. In other words, the concept of part expropriation, that governmental activity or regulation that substantially impinges on the use of private land can also amount to expropriation, is not generally recognized. There are signs that the High Court's interpretation of section 51(xxxi) is changing to recognize the concept of part expropriation so far as it applies to regulation that economically sterilizes the use of land.[51] Interference with private land emanating from governmental activity is simply a twin aspect of the same concept.[52] Generally, however, the state compulsory acquisition legislation has not compensated anything less than a loss of private proprietary interests through the government's acquisition of an area of land, and other losses which might be incidental to that. A person whose land is detrimentally affected by public projects in the vicinity must thus litigate under the tort of nuisance or another cause of action.[53] Access to compensation for loss caused by the amendment of a planning scheme (rezoning) is similarly limited.

STATE LEVEL—PLANNING COMPENSATION

Planning legislation often contains limited provision for compensation of losses caused by planning initiatives. In Australia, the following concepts are frequently employed in the discussion of compensation issues.[54]

"Severance" occurs when part of a land parcel is acquired for a public purpose. In addition to the value of the land that is taken, compensation must also be paid for the effects of the severance on the areas of the land parcel not taken. If a strip of land is acquired through a farm for the construction of a road, for example, operations could be adversely affected by the isolation of water supplies.[55] Compensation must be paid for such wider effects.

There is a broad and a narrow concept of "injurious affection."[56] From the broad view it is "the detrimental effect on private land of the public use or development of nearby land."[57] There could be a decline in property values connected with loss of amenity, for example, through noise and air pollution emanating from a new freeway. The narrow view is much closer to the idea of severance, where an area of a larger parcel is acquired, but here the issue is depreciation in the value of the remaining land caused by actual or intended use of the acquired land.[58] The broader concept of injurious affection thus correlates with one aspect of the concept of part expropriation. With respect to state projects, compensation is not available in Victoria within the broader concept. Interferences in the broader sense are not subject to constitutional challenge because, even if the broader idea of injurious affection were regarded at common law as a part-acquisition of property, the state parliaments have the sovereignty to ordain this according to British constitutional principles. Private citizens are thus left to suing under the tort of nuisance or negligence, and it is possible for state legislation to remove this right.[59]

"Planning blight" is the term used for the decline in land values that can occur when a new development is proposed for discussion, but no formal steps are yet taken to reserve the land for public purposes.[60] The state government might raise for discussion the desirability of building a new prison and propose a number of alternative sites. Generally, there is no right to compensation for losses suffered by those who sell their land at a depreciated value during the period of discussion. In Victoria, the planning minister has the power to declare land to be land proposed for public reservation and to pay compensation,[61] but this is discretionary.

Loss of development opportunities can occur when a planning scheme is amended—that is, through rezoning. Planning controls could be introduced in an environmentally sensitive area, for example, which severely limit or remove altogether existing rights to construct buildings. Most jurisdictions preserve "existing use rights," also known as "nonconforming use rights,"[62] which protect within narrow parameters uses that were legitimately made of the land before rezoning.

Governmental powers of compulsory acquisition are distinguished from the procedures[63] by which the process is achieved. In Victoria there are many sources of power to acquire land compulsorily that are relevant to land use planning. For example, section 42(2)(b) of the Transport Act of 1983 (Vic) confers on the Public Transport Corporation and the Roads Corporation a power to acquire land compulsorily for transport purposes. For the specific purposes of land use planning there is a broad power of acquisition in section 172 of the Planning and Environment Act of 1987 (Vic), allowing the minister for planning to acquire land compulsorily if the land is:

- required for the purposes of any planning scheme;
- used for any purpose not in conformity with the planning scheme, even if not actually prohibited by it;[64]
- vacant and unoccupied;[65] or
- in an area for which the governor in council has made a declaration that it is desirable to compulsorily acquire land to enable the better use, development, or planning of the area.

There is a potential compensation claim where planning permission sought for private development of the reserved land is refused on the ground that the land is already reserved for a public purpose.[66]

STATE LEVEL—COMPULSORY ACQUISITION PROCEDURES

In Victoria, the first step in compulsory acquisition is reservation of the land for a future public purpose. Reservation is achieved through amendment of the relevant planning scheme.[67] The planning scheme amendment procedures afford opportunities to affected landowners, and others, to object to the total project through the planning procedures described above. The new standardized planning schemes in Victoria, the

Victoria Planning Provisions, provide two categories of reserved land. First, public land already dedicated[68] to an *existing* public purpose is zoned as one of a variety of "public land zones." They are "public use," "public park and recreation," "public conservation or resource," or "road." Second, private land that is to be acquired for a planned public purpose is now included in a "public acquisition overlay," the purpose of which is "to reserve land for a public purpose and to ensure that the use or development of land do not prejudice the purpose for which the land is to be acquired." There are some exceptions to the general principle that acquisition must be preceded by reservation, such as when the land has already been offered for sale privately.[69]

Those who hold proprietary rights in the land are entitled to compensation assessed as of the date of acquisition. The compensation is calculated on what the market value[70] of the interest would be if the land had not been reserved for a public purpose.[71] The difficulty of assessing this is relieved to some extent, if formalistically, by specification of the "underlying zone."[72] There is a widely held view that the correct basis of calculation is the market value of the land when being put to the *highest and best use* that could be made of it, although that use was not being pursued at the time of acquisition. In *Equity Trustees Executors and Agency Co. Ltd. v. Melbourne and Metropolitan Board of Works*,[73] Gobbo J made it clear that ascertaining the *highest and best use* involves a range of factors: "it requires . . . that the land be considered with all its attributes, existing and potential, at the relevant moment for assessment of value."[74] The underlying zone of the land in that case was Special Conservation in order to complement adjoining river parkland. His Honor thus found it irrelevant that its *highest and best use* could have been subdivision of the land into five allotments in 1975, when it was still zoned rural.

The Victorian legislation thus intends the ascertainment of an objective market value of the estates and interests in the land being acquired. There was a traditional valuation principle, however, that the primary focus should be the value of the land to the owner and not to the acquirer.[75] Paying some respect to this principle, the Victorian legislation contains[76] supplementary factors for assessing special values held in the land by the owner:

- special value to the claimant generally,
- any loss attributable to severance,
- any loss attributable to disturbance,

- enhancement or depreciation in value of interests in other land adjoining or severed from the acquired land by reason of the implementation of the purpose for which the land was acquired (thus encompassing the narrower concept of "injurious affection"), and
- any legal, valuation, and other professional expenses necessarily incurred by the claimant by reason of the acquisition of the interest.

"Special value" is defined to mean "in relation to an interest in land, . . . the value of any pecuniary advantage, in addition to market value, to a claimant which is incidental to his ownership or occupation of that land." Thus it has no relevance to sentimental or emotional attachments. Eccles and Bryant illustrate compensatable "special value" with the example of homes fitted out for wheelchair access by owners with disabilities who would suffer pecuniary loss if they were required to fit out their new homes at their own expense.

"Loss attributable to disturbance" is described as pecuniary loss suffered as the natural, direct, and reasonable consequence of the acquisition, which is incidental to ownership or occupation of the land but additional to its market value. This is directed at pecuniary loss and has no relevance to sentimental or emotional attachments. The losses generally compensated under this provision include removal costs and the costs of dismantling and reassembling machinery.[77]

"Solatium" is a further head of claim for compensation that does recognize sentimental or emotional attachment. Section 44 of the Land Acquisition and Compensation Act provides that "compensation may be increased by such amount, not exceeding 10% of the market value of the land, by way of solatium as is reasonable to compensate the claimant for intangible and non-pecuniary disadvantages resulting from the acquisition." In assessing this, all relevant circumstances applicable to the claimant must be taken into account, including the length of time the claimant had occupied the land, the age of the claimant, and the number, age, and circumstances of any other people living with the claimant where the land is the claimant's principal place of residence. Section 100 of the Planning and Environment Act makes similar provision with respect to the acquisition of a residence for planning purposes.[78]

Disputes about the assessment of compensation to be paid are directed to two possible forums. If the amount in dispute is less than $50,000, the issue is dealt with by the VCAT. If the amount in dispute is more than $50,000, it may, at the option of the claimant, be dealt with by VCAT or by the Supreme Court of Victoria. Any party may apply for the issue to be dealt with by the Supreme Court, regardless of the amount in dispute, if it raises questions of unusual difficulty or general importance.[79]

Naturally, it is also possible for the proprietors of estates and interests in land to agree on a value voluntarily by negotiation with the acquiring authority.

NATIONAL LEVEL—COMPULSORY ACQUISITION

The Australian constitution makes express provision for the acquisition of property for the purposes of the Commonwealth government, and thus the general British constitutional principle that parliament has sovereignty to acquire private property without compensation is submerged to the extent that the express provision applies.

Section 51(xxxi) provides that the Australian parliament has the power

> to make laws for the peace, order and good government of the Commonwealth with respect to:—
>
>> (xxxi) The acquisition of property on just terms from any State or person for any purpose in respect of which the Parliament has power to make laws.

This constitutional provision is supplemented by legislative provision for liability to pay compensation and procedures by which an acquisition of land is made.[80] Conventionally it has been considered that the entitlement to compensation under this legislation relates to the acquisition of a proprietary estate or interest in land within conventional classifications, such as full ownership or an easement. In other words, the Act does not provide compensation for part expropriations, either by governmental interference with the citizen's enjoyment of his or her private land, for example, by noise emanating from an air force base, or by a regulatory restriction of private land use, which effectively sterilizes the land's economic value.

Until recently, interpretation of "the acquisition of property" in section 51(xxxi) of the constitution has been similarly limited. However, in *Newcrest Mining (WA) Ltd. v. Commonwealth of Australia*,[81] the High Court of Australia has opened potential new directions in the treatment of the law of compulsory acquisition related to this issue. *Newcrest*[82] concerned mining leases that had been granted prior to 1978 over Crown land in the area of Coronation Hill in the Northern Territory. The area had long been considered for inclusion in the Kakadu World Heritage area. This was first initiated by the Fraser Liberal government in 1979 in recognition of its international environmental value. The plaintiff company acquired its mining leases in 1987 from BHP Minerals Ltd. Until 1991 the plaintiff company was in fact named BHP Gold Mines Ltd. In 1991 the cabinet of the Commonwealth government decided on the basis of a Resource Assessment Commission (RAC) report[83] to prevent mining in the Kakadu Conservation Zone, including Coronation Hill, largely in view of the spiritual and cultural importance of Coronation Hill to the Jawoyn people, who are the traditional Aboriginal owners of the land.[84] The report also concluded that the environmental impacts of the mine beyond the prospective mining site would include loss of the opportunity to preserve the entire catchment area of a tropical river, at least for the life of the mine, and could challenge the ecological integrity of the Kakadu National Park with which the area is biophysically linked, affecting future possibilities for listing the area as World Heritage.[85] The area is also the habitat of endangered and vulnerable species.[86]

The mine site itself was to occupy 13 square kilometers and it was proposed to extract the ore by open cut method, employing cyanide leaching.[87] Levels of radiation were also anticipated because of the presence of uranium. The RAC suggested methods of mitigating the ecological impact of mining if it were to go ahead.[88] These suggestions were directed to protection of the surrounding area. Even if they were adopted, the ecology of the site itself would have been changed beyond recognition.

The Commonwealth government made proclamations in 1989 and 1991 that added the relevant Crown land to Kakadu National Park. The National Parks and Wildlife Act of 1975 had already been amended in 1987 to provide that there would be no operations for the recovery of minerals in Kakadu National Park, and further that there would be no liability to pay compensation for that reason. The plaintiff contended that the effective termination of its right to mine was an acquisition of property by the Commonwealth, which entitled it to compensation on just terms, as provided in section 51(xxxi) of the Australian constitution.

In the High Court, the majority of justices[89] accepted the plaintiff's contention with respect to those mining leases that were valid at the time of their "acquisition." The different ruling of the minority[90] followed from their conclusion that the power to make laws for the government of a territory[91] is not subject to section 51(xxxi) in view of an earlier High Court decision[92] that they declined to overrule. One member of the majority, Toohey J, also declined to overrule the case, but found, as the majority had, that there was an acquisition of property, and it was effectuated through laws and proclamations that could also be characterized within legislative powers in section 51 of the Australian constitution.[93] The unique conclusion of Toohey J was that laws amenable to dual classification, as a law with respect to a territory under section 122 and as a law with respect to one of the heads of power in section 51, were still subject to the qualification of legislative power in section 51(xxxi) requiring just terms.

That the mining leases were "property" was not disputed. That suppression of their use could amount to *acquisition* by the Commonwealth was in contention. In the result, the majority concluded that a benefit was acquired by the Commonwealth when it terminated mining operations at Coronation Hill because it effectively acquired the unexpired term of the mining leases, thus enlarging its reversionary interest. In other words, the Commonwealth gained a benefit of a proprietary nature when its underlying ultimate or radical title to the land was freed of the effective exercise of the mining company's proprietary rights in it.[94] Thus there was a compulsory acquisition requiring the provision of "just terms" within the meaning of section 51(xxxi).

With respect to the correct judicial approach to deciding whether a compulsory acquisition has taken place, *Newcrest*[95] confirmed that if some benefit or advantage is acquired by the Commonwealth, there is an acquisition for the purpose of section 51(xxxi), and the corresponding loss of the private citizen will have to be compensated unless an exception can be found that exempts it.[96]

THE RELEVANT CONCEPT OF PROPERTY
AND ABORIGINAL LAND RIGHTS

Whether the extinguishment of Aboriginal native title[97] by the Commonwealth amounts to an expropriation within the meaning of section 51(xxxi) was raised indirectly in *Newcrest*.[98] It is quite reasonable to expect that extinguishment would be an expropriation. For one thing, native title depends upon a traditional indigenous connection to the land, generally entailing occupation of it.[99] At common law, possessory rights are intrinsically proprietary, and expropriation of them leads to compensation under section 51(xxxi).[100] Second, *Newcrest* confirmed the vital question to be whether the Commonwealth has acquired a valuable right and the citizen has suffered some corresponding loss. As a matter of principle, the decision supports the view that extinguishment of native title is an acquisition for the purposes of section 51(xxxi) because

extinguishment confers a benefit on the Crown itself—the Crown's ultimate or radical title is no longer burdened by the indigenous interest—
and lost native title right would clearly have been a valuable right in the
hands of those entitled to it, as recognized by the common law.

Although native title rights were not directly relevant to any issues in
contention between the parties, in his judgment in *Newcrest*, Gummow
J considered that the extinguishment of native title does not engage section 51(xxxi) because the "characteristics of native title as recognised at
common law include an inherent susceptibility to extinguishment or
defeasance by the grant of freehold or of some lesser estate which is
inconsistent with native title rights; this is so whether the grant be supported by the prerogative or by legislation."[101] Although other members
of the majority in *Newcrest* agreed in general terms with Gummow J,
some added their own brief comments on the native title question, which
indicate that the issue is by no means closed.[102]

In any case, as a matter of practice, the question has largely been
resolved in legislation. The Native Title Act of 1993 (Cth) was introduced
after the *Mabo Case*[103] and then extensively revised amid political controversy after *Wik and Thayorre Peoples v. Queensland*.[104] The so-called
Wik Amendment initiated a retrospective validation or confirmation of
European titles in Australia. The Act now provides rights to compensation upon impairment or extinguishment of Native Title in the following
situations:

- validation of "Past Acts,"
- confirmation of extinguishment by "Previous Exclusive Possession
  Acts,"
- validation of "Intermediate Period Acts," and
- authorization of "Future Acts" with respect to new projects.[105]

The legislation thus largely counters the practical obstacle to identify-
ing extinguishment as an expropriation that concerned Gummow J in
Newcrest.[106]

EXCLUSION FROM THE SCOPE OF SECTION 51(XXXI)
OF GOVERNMENTAL REGULATION THAT AFFECTS "VALUE"

In the jurisprudence of the Australian High Court on expropriation there
remains an unsettled issue about how a distinction is to be made between,
on the one hand, an expropriation, and on the other, the ordinary regu-

lation of property rights and the maintenance of legal institutions that accompany governmental authority under a modern democratic constitution. We will see that the court has unnecessarily complicated its task in this respect and, through minor rearrangement of juridical material already available to it, a clearer distinction might yet be made. Again the *Newcrest Decision*[107] is pivotal in this respect.

The basic purpose of section 51(xxxi) is to enable the Australian parliament to pass laws that make arrangements for the acquisition of property needed by government for purposes it may pursue under other heads of power in the constitution.[108] These laws must comply with the express safeguard that the acquisitions be on "just terms." However, the High Court has considered that certain styles of "acquisition" or "disposition" of property will not, as exceptions, create liability for compensation. Examples of these include taxation under section 51(ii) and the sequestration of a bankrupt's property under section 51(xxvii), which most will agree are not expropriations. The quest for the High Court is to discover a principle for distinguishing such "acquisitions" and "dispositions" from those that ought to be unconstitutional if compensation is not paid. The prevalent approach of the High Court has been to ask whether in relation to the acquisition or disposition of property in question the provision of compensation on "'just terms' is an inconsistent or incongruous notion."[109] For example, with respect to the acquisition of property involved in exacting a fine or penalty, it has been considered that payment of compensation on just terms to the person from whom the fine or penalty is exacted would be an "inconsistent or incongruous notion."

The topical issue is not the conclusion reached with respect to taxation, bankruptcy, and penalties, but rather the usefulness of a test based on "incongruity" for all but the most obvious cases. Not surprisingly, the search for a unified explanation of the incongruity, and thus a principle for determining its presence or absence in novel cases, has eluded both commentators[110] and judges of the greatest eminence. In these cases, the cultural and historical relativity of the "incongruity test" is clearly revealed. Take, for example, the dynamics of one leading case in this field, *Re Döhnert Müller Schmidt & Co.*[111] The Commonwealth government had appointed a controller to administer the firm in the first days of World War II on the basis that it was "enemy property." The firm was a wool buyer, operating between Australia and Leipzig, Germany. The controller liquidated its assets and paid the proceeds into a fund held by the court. In 1953 an application was made for the fund to be paid out, ultimately for the benefit of the Commonwealth government.

Dixon CJ, with whom the other judges concurred, outlined the significance of the requirement for "just terms" in section 51(xxxi). It is a safeguard and applies to all acquisitions of property falling within its scope. On the one hand, the sequestration of a bankrupt's property under laws made pursuant to section 51(xvii) does not fall within its scope, but on the other hand, the acquisition of land for a Bankruptcy Office would. The Commonwealth claimed entitlement to the assets of the German-Australian firm as a war prize through exercise of its defense power in section 51(vi), or by way of reparations through its external affairs power in section 51(xxix). However, the question remained of how to justify the removal of the exercise of these powers from the scope of section 51(xxxi). Dixon CJ concluded that section 51(xxxi) "covers laws with respect to the acquisition of real or personal property for the intended use of any department or officer of the Executive Government of the Commonwealth in the course of administering laws made by the Parliament in the exercise of its legislative power."[112] This is now a very conservative expression of the scope of section 51(xxxi), but commentators still cite the case when using war prize and reparations as examples of "acquisitions" outside the scope of section 51(xxxi),[113] and the judgment of Dixon CJ is often invoked for other purposes.[114]

More revealing, and at the same time demonstrating the limitations of a distinction based on "incongruity,"[115] is the concluding comment of Taylor J: "that enemy property could validly be seized only under legislation which provided compensation to the expropriated owners would, in my opinion, be *the height of absurdity.*"[116] In other words, an acquisition is excluded from the reach of section 51(xxxi) when it makes sense to exclude it. Clearly, this approach is highly questionable. Taxation, the sequestration of a bankrupt's property, and fines are on virtually all views properly not to be regarded as expropriations, but the "characterization approach," based on little more than evaluations of the incongruity or high absurdity of a contrary finding, suffers extreme cultural and historical relativity. The case of *Döhnert Müller Schmidt & Co.*[117] yielded a clear answer for Taylor J, but today, we would surely ask whether the firm and its proprietors were in fact enemies, or whether its proprietors were political refugees, first from the Nazis and then from the East German totalitarian governments, and whether the seizure of their property did no more than deny refugees their assets and legitimate means of subsistence. Their possible status as refugees is not revealed in the specific facts of the case, but at a general level the situation illustrates the point that the legitimacy of decisions based on an "incongruity" or "high absurdity" approach is not likely to be durable.

Similarly, the "incongruity" approach does not help when faced with new problems in more recent cultural contexts. Issues such as the division of family property upon divorce, the expropriation of native title, and constraints on land use for the benefit of the environment are just such problems. A decision based simply on the "incongruity" or "high absurdity" of the contrary conclusion would not be found convincing in an atmosphere of charged political tension. This approach would provide no guidance to resolution of the basic issues in dispute if, for example, a Commonwealth law made under the external affairs power in section 51(xxix) required retention of forest on private land, in implementation of the Climate Change Convention or the Biodiversity Convention, and landowners claimed that this amounted to an expropriation within the meaning of section 51(xxxi).

These considerations point to the need for a broader jurisprudential base for the application of section 51(xxxi). One might start this search with statements in the High Court about the need to spread the cost of individual sacrifices for the common good across the community. In *Mutual Pools & Staff Pty. Ltd. v. Commonwealth*[118] McHugh J said that section 51(xxxi) is "a guarantee that the property of a State or an individual citizen will not be sacrificed for the public welfare of the Commonwealth."[119] On the other hand, if every disadvantage suffered by a citizen as a result of a public initiative had to be compensated, no matter how slight, it would be impossible to implement programs for the broader community good. In *Mutual Pools*, Brennan J recognized this when he said that it "would be erroneous to elevate the constitutional guarantee of just terms to a level which would so fetter other legislative powers as to reduce the capacity of the Parliament to exercise them effectively."[120]

The relativity of interest between the individual and the community, which is implicit in these statements, has also been recognized in deciding what level of compensation amounts to "just terms." In *Grace Brothers Pty. Ltd. v. Commonwealth*,[121] the High Court referred to the balance between citizen and community in ascertaining what are "just terms." Latham CJ remarked that legislation effecting an acquisition should not be invalid unless a reasonable man could not regard the terms of acquisition as being just: "Justice involves consideration of the interests of the community as well as of the person whose property is acquired."[122] The issue for the court is thus to discern significant personal sacrifices required of an individual citizen which deserve compensation by the broader community benefiting from the relevant public initiative, and to assess the extent of that compensation.

The Australian High Court has adopted different approaches to guide this inquiry. I have referred above to the prevalent High Court approach of asking whether it is "incongruous" to describe a law as one effecting an acquisition of property for the purposes of section 51(xxxi). This "incongruity approach" has on occasion been supplemented by other approaches.

In *Mutual Pools* Brennan J saw no expropriation if the "the acquisition is a necessary or characteristic feature of the means which the law selects to achieve its objective and the means selected are appropriate and adapted to achieving an objective within power, not being solely or chiefly the acquisition of property."[123] On the other hand, where the sole or dominant character of a law is the acquisition of property, it must be supported by section 51(xxxi) and provide "just terms." This criterion is so open-ended that its literal terms could exclude from the reach of section 51(xxxi) a vast range of activities conventionally thought to be expropriations. It is possible to imagine a scenario in which such a classical[124] expropriation as the compulsory acquisition of land for the construction of a road could become obfuscated by application of this test. In effect, this approach hardly differs from the "incongruity approach."

Another approach has been to consider whether the law merely provides for the recognition of responsibilities and the adjustment of competing interests. In *Australian Tape Manufacturers Association Ltd. v. Commonwealth*[125] Mason CJ, Brennan, Deane, and Gaudron JJ said,

> In a case where an obligation to make a payment is imposed . . . *as a genuine adjustment of the competing rights, claims or obligations of persons in a particular relationship or area of activity*, it is unlikely that there will be any question of an "acquisition of property" within s. 51(xxxi) of the Constitution.[126]

A clear example might be a law under section 51(xxi) (marriage) founding a system for the adjustment of formal and informal interests in the property of married spouses upon divorce, in view of future responsibilities, such as the care of children resulting from the marriage.

At a more general level, this approach opens the way to recognition of a distinct role for obligations and responsibilities in deciding whether a governmental initiative effects an expropriation and, if so, the extent of compensation due. It would be possible for the High Court to adopt a formula for balancing the interests of the community and the citizen that draws into account the responsibilities of a citizen in a democratic nation among those "competing rights, claims or obligations" that can be dealt with in legislation without the measure constituting an expropriation.[127] Deane and Gaudron JJ adopted such an amalgamation when they classified a category of laws that "consists of laws which provide for the creation, modification, extinguishment or transfer of rights and liabilities as . . . a means for enforcing, some *general regulation of the conduct, rights and obligations of citizens* in relationships or areas which need to be regulated in the common interest,"[128] and thus are unlikely to be expropriations.

The effect of this would be that so far as citizens are obliged to use, or not to use, their property in a particular way, a law which manifests that responsibility takes nothing away. This was seen at a microlevel in *Mutual Pools,* where the plaintiff was in any case obliged on civil law unjust enrichment principles to refund money to customers, so a law requiring this to be done was not an expropriation.[129] A similar train of logic can apply at the social macrolevel.

To test further the explanatory power of a formulation based on social responsibility in the macrosense, we might consider the clear example of taxation. When government exacts a tax, it acquires some of the property of the taxpayer, and thus, a taxation law should prima facie amount to an expropriation within section 51(xxxi). We saw above that the power to extract taxes from citizens[130] is regarded as an independent source of power to acquire property because it would be "incongruous" to find otherwise, and thus the requirement of compensation in section 51(xxxi) is irrelevant. Taxation is thus generally regarded as an obvious case. Nevertheless, a great deal of artificiality has been drawn into the juristic explanation of why a law to "acquire money for public purposes" is so obviously not an expropriation.[131]

We might consider some of the observations made about taxation in *Mutual Pools.*[132] Mason CJ sought the explanation in the nature of "just terms," observing that "of its nature 'taxation' presupposes the absence of the kind of *quid pro quo* involved in the 'just terms' prescribed by s[ection] 51(xxxi)."[133] This view sits easily within characterization and incongruity tests explored above. This test could also exclude activities conventionally thought to be expropriations from the reach of section 51(xxxi). It is difficult to envisage the quid pro quo flowing to a landowner whose property is acquired for a road, apart from the compensation itself, yet this is a classical example of expropriation[134] and the concept of "just terms" applies easily to it. If the quid pro quo referred to in the passage is the compensation payable, then the test is circular, effectively stating that an acquisition falls within section 51(xxxi) when we can imagine compensation being paid.

Dawson and Toohey JJ were unable to accept that money constitutes property, at all events for the purposes of section 51(xxxi): "money merely represents value and it is hardly *sensible* to speak of the acquisition of value on just terms . . . if money were property for the purposes of s. 51(xxxi), no distinction could be drawn between an acquisition of property and a tax."[135] Whether it is "sensible" to speak of money as property for purposes of the constitution depends very much on one's view of the objective of protecting private property rights. It is a conventional liberal view that the civil right to private property secures for the citizen the material resources required to enjoy the other liberal freedoms and to facilitate a self-reliant way of life without dependence upon a paternalistic state.[136] To strive for self-fulfillment or self-development, a citizen needs private assets. Even as "value," money is plainly such an asset. However, the individual citizen cannot strive for private fulfillment, let alone exist, without community. Membership of community entails social responsibilities.

This brings us back to the position already acknowledged in different places by the Australian High Court. The concept of "just terms" is arrived at through consideration of the interests of both the community and the individual. A law that expresses or gives content to an obligation or a responsibility that the citizen should in any case fulfill does not disadvantage the citizen, and cannot be an expropriation. Taxation laws can thus quite logically be explained as laws giving content to the citizen's responsibility within a democratic society to contribute financially to the maintenance of community, without which he or she can have no real social existence. They are not an expropriation.

Judicial acknowledgment of the responsibility to contribute through taxation to the maintenance of civil society would not be a large step for the High Court to take. It is also a citizen's responsibility to satisfy civil liabilities. If the citizen falls short in this respect, then, in the last resort, an administrator has to be appointed to take charge of assets for the benefit of creditors. The social responsibility explanation of compulsory acquisitions and dispositions of a citizen's property thus holds for the conventional exemptions from the reach of section 51(xxxi). One exemption from the reach of section 51(xxxi) not explained by consideration of the citizen's responsibilities is the confiscation of private assets by way of war prize or reparations. As I have suggested, the position of a political refugee should be considered differently now, especially in view of the rapid growth of international humanitarian law within the United Nations framework.[137]

With respect to our more problematical example of a constraint on the actions of a private landowner enforced by legislation for environmental reasons, the explanation based on responsibility still holds true. If the legal constraint expresses limitations on use of the land that exist for inherent ecological reasons, then the landowner has sacrificed nothing by adhering to it. For one thing, the owner never held property with a greater value than the land with its particular ecological potential, and further, a citizen in a modern democracy in the twenty-first century must surely have a responsibility to use his or her property in an ecologically sustainable way.[138]

PART EXPROPRIATION

The majority in the *Newcrest Decision*[139] concluded that suppression of use of the mining leases amounted to an acquisition of them. A benefit was acquired by the Commonwealth because it effectively acquired the unexpired term of leases, thus enlarging its reversionary interest. The issue over which the majority and minority justices disagreed was the question of whether the guarantee in section 51(xxxi) applied to acquisitions of property in the Northern Territory and, it will be recalled, a majority concluded that it did; certainly if the acquisition could also be characterized within one of the other powers in section 51, such as external affairs and the implementation of treaties.[140]

That the mining leases were "property" was not disputed. That suppression of their use could amount to acquisition by the Commonwealth was not seriously doubted either. In arriving at this point, some members of the court discussed the issue that the Commonwealth had effectively "sterilized" the mining interests without formally acquiring them, thus raising the issue of part expropriation or a "partial taking" as it was described in *Causby*.[141] Gummow J drew attention[142] to the finding of Dixon J in *Bank of New South Wales v. Commonwealth*[143] that an indirect acquisition of "the substance of a proprietary interest"[144] can amount to an expropriation. In that case, the Commonwealth sought, through the Banking Act of 1947 (Cth), to arrange for the business of private banks to be taken into the hands of agents of the Commonwealth so that "in a real sense, although not formally," the banks and their shareholders were effectively deprived of "the reality of proprietorship." Gummow J concluded that "there was an effective sterilisation of the rights constituting the property in question. . . . The vesting in the Commonwealth of the minerals . . . and the vesting of the surface . . . had the effect, as a legal and practical matter, of denying to Newcrest the exercise of its rights under the mining tenements."[145]

The language of "sterilization" was also adopted by Brennan CJ[146] and less significantly by McHugh J.[147] Although the decisive point was that the Commonwealth had effectively regained the unexpired period of the mineral tenancies,[148] the possibility that regulation of land use for reasons of ecological sustainability might be considered an expropriation of "the reality of proprietorship," requiring compensation from the very limited funds available for conservation and environmental protection, inspired Sperling[149] to express very pertinent concerns that by conceiving limitation of the use of the mining leases as an acquisition, the High Court had deviated from its approach in the *Franklin Dam Case*.[150] In that case, the Commonwealth had exercised its constitutional powers to prevent the state of Tasmania from constructing a hydroelectric dam in a wilderness area that had been listed under the World Heritage Convention. Section 51(xxxi) of the Australian constitution also extends to acquisitions of property from states, requiring that they also be on just terms. Mason J considered that the Commonwealth had made no acquisition of a proprietary right from the state of Tasmania although the restriction of use to wilderness was clearly stringent.[151] While a member of the majority on other crucial points, Deane J considered that severe restriction of the use of land could amount to expropriation,[152] and drew attention to an earlier statement of Stephen J that whatever approach is adopted, the universality of the problem of restricting "free enjoyment of proprietary rights" must eventually be dealt with as an expropriation problem.[153]

Sperling rightly argued that if in consequence of the *Newcrest Decision*,[154] the public regulation of private land use for the purposes of environmental protection might now be construed as full or part sterilization of the relevant private interest in the land, and in turn, be characterized as an acquisition of property requiring compensation, then a concept of public interest must be introduced to the equation.[155] As I have pointed out above,[156] the High Court has already considered that there is no expropriation where the law expresses or balances an existing obligation or responsibility and that the concept of "just terms" involves a balancing of private and community interests.

Environmental responsibilities are a further factor for consideration in this respect. In contrast to the owner's powers of exclusion and assignment, so far as the owner's power to use land is concerned, in the twenty-first century the conventional common law idea of "free enjoyment of proprietary rights" has entered the realm of fiction. We know now that human activity has ecological constraints. The thought that there may be limitless "improvement" of property has no foundation in scientifically verifiable reality. The complexity of ecosystems, and the uncertainty of predictions about the effects of human activity on them, have led to international development of the precautionary principle within the concept of sustainable development. The sum of these considerations is that a property owner who does not recognize the ecological limitations of the property, and ignores authoritative advice on the point, must inevitably be restrained by law. It defies language to describe this as a "sterilization" of the property. A law that requires the ecological constraints of the property to be recognized takes nothing away because the owner was never entitled to use it in a contrary way in the first place. The owner is not being required to sacrifice anything. At the same time, it is the land itself and the environment that benefit directly. The public and the Commonwealth benefit only indirectly. The future generations of people who will hold interests in the land also benefit.

A similar view was adopted most recently, at the United Nations—FIG[157] *Workshop on Land Tenure and Cadastral Infrastructures for Sustainable Development.*[158] One of the conclusions reached by the international experts working together on these issues was that

> [t]he property rights in land do not in principle carry with them a right to neglect or destroy the land. The concept of property (including ownership and other proprietary interests) embraces social and environmental responsibility as well as relevant rights to benefit from the property. The registration of property in land is thus simultaneously a record of who is presumed to bear this responsibility and who is presumed to enjoy the benefit of relevant rights. The extent of responsibility is to be assessed by understanding the social and environmental location of the land in the light of available information and is subject to express laws and practices of the appropriate jurisdiction.[159]

It is sometimes protested that the owner has acquired the land in question with certain plans and expectations, such as clearing it of trees and cultivating it, but these human intentions have little bearing on the best ecological course of action, objectively assessed. One might equally point out that someone who wants cleared farmland should acquire cleared land, rather than acquiring forested land and clearing it. People often acquire property that does not meet their expectations. Purchasers should ensure that property being purchased will meet their expectations, and it is unusual to hear of public compensation being requested when the property's true limitations are recognized. The purchasers of second-hand motor vehicles would never dream of this right. Consumer protection rights, and legal remedies for misrepresentation of the fitness of an acquisition for its purpose, are generally asserted against the vendor, not against the government. A person acquiring land may engage consultants to advise on the state of buildings, the environmental capacities of the land, the quality of its groundwater, and so forth. If this advice is not sought, or incorrect advice is obtained, this is not a situation for public compensation. This would require the community to underwrite private environmental assessments, whereas the true remedy is against the expert. In view of this, it is arguable that restraint of the Newcrest mining operation in Kakadu was not a compensatable expropriation, but rather a law compelling the company to respect environmental qualities of the land that it should have recognized, just as the international community did. Environmental responsibilities should also be drawn into calculation of compensation payable.[160]

Recognition of the environmental responsibilities of the private property owner to confine uses within the constraints of ecological sustainability as a basic juristic presumption need not be entirely disadvantageous to private landowners. Indeed, the recognition of a concept of part expropriation, toward which the High Court has signaled movement,[161] can bring other advantages to them. For one thing, excessive overregulation for reasons other than inherent environmental constraints would be open to challenge as an expropriation. Further, the concept of part expropriation[162] also carries with it the right to compensation for environmental interferences with private property that are sponsored by the public sector.

Noise provides a good illustration of such interferences because it is measurable. Take, for example, an airport extension sponsored by the Commonwealth that exposes residences to inordinate noise levels. This should also be considered a curtailment of "free enjoyment of proprietary rights," indeed a removal of the proprietary right to quiet enjoyment, and give rise to a right to compensation within section 51(xxxi). The Commonwealth has obtained a benefit through using surrounding private land for the dissipation of noise generated in the course of its profitable enterprise. It remains to determine at what degree or intensity of environmental interference the governmental activity becomes an unconstitutional expropriation. In *Newcrest*,[163] Kirby J invited an international comparative examination of these issues when he reminded us that "ordinarily, in a civilised society, where private property rights are protected by law, the government . . . may not deprive a person of such rights without a legal process which includes provision for just compensation."[164] It was concluded by the German Administrative Court in the *Munich Airport Case*[165] that "unreasonable intrusion" required compensation, or noise treatment works, but complete acquisition was required where the intrusion was so unbearable that meaningful usual use of the land could not be made.[166] The Court declined to specify decibel levels for the expropriation threshold,[167] but noted that in ascertaining relevant noise toleration levels it was correct to take into account human health needs for a sound sleep, occasionally with the window open, and thus the noise level at which the autonomic reaction of the human nervous system awakens one (55 dB[A]) was acknowledged as a valid maximum tolerable nighttime level, and that at which communication is interfered with (65 dB[A]) was acknowledged as a valid maximum tolerable daytime level.[168]

In the *Newcrest Decision*[169] the High Court has taken on board the concept of part expropriation. In the explication of this concept, recognition should be made of the ecological constraints on land use when assessing whether environmental regulation has effected an unconstitutional "sterilization." The law's perfect world of indestructible land and unlimited development potential does not exist in nature. On the other side, the concept of part expropriation brings with it the advantage of imposing a constitutional constraint on public projects that create environmental interferences. The recognition of this second, twin aspect of the concept of part expropriation would benefit private landowners. It would also provide a strong incentive to executive government to treat with greater seriousness the precautionary environmental impact assessment procedures that should identify in advance such environmental risks, and thus alert decision makers to possible expropriation risks,[170] rather than being seen as a mere formal obstacle to be overcome in implementing a decision already made.[171]

Current Issues in Compensation

Many topical issues have been stimulated with respect to expropriation and compensation by environmental questions, as my coverage has shown. This is the case with land use planning and other environmental controls.

When the movement toward land use planning was first gathering momentum in the more urbanized areas of Australia, other public measures, such as sanitation and public health law, were being adopted to curb the excesses of the Industrial Revolution, against which the English common law had proven ineffective.[172] Environmental protection, or "smoke" and "nuisance" problems as they were then called, was a major motivation for the adoption of land use planning. As environmental protection has risen to new challenges, the planning system has grown in sophistication and now appears to be the most viable system around which to organize most environmental and spatial information as well as systems of environmental legal rights and responsibilities. The central role for planning in protection of the environment has been recognized internationally at least since the *Stockholm Declaration* of 1972.[173] Planning law is conventionally a responsibility of the state governments in Australia, and local municipal government has a very significant role in the development and implementation of individual planning schemes as well as the grant of planning permission in accordance with them. Despite the enormous potential for fragmentation in such a decentralized field, analogous systems have nevertheless been adopted by the Australian states and territories, involving the exercise of similar discretions and the provision of appeals. In this decision making, environmental considerations are particularly important. Commonwealth involvement in planning has generally been restricted to resource use planning, using a narrow range of constitutional powers to implement its will. This involvement is expected to contract yet further with new legislation that is said to embody a new understanding, reached between the Commonwealth and the states and territories, of a different role for the national government in environmental protection.[174]

Land use planning does not generally give rise to private compensation rights. In the background is the long obsolete constitutional principle that a British Parliament has sovereignty to take a subject's property without compensation, which still applies at the state level. By virtue of statutory provision, compensation is payable when a tangible area of land is compulsorily acquired and for associated disturbances. Part expropriations, such as interference with the enjoyment of land through public projects and excessive overregulation of land use, are not generally recognized at the state level. Thus, there is no clear right to compensation if land use planning processes arrive at the decision to allow nearby a development that creates environmental interferences. The remedy is an action in the tort of nuisance or negligence, but the elements of these actions hardly represent contemporary environmental ethics, and more recently the astounding suggestion has been made in *Gillingham Borough Council v. Medway (Chatham) Dock Co. Ltd.*[175] that planning approval might actually provide statutory authority to the otherwise tortious act.

With respect to compulsory acquisition in the more conventional sense, at the state level the British constitutional principle prevails, and compensation rights must be created by legislation. This legislation also does not generally recognize part expropriation. The Commonwealth government is expressly bound by a guarantee of "acquisition on just terms" in section 51(xxxi) of the Australian constitution, so the obsolete British principle is not so relevant at the federal level. However, the Australian High Court has clearly been searching for some time for a comprehensive juristic explanation of how governmental intrusions on an individual's property rights can be distinguished from the constraints applied for legitimate social and environmental reasons in modern democratic government. Simply taken on its facts, and removed from other developmental trends in the High Court's search, the recent decision in *Newcrest*[176] recognized the constitutional entitlement to compensation of a mining company that was restrained from implementing its plans to use cyanide leaching processes[177] in an area of internationally acknowledged environmental significance. On the other hand, the High Court showed equivocation about a constitutional right to compensation for the traditional Aboriginal owners of the same land if their native title rights were to be extinguished.

Considering the *Newcrest Decision*[178] at a higher level, in terms of the more abstract principles enunciated, the case could stimulate some promising developments. Justice Kirby has effectively invited comparative legal analysis of the compulsory acquisition systems of civilized societies,[179] and this could assist the search for a comprehensive explanation of the distinction between governmental intrusions on an individual's property rights, on the one hand, and constraints on use and appropriations of property for legitimate social and environmental reasons in modern democratic government, on the other. Reconsidering earlier High Court authorities, one may extract from them juridical attempts to strike a balance between requiring individuals to make undue sacrifices to the national good, while on the other side excepting from a right to compensation the discharge of civil obligations and responsibilities that fall to the citizen in a modern democratic society. In the twenty-first century, this includes the ecological and social constraints on the use of land that we find expressed in environmental and planning law. So far as environmental regulation expresses the ecological limitations of the land in question, it effects no expropriation when it requires the landowner to observe them. Interestingly, this resembles the approach taken under the postwar German constitution. When it comes to the administration of land use, Australia and Germany already share much in the common origin of their land title registration systems,[180] and the German approach to expropriation is easily adapted to the concept of property employed in such systems.[181]

Through this approach, for which there is already promise in High Court jurisprudence, undue interference by the Commonwealth government with existing urban environmental qualities, in airport environs, for example, could also be scrutinized through the constitutional protection of private property. There is, as I have mentioned, ample legal material from which the Australian High Court could fashion the dual aspects of a concept of part expropriation—on the one hand, protection from excessive overregulation that effectively takes the reality of proprietorship, so far as it does not express the social and environmental responsibilities of a citizen in a democratic society to make beneficial use of the property; and, on the other hand, to protect the citizen's beneficial use and enjoyment of property from undue environmental interference caused by governmental projects. In this respect, and also with great relevance to the constitutional protection of native title, the conventional liberal justification of private property, as the assets required by a private citizen to lead a self-reliant life, and to find self-fulfillment and self-development in a modern democratic society without undue reliance on a paternalistic state for welfare, helps us to focus the purpose of a constitutional protection of private property.[182] The absence of such assets has often been regarded as the seat of many problems experienced by Aborigines in Australia today, and the recognition of native title is a major component of the answer to that.[183] It is thus difficult to see how native title could not be entitled to constitutional protection when other forms of property in unalienated Crown land are.

So, with these drawbacks and uncertainties in mind, the law of expropriation in Australia might not yet be considered fully mature, but it could still emerge as a significant model in the Asia-Pacific region.

Notes

1. The relevant abbreviations are: New South Wales, NSW; Tasmania, Tas; Victoria, Vic; Queensland, Qld; South Australia, SA; and Western Australia, WA.

2. Australian constitution of 1901. Australian legislation can be accessed at http://law.agps.gov.au/Welcome.html.

3. Statute of Westminster Adoption Act of 1942 (Cth). See now Australia Act of 1986 (Cth). The Australian Commonwealth jurisdiction is generally abbreviated as Cwth or Cth.

4. The relevant abbreviations are: Australian Capital Territory, ACT; and Northern Territory, NT.

5. Section 51(i), Australian constitution of 1901, and see *Murphyores Inc. Pty. Ltd. v. Commonwealth* (1976) 136 C.L.R. 1.

6. Respectively, sections 51(xxix) and (xx), Australian constitution of 1901, and see *Commonwealth v. Tasmania* (Franklin Dams Case) (1983) 46 A.L.R. 625.

7. This contrasts with approaches in other systems. For example, in the postwar German constitution the liberal concept of private property encompasses a corresponding social responsibility in the use of what one owns: Article 14 II *Grundgesetz* (constitution of the Federal Republic of Germany of May 23, 1949, German Federal Statutes, 1). The new constitutions of the *Länder* of former East Germany, and of former Warsaw Treaty countries, are also interesting in this respect.

8. J. B. McLoughlin, *Shaping Melbourne's Future? Town Planning, the State and Civil Society* (Melbourne: Cambridge University Press, 1992).

9. M. Raff, "Environmental Obligation and the Western Liberal Concept of Property," *Melb. U.L.Rev.* 22 (1998): 657.

10. M. Raff, *German Real Property Law and the Conclusive Land Title Register,* Ph.D. Thesis (Law), University of Melbourne, August 1999. The legislation of the state and territory jurisdictions that implements land title registration is Transfer of Land Act of 1958 (Vic); Real Property Act of 1900 (NSW); Land Title Act of 1994 (Qld); Real Property Act of 1886 (SA); Transfer of Land Act of 1893 (WA); Land Titles Act of 1980 (Tas); Land Title Act of 1925 (ACT); Real Property Act of 1986 (NT).

11. See generally A. J. Bradbrook and M. A. Neave, *Easements and Restrictive Covenants in Australia,* 2nd ed. (Sydney: Butterworths, 2000).

12. Subdivision Act of 1988 (Vic). Victorian legislation can be found at http://www.dms.dpc.vic.gov.au/.

13. *Stockholm Declaration* 1972, UN Doc A/Conf 48/14 Rev 1 (June 16, 1972) in (1972) 11 I.L.M. 1416.

14. On intergenerational equity, see Principle 2.

15. *Rio Declaration, Climate Change Convention, Biodiversity Convention* and *Statement of Forest Principles,* in United Nations Conference on

Environment and Development (UNCED), *The Earth Summit,* ed. S. P. Johnson (London: Graham & Trotman/Martinus Nijhoff, 1993).

16. See, for example, *Agenda 21,* Chapter 7, "Promoting Ecologically Sustainable Human Settlement," para. 7.30.

17. World Commission on Environment and Development, *Our Common Future* (Oxford University Press, 1987). See also Expert Group on Environmental Law of the World Commission on Environment and Development, *Environmental Protection and Sustainable Development—Legal Principles and Recommendations* (London: Graham & Trotman/Martinus Nijhoff, 1986). In his separate decision in the "Case Concerning the Gabcikovo-Nagymaros (Hungary/Slovakia)," *International Legal Materials* 37 (1998): 162, the vice president of the International Court of Justice, Judge Weeramantary, maintained that the concept of sustainable development has long been a customary principle of international law.

18. Intergovernmental Agreement on the Environment (IGAE), scheduled to the National Environment Protection Council (Victoria) Act of 1995 (Vic), which mirrors the National Environment Protection Council Act of 1994 (Cth) and identical legislation in the other states and territories. The Principles of ESD and the Precautionary Principle are now set in sections 3A and 391 respectively of the Environment Protection and Biodiversity Conservation Act of 1999 (Cth), which commenced on July 16, 2000.

19. See W. Gullett, "Environmental Protection and the 'Precautionary Principle,'" *Environmental and Planning Law Journal* (Australia) 14 (1997): 52.

20. See Experts Group of the World Commission on Environment and Development, *Environmental Protection and Sustainable Development—Legal Principles and Recommendations* (Graham & Trotman/Martinus Nijhoff, 1987), 58.

21. In the Australian Capital Territory, the Land (Planning and Environment) Act of 1991 (ACT) applies generally, but with respect to the City of Canberra, the Commonwealth legislation Australian Capital Territory (Planning and Land Management) Act of 1988 (Cth) also has relevance. For the Northern Territory, see Planning Act of 1993 (NT). For New South Wales, see Environmental Planning and Assessment Act of 1979 (NSW). For Queensland, see Integrated Planning Act of 1997 (Qld). For South Australia, see Development Act of 1993 (SA). For Tasmania, see Land Use Planning and Approvals Act of 1993 (Tas). For Western Australia, see Town Planning and Development Act of 1928 (WA). WA also has some regional development legislation, such as the Metropolitan Region Town Planning Scheme Act of 1959 (WA), the Swan Valley Planning Act of 1995 (WA), the East Perth Redevelopment Act of 1991 (WA), and the Subiaco Redevelopment Act of 1994 (WA).

22. R. Freestone, *Model Communities—The Garden City Movement in*

Australia (Melbourne: Nelson, 1989). Reference was made in Victorian parliamentary debates of this period to the growing town planning movement as a justification for reforms. For a detailed history of Planning Law in Victoria, see M. Raff, "A History of Land Use Planning Legislation and Rights of Objection in Victoria," *Monash U.L.Rev.* 22 (1996): 90.

23. L. Sandercock, *Cities for Sale—Property, Politics and Urban Planning in Australia* (Melbourne: University Press, 1975), 12, 16, 21.

24. In Queensland, a planning scheme cannot prohibit developments or uses of premises but only regulate them: section 2.1.23, Integrated Planning Act of 1997 (Qld).

25. In New South Wales, there is a hierarchy of *Environmental Planning Instruments*—State Environmental Planning Policies, Regional Environmental Plans, Local Environmental Plans, and Development Control Plans: Environmental Planning and Assessment Act of 1979 (NSW). The combined effect of these instruments is to create a series of zones recorded on maps in which particular developments are permitted or prohibited: see G. McLeod (ed.), *Planning Law in Australia,* LBC Information Services, Sydney (looseleaf), 1.240.

26. In Queensland, a planning scheme must incorporate five elements: (a) coordination and integration of matters dealt with by the planning scheme; (b) identification of desired environmental outcomes for the planning scheme area; (c) measures that facilitate the desired environmental outcomes; (d) performance indicators to assess achievement of the desired environmental outcomes; and (e) a benchmark development sequence: s 2.1.3. (1) Integrated Planning Act of 1997 (Qld). Thus, in principle, so long as these elements are achieved there is no express requirement for a map. The Brisbane Town Plan does, however, comprise policy, text, and zoning scheme maps: reproduced in ibid., 1.2190.

27. For a more comprehensive explanation of Victoria's Planning System see D. Eccles and T. Bryant, *Statutory Planning in Victoria* (Sydney: Federation Press, 1999). Yet more detailed is T. Bryant, R. Byard, and G. Testro, *Planning and Environment Service (Victoria),* Butterworths, 1995 (looseleaf).

28. Planning and Environment (Planning Schemes) Act of 1996 (Vic).

29. Section 12, Planning and Environment Act of 1987 (Vic). See M. Raff, "The Renewed Prominence of Environmental Impact Assessment," *Environmental and Planning Law Journal* (Australia) 12 (1995): 241, 251ff.

30. VCAT replaced the Administrative Appeals Tribunal as the appellate body in planning and environmental matters in July 1998: Victorian Civil and Administrative Tribunal Act of 1998 (Vic). See text below following note 41.

31. Section 60 Planning and Environment Act of 1987 (Vic). See M. Raff, "Renewed Prominence of Environmental Impact Assessment," 250ff.

32. In Victoria, State Environment Protection Policies (SEPPs) are made

by the Environment Protection Authority under the Environment Protection Act of 1970 (Vic), which provides statutory underpinning for the regulation of pollution discharge. Section 84B of the Planning and Environment Act of 1987 (Vic) requires that VCAT "must take account of and give effect to any relevant State environment protection policy declared in any Order made by the Governor in Council under s 16 of the Environment Protection Act 1970."

33. For example, see *Nalder v. Penney & Lang Pty. Ltd.* (1994) 13 Administrative Appeals Tribunal Reports 337, in which the Administrative Appeals Tribunal (forerunner of VCAT) refused to approve a residential development inside the prescribed buffer area around an abattoir because it would be affected by smells.

34. (1995) 15 Administrative Appeals Tribunal Reports 35.

35. Flora and Fauna Guarantee Act of 1988 (Vic).

36. *World Charter for Nature*, UN GA Res 37/7, November 9, 1982, also in (1983) 22 I.L.M. 455.

37. Town and Country Planning Act of 1961 (Vic).

38. *National Trust of Australia (Vic) v. Australian Temperance and General Mutual Life Assurance Society Ltd.* (1976) V.R. 592. In view of the complete replacement of legislation at the heart of this case (Town and Country Planning Act of 1961 [Vic]), one might consider that it has been accorded undue respect in the later cases of *Lyth v. City of Greater Geelong* (1994) 13 Administrative Appeals Tribunal Reports 289 and *Salmal Constructions Pty. Ltd. v. Richards* (1998) 99 Local Government and Environment Reports of Australia 423.

39. *Turner v. City of Echuca* (1994) 12 Administrative Appeals Tribunal Reports 317.

40. *Lawonnue Pty. Ltd. v. City of Port Phillip and Macrae* (1999) 2 Victorian Planning Reports 4. See also *K. A. Reed Group Pty. Ltd. v. National Trust* (1999) 1 Victorian Planning Reports 267, *Heritage Planning & Design v. Howie* (1998) 22 Administrative Appeals Tribunal Reports 224. There are also systems for listing cultural heritage outside the land use planning system. In Victoria this is contained chiefly in the Heritage Act of 1995. At the national level, the Environment Protection and Biodiversity Conservation Act of 1999 (Cth), the Aboriginal and Torres Strait Islander Heritage Protection Act of 1984 (Cth), and the Australian Heritage Commission Act of 1975 (Cth) are the main sources of heritage protection.

41. VCAT replaced the Administrative Appeals Tribunal (AAT): see above, note 30. In New South Wales the equivalent appeal body is the Land and Environment Court: Land and Environment Court Act of 1979 (NSW). In Queensland it is the Planning and Environment Court: Local Government (Planning and Environment) Act of 1990 (Qld) and Integrated Planning Act of 1997 (Qld). In South Australia it is the Environment Resources and Devel-

opment Court: see Environment Resources and Development Court Act of 1993 (SA). In Tasmania it is the Resource Management and Planning Appeal Tribunal: Resource Management and Planning Appeal Tribunal Act of 1993 (Tas). In the Australian Capital Territory it is the Administrative Appeals Tribunal: Administrative Appeals Tribunal Act of 1989 (ACT). In the Northern Territory it is the Planning Appeals Tribunal: Planning Act of 1993 (NT). In Western Australia there is a choice of appeals to the relevant minister or to the Town Planning Appeal Tribunal: Town Planning and Development Act of 1928 (WA). Note that appeals are not available to third parties in WA unless a planning scheme expressly provides one, and this is very rare: G. McLeod (ed.), *Planning Law in Australia*, 2.3010.

42. There are procedures for exempting decisions from the right of appeal: section 82(2) and (3), Planning and Environment Act of 1987 (Vic).

43. Section 98(1), Victorian Civil and Administrative Tribunal Act of 1998 (Vic). Among the common law principles of administrative law, the principles of natural justice require that the parties be afforded a fair opportunity to present their cases before an adjudicator who has no real or apparent personal interest in the matter.

44. In Victoria *The Good Design Guide for Medium-Density Housing* first set out standards of energy efficiency for buildings, for example. This has now been revised as *ResCode,* which is incorporated into Victoria's planning schemes by reference.

45. See, for example, the Leichhardt (NSW) Interim Development Control Plan No. 17, *Energy Efficient Housing,* set out in G. McLeod (ed.), *Planning Law in Australia,* 1.450ff.

46. House of Representatives Standing Committee on Environment and Heritage, *Inquiry into Public Good Conservation—Imposition of Environmental Measures Imposed on Landholders,* at http://www.aph.gov.au/house/committee/environ. See also D. Farrier, "Vegetation Conservation: The Planning System as a Vehicle for the Regulation of Broadacre Agricultural Land Clearing," *Melb. U.L.Rev.* 18 (1991): 26; N. Nearn, "Bushland Protection Through Planning Controls in New South Wales," *Environmental and Planning Law Journal* (Australia) 12 (1995): 318; and E. Lee, M. Baird, and I. Lloyd, "SEPP 46—Protection and Management of Native Vegetation," *Environmental and Planning Law Journal* (Australia) 15 (1998): 127.

47. D. C. Pearce and R. S. Geddes, *Statutory Interpretation in Australia,* 3rd ed. (Sydney: Butterworths, 1988), 101–103, and *Springhall v. Kirner* (1988) V.R. 159, 165. See text above following note 7.

48. Section 51(xxxi) is set out below, in text following note 79.

49. *New South Wales v. Commonwealth* (Wheat Case) (1915) 20 C.L.R. 54, per Griffith CJ at 66 and per Barton J at 77.

50. Land Acquisition and Compensation Act of 1986 (Vic); Lands Acquisition Act of 1989 (Cth); Lands Acquisition Act of 1994 (ACT); Lands

Acquisition Act of 1996 (NT); Land Acquisition (Just Terms Compensation) Act of 1991 (NSW); Acquisition of Land Act of 1967 (Qld); Land Acquisition Act of 1969 (SA); Land Acquisition Act of 1993 (Tas); and Land Administration Act of 1997 (WA).

51. *Newcrest Mining (WA) Ltd. v. Commonwealth of Australia* (1997) 147 A.L.R. 42, discussed more fully in text below, following note 81.

52. In *United States v. Causby* 328 U.S. 256 (1946), interference with use of land by low-flying aircraft amounted to a "partial taking" (at 265) within the meaning of the Fifth Amendment to the United States constitution.

53. For a brief overview, see G. M. Bates, *Environmental Law in Australia,* 4th ed. (Sydney: Butterworths, 1995), 50–57. For more detailed coverage, see H. Luntz and D. Hambly, *Torts—Cases and Materials,* 4th ed. (Sydney: Butterworths, 1995); or F. Trindade and P. Cane, *The Law of Torts in Australia* (Melbourne: Oxford University Press, 1999).

54. See Eccles and Bryant, *Statutory Planning in Victoria,* 2nd ed. (Sydney: Federation Press, 1999), 152–158.

55. Ibid., 155–156.

56. D. Brown, *Land Acquisition,* 4th ed. (Sydney: Butterworths, 1996), 138.

57. Ibid., 154.

58. Ibid. See also G. L. Fricke, *Compulsory Acquisition of Land in Australia,* 2nd ed. (Sydney: Law Book Co., 1982), 102.

59. See, for example, section 36, Australian Grands Prix Act of 1994 (Vic).

60. Eccles and Bryant, *Statutory Planning in Victoria,* 156–157.

61. Section 113, Planning and Environment Act of 1987 (Vic).

62. Section 6, Planning and Environment Act of 1987 (Vic) and clause 63, General Provisions, *Victoria Planning Provisions.* See also B. Kennedy, "The Future of Existing Use Rights in Victoria," *Environmental and Planning Law Journal* (Australia) 12 (1995): 400. See generally, Eccles and Bryant, *Statutory Planning in Victoria,* 49–50.

63. These are contained in the Land Acquisition and Compensation Act of 1986 (Vic); see further text below following note 65.

64. To rely upon this head of power, the minister or responsible authority must believe it desirable that the use should not be continued or, as the case requires, that the land should be put to an appropriate use in order to achieve the proper development of any area in accordance with the planning scheme.

65. The proviso set out in note 64 must also be satisfied here.

66. See Eccles and Bryant, *Statutory Planning in Victoria,* 165–166.

67. Section 5(1), Land Acquisition and Compensation Act of 1986 (Vic).

68. Dedication and administration of existing public land is governed by the Crown Land (Reserves) Act of 1978 (Vic), as well as a range of other leg-

islation, such as the National Parks Act of 1975 (Vic) and the Conservation Forests and Lands Act of 1987 (Vic), among others.

69. The exceptions are discussed in Eccles and Bryant, *Statutory Planning in Victoria*, 160–161.

70. "Market value" is defined in section 40 of the Land Acquisition and Compensation Act of 1986 (Vic) to mean "in relation to any interest in land on a particular date, . . . the amount of money that would have been paid for that interest if it had been sold on that date by a willing but not anxious seller to a willing but not anxious purchaser."

71. How this is achieved is discussed in Eccles and Bryant, *Statutory Planning in Victoria*, 162.

72. See section 201, Planning and Environment Act of 1987 (Vic).

73. (1994) 1 V.R. 534.

74. Ibid., at 541. On "highest and best use," see further D. Brown, *Land Acquisition*, 105–107.

75. *Pastoral Finance Association Ltd. v. Minister* (1914) A.C. 1083. See also D. Brown, *Land Acquisition*, 99–103.

76. Section 41, Land Acquisition and Compensation Act of 1986 (Vic).

77. Eccles and Bryant, *Statutory Planning in Victoria*, 163.

78. Outlined above in text, following note 63.

79. Section 81, Planning and Environment Act of 1987 (Vic), and Eccles and Bryant, *Statutory Planning in Victoria*, 168.

80. Lands Acquisition Act of 1989 (Cth). The provisions of this Act generally resemble those of the Land Acquisition and Compensation Act of 1986 (Vic) discussed above.

81. (1997) 147 A.L.R. (referred to henceforth simply as *Newcrest*).

82. Ibid.

83. Resource Assessment Commission (Cth), *Kakadu Conservation Zone Inquiry Final Report*, AGPS. May 1991 (Parliamentary Paper No. 110 of 1991) ("*Kakadu Conservation Zone Inquiry* Vol. 1").

84. B. Galligan and G. Lynch, "Integrating Conservation and Development: Australia's Resource Assessment Commission and the Testing Case of Coronation Hill," *Environmental and Planning Law Journal* (Australia) 9 (1992): 181, 190–192, also available in B. Galligan and G. Lynch, *Integrating Conservation and Development: Australia's Resource Assessment Commission and the Testing Case of Coronation Hill*, Discussion Paper No. 14, Federalism Research Centre, Australian National University, March 1992.

85. *Kakadu Conservation Zone Inquiry* Vol. 1, 123.

86. Resource Assessment Commission (Cth), *Kakadu Conservation Zone Inquiry Final Report*, AGPS, May 1991 (Parliamentary Paper No. 111 of 1991) ("*Kakadu Conservation Zone Inquiry* Vol. 2"), 15ff.

87. *Kakadu Conservation Zone Inquiry* Vol. 2, 95ff. Cyanide leaching is

the process that was employed at the joint venture project of the Australian company Esmeralda Exploration and the Romanian company Remin from which the recent environmental crisis in the Danube river system was reported to have emanated: S. Mann and B. Fitzgerald, "Cyanide Spill Rocks Miner," *The Age* (Melbourne), February 10, 2000, 1. This introduces a paradoxical element to the idea of expropriation through "sterilization" of the economic viability of land.

88. *Kakadu Conservation Zone Inquiry* Vol. 2, 63ff.

89. Gaudron, Toohey, Gummow, and Kirby JJ.

90. Brennan CJ, Dawson, and McHugh JJ.

91. Section 122, Australian constitution.

92. *Teori Tau v. Commonwealth* (1969) 119 C.L.R. 564.

93. Specifically, the external affairs power in section 51(xxix). The laws implemented the World Heritage Convention.

94. *Newcrest,* per Brennan CJ at 48, per McHugh J at 81, per Gummow J (Gaudron and Toohey JJ agreeing) at 129.

95. *Newcrest.*

96. See generally D. F. Jackson and F. Lloyd, "Compulsory Acquisition of Property," *AMPLA Yearbook* 75 (1998), and G. Griffith and G. Kennett, "Constitutional Protection Against Uncompensated Expropriations of Property," *AMPLA Yearbook* 49 (1998).

97. First recognized by the Australian High Court in *Mabo v. State of Queensland* (No 2) (1992) 175 C.L.R. 1 ('*Mabo*'). Only Deane and Gaudron JJ expressly dealt with the question, concluding (at 111) that "extinguishment of [native title] rights would constitute an expropriation of property, to the benefit of the underlying estate, for the purposes of section 51(xxxi)."

98. *Newcrest.*

99. Toohey J in *Mabo, Newcrest,* at 206–214, grounded "common law aboriginal title" in indigenous possession of the land. This approach has been adopted in Canada to support the concept of common law aboriginal title recognized there: *Delgamuukw v. British Columbia* (1997) 153 D.L.R. (4th) 193. See case note by M. Tehan in *Melb.U.L.Rev.* 22 (1998): 763.

100. *Minister of State for the Army v. Dalziel* (1944) 68 C.L.R. 261. See also *Perry v. Clissold* (1907) A.C. 73.

101. *Newcrest,* 112–113.

102. Toohey J, *Newcrest,* 71. Kirby J, ibid., 143, indicated inclination to view extinguishment of native title as an expropriation if the text of the constitution required that.

103. Above, note 97.

104. (1997) 141 A.L.R. 129.

105. For information about these schemes, see R. H. Bartlett, *Native Title in Australia* (Sydney: Butterworths, 2000).

106. Above, note 101.

107. *Newcrest.*

108. Generally in sections 51 and 52 of the Australian constitution. The text of section 51(xxxi) is set out above, in text following note 79.

109. Deane and Gaudron JJ (Mason CJ concurring) *In re DPP*; ex parte Lawler (1994) 179 C.L.R. 270, 285.

110. See D. F. Jackson and F. Lloyd, "Compulsory Acquisition of Property," 78–81, and G. Griffith and G. Kennett, "Constitutional Protection Against Uncompensated Expropriations of Property," 50, 64–67.

111. (1961) 105 C.L.R. 361.

112. Ibid., 372.

113. Ibid.

114. See, for example, Brennan CJ in *Newcrest,* 49.

115. Deane and Gaudron JJ, *In re DPP.*

116. (1961) 105 C.L.R. 361, 377 (my emphasis).

117. Ibid., 361.

118. (1994) 119 A.L.R. 577.

119. Ibid., 624. See also Brennan J in *Georgiadis v. Australian and Overseas Telecommunications Corporation* (1993) 119 A.L.R. 630, at 638.

120. Ibid., 594.

121. (1946) 72 C.L.R. 269.

122. Ibid. at 279–280, in agreement on this point with Starke J at 285, Dixon J at 291, and McTiernan J at 295.

123. (1994) 119 A.L.R. 594.

124. Blackstone, *Commentaries on the Laws of England,* 15th ed. (London: Cadell & Davies, 1809), Book I, 138–139.

125. (1993) 176 C.L.R. 480.

126. Ibid., 510 (my emphasis). Adopted in *Mutual Pools,* above, (1994) 119 A.L.R. 577 by Mason CJ at 587, Brennan J at 592, and alluded to by Deane and Gaudron JJ at 602. Adopted in *Nintendo Co. Ltd. v. Centronics Systems Pty. Ltd.* (1994) 121 A.L.R. 577 by Mason CJ, Brennan, Deane, Toohey, Gaudron, and McHugh JJ at 595, and, it seems, by Dawson J at 600.

127. In text above, at note 126.

128. *Mutual Pools* above, (1994) 119 A.L.R. 601(my emphasis).

129. Ibid., at 602.

130. Section 51(ii), Australian constitution.

131. Dixon CJ in *Commissioner of Taxation v. Clyne* (1958) 100 C.L.R. 246 at 263.

132. (1994) 119 A.L.R. 577.

133. Ibid., at 586.

134. Blackstone, *Commentaries on the Laws of England.*

135. (1994) 119 A.L.R., at 610 (my emphasis).

136. This is the view adopted in the interpretation of Article 14 of the

German constitution (*Grundgesetz für die Bundesrepublik Deutschland vom 23. Mai 1949* (BGBl. S. 1), the title of which is often translated as the German Basic Law). See the "Hamburg Dyke Case," *Neue Juristische Wochenschrift* 22 (1969): 309.

137. In text above, following note 117. See generally, *Minister for Immigration and Ethnic Affairs v. Teoh* (1994) 128 A.L.R. 353.

138. See text above, following note 13.

139. *Newcrest.*

140. In text above, following note 90.

141. *United States v. Causby* 328 U.S. 256 (1946).

142. *Newcrest,* at 99 and 129.

143. (1948) 76 C.L.R. 1.

144. Ibid., at 349.

145. *Newcrest,* at 130.

146. Ibid., at 47–48.

147. Ibid., at 81.

148. In text above, following note 93.

149. K. Sperling, "Going Down the Takings Path: Private Property Rights and Public Interest in Land Use Decision-Making," *Environmental and Planning Law Journal* (Australia) 14 (1997): 427.

150. *Commonwealth v. Tasmania* (1983) 46 A.L.R. 625.

151. Ibid., at 707–709. See also Murphy J at 738 and Brennan J at 795–796.

152. Ibid., at 824–833.

153. *Trade Practices Commission v. Tooth & Co. Ltd.* (1979) 142 C.L.R. 397, 414–415.

154. *Newcrest.*

155. K. Sperling, "Going Down the Takings Path."

156. In text above, following note 125.

157. Fédération International des Géomètres—International Federation of Surveyors.

158. Bathurst, Australia, October 17–23, 1999, http://www.sli.unimelb.edu.au/UNConf99/index.html.

159. *The Bathurst Declaration on Land Administration for Sustainable Development,* 6, available at http://www.ddl.org/figtree/pub/figpub/pub21/figpub21.htm.

160. See further, M. Raff, "Environmental Obligation and the Western Liberal Concept of Property," 686–687.

161. *Newcrest.*

162. Or "partial taking," as it was described in *United States v. Causby* 328 U.S. 256 (1946).

163. *Newcrest.*

164. Ibid., 150.

165. Entscheidungen des Bundesverwaltungsgerchts [BVerwGE—Decisions of the Federal Administrative Court] (1991) 37, 232.

166. Above, note 136.

167. BVerw GE, 382–383.

168. Ibid., 386.

169. *Newcrest.*

170. Consider, for example, the factual dynamic in *Botany Municipal Council v. Federal Airports Corporation* (1992) 109 A.L.R. 321.

171. M. Raff, "Ten Principles of Quality in Environmental Impact Assessment," *Environmental and Planning Law Journal* (Australia) 14 (1997): 207, 214–215.

172. See "The Contaminations of Great Cities," *The Register* (Adelaide), July 3, 1857.

173. *Stockholm Declaration* 1972.

174. Environment Protection and Biodiversity Conservation Act of 1999 (Cth).

175. (1993) Q.B. 343. See also "Public Law Rules over Private Law as a Standard for Nuisance: OK?" *Journal of Environmental Law* 4 (1992): 251.

176. *Newcrest.*

177. *Kakada Conservatory Zone Inquiry,* Vol. 2, above, note 86.

178. *Newcrest.*

179. Ibid., 150.

180. See M. Raff, *German Real Property Law.*

181. In text above, following note 158.

182. See text above, at note 136.

183. See, for example, Human Rights and Equal Opportunity Commission, *Bringing Them Home—Report of the National Inquiry into the Separation of Aboriginal and Torres Strait Islander Children from their Families,* Sydney, 1997.

References

Australia Act of 1986

Australian constitution, 1901

Lands Acquisition Act of 1989

Planning and Environment Act of 1987

D. Brown, *Land Acquisition,* 4th ed. Sydney: Butterworths, 1996.

D. Eccles and T. Bryant, *Statutory Planning in Victoria,* 2nd ed. Sydney: Federation Press, 1999.

"Public Law Rules over Private Law as a Standard for Nuisance: OK?" *Journal of Environmental Law* 4 (1992): 251.

M. Raff, "Environmental Obligation and the Western Liberal Concept of Property." *Melb. U. L. Rev.* 22 (1998): 657.

M. Raff, "Ten Principles of Quality in Environmental Impact Assessment." *Environmental and Planning Law Journal* 14 (1997): 207, 214–215.

L. Sandercock, *Cities for Sale—Property, Politics and Urban Planning in Australia.* Melbourne: University Press, 1975.

K. Sperling, "Going Down the Takings Path: Private Property Rights and Public Interest in Land Use Decision-Making." *Environmental and Planning Law Journal* 14 (1997): 427.

Chapter 2

Compensation System
in the People's Republic of China

ZHAN XIAN BIN

A compensation system in every country with a private ownership system is based on the constitution. In the People's Republic of China (PRC), a communist state adopting the state ownership system, the national system to redress damages is based on the constitution (Art. 41), but the compensation system is not. The constitution of the PRC has no compensation provision comparable to Clause 3 of Article 29 in the constitution of Japan. In other words, the provision for compensation is put in individual acts.

For example, there have been "The Rights to the Use of Land Ordinance in Shanxi Gansu Ningxia Remote Area," proclaimed in January 1944; "Compensation Act for Flood Control Construction in Henan Province," proclaimed by the Henan Province government in August 1952; "Expropriation Act for the Construction of the National Projects," proclaimed by the state council (cabinet) in November 1953; "Amendment for Country Cooperatives Projects Ordinance," proclaimed by the central government in September 1962; "Expropriation Ordinance for National Projects," proclaimed by the Standing Committee of the National People's Congress in June 1982; "Field Law of the PRC" (hereinafter cited as FL), proclaimed by the Standing Committee of the National People's Congress on June 18, 1985; "Fishery Law of the PRC" (hereinafter cited as FIL), proclaimed by the Standing Committee of the National People's Congress in January 1986; "Land Administration Law of the PRC"

Professor, Law School, Tsinghua University. *This article was translated by Shinji Yukikado, professor of law, Sapporo Gakuin University.*

(hereinafter cited as LAL), proclaimed by the Standing Committee of the National People's Congress in June 1986; "Law on Reinstatement of Land," proclaimed by the state council on November 8, 1988; and the "Law on Compensation, Resettlement Subsidies in Compulsory Land Acquisition for Big or Medium Water Supply and Hydroelectric Power Plants," proclaimed by the state council on February 15, 1991. We can find the provisions on compensation for loss caused by legal acts of national organizations or public officials in such laws. The compensation in provisions is not constitutionally requested, but permitted by a policy.

The principles of compensation in the above-mentioned laws are: (1) equality in burden; (2) payment for real loss (payment for the loss that has already been caused or will be probably caused, not for the uncertain loss that possibly will be caused); (3) payment for the loss of property, not for spiritual loss, emotional pain, and so on that will be included in damages; and (4) payment for the direct loss (the direct causation between the loss and the legal act).

Lands in the PRC are owned by the state and collectives (quasi-state), and people, enterprises, and organizations own only the rights to the use of land. Thus, the state can expropriate the rights to the use of state-owned lands for economic development, culture, national defense, public projects, and so on through administrative power in sovereignty. In the country, collective ownership to lands is changed to state ownership at first, and then the state expropriates the rights to the use of the lands of farmers and village enterprises. In the cities, since the land is owned by the state, the rights to the use of land owned by citizens, enterprises, and organizations can be directly expropriated. Accordingly, compensation on lands in the PRC is only for rights to the use of land.

This essay focuses on the compensation systems of the PRC in LAL, FL, Law on Reinstatement of Land, Ordinance on Compensation, Resettlement Subsidies in Compulsory Land Acquisition for Big or Medium Water Supply and Hydroelectric Power Plants, and so on.

Prerequisite to Compensation by Land Expropriation

Three factors—and expropriation in accordance with laws (legal expropriation), land expropriation in accordance with procedures in laws (legal procedure), and the existence of direct causation—are the prerequisites to administrative compensation.

LEGAL EXPROPRIATION

"Legal" land expropriation consists of two factors. First, the expropriated land must be used for economy, culture, national defense, social service, and construction sites based upon the national investment plan of fixed assets or national approval. This is prescribed in Articles 21 and 22 of LAL (proclaimed at the Sixteenth Meeting of the Standing Committee of the Sixth National People's Congress on June 25, 1986, and revised at the Fifth Meeting of the Standing Committee of the Seventh National People's Congress on December 29, 1988). They are as follows:

Article 21
    When the state needs to requisition land owned by collectives or to use state-owned land for economic, cultural or national defense construction projects and for initiating public works. . . .

Article 22
    Upon approval, construction units may apply for use of land needed for those state construction projects which are listed in the state fixed assets investment plan or which may be built in accordance with state provisions.

Second, the procedure of land expropriation must be legal. The organization in charge of construction (to utilize the expropriated land) has to apply to the bureaus of Land Management in the local government beyond the county level for land expropriation, together with the construction planning instrument or other instruments approved, according to the state basic construction procedure, by the State Land Administration or Bureau of Land Management of local government beyond the county level. In China, the central government and the local governments sometimes have conflicting functions, and sometimes have the same functions. Thus, to solve just one problem or to obtain approval for one project, one has to go through different formalities and apply to several departments. This is an important issue to be reformed in the administration system.

The procedure after receiving the application is prescribed in Article 25 of LAL:

The State Council may approve it in the case of the requisition of more than 1,000 mu (1 mu = 6.667 are) of cultivated land or more than 2,000 mu of other types of land for state construction. In the case of the requisition of land in the administrative areas of provinces or autonomous regions, the governments of the provinces or autonomous regions may approve. In the case of the requisition of less than 3 mu of cultivated land and less than 10 mu of other types of land, the people's governments at the county level may approve. The limits of approval authority of people's governments of municipalities under provinces and of autonomous regions shall be decided by the standing committees of people's congresses of the provinces and autonomous regions.

In the case of the requisition of land within the administrative areas of municipalities directly under the central government, the people's governments of the municipalities may approve. The limits of approval authority of the people's governments of districts and counties under centrally administered municipalities shall be decided by the standing committees of the people's congresses of the municipalities.

The above-mentioned two factors will cause the legal relation of administrative compensation. If even one of the two factors is lacking, the legal relation fails to exist.

DIRECT CAUSATION

Direct causation between the loss (not including spiritual pains) and land expropriation is also indispensable for administrative compensation. "Loss" means the decrease in the property, the disability of enterprise production, and loss of people's living conditions (houses and so on).

The Persons Compensated in Land Expropriation, Contents of Compensation, and Standards to Calculate Compensation

THE PERSONS COMPENSATED

The persons compensated are the individuals (natural persons) owning the land use rights, and enterprises (legal persons) (state, collective, and private enterprises having less than eight employees; joint ventures having relations with foreign capitals; enterprises having foreign stocks; foreign enterprises; and overseas Chinese enterprises) owning the land use rights. Article 10 of the present constitution of the PRC (proclaimed at the First Conference of the Fifth National People's Congress in 1982, and revised at the First Conference of the Seventh National People's Congress on April 12, 1988) provides as follows:

> Land in the urban areas of cities shall be owned by the state. Land in rural and suburban areas shall be owned by collectives except for the portions designated as owned by state according to law. Residential district, reserved district, and reserved mountain shall be owned by the collectives.

The state or collectives own all of the land in the PRC. So, not the ownership but the land use rights are expropriated for public good. Administrative compensation is paid for the land use rights lost. LAL has the provisions on the contents of compensation to individuals and enterprises (legal persons, public or collective organizations using land). For example, Article 30 provides as follows:

> All kinds of compensation and resettlement subsidies paid for requisitioned land on account of state construction, except for the compensation for individually owned attachments or young crops on the requisitioned land which shall be paid to such individuals, shall be used by the units being requisitioned to develop production, to provide employment for the extra labor force due to requisition of the land and as living subsidies for people who cannot be employed. Such funds shall not be used for other purposes and shall not be appropriated by any unit or individual.

THE CONTENTS OF COMPENSATION AND STANDARDS TO CALCULATE COMPENSATION

Since the differences in areas or races in the PRC (which has vast territory and fifty-six races) are reflected in the values of land, the differences make the compulsory unification of these values in the state inappropriate. So LAL has the fundamental provisions on contents of compensation and standards to calculate compensation. The people's congresses of the provinces, autonomous regions, and municipalities directly under the central government, with the power delegated by the National People's Congress, can only enact laws according to their values of land, which do not violate LAL. I will explain the contents of compensation and standards to calculate compensation of LAL, and the laws of provinces.

The Contents of Compensation and Standards to Calculate Compensation in Expropriation of Collective-owned Land

Compensation in the expropriation of collective-owned land is comprised mainly of payment for (1) land, (2) attachments or young crops owned by individuals, (3) living subsidies (see Art. 30 of LAL), and (4) expropriated land and resettlement subsidies.

1. The standard to calculate compensation in expropriation of collective-owned land: Article 27 of LAL provides, "The compensation for requisition of cultivated land shall be three to six times the average annual output value of the requisitioned land for the three years preceding such requisition." This is a fundamental provision on calculation. It also provides:

> Units using requisitioned land for state construction shall pay land compensation. The compensation for requisition of cultivated land shall be three to six times the average annual output value of the requisitioned land for three years preceding such requisition. Provinces, autonomous regions, and municipalities directly under the central government shall stipulate standards of compensation for requisition of other types of land with reference to the standard of compensation for requisition of cultivated land.

As a result, provinces, autonomous regions, and municipalities directly under the central government stipulate the standards of compensation reflecting their characteristics, according to this article of LAL. The standards of provinces are classified into three types.

(a) *Guangdong and Yunnan Provinces*. These provinces have a standard applying to paddy fields, vegetable fields, fruit fields, other cultivated land, and fields shortly after cultivation. In the case of vegetable fields, fruit fields, and cultivated land, the compensation is four to five times the output value in the year of expropriation. In the case of fields shortly after cultivation, it is three to four times the output value in the year of expropriation.

(b) *Shanxi, Zhejiang, Fujian, Shandong, and Hubei Provinces*. These provinces have a standard applying to administrative regions (cultivated land in the suburbs of big or medium cities, cultivated land in the suburbs of small cities, and cultivated land in the country). In the case of cultivated land in the suburbs of big or medium cities, the compensation is five to six times the average annual output value of the land for three years preceding such expropriation. In the case of cultivated land in the suburbs of small cities, it is four to five times the output value of the land in the year of expropriation. In the case of cultivated land in the country, it is three to five times the output value of the land in the year of expropriation.

(c) *Guangxi and Other Provinces.* These provinces have the same standard as that of LAL, explained above.

2. The standard to calculate compensation for attachments or young crops on the collective-owned land expropriated: Provinces, autonomous regions, and municipalities directly under the central government have their own provisions on attachments with the power delegated by Clause 2, Article 27 of LAL. In the provisions, real loss is regarded as a standard to calculate, and real loss is calculated according to the present price in each region.

Most of the provinces and so on have provisions that real loss is a standard to calculate young crops. But Henan Province has a provision that 60 to 80 percent of the output value of the cultivated land for three months is the standard on the basis of Article 30, LAL Implementation Law of Henan Province.

3. The standard to calculate resettlement subsidies: This is stipulated in Clause 2, Article 28 of LAL:

Resettlement subsidies for requisition of cultivated land shall be calculated according to the agricultural population needing to be resettled. The agricultural population needing to be resettled shall be calculated by dividing the amount of requisitioned cultivated land by the average amount of original cultivated land per person of the unit being requisitioned. The standard resettlement subsidy to be divided among members of the agricultural population needing resettlement shall be two or three times the average annual output value of each mu of the requisitioned cultivated land for the three years preceding such requisition. However, the highest resettlement subsidy for each mu of requisitioned cultivated land shall not exceed ten times its average annual output value for the three years preceding such requisition. Provinces, autonomous regions, and municipalities directly under the central government shall stipulate respective standards for resettlement subsidies for requisition of other types of land with reference to the standard resettlement subsidy for cultivated land.

Since there are many farmers and the area of cultivated land per farmer is small in Jiangsu Province, the compensation for expropriating 1 mu of cultivated land will be higher. Article 22 of LAL Implementation Law of Jiangsu Province provides as follows:

> The resettlement subsidy shall be three times the average annual output value of cultivated land for three years preceding the expropriation. In the case of less than 1 mu of cultivated land per one person before expropriation, the resettlement subsidy shall be four times the output value of the land in the year of expropriation. If 1 mu of cultivated land is decreased by 0.1 mu, the resettlement subsidy shall be two times the output value of 1 mu in the year of expropriation. However, it shall not exceed 10 times the output value of 1 mu in the year of expropriation.

And Article 19 of LAL Implementation Regulation of Jiagxi Province provides as follows:

> The resettlement subsidy in the expropriation of merchandise vegetable fields in municipalities directly under the central government and cities shall be calculated under ten times the average annual output value. In the case of expropriation of vegetable fields in the suburbs, the resettlement subsidy shall be calculated under eight times the average annual output value.

In the provinces of Heilong Jiang, Shanxi, Shan Dong, and Hubei, the province laws provide that the resettlement subsidy shall be calculated on that of cultivated land. The province laws in SiChuan, Zhejiang, and so on provide that "The subsidy shall be calculated on half of that of calculated land." And the province laws in Fujian and Hunan provide, "The subsidy shall be calculated on one to four times" (Fujian Province) and "two to three times" (Hunan Province) "the output value for the year preceding the expropriation."

The basic formula for calculating a resettlement subsidy is as follows:

Redundant Labor Force = Area of Cultivated Land
÷ (Area of Cultivated Land before Expropriation ÷ Labor Force Index of Expropriated Land Use Rights Owners)

Resettlement Subsidy per One Person in Redundant Labor Force
= Resettlement Subsidy ÷ Labor Force Index Given Resettlement Subsidy

4. The special provision on compensation for expropriated land and resettlement subsidies: The states have the provision in LAL on compensation for expropriated land and resettlement subsidies, to consider the state's financial circumstances and the living standard of the "peasants." Article 29 of LAL provides as follows:

> If land compensation and resettlement subsidies paid in accordance with Articles 27 and 28 of this law are still insufficient to maintain the original living standard of the peasants needing resettlement, the resettlement subsidy may be increased upon approval of people's governments of provinces, autonomous regions, or municipalities directly under the central government. However, the total land compensation and resettlement subsidy shall not exceed twenty times the average yearly output value of the requisitioned land for the three years preceding such requisition.

The Contents of Compensation and the Standards to Calculate Compensation in Expropriation of State-owned Land

The contents of compensation and the standards to calculate compensation in expropriation of state-owned land are dependent on the uses of the land before expropriation. The uses are generally classified into four types: (1) land for agricultural production; (2) land for nonagricultural production; (3) land for offices of state agencies, army, and nonprofit organizations; and (4) land for residence. The uses make the contents and compensation standards different.

The Contents of Compensation and the Compensation Standards

(a) The contents of compensation: Compensation for the expropriation of land for agricultural production is paid for attachments, young crops, investment in the land, and unemployment of workers engaged in agricultural production.

(b) The compensation standards: The compensation for the above-mentioned four losses is calculated via LAL in most provinces, autonomous regions, and municipalities centrally governed in the PRC. However, there are some provinces enacting their own compensation standard regulations on the basis of the standards of LAL. For example, Article 11 of the Land Administration Implementation Regulation of Hubei Province provides that "the compensation in the expropriation of land for agricultural production shall be calculated on the lower limit of compensation for collective-owned land expropriation."

Article 18 of the Land Administration Implementation Regulation of Guangdong Province provides as follows:

> The compensation in the expropriation of state-owned land or area such as farms, woods, and fisheries shall be calculated under 70 percent of the compensation in the expropriation of collective-owned land. The compensation standards of young crops and attachments on the expropriated land, and of resettlement subsidies shall be the same as those in the expropriation of collective-owned land.

Article 28 of the Land Administration Implementation Regulation of Heilong Jiang Province provides as follows:

> In the expropriation of state-owned cultivated land used by another organization, the compensation for the rights to the use shall be calculated four to five times its average annual output value for the three years preceding such expropriation, or instead of it the expropriating organization shall take the responsibility of securing resettlement for the farmers losing work. This regulation means that the compensation standards in the expropriation of state-owned land are the same as those in the collective-owned land expropriation. However, it shows that securing resettlement is the alternative to compensation for land.

The Contents of Compensation and the Compensation Standards in the Case of Expropriation of State-owned Land for Nonagricultural Production and Management

(a) The contents of compensation: The compensation is paid for attachments, loss by the cessation of agricultural production, and relocation cost of residents.

(b) The compensation standards: Compensation standards are dependent on local regulations. The compensation for attachments is calculated on the basis of real loss. When the expropriated enterprise cannot continue production, there are three types of provisions for compensation.

The first type of provision is that employees' salaries are compensated as a loss for the period of the stopped production. For example, Article 74 of the Taiyuen City Construction Management Regulation provides that "The expropriating organization shall pay compensation for relocation costs of the factory, enterprise and organization of commerce and industry, and employees' salaries while the production is stopped. However, the salary shall not exceed one month's amount."

The second type of provision shows that the loss for the period of the stopped production is calculated on the average profits of the expropriated enterprise. For example, Clause 2, Article 30 of the Shaanxi Province Regulation of Land Administration Implementation provides as follows:

> The reasonable compensation shall be paid to the expropriated enterprise whose production has become impossible or stopped, and besides, the organization using the expropriated land shall pay the average profits for the six months preceding the relocation for the period decided by the agreement with the expropriated enterprise.

The third provision shows that the types of organization using the land before expropriation decide the compensation standards. For example, Article 15 of the Beijing City Regulation of Construction Relocation Implementation provides:

> In the case of the state-owned organization, all of the loss caused by the shutdown or relocation shall not be compensated. In the case of the collective-owned organization and privately managed organization, the loss caused by the relocation shall be compensated by the organization newly using the expropriated land according to the provisions.

Moreover, if it is necessary to relocate the organization using the land before expropriation, the construction unit (new user of the expropriated land) shall be responsible for relocation. However, if the organization that used the land before expropriation moves by itself, the relocation cost shall be compensated by the construction unit (see Art. 34 of LAL).

The Contents of Compensation and the Compensation Standards in the Case of Expropriation of Land Used for Office of State Organs and So On

(a) The contents of compensation: Only the loss of attachments on the expropriated land is compensated in the case of expropriation of land for offices of state organizations, army, state enterprises, nonprofit organizations, and so on. This is provided in the local laws.

(b) The compensation standards: According to each set of local laws, the organization using the land after expropriation shall generally compensate for the reasonable investment and materials' costs calculated on the basis of the area of the demolished building. The expropriated organization can then move to a new place and build its office using the compensation.

The Contents of Compensation and the Compensation Standards in the Case of Expropriation of State-owned Land Used for Residence

(a) The contents of compensation: Loss of a residence, loss in living conditions caused by losing a residence, and relocation cost are compensated.

(b) The compensation standards: This is provided in each of the local laws. According to them, the department in charge of real estate appraises the demolished residence, and the compensation is calculated on the basis of the appraisal in general. However, compensation is never paid for an illegal residence.

The compensation for loss in living conditions caused by losing a residence is generally that of providing a new residence. Its standard is providing a new residence whose floor area is the same as that of the demolished residence. If the floor area of the demolished residence is too small, providing a new residence whose floor area is a little larger is permitted. When the resident rents a house until moving to a new residence, the organization using the land after expropriation shall pay 8 to 10 renminbi per person per month for rent. If the organization using the land after expropriation provides a prefabricated house, the rent will be paid by the organization. If the organization to which those losing residences belong temporarily provides housing, 4 to 6 renminbi per person per month for rent will be paid by the land-using organization. The compensation for rent ends when the residents move into new residences.

(c) The standard of compensation for relocation cost: Article 34 of LAL, as a general provision of relocation cost compensation, provides that "construction units which require state-owned land currently used by other units shall pay proper compensation to those units if losses are caused by the requisition, and shall be responsible for moving such units if necessary." Each local law has provisions on the standard of reasonable compensation. For example, Article 83 of the Taiyuen City Regulation for City Construction Management provides as follows:

> Construction units shall pay 30 to 50 renminbi in a lump sum on the basis of the distance to the new residence as relocation cost compensation. And construction units shall pay two times the above-mentioned relocation cost compensation to residents moving to a prefabricated house.

There are some local laws with provisions that residents relocating in cooperation with construction units are given "three days of paid vacation." There are many other provisions.

The Payment of Compensation in Land Expropriation and the Management of Compensation

THE PAYER OF COMPENSATION

Clause 1, Article 28 of LAL provides, "In addition to payment of compensation when requisitioning land for state construction, the land-using units shall also pay for resettlement subsidies." Accordingly, the organization using the expropriated land pays the compensation.

However, there are various local laws on how to pay compensation, reflecting the local circumstances in accordance with the principle of LAL. The ways to pay compensation are generally classified into three groups. First, the land-using units pay compensation and resettlement subsidies in a lump sum into bank accounts of persons being expropriated, or directly pay cash to them in a lump sum. Second, land-using units provide new attachments and young crops of the same quality and of the same number as those on the expropriated land. Third, in the case of the expropriation for the reconstruction of railways, roads, and drainage, the land having been used for railways and so on before expropriation is changed to cultivated land, being exchanged for the expropriated land. Any imbalance in the exchange is adjusted by compensation. Although land-using units pay compensation according to provisions, the state really pays compensation with construction costs through land-using units.

THE USE OF COMPENSATION

Article 30 of LAL provides that "all kinds of compensation and resettlement subsidies . . . shall not be used for other purposes and shall not be appropriated by any unit or individual." This provision shows that the persons being expropriated cannot perfectly and freely use the compensation and resettlement subsidies. The purposes for their use are limited to six: developing production; promoting the efficiency of cultivated land; enhancing reproduction and facilities' renewal of enterprises; providing employment for the extra labor force; providing living subsidies for people who cannot be employed; and providing newly built or rebuilt offices and residences (see Art. 30 of LAL).

The Management of Compensation

Each set of local laws has provisions on management of compensation to check the above-mentioned six purposes in accordance with Article 30 of LAL. Although the provisions are different, reflecting local circumstances, there are two groups. The first states that the compensation and resettlement subsidies are centrally managed by the organization being expropriated, and that they are used under the control of county or township governments. The second states that the organization being expropriated makes a plan to use the compensation and resettlement subsidies according to the plan reviewed and approved by the land management bureau of the municipality directly under the central government or county (including city) governments.

The Legal Responsibility
in Illegal Use of Compensation

Article 49 of LAL provides as follows:

> Units at higher levels or other units that unlawfully seize land compensation and resettlement subsidies paid to the units whose land has been requisitioned shall be ordered to return such funds and make compensation, and they may be fined concurrently. Disciplinary sanctions shall be adopted against those who bear the main responsibility, either by the units to which they belong or by offices at a higher level. Unlawful seizures by individuals shall be handled as in the case of graft.

When there are extenuating circumstances, disciplinary sanctions are adopted. However, in the case of no extenuating circumstances, Article 155 of the Criminal Law applies the embezzlement case. It provides as follows:

> If public officials embezzle public property, taking advantage of their official positions, they shall be sentenced to penal servitude for less than five years or detention. In the case of aggravating circumstances such as enormous sums being embezzled, they shall be sentenced to penal servitude for more than five years. Moreover, in the case of more aggravating circumstances, they shall be sentenced to penal servitude for an indefinite term or death.

The Compensation in the Special Expropriation of Land

The special expropriation of land in the PRC means (1) land acquisition for big or medium water supply and hydroelectric power plants, (2) temporary use of state-owned or collective-owned land for construction, and (3) occupation of state-owned forest for construction, development of mines, and so on, and the destruction of state-owned or collective-owned land for construction. Articles 5, 6, 7, 8, and 9 of the Law on Compensation, Resettlement Subsidies in Compulsory Land Acquisition for Big or Medium Water Supply and Hydroelectric Power Plants (proclaimed at the State Council on February 15, 1991) (hereinafter cited as the Law) provide for the contents and standards of compensation in abovementioned (1). The contents and standards of compensation are dependent on the scale of the plants. The compensation for attachments and young crops is also dependent on it.

THE COMPENSATION AND RESETTLEMENT SUBSIDIES IN THE CASE OF CONSTRUCTION OF BIG WATER SUPPLY AND HYDROELECTRIC POWER PLANTS

According to Articles 5 and 6, the compensation for cultivated land shall be three to four times the average annual output for the three years preceding expropriation, and resettlement subsidies shall be two to three times the average annual output for the three years preceding expropriation; the compensation and resettlement subsidies in the expropriation of non-cultivated land shall be paid by the governments of provinces, autonomous regions, and municipalities directly under the central government in accordance with the standard of cultivated land acquisition; and the compensation and resettlement subsidies shall be paid to the individual persons being expropriated, and the subsidies necessary to maintain the original living standard of people after expropriation of cultivated or non-cultivated land may be paid in accordance with a higher standard than that explained above. However, the total of compensation and resettlement subsidies shall be limited. To put it concretely, in the case of more than 1 mu of cultivated land occupied by one person, the total shall not exceed eight times the average output for the three years preceding expropriation. In the case of 0.5 to 1 mu occupied by one person, it shall not exceed twelve times the average output for the three years preceding expropriation. And in the case of less than 0.5 mu, it shall not exceed twenty times the average output for the three years preceding expropriation.

THE COMPENSATION AND RESETTLEMENT SUBSIDIES IN THE CASE OF CONSTRUCTION OF MEDIUM WATER SUPPLY AND HYDROELECTRIC POWER PLANTS

Article 7 of the Law provides that "the standard of compensation and resettlement subsidies shall be stipulated by the governments of provinces, autonomous regions, and municipalities directly under the central government referring to the standards provided in" LAL and Articles 5 and 6 of the Law. Accordingly, this standard is provided in each local law.

THE COMPENSATION FOR ATTACHMENTS AND YOUNG CROPS ON EXPROPRIATED LAND IN THE CASE OF CONSTRUCTION OF BIG AND MEDIUM WATER SUPPLY AND HYDROELECTRIC POWER PLANTS

Article 8 of the Law provides that "the standard of compensation for attachments and young crops shall be stipulated by the governments of provinces, autonomous regions, and municipalities directly under the central government." Each local government pays compensation according to local law on the basis of LAL.

THE COMPENSATION FOR TEMPORARY USE OF STATE-OWNED OR COLLECTIVE-OWNED LAND FOR CONSTRUCTION

When the state uses state-owned or collective-owned land for construction and returns the land to the owner after finishing the construction, using the land itself causes loss for that period. The compensation standards for such special land use are dependent on how the expropriated land has been used.

In the case of land use for storage sites for materials, roads, other temporary installations, erecting lines above ground, laying pipelines underground, and building other underground projects such as subways, Clauses 2 and 3, Article 33 of LAL apply. They provide as follows:

> 2. Storage sites for materials, transportation routes, and other temporary installations of construction projects shall be situated within the limits of the requisitioned land as far as possible. When additional land for temporary use is truly necessary, the construction units may apply to the agencies authorizing the use of land for projects, specifying the amount of land and the time limit for such temporary use, and shall sign temporary land

use agreements with agricultural collective economic organizations upon such applications being approved. Construction units shall pay compensation each year during the time limit based on the average annual output value of such land for the preceding three years. No permanent structures shall be erected on such land for temporary use. Construction units shall restore the production conditions of such land and return it promptly after the period of temporary use expires.

3. Requisition of land for the temporary uses of erecting lines above ground, laying pipelines underground, building other underground projects, carrying out geological prospecting, and so on shall be subject to the approval of local people's governments at the county level, and compensation shall be paid in accordance with the provisions of the preceding paragraph.

The Compensation for Occupation of State-owned Forest for Construction, Development of Mines, and So On, and the Destruction of State-owned or Collective-owned Land for Construction

Clause 3, Article 33 of LAL provides that "construction units shall ask for approval from local people's governments at the county level if land surveys are needed for choosing construction sites and shall pay proper compensation for any losses caused."

The Compensation for Land Subsidence Caused by Developing Underground Resources

LAL has no provision for this compensation. However, the local laws have the provisions. For example, Article 25 of the Jiangsu Province Regulation for LAL Implementation and Article 21 of the Henan Province Regulation for LAL Implementation contain these provisions.

The Compensation for Temporary Occupation of State-owned Forest for Facilities Construction and So On

Clause 3 of Article 9, Regulation for Forest Law Implementation of the PRC (approved by the state council on April 28, 1986, and enacted by the Ministry of Forest Industry on May 10, 1986), applies to this case. It provides as follows:

Units occupying forest shall pay compensation for real loss to the organization managing the forest. In the case of the occupation of the forest for less than one year, the compensation may be appropriately decreased. The people's governments of provinces, autonomous regions, and municipalities directly under the central government shall enact the regulations for compensation.

The Compensation of Reinstatement

Reinstatement means that when the other units using state-owned or collective-owned land for construction destroy the land, the land-using units or units in charge of construction reinstate it after construction. This is one kind of compensation. Article 19 of the Law on Reinstatement of Land (proclaimed by the state council on November 8, 1988) stipulates the definite content and standard of compensation for various cases. Article 14 of the same law provides as follows:

The units using state-owned or collective-owned land shall be responsible for the reinstatement of the land destroyed by themselves, and shall pay the compensation for the loss caused by the destruction to the units damaged. The latter compensation is for the loss of cultivated land, wood, and other land. In the compensation for the loss of cultivated land, the real loss shall be the average annual output for three years preceding the land destruction. The real loss to enterprises and individuals shall be paid every year. If the land-using units reinstate the land by themselves, the period for the compensation shall be decided according to the reasonable period stipulated in the agreement. In the case of other land, the compensation shall be based on the above-mentioned principles. The standard of compensation for attachments and young crops shall be stipulated by provinces, autonomous regions, and municipalities directly under the central government.

The real loss standard is generally adopted in the local laws.

The Points at Issue

Compensation in Land Expropriation According to the Local Laws Without any Provisions in the Constitution

Compensation by legal actions is for the special loss of property, but not for spiritual pains. Which provisions in the constitution of the PRC show these principles? We have no provisions such as Clause 3, Article 29 of the constitution of Japan, providing that "private property may be taken for public use upon just compensation therefor."

The relationship between the constitution and compensation provisions in laws provide the legal basis of compensation: (1) If compensation shall be constitutionally requested, and laws have no provisions for compensation, there is a problem in claiming the compensation is possible or not on the basis of the constitution. (2) If compensation shall be not constitutionally requested, and laws have the provisions for compensation, the compensation is permitted by a policy. It is naturally possible to abolish the policy. Then if laws have no provisions for compensation, it is naturally possible to make provisions in laws.

Accordingly, because the constitution of the PRC has no provision for compensation, LAL, FL, and other individual laws have compensation provisions as a policy. The above-mentioned (2) applies to the PRC.

However, there are some scholars who think that the constitution has a provision for compensation. They argue that the provision is Clause 3, Article 41 of the constitution, providing that "People whose rights are violated and damaged by state organizations or public officials have the right to claim the damage according to laws," and that this provision includes compensation. So even when there is no provision in a law, claiming compensation is possible on the basis of the constitution, according to this opinion.

In the constituion of Japan, Article 17 on damages provides that "every person may sue for redress as provided by law from the state or public entity, in case he has suffered damage through an illegal act of any public official." On the other hand, Clause 3 of Article 29 for compensation provides that "private property may be taken for public use upon just compensation therefor." The difference between Articles 17 and 29 is whether the actions of state organizations and public officials are legal or illegal. I think that trying to put compensation into Article 41 of the constitution of the PRC ignores the difference. And I am concerned about the possible revision of laws to abolish the compensation provisions to protect not people's rights but administrative authority, because the constitution has no provision for compensation.

COMPENSATION AS A NATIONAL POLICY

I think that the right to claim compensation is not guaranteed by the constitution of the PRC. I understand that the individual laws such as

LAL, FL, the Law of Road Management, and so on have compensation provisions as a national policy, and that the state makes the provisions as a favor for people. For example, Articles 24 through 34 of LAL show this, and Article 31 provides as follows:

> Land administration departments of local people's governments at or above the county level shall coordinate the units being requisitioned, units using requisitioned land and other units concerned to help resettle the extra labor force due to requisition of land for state construction by developing agricultural and sideline production, and setting up township (town) or village enterprises. If there are still people who cannot be resettled, the qualified persons among them may be given work in the units using the requisitioned land or other units under collective ownership or ownership by the whole people, and the corresponding resettlement subsidy shall be transferred to the units that absorb such a labor force.
>
> If all the land of the unit is requisitioned, members originally registered in agricultural households may change their status to nonagricultural households upon approval of the people's governments of provinces, autonomous regions, or municipalities directly under the central government. People's governments at or above the county level may consult with the relevant township (town) or village to decide upon the settlement of the original collective-owned property and the compensation and resettlement subsidies received, which shall be used for organizing production and as living subsidies for those who cannot be employed, but shall not be distributed privately.

The provisions (on the compensation, resettlement subsidies, living subsidies, registration of nonagricultural households, relocation, and so on) is based on the policy of giving benefits to people and are often found in the laws such as FL, the Law of Road Management, and so on. Compensation means benefits from the state. I think this is because the history of the PRC in giving priority to duties does not permit the right to compensation. Or can I inversely say that the nonstipulated right exists because of the history?

Conclusion

The national liability system to redress damages and to compensate loss have developed among countries having a system of private ownership. The PRC (founded on October 1, 1949) has a system of national ownership and owns most of the productive means. It is because of Chinese values that there are no conflicts between the people and administrative authority, and if any, they will be resolved not by courts but by the administrative authority itself, because the people are the master of the state, and the state organizations represent the interests of the people. So the people of the PRC have not been conscious of the function of the law to guarantee their rights and benefits. In other words, they have recognized that the state of the people should be exempted from redressing damages of people caused by public officials as servants in doing their work for people. Although the PRC has been introducing the market system and private ownership system, the state, or people, still own the land in the public ownership system. The people have no ownership of land, but have rights to the use of land (see Art. 2 of LAL). So if the state exercises administrative power in sovereignty over state-owned land for economy, culture, national defense, and public projects, it violates not private ownership but the right to the use of land. Accordingly, since land expropriation in the PRC is not the expropriation of land ownership but that of land use rights, the compensation in the expropriation of land is not for land ownership but for land use rights, and paying that compensation is based on national policy.

Chapter 3

Government as Ground Landlord and Land Use Regulator: The Hong Kong Experience

ANTON COORAY

Hong Kong was first occupied by the British in 1841 and became a Crown colony in 1843. It remained under British administration until July 1, 1997, when sovereignty over Hong Kong was handed back to the People's Republic of China.[1] In pursuance of the Sino-British Joint Declaration of 1984, China enacted the Basic Law of Hong Kong, which guarantees that Hong Kong will continue its system of government and way of life for at least fifty years after 1997.[2] As a Special Administrative Region of the People's Republic of China, Hong Kong enjoys a "high degree of autonomy" and has been empowered to exercise executive, legislative, and independent judicial powers.[3] The Basic Law confers extensive powers on Hong Kong except certain powers in relation to foreign affairs and defense, which are within the jurisdiction of the Chinese central government.[4] The "One Country-Two Systems" concept, which underlies the Basic Law, ensures that the Chinese socialist system and policies will not be practiced in Hong Kong and that the previous capitalist system and way of life will remain unchanged for fifty years from 1997.[5]

The Basic Law provides for a system of government modeled on the pre-1997 system. It continues the colonial model of an "executive-led system" of government, in which the legislature plays only a secondary part. At the apex of the government structure is the chief executive, selected in Hong Kong and appointed by the Chinese central government, and accountable to the Chinese central government and to Hong Kong.[6] Legislative power is vested in the Legislative Council, an elective body.

Professor, Faculty of Law, City University of Hong Kong.

While, in theory, any member of the Legislative Council may introduce a legislative measure, only the government has the power to introduce legislation relating to public expenditure, political structure, or the operation of the government. It is only with the written consent of the chief executive that a member of the Legislative Council may introduce a private member's bill relating to government policies.[7] However, the Legislative Council is by no means an unimportant part of government. The government cannot enact legislation or implement any financial measures without Legislative Council approval. Significantly, the Legislative Council today, unlike its predecessor under British administration, has the power to impeach the chief executive.[8]

An executive council appointed by the chief executive from among principal government officers, members of the Legislative Council, and public figures[9] has the principal function of assisting the chief executive in policy making.[10] The public service performs a central part in Hong Kong's system of government. The Basic Law, however, does not clearly demarcate functions among the chief executive, the Executive Council, and the public service.[11]

The judiciary is kept clearly separate from the executive and legislative branches of the government. The Basic Law explicitly sets out the need for courts to exercise judicial power independently, free from any interference.[12] Judicial appointments must be made on the basis of judicial and professional qualities.[13] The chief executive must act on the recommendation of an independent judicial service commission in making judicial appointments.[14] Judges may be recruited from other common law jurisdictions, save that the chief justice of the Court of Final Appeal and the chief judge of the High Court must be Chinese citizens who are permanent residents of Hong Kong.[15]

The Basic Law guarantees the continuation of the judicial system previously practiced in Hong Kong, subject to the creation of a new court of final appeal to replace the Privy Council as Hong Kong's highest appellate tribunal.[16] In criminal or civil proceedings, the principles previously applied in Hong Kong and the rights previously enjoyed by parties will be maintained.[17] On the basis of the system previously applied, the government must make provisions for local lawyers and lawyers from outside Hong Kong to work and practice in Hong Kong.[18]

The Basic Law guarantees the continuation of Hong Kong's common law system of administration of justice.[19] Common law and equity will continue to be sources of law, and Hong Kong's courts, structured on the U.K. model, are free to refer to precedents from other common law jurisdictions.[20] The Basic Law guarantees fundamental rights and freedoms and provides that the International Covenant on Civil and Political Rights will remain in force in Hong Kong.[21]

One of the general principles enunciated in the Basic Law is that Hong Kong must protect the right of private ownership of property in accordance with the law.[22] In this context, private property rights do not mean freehold property rights, of which there are none in Hong Kong. The only exception would be the possibility of acquiring ownership of land by adverse possession. A person may acquire possessory title against the government by adverse possession for a period of sixty years under the Limitation Ordinance.[23] There are no known instances of anyone successfully setting up possessory title against the government.[24] Apart from the unlikely exception of land held on possessory title, the highest form of property rights in Hong Kong is to hold property on lease from the government. All land in Hong Kong belonged to the Crown before July 1, 1997, and passed into the hands of the People's Republic of China. However, it is the Hong Kong government that is responsible for the management of land and natural resources in Hong Kong. The Hong Kong government may lease the land and will be exclusively entitled to the proceeds of such land leases, as before 1997.[25]

It is in this light that we will now proceed to examine the land use regulation system in Hong Kong and the system of compensation for deprivation of property rights. The only observation that needs to be made at the outset is that Hong Kong's land use regulation system is largely modeled on the U.K. experience.

Hong Kong's Landholding System

Land has always been a valuable resource, if not the only valuable natural resource, in Hong Kong, and has always remained government property. Upon the formal British occupation of Hong Kong in 1841, when it was not clear whether the British would have a permanent foothold in the island, one of the first steps taken by the administration was to make a declaration of its land policy. The Public Notice and Declaration of May 1, 1841, stated as follows: "With a view to the reservation to the Crown of as extensive a control over the lands as may be compatible with the immediate progress of the establishment, it is now declared that the number of allotments to be disposed of from time to time, will be regulated with due regard to the actual public wants."[26]

The first land sale took place in May 1841. Captain Eliot, the British plenipotentiary, authorized the auction sale of leasehold interests in land and gave an assurance that subject to approval of the Imperial Government, he would allow the leasehold interests to be converted to freehold estates. This promise, however, was frustrated by an order from the Imperial Government in 1843, the year when, as a result of a Sino-British Treaty,[27] Hong Kong became a Crown colony.[28] The secretary of state directed Pottinger, the first governor of Hong Kong, that land was not to be granted in perpetuity, or for a greater length of time than was thought necessary to induce tenants to erect substantial buildings (seventy-five years), and that renewals were to be at the governor's discretion.[29] The secretary of state also directed that grants were to go to the highest bidder.

The practice of granting land leases to the highest bidder for a term of seventy-five years had its first change in 1849, when Governor Bonham allowed the grant of leases for terms of 999 years, virtually freehold. The governor also directed that the bidding was not to be for the annual rent, but for the payment of a single premium.[30] In 1860, when the British administration secured what is now known as Urban Kowloon in perpetuity from China to accommodate the increased demand for land,[31] the government granted 999-year leases to established Chinese residents of that area. New grants of land in Urban Kowloon, however, were on short-term leases.[32]

In 1898 the secretary of state disapproved of long leases and ordered that leases must be granted for a period of seventy-five years only.[33] When the British secured, through the Convention of Peking in 1898,[34] a ninety-nine-year lease of the New Territories of Hong Kong, the government could not grant land leases exceeding ninety-nine years, in order that all land leases in the New Territories would terminate at least three days before July 1, 1997.

In 1946 it was decided that when a nonrenewable seventy-five-year lease (meaning a lease without an express right of renewal) came to an end, a renewal would only be granted by way of a new lease, and not by way of an extension of time for the old lease. This meant that the government was able to draft a new land lease incorporating terms that it thought must govern the use and development of land in a particular area. The Executive Council proposed a "policy of fuller development for the whole district and the exercise of compulsion to build to an extent compatible with the class of the area," and the government decided that "the adequate development of the leased area in accordance with the needs of the community would be a condition precedent to the grant of any new Crown lease."[35]

In 1947 the secretary of state authorized the leasing of land for community purposes, such as educational institutions, by way of private treaty at reduced premium.[36] In 1960 the government began to auction government land according to a land disposal program, in place of the old system whereby the government auctioned land on an ad hoc basis whenever there was demand for particular sites.[37] Today, most government land is sold (i.e., given on lease) by public auction or tender. However, land is granted at a nominal or reduced premium to nonprofit institutions that provide housing, educational, and charitable facilities.[38]

The position today, endorsed by the Basic Law, is that the state (i.e., the People's Republic of China) owns all land in Hong Kong, land that was previously owned by the British Crown. Just as the Hong Kong colonial government managed land before July 1, 1997, the government of the Hong Kong Special Administrative Region is responsible for the management, use, and development of land and for the grant of land leases. The Basic Law guarantees that revenues derived from such land management are exclusively at the disposal of Hong Kong government.[39]

Government Leases as a Means of Regulating the Use and Development of Land[40]

Being the sole ground landlord,[41] the government is able to regulate the location, manner, and intensity of land use developments. As we have seen above, the government has in recent times incorporated lease conditions designed to implement its land development policies in respect of different areas of Hong Kong. Today, the government implements its land use policies mainly in the following ways:

First, the government has divided Hong Kong into three population density zones. While density controls in zone 1 are effected through the Planning Regulations made under the Buildings Ordinance,[42] density controls in the other two zones are implemented through lease conditions.[43] Since 1956 it has been the practice of the Hong Kong government to follow the density zoning guidelines quite rigidly when renewing leases or granting new leases.[44]

Second, as noted elsewhere in this essay, first-generation outline zoning plans do not contain enforcement provisions and depend on the Buildings Ordinance controls and lease controls for implementation.[45] When planning permission is granted for a development, it is usual for the permission to be given subject to conditions, which set out the planning parameters.[46] If a developer has to obtain a new lease of land or a modification of an existing lease to carry out the development, the government will insist on incorporating the planning conditions into the lease.[47] Thus the government, as the landlord, is in a position to ensure that the development is carried out in accordance with the planning permission granted by the government in its capacity as the planning authority. Government's ability to exercise powers of landowner as well as planning authority led a judge of the High Court[48] to observe that "a peculiar, if not unique, feature of life in Hong Kong is that the government is the sole ground landlord. It is the provider of land and can combine the functions of landlord and planning authority. Thus Hong Kong government can do what many planning officers in the UK would give their eye-teeth to be able to do."[49]

Third, apart from lease conditions, which give effect to density controls and planning controls, the government has over the years developed a number of standard lease conditions, particularly those imposing environmental protection measures.[50] These lease conditions are an important means of ensuring that certain accepted standards of amenity and community benefits are maintained throughout the territory.

Fourth, leases have been used in Hong Kong to lay down specific requirements in respect of particular land grants. They determine the particular manner in which the land may be developed. A lease may restrict the use of the land only for "private residential purposes"[51] or "Industrial or godown [warehouse] purposes";[52] or it may restrict permissible buildings to "detached or semi-detached residential premises of European type";[53] or it may permit only a residential building not exceeding "thirty-five feet in height and, except with the consent of the Governor-in-Council first obtained, not more than one house."[54] It may be noted in passing that in the early years of Hong Kong, the government used lease conditions permitting only European-type houses as a means of preserving certain residential areas for the Europeans, from which the Chinese were excluded.[55] In later years, explicit legislation was passed to provide for exclusive residential areas for Europeans,[56] and such segregating legislation remained in the statute book until 1946.[57]

How Effective are Lease Conditions in Land-Use Regulation?

A government lease, just like a private lease, is governed by the law of contract.[58] Courts will give effect to lease conditions, unless they are "unconscionable."[59] What is more, public law principles relating to judicial review such as legitimate expectation or unreasonableness are not relevant in determining the meaning and scope of lease conditions.[60] Because a lease is a private contract, once the parties have signed a lease agreement they are bound by the terms of contract.[61]

The principal advantage of lease control is that leases are enforceable. If the lessee acts in breach of lease conditions, the government may exercise its contractual right to reenter the land[62] or invoke civil law remedies such as injunction.[63] A breach of lease covenants may in certain circumstances amount to a criminal offense.[64]

The principal disadvantage of lease control as a means of land use regulation is that lease controls are site-specific. It is only if and when new leases are granted or old leases come up for renewal or modification that the government will be able to implement its regional land use policies by imposing lease conditions. In other words, the government has no power to unilaterally change terms of agreement in an existing lease.

Requests for modification of lease offer an opportunity for the government to introduce restrictive lease conditions. A landowner may secure planning permission for a development of such intensity as is not permitted by the existing lease. For instance, while the existing lease may stipulate that the buildings on the land must be no more than three stories high, the landowner might succeed in obtaining planning permission for a fourteen-story building. The landowner will not be able to carry out the permitted development until the government modifies the restrictive lease conditions. For the grant of enhanced developmental rights, the government will demand the payment of a premium representing a percentage of the difference between the existing value of the land and the value of land with the new development rights.[65] The government will not only exact a premium, but also impose conditions[66] subject to which the newly granted development rights may be exercised.

Regulation of Land Use Developments Through Building Legislation

Just like lease conditions, building controls are site-specific. Although enacted with the primary objective of making buildings safe, the Buildings Ordinance also enables the Building Authority to take certain planning considerations into account when exercising its approval powers.

First, the Building Authority will not permit the construction of a building that contravenes any requirements set out in the Town Planning Ordinance, such as when a proposed building is not permitted under the relevant development plan.[67] The Building Authority will, for example, reject any plans of building works that do not comply with planning conditions imposed by the Town Planning Board. The Court of Appeal held recently that while the Building Authority must reject any proposed building if it is inconsistent with a plan prepared under the Town Planning Ordinance, the Building Authority may nevertheless approve such a building if the inconsistency is insignificant.[68]

Second, the Building Authority has the discretion to reject a plan of building works if it would result in a building differing in height, design, type, or intended use from buildings in the immediate neighborhood or previously existing on the same site.[69] The Building Authority is thus able to ensure congruity of a neighborhood, which is essentially a planning function.[70] Third, the Building (Planning) Regulations[71] enable the Building Authority to take planning considerations into account. These regulations set out the appropriate plot ratio and site coverage for various classes of building sites. It is through these specifications that the regulations implement the density controls in residential zone 1 prescribed by the government.[72]

The Building Authority is able to enforce the requirements set out in the Buildings Ordinance, and through it the requirements of the Town Planning Ordinance, only when permission is sought for a new building or for a material change in the use of a building necessitating structural alternations.[73] There are instances in Hong Kong where the use of a building is materially changed without carrying out any building works, for instance, from a private residence to a motel. In such a situation the Building Authority has no enforcement powers. It is only where some building works have been carried out without prior approval that the Building Authority has enforcement powers, such as the power to require alteration or demolition of a building. If the change of use, not involving any building works, is permitted under the lease, there is no way of preventing the change of use[74] unless it is forbidden under an enforceable plan made under the Town Planning Ordinance.[75]

Regulation of Land Use Under Planning Legislation[76]

The Town Planning Ordinance is a relatively short statute, made up of a mere twenty-six sections. When passed in 1939, it provided for the establishment of a Town Planning Board, entrusted with the task of preparing draft outline zoning plans as directed by the governor in council (equivalent of today's chief executive). In 1974, an amendment of the ordinance introduced a planning permission system.[77] In 1991, the planning permission system was further improved by introducing an independent Town Planning Appeal Board.[78] In the same year, provision was made authorizing the Town Planning Board to make draft plans for any areas of Hong Kong, and not only for existing and potential urban areas of Hong Kong as before.[79] Most important, the 1991 amendment introduced enforcement provisions intended mainly to regulate land uses in rural areas.[80]

The Town Planning Ordinance empowers the government to regulate the use and development of land in the following ways:

1. The Town Planning Board may make development plans that demarcate areas for various land uses, such as residential, commercial, or industrial.
2. A development plan may provide that certain specified uses are permitted as of right, while others will require planning permission.
3. Any breach of a Second-Generation Outline Zoning Plan or a Development Permission Area Plan is a punishable offense, and the Director of Planning may take enforcement action in respect of such breaches.

STATUTORY DEVELOPMENT PLANS

Currently, there are two types of statutory development plans: Outline Zoning Plans and Development Permission Area Plans.[81] Although these two types of plans follow the same format, there are significant differences between them as regards enforcement, which will be examined under "Enforcement of Planning Controls."

A development plan consists of two parts: a map and a set of notes. The map shows the area of land covered by the plan and divides it into a number of zones. The notes describe what developments may be undertaken in each of the zones, either as of right or upon obtaining planning permission.[82] Each development plan also carries a nonstatutory explanatory statement, for the purpose of explaining the planning intention of each zone. It has been held that although the explanatory statement is not a constituent part of a development plan, it is permissible for the planning authorities to derive assistance from it in order to better understand the plan.[83]

The procedure for making development plans envisages public participation of a limited nature. A draft plan made by the Town Planning

Board must be published, giving an opportunity for any person affected by the plan to submit a written statement of objection. A written statement of objection must state the reasons for the objection and propose any such measures as the objector wishes the Town Planning Board to take in order to meet the objection. For instance, the objector may object to the inclusion of his or her land in a green belt zone and request an upzoning of it to a small-scale residential zone. The Town Planning Board must consider any objections it receives and may propose amendments to meet the objection. If the Town Planning Board proposes any amendment of the plan, it must give public notice of it, enabling any landowner who is affected by the proposed amendment to object to it. For instance, a neighboring landowner, who does not wish to have the peace and quiet of her or his neighborhood disturbed, might object to the upzoning on the ground that the green belt serves a useful purpose in checking urban sprawl. After hearing the original objectors and further objectors, the Town Planning Board must submit the draft plan, with or without amendments, to the chief executive for approval.

INTERACTION BETWEEN STATUTORY PLANS AND NONSTATUTORY PLANS

Statutory plans operate in the backdrop of nonstatutory plans. The nonstatutory plans at territorial level are policy statements. There are two territorial-level nonstatutory plans, namely, the Territorial Development Strategy and the Hong Kong Planning Standards and Guidelines. The latter sets out standards and guidelines that must be followed in any land use development project. It has eleven chapters dealing with subjects such as environment, residential densities, and conservation.

Nonstatutory plans at the subregional level set out medium- and long-term planning strategies for the five subregions into which Hong Kong has been divided. These subregional plans, which are based on the Territorial Development Strategy, guide the preparation of plans for districts within each region. Each subregion is divided into a number of districts. A map-based development strategy is prepared for each district, within the planning strategy for the subregion. The district plan known as the outline development plan provides the basis on which a number of local statutory development plans may be prepared.

Thus, while the Town Planning Ordinance provides for only two types of statutory plans, which are in effect local plans, it is difficult to understand the statutory plan-making process without reference to the nonstatutory plans, which set out the government's planning polices and the preferred areas for particular developments. The nonstatutory plans may be said, in that sense, to provide unity among statutory development plans.

PLANNING PERMISSION

The Town Planning Ordinance was amended in 1974 to introduce a system of planning permission. Prior to 1974, there was in place some sort of a nonstatutory planning permission system, which was described by Leonard J in the case of *Singway Co. Ltd. v. The Attorney General*[84] (1974) as a system of "control by consultation."[85] That system of "control by consultation," or the "planning permission system," as the applicant described it, operated in the following manner.

The pre-1974 outline zoning plans were in the form of a zone-based map with brief annotations on it. The annotations sought to introduce an element of flexibility to an otherwise rigid system of zoning. The annotations on the plan in question in the *Singway* case, for example, stated that "on land designated 'residential' certain non-industrial uses such as shops, hotels, open spaces, petrol filling stations, government, institutional, community and utility uses may be permitted." This attempt by the Town Planning Board to make the zoning system flexible was laudable but, as Leonard J held in the *Singway* case, invalid under the ordinance for the following two reasons:

First, the Town Planning Ordinance empowered the Town Planning Board to show or make provision for zones for various uses such as residential, commercial, or industrial.[86] It did not authorize the Town Planning Board to do any more than that. As a result, the Town Planning Board had no power to describe what types of land development might be carried out in a particular zone. Therefore annotations could not validly form part of the plan.

Second, the notes, even if they could have been incorporated into the plans validly, were uncertain in their operation. The notes did not state clearly what uses might be permitted in a particular zone. The notes in respect of each zone listed a number of uses that had nothing in common among them and stated that uses "such as" those on the list "may be permitted." The notes were therefore "clearly vague and purposely vague,"[87] not only because they failed to specify clearly what types of development might be permitted, but also because they failed to specify how, when, and to whom an application for planning permission may be made.

The decision in the *Singway* case prompted the government to amend the Town Planning Ordinance in two important respects.[88] First, it amended section 4(1) of the Ordinance, empowering the Town Planning Board to incorporate descriptive notes into development plans.[89] Second, it introduced a planning permission system whereby the Town Planning Board was empowered to grant planning permission in accordance with the relevant development plan.

Sections 16 and 17, inserted into the Ordinance in 1974 and setting out the planning permission procedure, were amended and further expanded in 1991.[90] Currently, an application for planning permission is considered, in the first instance, by one of the two planning committees of the Town Planning Board. Any applicant aggrieved by the determination of the planning committee may apply to the Town Planning Board for a review of such determination. Where the Town Planning Board on review refuses to grant planning permission, or grants planning permission subject to conditions not acceptable to the applicant, the applicant may appeal to the Town Planning Appeal Board. The Town Planning Appeal Board may confirm, reverse, or vary the decision of the Town Planning Board. It has the power to exercise an independent planning judgment and may disagree with the Town Planning Board's interpretation of relevant factors.[91] The Appeal Board's decision is final and may only be questioned by way of an application for judicial review.[92]

When Is Planning Permission Required?

Hong Kong does not have a pure planning permission system as in the United Kingdom, where no land use development may be carried out without first obtaining planning permission, unless the proposed development is an exempted development. In the United Kingdom, the requirement of planning permission is mandatory whether or not the development site is governed by a development plan. In Hong Kong, on the other hand, the planning permission provisions are applicable only in such areas as are covered by statutory development plans.[93] A landowner who wishes to develop her or his land, which is not governed by a statutory development plan, may proceed with such development so long as it is permitted by the relevant land lease and by the Building Authority. A landowner who wishes to carry out any development on a land governed by a statutory development plan must ensure that the proposed development is permissible under the relevant plan. A development is permissible under a statutory development plan in one of three ways:

1. The notes of every statutory development plan in respect of a specified zone designate certain uses as always permitted.[94] Such uses may be carried out as of right without any need for planning permission. Notes of specified zones adopt a two-column format and will list the always permitted uses in column 1 of the notes.

2. The notes of a statutory development plan in respect of a specified zone designate certain uses, which may be undertaken upon obtaining planning permission from the Town Planning Board.[95] Such uses are listed in column 2 of the notes. An application may be made to the Town Planning Board for permission to carry out a column 2 use.

3. The notes of a statutory development plan in respect of an "unspecified zone" or an "undetermined zone" stipulate that no development may be carried out in the zone without obtaining planning permission.[96] Unspecified zones do not adopt the two-column format for the reason that the Town Planning Board has not yet finalized a definite development program for areas covered by such zones.[97] The Explanatory Statement relating to "Unspecified Zones" now usually provides some indications as to what sort of developments are likely to be considered favorably in such zones. For instance, the explanatory statement of the Draft San Tin Development Permission Area Plan[98] states in respect of one of the three subareas of the unspecified zone that "in view of the high concentration of fish ponds in the area, agricultural uses will be encouraged. . . . The planning objective for the sub-area is to promote conservation and environmental improvement of this lowland rural area." The Town Planning Board may grant planning permission only to the extent shown, provided for, or specified in the plan.[99] It has no authority to deviate from the plan and grant planning permission for a nonconforming use, unlike in the United Kingdom, where the determination must be made in accordance with the relevant plan, if any, unless material considerations indicate otherwise.[100]

Who Can Make an Application for Planning Permission?

The Town Planning Ordinance does not require the applicant for planning permission to be the owner of the proposed development site. As in the United Kingdom, it is possible for a person to make an application for planning permission in respect of someone else's land. However, in the United Kingdom, the applicant must notify the landowner of his or her application for planning permission, giving the owner the opportunity to make representations. Moreover, the U.K. legislation recognizes that members of the public have a right to make representations regarding planning applications. In Hong Kong, planning applications are a matter between the applicant and the Town Planning Board. There is no provision for anyone else to participate in the planning permission process.

The Town Planning Board, however, requires an applicant who does not own the development site to state in the application whether she or he has obtained the landowner's consent.[101] In fact, whether the applicant has a proprietary interest in the land in question is a relevant planning consideration, because the feasibility of the implementation of a planning permission is a material consideration that the Town Planning Board may take into account.[102] For instance, where the applicant is seeking permission to develop a comprehensive development area, it is crucial whether the applicant has a reasonable chance of implementing the planning permission by acquiring all the land in the zone, or by entering into a joint enterprise with other landowners.

Consideration of Planning Applications

The Town Planning Board considers an application for planning permission, in the first instance, in the absence of the applicant.[103] If the applicant is aggrieved by that decision, he or she may ask the Town Planning Board to review it.[104] The applicant may appeal against the Town Planning Board's decision on review to the Town Planning Appeal Board.[105] In considering an application for planning permission, the Town Planning Board solicits views of relevant government agencies such as the Environmental Protection Department, Land Administration, Buildings Department, Commissioner for Transport, and the Director of Fire Services. To make up for the absence of direct public participation, the Town Planning Board relies on relevant government officers to carry out a survey of local views.

Planning permission is usually granted subject to conditions, including a condition that it will lapse unless work commences within three years of the grant of permission. For good cause shown, the Town Planning Board may extend the validity period.[106]

To assist applicants for planning permission the Town Planning Board has published a set of guidance notes, which are intended to help applicants in the process. The guidance notes describe the nature of a development plan and explain when an application for planning permission may be made. Another document entitled "Supplementary Information to be Provided for a Section 16 Application" sets out additional information that must be submitted if the application is for certain uses, such as a bank, school, or warehouse. The required information includes technical assessments such as environmental, drainage, landscape, and visual impact assessments.

For the development of a comprehensive development area zone,[107] the application must be made on the basis of a master layout plan, which in considerable detail sets out the layout of the different components of the comprehensive development, such as residential uses, commercial uses, parking lots, and open spaces.

The Town Planning Board has also issued nineteen guidelines. Of the nineteen guidelines, the first fourteen deal with the criteria that the Town Planning Board will follow in considering particular types of development in certain zones. For instance, Guideline 1 deals with showroom uses in industrial buildings in industrial zones. Guideline 10 deals with developments in green belt zones. The last five guidelines deal with procedural matters, such as submission of a master layout plan for developments in a comprehensive development area zone (Guideline 18) and the procedure for minor amendments to a development proposal for which planning permission has already been granted (Guideline 19A).

In considering whether to grant planning permission, the Town Planning Board must rigidly adhere to the relevant plan. Unlike in the United Kingdom, where the planning authority may grant planning permission inconsistently with any relevant development plan,[108] in Hong Kong, the Town Planning Board may grant planning permission only to the extent shown, provided for, or specified in the plan.[109] However, this does not mean that the planning authorities in Hong Kong must turn a blind eye to any other planning considerations, which may be material to the determination of a planning permission application.

Unlike in the United Kingdom,[110] the planning authorities in Hong Kong are not by statute required to take into account material considerations other than the relevant statutory development plan. The Town Planning Board, however, clearly states in its statutory development plans that it will take into account all material considerations. A typical explanatory statement will provide as follows: "Planning applications to the [Town Planning] Board will be assessed on individual merits. In general, the Board's consideration of the planning applications will take into account all relevant planning considerations, which may include the departmental outline development plan/layout plans and the guidelines published by the Board." The Town Planning Appeal Board has at least impliedly recognized the importance of giving due weight to all the material considerations.[111] The Privy Council has quite clearly stated that although the statute is silent on the matter, the Town Planning Board and the Town Planning Appeal Board must take all material considerations into account.[112]

A Presumption in Favor of Development?

In the United Kingdom it is generally agreed that the purpose of planning legislation is more to facilitate development than to restrict or control development. The 1986 White Paper "Building Business, Not Barriers"[113] stated that whenever possible development should be encouraged. It recognized that there is always a presumption in favor of development, unless that development would cause demonstrable harm to interests of acknowledged importance.[114]

In 1993, it was argued before the Town Planning Appeal Board that as in the United Kingdom there was in Hong Kong a presumption in favor of development. The Appeal Board,[115] while appreciating the differences between the two planning regimes, was prepared to proceed on the basis that planning permission should be granted to the extent shown, provided for or specified in the plan, having regard to all material considerations, unless there were good reasons to refuse planning permission. In a later case[116] the Appeal Board said that since the Town Planning Ordinance imposes restraints on enjoyment of land without compensation,[117] planning permission should be granted unless there are valid planning objections.

The guidelines issued by the Town Planning Board are useful in determining what sort of development is encouraged in various zones. By indicating that certain kinds of developments will be considered favorably, the guidelines seem to give rise to some sort of presumption in favor of such developments. The Guidelines for Office Buildings in Industrial Zones,[118] for example, provide that favorable consideration may be given to proposed office buildings on sites within the older part of an industrial area requiring renewal or restructuring and where the building will bring about significant improvements to the general amenity and environment of the area.[119] Similarly, the Guidelines for Office Development in Residential (Group A) Zone provide that in general the Town Planning Board will consider favorably planning applications for office developments, which produce specific environmental and planning gains.[120]

The green belt zones, by way of contrast, are based on a presumption against development. The relevant guidelines[121] state that there is a general presumption against development in a green belt zone and that an application for new developments in a green belt zone will be considered in exceptional circumstances only and that they must be justified on strong planning grounds. Similarly, the Guidelines for Open Storage and Port Back-up Uses[122] state that there is a general presumption against development on sites below 2,000 square meters for port back-up uses and below 1,000 square meters for open storage uses in rural areas. The Protection of the Harbor Ordinance (1997) sets out the only statutory presumption against development. It states that the harbor is to be protected and preserved as a special public asset and a natural heritage of the Hong Kong people, and for that reason there is a presumption against reclamation in the harbor.[123]

ENFORCEMENT OF PLANNING CONTROLS

An amendment of the Town Planning Ordinance in 1991 introduced enforcement provisions.[124] The 1991 amendment was intended to deal with the deteriorating land use situation in the rural areas of Hong Kong. Unregulated and undesirable land uses in rural Hong Kong escaped enforcement for the following reasons.

First, much of the land in the New Territories, rural Hong Kong, is governed by what are known as block Crown leases. In 1898 when the British administration acquired a ninety-nine-year lease of the New Territories, the government conducted a survey of land ownership. As Hong Kong did not, and does not, recognize freehold landownership, the government granted a ninety-nine-year lease to each of the landowners. Instead of granting a separate lease to each of the landowners, the government made a block Crown lease for a district, indicating on a schedule the existing land use on each of the land lots. In 1983 it was held by the High Court that these block Crown leases contained only one restriction, namely, that no buildings, other than a building for agricultural purposes, could be built on land lots designated as agricultural lots.[125] The High Court held that the use of agricultural land for storage purposes was not prohibited under block Crown leases. This meant that lease controls were virtually ineffective in the New Territories to control undesirable land uses, such as container yards and dumping grounds, not involving any building works.

Second, the Buildings Ordinance was similarly of little assistance in controlling the environmentally disastrous land uses in the New Territories because those land uses, mainly storage of containers, building materials, and dumping of waste, did not involve building works and therefore were outside the remit of the Buildings Ordinance.

Third, what is worse, the Town Planning Ordinance itself had no application in the rural New Territories. Before its amendment in 1991, the Town Planning Ordinance empowered the Town Planning Board to make plans for existing or potential urban areas only. This meant that large tracks of the New Territories remained outside the scope of the ordinance. As we have seen in our discussion on planning permission, no planning permission is required for any land use development effected in any area not governed by a statutory development plan.

The 1991 amendment sought to remedy the situation by enabling the Town Planning Board to make plans for any area of Hong Kong, as directed by the governor-general (today the chief executive) and by introducing enforcement provisions. In this process, the amending ordinance introduced two new statutory plans: interim development permission area plans and development permission area plans.

Interim Development Permission Area Plans

The director of planning was given the power to make these plans any time between the first public notification of the amendment bill and the coming into force of the amendment ordinance.[126] The idea was to prevent landowners from changing the use of their lands while the bill was going through the approval process in the Legislative Council. Thirty such plans were made. As shown below, all of these plans were replaced by development permission area plans, and the repealed plans are of little relevance today.

Development Permission Area Plans

The Town Planning Board could make these plans any time after the commencement of the amendment ordinance on January 25, 1991. All thirty interim development permission area plans made by the director of planning were replaced by development permission area plans within six months of January 25, 1991. Development permission area plans can be made for any area of Hong Kong other than areas that are or were governed by an outline zoning plan. In effect development permission area plans are principally meant for rural areas of Hong Kong.

ENFORCEMENT UNDER DEVELOPMENT PERMISSION AREA PLANS

The Town Planning Ordinance, as amended in 1991, provides that it is an offense to commence or undertake any unauthorized development while a development permission area plan is in force.[127] It also provides that if there is or was an unauthorized development the director of planning may serve any of three kinds of notices to control such unauthorized developments. These notices are:

1. Enforcement notice.[128] This is a notice requiring the unauthorized development to be stopped or regularized[129] by a specified date.
2. Stop notice.[130] This is a notice that requires the addressee to stop an unauthorized development by a date earlier than that specified in an enforcement notice, where the unauthorized development is a health or safety hazard, adversely affects the environment, or would make it impracticable to reinstate the land within a reasonable time.
3. Reinstatement notice.[131] This is a notice that may be issued where an enforcement notice has already been issued. It requires the land to be reinstated to the condition it was before the gazetting of the development permission area plan. Where the development permission area plan has replaced an interim development permission area plan within six months of the coming into force of the 1991 amendment of the ordinance, reinstatement may be to the condition the land was at the time of the gazetting of the interim plan.[132]

A development is an unauthorized development unless:

1. it is an existing use, that is, a use in existence at the time the plan was gazetted;
2. it is permitted by the plan, meaning a use always permitted (permitted as of right) under the plan; or
3. it is permitted by the Town Planning Board by a grant of planning permission. Any planning permission granted by the director of planning in respect of a land under an interim development permission area plan,[133] which is now governed by a development permission area plan, is also an authorized development.[134]

ENFORCEMENT UNDER OUTLINE ZONING PLANS

As regards enforcement provisions, outline zoning plans may be divided into two categories, and the present author wishes to call them 'first-generation outline zoning plans' and 'second-generation outline zoning plans.' By a first-generation outline zoning plan we mean an outline zoning plan that covers an area of Hong Kong for the first time. All outline zoning plans that had been made before the 1991 amendment of the Town Planning Ordinance fall into this category. Any outline zoning plan made after the 1991 amendment covering an area that had not previously been governed by a development permission area plan also falls within the definition of first-generation outline zoning plans.

The enforcement provisions introduced in 1991 do not apply to first-generation outline zoning plans. They apply only to second-generation outline zoning plans, meaning outline zoning plans that are made to replace development permission area plans. Development permission area plans were introduced in 1991 to be in force for three years, with a possible additional year to be granted by the chief executive.[135] When a development permission area plan is replaced by an outline zoning plan, the enforcement provisions continue to apply under the new plan.[136] Thus, enforcement provisions apply in respect of second-generation outline zoning plans.

COURTS AND ENFORCEMENT OF PLANNING CONTROLS[137]

The new powers of enforcement created by the 1991 amendment of the Town Planning Ordinance have enabled courts to be involved in the enforcement process in three ways:

1. Any land use development in contravention of a development permission area plan or a second-generation outline zoning plan is an unauthorized development, and any offender may be prosecuted in a Magistrate's Court.[138]
2. Failure to comply with any notice issued by the director of planning in the exercise of his powers of enforcement is an offense, and the offender may be prosecuted in a Magistrate's Court.[139]
3. Apart from the original criminal jurisdiction conferred on the Magistrate's Courts under (1) and (2) above, and the resultant appellate jurisdiction exercised by the Court of First Instance, there may also be occasion for judicial review applications questioning the legality of the exercise of an enforcement power. Judicial review applications are heard in the Court of First Instance, subject to an appeal to the Court of Appeal and a further appeal to the Court of Final Appeal.

The courts need to ensure that not only the will of the legislature is given effect, but also that rights of the individual are protected against unlawful invasion. In one of the early cases on enforcement the court observed as follows: "Deterrence is an important consideration if the legislation is to be effective. Heavy fines could encourage landowners to be more vigilant to prevent unauthorized developments."[140] Where, however, a magistrate has imposed a high penalty as a deterrent not called for in the circumstances of the case, the sentence would be reduced on appeal.[141]

Courts have held that an enforcement notice must be in strict accordance with the relevant statutory provision. An enforcement notice is invalid if it informed the recipient that he or she could comply with the notice by discontinuing the unauthorized use without advising her or him that in the alternative she or he might comply with the notice by obtaining planning permission.[142] On the other hand, an enforcement notice is not invalid merely because it does not classify the unauthorized development as an operational development or a material change of use: all that is required is that the notice informs the recipient what wrong she or he has done and what she or he could do to put things right.[143]

An enforcement notice would be invalid if it does not give reasonable time to the recipient to comply with it, because of the penal consequences of noncompliance with such notice.[144] Similarly, in determining whether the recipient has taken reasonable steps to comply with the notice, the court must be mindful that failure to comply with a notice is an offense.[145]

While persons prosecuted for enforcement offenses have on occasion been successful in challenging the validity of the prosecution, no judicial review application has met with success. In one case, the application for judicial review was rejected mainly because of undue delay[146] and in another, because the director of planning had not acted irrationally in the exercise of his discretion.[147]

Compensation for Expropriation of Property Rights

In Hong Kong the government is the universal landlord and grants land for various uses by way of lease. There being no privately owned land, it is inaccurate to talk of compulsory acquisition of property by the government. In Hong Kong the preferred terminology is resumption of land, meaning appropriation of leased land by the government before the expiry of the lease. However, compulsory acquisition is the correct terminology where the government decides to appropriate land held on a possessory title. Any person who proves that he or she has had possession of government land for sixty years adverse to the interests of the government will defeat the government's title to that land and will, as a result, become its freeholder. There is, however, no reported instance of anyone successfully setting up possessory title against the government.[148]

The principal enactment relating to the resumption of government land is the Lands Resumption Ordinance. There are several ordinances that provide for resumption of land under the Lands Resumption Ordinance. For instance, the Land Development Corporation Ordinance, which established a Land Development Corporation to implement development programs for urban renewal, provides that the corporation may request the government to resume land needed for its development projects. The chief executive may resume such land, acting under the Lands Resumption Ordinance.[149] The Town Planning Board may recommend the resumption of any land for the purpose of implementing a development plan made under the Town Planning Ordinance, and any such resumption by the chief executive will be under the Lands Resumption Ordinance.[150]

There are several other ordinances that enable the government to resume government land. For instance, the chief executive may resume any land for the purpose of implementing a road work scheme or a railway scheme,[151] and may order the resumption of any land within a marine park required for a public purpose.[152] The government may acquire property held on a possessory title under the Land Acquisition (Possessory Title) Ordinance, which has provisions very similar to those of the Lands Resumption Ordinance.[153]

While Lands Resumption Ordinance and the other ordinances referred to above enable the government to take away land from its lawful owner, the Mining Ordinance provides for the withdrawal of a property right enjoyed by a landowner. The chief executive may at any time, by notice in the gazette, declare any area to be closed to prospecting or mining. If as a consequence of such a notice, a landowner's right to prospect or mine is adversely affected, she or he has a right to claim compensation for any disturbance caused by the chief executive's action.[154] Of course, if the government resumes any land given on a mining lease, the landowner will be entitled to claim compensation for the loss of her or his property.[155]

Legislation relating to reclamation illustrates a situation where a landowner will be able to claim compensation for loss caused to him or her as a result of what the government does outside his or her land. A landowner may be compensated for the loss of marine access rights, occasioned by reclamation of the sea.[156] The Roads Ordinance and the Railways Ordinance recognize the right of landowners to claim compensation in respect of restrictions placed on the enjoyment of their property rights due to the building of roads or railways.[157] The Electricity Networks (Statutory Easements) Ordinance[158] provides another good example of compensation for injurious affection, where the claimant's land has not been resumed. Under the Lands Resumption Ordinance a landowner may be able to claim compensation for the loss of an easement, when the government resumes the land subject to the easement. Apart from a few instances, such as the above, Hong Kong ordinances do not recognize a freestanding right of compensation on account of injurious affection.

Resumption of Land under Lease Terms

The government may resume land as provided for in the lease agreement. It is usual for leases to contain a provision that enables the government to reenter land for breach of lease conditions. Where land is resumed for a breach of lease conditions, the lessee is not entitled to any compensation.

Leases also contain a provision that authorizes the government to acquire land for a public purpose. A typical resumption for a public purpose clause would provide as follows: "The Government shall have full power to resume, re-enter upon and re-take possession of all or any part of the lot if required for the improvement of Hong Kong or for any other public purpose whatsoever (as to which the decision of the Chief Executive shall be conclusive)." The lease will also provide that where land is resumed for a public purpose in pursuance of the government's contractual right, the director of lands has the exclusive authority to determine the amount of compensation payable for the loss of land and any buildings on it. Since under such lease provisions the amount of compensation is determined by the director of lands, against whose decision there is no appeal, the government rarely relies on its contractual right of resumption. Instead, the government exercises its statutory powers of resumption, which are subject to procedures designed to safeguard the rights of anyone who has a legally protected interest in the resumed land.

Resumption of Lands
under the Lands Resumption Ordinance

Without prejudice to the government's contractual right to resume land,[159] the government may resume land for public purposes.[160] The Lands Resumption Ordinance defines resumption for a public purpose by stating three specific purposes, including resumption of property to improve the sanitary conditions of a property, followed by the following words: "resumption for any purpose of whatsoever description whether ejusdem generis with any of the above purposes or not, which the Chief Executive in Council may decide to be a public purpose."[161] It is not necessary for the chief executive to specify the particular purpose for which the land is required and it is enough for the resumption notice to state that the land is required for a public purpose. The notice containing such statement is conclusive evidence that the resumption is for a public purpose.[162]

Land Resumption Procedure

Land resumption procedure begins with an order made by the chief executive that he has decided to resume a particular land for a public purpose. The chief executive must give public notice of the decision declaring that the land will be resumed one month or some other prescribed period after the date of the notice. The notice must be served on the owner and must be conspicuously displayed on the affected land.[163] Before the expiration of the period of public notice, the owner and any other person having an interest in the land may agree to a voluntary purchase of the land. If the director of lands and the affected claimants are able to agree on the terms of the purchase, the resumption procedure will be abandoned.[164] Where no agreement has been reached, the land reverts to the government at the expiration of the notice period.[165]

The director of lands must, within twenty-eight days of such reversion, make an offer of compensation to "the former owner or any person having a [registered] estate or interest in the land immediately before reversion" or require them, by notice, to submit a compensation claim.[166] If the director of lands and the affected parties fail to reach a timely agreement on the amount of compensation, the director of lands or the claimants may refer their dispute to the Lands Tribunal for settlement.[167]

Even after agreeing to compensation with the government, a claimant may submit a fresh claim to the government under section 8 of the Lands Resumption Ordinance. This section is particularly helpful to claimants who would have been unaware of the notice of resumption. An important class of claimants who benefit from this section are those whose interests in the land had not been registered. Since the director of lands is required by section 6 of the ordinance to notify only those who have a registered interest in the resumed land for the purpose of negotiating compensation terms, those with any unregistered interests can use section 8 to lodge their compensation claims.

Grounds on Which Compensation May Be Claimed

Compensation is payable only as provided by the ordinance, and no action may be taken in any court of law for damages or any other relief in respect of loss resulting from a land resumption.[168] The Lands Tribunal has exclusive jurisdiction to determine any compensation claims[169] and must determine the amount of compensation (if any) payable on the basis of the loss or damage suffered by the claimant due to the resumption of the land specified in the claim. There are three main heads of compensation: (1) compensation for deprivation of property; (2) compensation for severance and disturbance; and (3) compensation payable to neighbors.

1. Compensation for deprivation of property. In determining compensation payable for deprivation of property, the Lands Tribunal must assess the value of the land resumed at the date of resumption.[170] The value of the land resumed is taken to be the amount that the land, if sold by a willing seller in the open market, might be expected to realize.[171] Therefore, the landowner will be able to claim compensation not only on the basis of the actual use of the land, but also on the basis of the best use to which the land may reasonably be put.[172] The open market rule proceeds on the fictional assumption that the land is available for sale on the open market, although in fact the land has been taken away from the landowner. As a result, the *Pointe Guorde* principle[173] mandates that no account must be taken of any increase or decrease in the value of the land wholly due to the purpose for which the land is being resumed.[174] No account must be taken of the fact that the land is affected by a statutory plan made under the Town Planning Ordinance.[175] It must also ignore any enhancement of value conferred by such a statutory plan.[176] The landowner is not entitled to claim damages as a solace to injured feelings, as result of the compulsory taking: the Lands Resumption Ordinance expressly states that no allowance must be made on account of the resumption being compulsory.[177]

2. Compensation for severance and disturbance. Apart from compensation paid for deprivation of property, the owner and others having an interest in the resumed land may obtain compensation for other consequential losses, namely, compensation for severance and disturbance. Compensation is payable for loss or damage suffered by the landowner due to the severance of the land resumed or any building erected thereon from any other land owned by him or her, or building erected thereon, contiguous or adjacent thereto.[178] *Suen Sun-yau v. Director of Buildings*

and Lands,[179] where the government had resumed 2,526.3 square meters and left the landowner with a mere 63.7 square meters of landlocked land, provides a textbook case of loss resulting from severance. A landowner or other person having an interest in the land may claim compensation for what is popularly known as "disturbance."[180] The Lands Resumption Ordinance provides that compensation must be paid for any loss caused to any business conducted by a claimant on the resumed land, due to the removal of the business from there. Compensation is also payable in respect of expenses in moving from the premises or in acquiring alternative premises.[181]

3. Compensation payable to neighbors. Compensation payable under headings (1) and (2) is payable to the owner and other persons having an interest in the resumed land. Here, we deal with the rights of persons having a proprietary interest in some other related land. The Lands Resumption Ordinance provides that where the resumed land is subject to an easement, the owner or occupier of the dominant tenement will be able to claim compensation.[182] There are no reported instances where compensation has been awarded for deprivation of a neighbor's easement rights as a result of land resumption.

RESUMPTION OF LAND IN CONNECTION WITH ROAD WORKS AND RAILWAY WORKS

Road works and railways are major infrastructural developments that call for a balancing of the wider interests of the community and property interests of private landowners.[183] The Roads (Works Uses and Compensation) Ordinance[184] and the Railways Ordinance[185] provide for public notification of proposed road or railway works, enabling affected persons to make objections and representations. Both ordinances enable the chief executive to order the resumption of land for the purposes or road works or railway works.[186] Where land is resumed under either of the ordinances, compensation is paid as if the claim is made under the Lands Resumption Ordinance.[187]

In addition to compensation payable for resumption of land, both ordinances provide for compensation on account of injurious affection. The Roads (Works, Uses and Compensation) Ordinance was enacted in 1982 to replace the Street Alteration Ordinance of 1970, and one of the defects of the 1970 ordinance was the vagueness of its compensation provisions. The 1970 ordinance gave the owners and occupiers of land a right to claim compensation where "any pecuniary loss or damage" was likely to be caused by the proposed road works. The 1982 ordinance narrowed the scope of compensation claims by stating that compensation would only be paid to the extent specified in the schedule to the ordinance. The Railways Ordinance also follows this model of demarcating the scope of compensation claims.[188] Items specified in the schedule include: subjecting a land to an easement in favor of the road works or railway works,[189] the extinction of an easement owing to the resumption of adjacent land,[190] the restriction of road access to land,[191] restriction of private rights over foreshore or seabed,[192] and loss or damage resulting from works and associated activities.[193] Both ordinances provide for the secretary for transport to make an offer of compensation to the affected persons, and for the referral of the matter to the Lands Tribunal if the claimant disputes the compensation settlement.[194]

Both ordinances enable a landowner whose land use rights have been adversely affected to have her or his land resumed. For instance, where the Building Authority refuses to approve any building works because they are incompatible with proposed road works or railway works, the owner of the proposed building site has the right to require that her or his land be resumed.[195] Similarly, a landowner who is adversely affected by the resumption of an adjacent land may require her or his land to be resumed.[196] The chief executive determines in his discretion whether or not to comply with the request for resumption. This right to have one's land resumed is similar to the right known elsewhere as the right to a purchase notice.[197]

AIRPORT HEIGHT RESTRICTIONS

The Hong Kong Airport (Control and Obstructions) Ordinance, which provides for the control of building heights and lighting to ensure air traffic safety,[198] entitles landowners to claim compensation for losses attributable to airport height restrictions. The secretary for planning and lands may declare areas where buildings are prohibited or where building heights are controlled.[199] The chief executive may order the demolition or the reduction in height of a building in such areas. The effect of such an order is that the value of the land is adversely affected. The landowner may claim compensation for the diminution of the land value and also for the loss of enjoyment of the land.[200] He or she is also entitled to be compensated for any building works required for compliance with such an order.

RECLAMATIONS

Reclamations have played a significant role in land development policy from the early years of Hong Kong's history. Large-scale reclamations have provided valuable space for the ever-expanding built environment, including Hong Kong's new international airport. The community's concern over extensive reclamations is reflected in the Protection of the Harbor Ordinance, which creates a presumption against reclamation.[201]

Reclamations are governed by the Foreshore and Seabed (Reclamations) Ordinance, which provides for public notification of reclamations, procedures for objection making, and payment of compensation.[202] Reclamations do not directly lead to compensation claims for resumption because the sea, which is the subject of reclamation, is not privately owned. Of course, if any land is resumed in connection with a reclamation, compensation claims will arise under the Lands Resumption Ordinance.

Compensation claims arising from reclamations are for interference with neighboring property rights. Any person who claims to be "injuriously affected" by a reclamation, for example, because of the loss of right of access to the sea,[203] may claim compensation.[204] There is no statutory definition of injurious affection and the following meaning has been suggested: "The loss in value to the land retained by the claimant caused by the extinguishment of his interest, right or easement over the foreshore and sea-bed affected by the reclamation."[205] It is usually a land that is contiguous to the area of the sea to be reclaimed that may be injuriously affected, although contiguity is not an indispensable requirement.[206]

It is possible that a reclamation may not injuriously affect a neighboring land, but may in fact increase its value. In such a situation, should there be a deduction in the amount of compensation payable to take account of the betterment resulting from the reclamation of the sea? The government's right to a setoff for betterment has been conceded in litigation, but Hong Kong courts are yet to determine whether the government has a legal right to a setoff.[207] Compensation amount is agreed between the claimant and the director of lands. Where they cannot agree, the matter must be referred to the Land Tribunal for determination.[208]

It is not unusual for a land lease agreement to take away the right to compensation. A typical lease provision will state that the lessee will have no right over or in respect of the government-owned foreshore or the seabed, and that he or she has no right of access to the sea. It will also provide that the lessee will not have any right to object to any reclamation, or to claim compensation in respect of any loss of marine access or any injurious affection resulting from any reclamation or from the grant of any government lease of the foreshore or seabed.

COUNTRY PARKS AND MARINE PARKS

The Country Parks Ordinance provides for the designation, control, and management of country parks,[209] while the Marine Parks Ordinance provides for designation, control, and management of marine parks.[210] Country parks and marine parks are important components of nature conservation strategy. In country parks and marine parks, developmental activities are kept to a bare minimum. No new developments may be carried out in a country park or a marine park without the approval of the Country and Marine Park Authority.[211]

No compensation is payable to the owner of any land because the development value of the land is affected by the designation of a country park.[212] Compensation is payable where approval has been refused for a new development or where an occupier has been required to cease or modify an existing land use.[213] In calculating the amount of compensation payable, account will be taken of the loss of land value because of the restriction on the claimant's use of land.[214]

The Country Parks Ordinance has no provisions for resumption of land. Any resumption of land within a country park will have to be under the Lands Resumption Ordinance. The amount of compensation payable to the landowner under the Lands Resumption Ordinance, on the basis of market value, will be affected by the fact that the land has little development potential, as it is within a country park. The affected landowner may, however, make a supplementary claim under the Country Parks Ordinance for the diminution of the value of her or his land. If both claims succeed, the landowner will be able to obtain compensation representing the market value of the land, as if the land was not affected by the development restrictions in force in the country park.[215]

The Marine Parks Ordinance provides that the chief executive may, under the Lands Resumption Ordinance, resume any land that is required for the purpose of any marine park or marine reserve.[216] The affected persons will be able to pursue their compensation claims under the Lands Resumption Ordinance. Unlike under the Country Parks Ordinance, no compensation is payable for any loss caused by restrictions imposed on land use within a marine park or marine reserve. The ordinance provides that no damages may be recovered for extinguishment, modification, or restriction of rights, personal disturbance, inconvenience, or damage to or loss in the value of any land, trade, or business.[217]

AN OVERVIEW OF COMPENSATION PROVISIONS

Provisions under various statutes in Hong Kong provide for compensation to be paid in respect of resumption of land as well as lesser interferences with property rights. The following concluding observations may be made about Hong Kong's approach to compensation.

First, no compensation is payable where a person's land is adversely affected by the fact that his or her land is brought within a plan made under the Town Planning Ordinance[218] or the Marine Parks Ordinance.[219] Compensation is payable only where the chief executive decides to resume land under the Lands Resumption Ordinance for the purpose of implementing a plan made by the Town Planning Board,[220] or for the purpose of a marine park or marine reserve.[221]

In the case of *Lam Kit v. Director of Lands* (1994),[222] the Lands Tribunal held that owners of land in an area brought within a comprehensive redevelopment area zone[223] for an urban improvement scheme could not claim compensation on the ground that their land values were adversely affected by the zoning.

Second, the Lands Resumption Ordinance does not restrict payment of compensation to the loss of property, but will also permit compensation for disturbance and severance resulting from the resumption. Certain other ordinances recognize the right of landowners to receive compensation for interferences with their land use rights where their land has not been resumed. A good example is the Electricity Network (Statutory Easements) Ordinance,[224] which provides for the creation of electricity easements over land and the payment of compensation to landowners over whose land an electricity network passes. Another example is provided by legislation relating to reclamations. The Foreshore and Seabed (Reclamations) Ordinance confers a right to compensation on persons who are "injuriously affected" by a reclamation. This right is somewhat analogous to a dominant landowner's right to compensation for the loss of an easement resulting from the resumption of the servient land, as under the Roads Ordinance or the Railways Ordinance.

Third, it is usual for Hong Kong legislation providing for compensation to state that the right to compensation and the calculation of compensation must be in strict accordance with the relevant statute and thereby exclude any other claims for compensation.[225] A good example is the case of *Yicon Ltd. v. China Light & Power Co. Ltd.*,[226] decided under the Electricity Networks (Statutory Easements) Ordinance. Under that ordinance, the land affected by the laying of an electricity network is defined as any land within a 25-meter corridor on either side of a line drawn from the center of the transmission line. The applicants, whose land fell outside the statutory corridor, argued in support of their compensation claim that even land outside the 25-meter zone is capable of being affected by an electricity network. The Lands Tribunal held that compensation payment was wholly governed by statute and that unless the land was within the area defined by the statute, no compensation claim could be made.

Fourth, in determining the amount of compensation payable, the Lands Tribunal has consistently followed principles of valuation operative in common law jurisdictions, so long as they can be invoked consistently with the governing statutory criteria. The central principle is the payment of open market value.[227] Article 105 of the Basic Law recognizes the right to compensation in the following terms: "The Hong Kong Special Administrative Region shall, in accordance with law, protect the right of individuals and legal persons to the acquisition, use disposal and inheritance of property and their right to compensation for lawful deprivation of their property. Such compensation shall correspond to the real value of the property concerned at the time and shall be freely convertible and paid without delay." Cruden argues that the Basic Law, when referring to "real value" of resumed land, does not intend to introduce a new, unfamiliar basis for compensation. It only reiterates that the existing principles of valuation developed by the Lands Tribunal will continue to apply as they did before the Chinese resumption of sovereignty over Hong Kong.[228]

Fifth, is there room in Hong Kong for the reception of the American concept of "inverse condemnation"? The answer depends on the extent to which the entrenched written constitution of Hong Kong protects property rights, including the right not be interfered with in the exercise of such rights. Article 6 of the Basic Law states that Hong Kong must protect the right of private ownership of property in accordance with law. Article 105, which is quoted above, protects landowners' rights to compensation for deprivation of their property. It has been argued that "deprivation of property" must be construed in the light of American jurisprudence in order to cover takings that may fall short of total deprivation of property.[229]

Sixth, while statutory provisions are relevant in determining the amount of compensation payable where the claimant and the government cannot agree on a settlement, it is often the case that compensation awards are mutually agreed upon. In such cases it is very likely that the claimants would be awarded compensation in excess of their legal entitlement, in order to avoid recourse to the Lands Tribunal. The Land Development Corporation Ordinance, for example, provides that the chief executive will not exercise his right to resume land affected by a land development scheme, unless he is satisfied that the corporation has taken all reasonable steps to acquire the property without resorting to resumption of land, for instance, by negotiating for the purchase of the land on terms that are fair and reasonable.[230] No such duty has been imposed on the Urban Renewal Authority, which will be established replacing the corporation when the Urban Renewal Ordinance, No. 63 of 2000, which was passed in July 2000, is brought into effect.

Seventh, even where land has been resumed, the government has found it convenient to offer terms of compensation better than what the claimants are legally entitled to. Particularly where the government needs to acquire large areas of land, payment of such generous amounts of compensation aids swift land acquisition. The government has, for the award of such ex gratia payments, developed a set of administrative guidelines. These unpublished guidelines are discussed in Cruden's book, and are a very important source for computation of compensation.

Land Use Planning in Hong Kong: The Future

Land use developments in Hong Kong are regulated principally under three sets of legislation: the Town Planning Ordinance, the Buildings Ordinance, and legislation relating to land leases. The Hong Kong government exercises powers under all these statutes and takes strength from the fact that all land in Hong Kong is state-owned. On the planning front, while the Town Planning Ordinance remains the principal statute, the government exercises planning-related powers under certain other statutes, all of which have been briefly examined above under compensation.

The Roads Ordinance and the Railways Ordinance enable the secretary of transport to prepare a scheme of road works or railway works.[231] A road works scheme may be referred to the Town Planning Board for the purpose of considering objections, as if the scheme were a draft plan prepared by the Town Planning Board.[232] The Railways Ordinance, on the other hand, does not involve the Town Planning Board in the consideration of objections. A scheme approved under the Roads Ordinance or the Railways Ordinance is as effective as if it were a plan prepared and approved under the Town Planning Ordinance.[233]

Plans prepared under the Country Parks Ordinance and the Marine Parks Ordinance are an important source of land use regulation as tending to conserve natural resources. Draft plans of country parks or marine parks are prepared under the two relevant statutes, which set out the powers of control and regulation in respect of those parks. Where a country park is wholly or partly within an area governed by a development plan made by the Town Planning Board, the plan clearly states that the land covered by the country park is not governed by the Town Planning Ordinance.

There is no prospect of a comprehensive town planning statute that will bring all the different specialized planning type agencies together with the central planning authority. The efforts of the government have been directed toward improving the relevant statutes individually.

There have been consistent demands for a comprehensive review of the Town Planning Ordinance to provide for more public participation and transparency in the planning process. After years of study and public consultation, the government introduced a town planning bill in the Legislative Council in the 1999–2000 session, but the administration and the Legislative Council could not agree on some of the basic principles underlying the proposed planning regime. As a result, the bill has been allowed to lapse.

The main proposals for reforms in the bill may be outlined here.[234] The first proposed change relates to plan making. Under the proposed legislation, members of the public will be given an opportunity to make representations in favor of the plan or against it. All representations must be made available for public inspection. Those who make adverse representations have a right to be heard along with those who have commented on adverse representations. Thus the ordinance will have a single-stage objection hearing.[235]

As regards the planning permission system, the proposed reforms envisage the publication of "bad neighbors" developments, requiring the applicant to obtain the consent of the landowner to make the application, and requiring the successful applicants to guarantee compliance with planning conditions.

The enforcement provision will likely remain largely unchanged. The only significant change perhaps will be increased fines.

There have been more radical demands for reform, including the setting up of an independent Planning Authority in place of the Town Planning Board, which is a statutory body consisting of official members and appointed nonofficial members. It remains to be seen whether such radical reforms will be acceptable to the administration, private land developers, and the community at large.

Appendix

CONSTITUTIONAL PROVISIONS RELEVANT TO LAND LEASES
AND COMPENSATION FOR DEPRIVATION OF PROPERTY RIGHTS

THE BASIC LAW OF THE HONG KONG SPECIAL
ADMINISTRATIVE REGION OF THE PEOPLE'S
REPUBLIC OF CHINA

Article 5
The socialist system and policies shall not be practised in the Hong Kong Special Administrative Region, and the previous capitalist system and way of life shall remain unchanged for 50 years.

Article 8
The laws previously in force in Hong Kong, that is, the common law, rules of equity, ordinances, subordinate legislation and customary law, shall be maintained, except for any that contravene this Law, and subject to any amendment by the legislature of the Hong Kong Special Administrative Region.

Article 11
In accordance with Article 31 of the Constitution of the People's Republic of China, the systems and policies practised in the Hong Kong Special Administrative Region, including the social and economic systems, the system for safeguarding the fundamental rights and freedoms of its residents, the executive, legislative and judicial systems, and the relevant policies, shall be based on the provisions of this Law.

No law enacted by the legislature of the Hong Kong Special Administrative Region shall contravene this Law.

Article 39
The provision of the International Covenant on Civil and Political Rights, the International Covenant on Economic, Social and Cultural Rights, and

international labour conventions as applied to Hong Kong shall remain in force and shall be implemented through the laws of the Hong Kong Special Administrative Region. The rights and freedoms enjoyed by Hong Kong residents shall not be restricted unless as prescribed by law. Such restrictions shall not contravene the provisions of the preceding paragraph of this Article.

Article 7
The land and natural resources within the Hong Kong Special Administrative Region shall be State property. The Government of the Hong Kong Special Administrative Region shall be responsible for their management, use and development and for their lease or grant to individuals, legal persons or organizations for use or development. The revenues derived therefrom shall be exclusively at the disposal of the government of the Region.

Article 120
All leases of land granted, decided upon or renewed before the establishment of the Hong Kong Special Administrative Region which extend beyond 30 June 1997, and all rights in relation to such leases, shall continue to be recognized and protected under the law of the Region.

Article 121
As regards all leases of land granted or renewed where the original leases contain no right of renewal, during the period from 27 May 1985 to 30 June 1997, which extend beyond 30 June 1997 and expire not later than 30 June 2047, the lessee is not required to pay an additional premium as from 1 July 1997, but an annual rent equivalent to 3 per cent of the rateable value of the property at that date, adjusted in step with any changes in the rateable value thereafter, shall be charged.

Article 122
In the case of old scheduled lots, village lots, small houses and similar rural holdings, where the property was on 30 June 1984 held by, or, in the case of small houses granted after that date, where the property is granted to, a lessee descended through the male line from a person who was in 1898 a resident of an established village in Hong Kong, the previous rent shall remain unchanged so long as the property is held by that lessee or by one of his lawful successors in the male line.

Article 123
Where leases of land without a right of renewal expire after the establishment of the Hong Kong Special Administrative Region, they shall be dealt with in accordance with laws and policies formulated by the Region on its own.

Article 6
The Hong Kong Special Administrative Region shall protect the right of private ownership of property in accordance with law.

Article 105
The Hong Kong Special Administrative Region shall, in accordance with law, protect the right of individuals and legal persons to the acquisition, use, disposal and inheritance of property and their right to compensation for lawful deprivation of their property.

Such compensation shall correspond to the real value of the property concerned at the time and shall be freely convertible and paid without undue delay.

The ownership of enterprises and the investments from outside the Region shall be protected by law.

Article 29
The homes and other premises of Hong Kong residents shall be inviolable. Arbitrary or unlawful search of, or intrusion into, a resident's home or other premises shall be prohibited.

Article 40
The lawful traditional rights and interests of the indigenous inhabitants of the "New Territories" shall be protected by the Hong Kong Special Administrative Region.

Notes

1. For the history and main features of Hong Kong's constitutional law, see Peter Wesley Smith, *Constitutional and Administrative Law in Hong Kong,* 2nd ed. (Hong Kong: China & Hong Kong Law Studies, 1994).
2. For a thorough and thought-provoking account of the Basic Law, see

Yash Ghai, *Hong Kong's New Constitutional Order*, 2nd ed. (Hong Kong: Hong Kong University Press, 1999). Constitutional documents of Hong Kong before and after 1997 are published, with an introduction and an index, by the present author, in *Texts of Constitutions—1*, in R. Blanpain (ed.), *International Encyclopaedia of Laws* (Kluwer International, 1998).

3. Basic Law, Article 1.

4. See Yash Ghai, *Hong Kong's New Constitutional Order*, chapter 4, "Sovereignty and Autonomy: The Framework of the Basic Law."

5. See M. J. A. Cooray, "Hong Kong in China: The Promise of 'One Country: Two Systems,'" *McGill Law Journal* 42 (1997): 751–760, and the book reviewed, Roda Mushkat, *One Country, Two International Personalities* (Hong Kong: Hong Kong University Press, 1997).

6. See generally Yash Ghai, *Hong Kong's New Constitutional Order*, chapter 6, "The Political and Administrative System."

7. Basic Law, Article 75.

8. For the impeachment procedure, see Basic Law, Article 73(9).

9. Basic Law, Article 55.

10. Ibid., Article 54.

11. See generally Yash Ghai, *Hong Kong's New Constitutional Order*, chapter 6, "The Political and Administrative System."

12. Basic Law, Article 85.

13. Ibid., Article 92.

14. Ibid., Article 88.

15. Ibid., Articles 90, 92.

16. Ibid., Article 81.

17. Ibid., Article 87.

18. Ibid., Article 94.

19. Ibid., Article 8.

20. Ibid., Article 84.

21. See M. J. A. Cooray, "International and Domestic Sources of Human Rights in Harmony? The Hong Kong Experience," *Yearbook Law & Legal Practice in East Asia* 4 (1999): 71–94.

22. Basic Law, Article 6.

23. Cap 347.

24. See the secretary for lands and works moving the second reading of the Land Acquisition (Possessory Title) Bill in the Legislative Council on June 29, 1983, *Debates of the Hong Kong Legislative Council (1982–83 session)*, 1045.

25. Basic Law, Article 7.

26. Hong Kong Government Gazette, vol. 1, no. 1, May 1, 1841, 11. For the early history of Hong Kong see J. W. Norton-Kyshe, *The History of the Laws and Courts of Hong Kong*, 2 vols. (Hong Kong: Vetch and Lee, 1970, reissue of 1898 ed.).

27. The Treaty of Nanking of 1842; see Peter Wesley-Smith, *Constitutional and Administrative Law in Hong Kong*, 35.

28. Hong Kong remained a Crown colony until July 1, 1997, when the People's Republic of China resumed its sovereignty over Hong Kong.

29. See Roger Bristow, *Land Use Planning in Hong Kong: History, Policies and Procedures* (Hong Kong: Oxford University Press, 1984), 25.

30. Ibid., 27.

31. As a result of the Convention of Peking in 1860. For the Convention, see Peter Wesley-Smith, *Constitutional and Administrative Law in Hong Kong*, 39.

32. See Bristow, *Land Use Planning in Hong Kong*, 28–29.

33. See ibid., 38.

34. See Peter Wesley-Smith, *Unequal Treaties 1898–1997: China, Great Britain, and Hong Kong's New Territories* (Hong Kong: Oxford University Press, 1983).

35. Bristow, *Land Use Planning in Hong Kong*, 67.

36. Ibid.

37. Ibid., 85.

38. See *Hong Kong 1998*, 218.

39. Basic Law, Article 7.

40. See generally *Halsbury's Laws of Hong Kong*, vol. 25 *Town Planning*, [385.060]–[385.066].

41. In *Shun Shing Hing Investment Co Ltd. v. Attorney General* (1983) HKLR 433, Hunter J at 434 described the Hong Kong government as the sole ground landlord. That description fits the Hong Kong government today.

42. Building (Planning) Regulations.

43. See *Town Planning in Hong Kong: A Quick Reference* (Planning Department, 1995), 37–39.

44. Bristow, *Land Use Planning in Hong Kong*, 194.

45. See "Enforcement under Outline Zoning Plans," *infra*.

46. See "Consideration of Planning Applications," *infra*.

47. The director of lands, who is responsible for the grant of leases, is an official member of the Town Planning Board and is able to contribute to the Town Planning Board's discussions on enforceability of proposed conditions through lease conditions. Planning conditions requiring off-site improvements, such as building a footbridge, are not easy to implement through the lease.

48. Under the Basic Law, the Court of First Instance is the equivalent of the former High Court.

49. *Shun Shing Hing Investment Co. Ltd. v. Attorney General* (1983) HKLR 433, at 434 per Hunter J (HC).

50. See *Secan Ltd. v. Attorney General* (1995) 2 HKLR 523; [1995] 2 HKC 629 (CA).

51. *Donald W. Shields (No. 2) v. Mary Chan* (1972) HKLR 121 (FC) and *The Attorney General v. Lo Hoi-ming* (1965) HKLR 1152 (HC).

52. *Mexx Consolidated (Far East) Ltd. v. Attorney General and Anor.* (1987) HKLR 1210 (HC).

53. *Wong Bei-nei v. Attorney General* (1973) HKLR 582 (HC).

54. *Real Honest Investment Ltd. v. Attorney General* (1997) 2 HKC 182 (CA).

55. Bristow, *Land Use Planning in Hong Kong,* 39–40.

56. Hill District Reservation Ordinance No. 4 of 1904 explicitly prohibited Chinese from residing in the Hill District. Under increasing pressure from the affluent and influential Chinese, the government made the prohibition less discriminatory and restrictive by enacting the Peak District (Residence) Ordinance of 1918. To a similar effect was Cheung Chau (Residence) Ordinance No. 14 of 1919.

57. Peak District (Residence) Repeal Ordinance No. 10 of 1946 and Cheung Chau (Residence) Repeal Ordinance No. 11 of 1946. See *Halsbury's Laws of Hong Kong,* Chapter 25, *Town Planning,* "[385.020] Land-use control as a means of racial segregation."

58. *Wang Wah Chong Investment Co. Ltd. v. Attorney General* (1981) HKLR 336; (1981) 1 WLR 1141 (PC).

59. *Lok On Co. Ltd. v. Attorney General* (1986) HKLR 857, at 859 (CA).

60. *Canadian Overseas Development Co. Ltd. v. Attorney General* (1991) 1 HKC 288 (CA).

61. See generally Anthony M. W. Law, "Judicial Review of Government Leases in the Hong Kong Special Administrative Region," *Hong Kong Law Journal* 29 (1999): 240–266.

62. Leases contain a provision enabling the government to reenter land for breach of covenant.

63. As in *Attorney General v. Fulton Corporation* (1963) HKLR 176 (FC).

64. Summary Offences Ordinance (Cap 228), section 4(25).

65. Public law principles do not apply to the determination of the amount payable as premium: *Hang Wah Chong Investment Co. Ltd. v. Attorney General* (1981) HKLR 336, at 342; (1981) 1 WLR 1141, at 1146 (PC).

66. Such as requiring the developer to take environmental protection measures: *Secan Ltd. v. Attorney General* (1995) 2 HKLR 523; (1995) 2 HKC 629(CA).

67. Buildings Ordinance (Cap 123), section 16(1)(d).

68. See *Building Authority v. Head Step Ltd.* (1995) 6 HKPLR 87 (CA).

69. Buildings Ordinance (Cap 123), section 16(1)(g).

70. See Kemal Bokhary, "Section 16(1)(g) of the Building Ordinance (Cap 123)—A Shooter's Guide," *Hong Kong Law Journal* 19 (1989): 314–330.

71. Building (Planning) Regulations.

72. See the discussion of density control at "Government Leases as a Means of Regulating the Use and Development of Land," *supra*.

73. Approval of the Building Authority is required for "building works," and if a material change of use of a building is effected without any "building works," the Building Authority has no jurisdiction in respect of such change of use.

74. Some examples are given in *Comprehensive Review of the Town Planning Ordinance: Consultative Document* (Hong Kong: Planning Environment and Lands Branch, 1991), 52, 63.

75. Enforceable plans are development permission area plans and second-generation outline zoning plans. See "Enforcement under Development Permission Area Plans" and "Enforcement under Outline Zoning Plans," *infra*.

76. See *Halsbury's Laws of Hong Kong*, 'Town Planning' and 'Environment' by the present author.

77. Town Planning (Amendment) Ordinance No. 59 of 1974.

78. Town Planning (Amendment) (No. 2) Ordinance No. 101 of 1991.

79. Town Planning (Amendment) Ordinance No. 4 of 1991.

80. Ibid.

81. For the Interim Development Permission Area Plans made in 1990 and replaced by Development Permission Area Plans in 1991, see "Interim Development Permission Area Plans," *infra*.

82. The notes in respect of specified zones adopt a two-column format. Uses listed in column 1 are always permitted. Uses listed in column 2 may be permitted by the Town Planning Board upon application. Uses that are not listed in either column are not permissible in the zone at all.

83. *Henderson Real Estate Ltd. v. Lo Chai-wan* (1996) 7 HKPLR 1; (1997) HKLRD 258 (PC).

84. (1974) HKLR 275 (HC).

85. Ibid., at 290.

86. Town Planning Ordinance, section 4(1) in its original form.

87. (1974) HKLR 275, at 299.

88. See Town Planning (Amendment and Validation) Ordinance No. 59 of 1974.

89. Section 4(1) of the Town Planning Ordinance was amended to provide that in addition to designating zones, the Town Planning Board may show or make provision for "any matter whatsoever . . . by means of such diagrams, illustrations, notes or descriptive matter as the Board thinks appropriate."

90. See Town Planning (Amendment) (No. 2) Ordinance No. 101 of 1991.

91. *Henderson Real Estate Agency Ltd. v. Wo Chai Wan* (1996) 7 HKPLR 1, 11; (1997) HKLRD 258, 266, per Lord Lloyd of Berwick (PC).

92. *Henderson Real Estate Ltd. v. Wo Chai Wan* (1996) 7 HKPLR 1; (1997) HKLRD 258 arose out of a judicial review application disputing the

relevant decision of the Appeal Board reversing the Town Planning Board's decision.

93. Section 16(1) of the Town Planning Ordinance states that "where a draft plan or approved plan . . . provides for the grant of permission for any purpose, an application for the grant of such permission shall be made to the [Town Planning] Board."

94. Always permitted uses in a Residential Group A zone include flat, house, market, post office, and private club. They are listed in column 1 of the notes.

95. Uses that require planning permission in a Residential Group A zone include educational institution, hospital, hotel, and public utility installation. They are listed in column 2 of the notes.

96. In an unspecified zone certain uses, such as amenity area, cycle track, and taxi rank, are always permitted. But these are insignificant from the standpoint of a private developer.

97. The Explanatory Statement in the approved Tai Tam and Shek O Outline Zoning Plan No. S/H18/2 states that the undetermined zoning is intended to denote areas where further detailed planning study is required to identify the future uses of the land.

98. Plan No. DPA/YL-ST/1.

99. Town Planning Ordinance, section 16(4).

100. Section 54A of the Town and Country Planning Act, 1990 (U.K.). It has been held that the planning authority may grant planning permission for a nonconforming use if there are compelling material considerations supporting such use: *St. Albans District Council v. Secretary of State for the Environment* (1993) JPL 374. For similar observation on the Scottish equivalent of s54A, see *City of Edinburgh Council v. Secretary of State for Scotland and Anor.* (1998) 1 All ER 174, at 184 (House of Lords), where it was said that there is a presumption in favor of the development plan. The decision of the House of Lords correctly represents English law: *R. v. Leominster District Council,* ex parte Pothecary (1998) JPL 335 (CA). See also *James v. Secretary of State for the Environment and Saunders* (1998) 1 PLR 33.

101. The application forms require such information.

102. *Sovmots Investments Ltd. v. Secretary of State for the Environment* (1979) AC 144 (HL).

103. Town Planning Ordinance, section 16(3). The preliminary consideration of a planning application is normally not by the full board, but by one of its two planning committees.

104. Ibid., section 17(1).

105. Ibid., section 17(B)(1).

106. See *Town Planning Board Guidelines for Renewal of Planning Permission and Extension of Time for Compliance with Planning Conditions* TPB PG-No. 21.

107. A comprehensive development area is an area designated for comprehensive planning for purposes such as urban renewal: see *Town Planning Board Guidelines for Designation of "Comprehensive Development Area" (CDA) Zones and Monitoring the Progress of "CDA" Developments,* TPB PG-No. 17.

108. In England, the Town and Country Planning Act is said to embody a rebuttable presumption in favor of the plan. As a general rule, an application for planning permission will be determined in accordance with the policies set out in the development plan, unless there are material considerations, which indicate that in the particular case the provisions of the plan should not be followed. See *City of Edinburgh Council v. Secretary of State for Scotland and Anor.* (1998) 1 All ER 174, at 184 per Lord Clyde (HL) followed in *R. v. Leominster District Council,* ex parte Pothecary, (1998) JPL 335 (CA).

109. Town Planning Ordinance, section 16(4).

110. The Town and Country Planning Act (U.K.) provides that the local planning authorities must have regard to the provisions of the development plan, so far as material to the application, and to any other material considerations: section 70(2). It adds that where, in making any determination under the Planning Act regard is to be had for the development plan, the determination must be in accordance with the plan unless material considerations indicate otherwise: section 54A. The U.K. planning permission system has been described as a "plan-led" system. See Victor Moore, *A Practical Approach to Planning Law,* 7th ed. (London: Butterworths, 2000), 202.

111. See Appeal No. 4 of 1993 reported in *Town Planning Appeal Board Decisions, Volume 1 (1992–1993),* 75–81, at para. 20.

112. See *Henderson Real Estate Agency Ltd. v. Lo Chai-wan* (1996) 7 HKPLR 1; (1997) HKLRD 258 (PC).

113. Cmnd 9794 of May 1986.

114. This has been reaffirmed in PPGI *General Policy and Principles,* para. 5. See also *Cranford Hall Parking Ltd. v. Secretary of State for the Environment* (1989) JPL 169.

115. In Case No. 5 of 1993.

116. Case No. 6 of 1994.

117. See "An Overview of Compensation Provisions," *infra.*

118. TPB PG-No. 3A.

119. Ibid., para 2.6.

120. TPB PG-No. 5, para 3.

121. TPB PG-No. 10.

122. TPB PG-No. 13.

123. Ordinance No. 106 of 1997 (Cap 531), section 3.

124. Town Planning (Amendment) Ordinance, No. 4 of 1991. See Anton Cooray, "Enforcement of Planning Control in Rural Hong Kong: Reflections

on Recent Legislative Reforms," *Asia Pacific Law Review* 1, no. 1 (1992): 108–117.

125. *Attorney General v. Melhado Investment Ltd.* (1983) HKLR 327 (HC).

126. The town planning (amendment) bill was gazetted on July 27, 1990, and presented to the Legislative Council on November 7, 1990. The amendment ordinance came into operation on January 25, 1991.

127. Town Planning Ordinance, section 21.

128. Issued under section 23(1) of the Town Planning Ordinance.

129. An unauthorized development may be regularized by obtaining planning permission.

130. Issued under section 23(2) of the Town Planning Ordinance.

131. Issued under section 23(3) of the Town Planning Ordinance.

132. Town Planning Ordinance, section 23(4). The amendment ordinance came into effect on January 25, 1991, and all the interim development permission area plans were replaced by development permission area plans within six months of that date.

133. Under section 26(1)(b) of the Town Planning Ordinance.

134. See section 23(5) of the Town Planning Ordinance.

135. Town Planning Ordinance, section 20(5).

136. Ibid., section 20(6).

137. See Anton Cooray, "Enforcement of Planning Control in Hong Kong," *The New Gazette* (June 1995): 50–52.

138. Sections 21 and 20(8) of the Town Planning Ordinance. See "Enforcement under Development Permission Area Plans" and "Enforcement under Outline Zoning Plans," *supra*.

139. Section 23(6) of the Town Planning Ordinance.

140. *R. v. Tang Ying Yip* (1995) 2 HKC 277, per Litton J (HC).

141. *R. v. Chung Pak Chun*, MA 928 of 1993 decided on January 18, 1994 (unreported). The High Court reduced the fine and set aside the default imprisonment, which could not have been imposed validly.

142. *R. v. Tai Tong Lychee Valley Co. Ltd.* (1997) 2 HKC 64 (HC). Not to inform the recipient that he might be able to regularize his unauthorized development by obtaining planning permission would be repugnant to the concept of fairness: *Department of Justice v. Hung Wan Construction Co. Ltd.* (1997) 3 HKC 150 (HC).

143. *R. v. Tang Ying Yip* (1995) 2 HKC 277 (HC).

144. Ibid.

145. *R. v. Tai Tong Lychee Valley Co. Ltd.* (1997) 2 HKC 64 (HC).

146. *In re Man Wai Hung et al.*, MP 3144 of 1994, decided on January 20, 1995 (unreported) (HC).

147. *Tse Kwei King and Cheung Kam v. Attorney General*, MP 1509 of 1993, decided on December 21, 1993 (unreported) (HC).

148. See secretary for lands and works moving the second reading of the Land Acquisition (Possessory Title) Bill, June 29, 1983, *Debates of the Hong Kong Legislative Council (1982–83 session),* 1045.

149. Cap 15. A new Urban Renewal Authority under the Urban Renewal Authority Ordinance will replace the Land Development Corporation. The new ordinance was passed by the Legislative Council and signed by the chief executive in July 2000, but has not yet been brought into effect by the secretary for planning and lands.

150. See Town Planning Ordinance, section 4(2).

151. See "Resumption of Land in Connection with Road Works and Railway Works," *infra.*

152. See "Country Parks and Marine Parks," *infra.*

153. Cap 130, section 3.

154. Mining Ordinance, sections 11, 12.

155. Mining Ordinance, section 65.

156. See "Reclamations," *infra.*

157. See "Resumption of the Land in Connection with Road Works and Railway Works," *infra.*

158. Cap 357.

159. Lands Resumption Ordinance (Cap 124), section 22.

160. Ibid., section 3.

161. Ibid., section 2.

162. Ibid., section 19.

163. Ibid., sections 3, 4.

164. Ibid., section 4A.

165. Ibid., section 5.

166. Ibid., section 6(1).

167. Ibid., section 6(3).

168. Ibid., section 9. See also *Re an application by KOY Investments Ltd.* (1983) HKLR 28.

169. Lands Tribunal Ordinance (Cap 17), section 8.

170. Lands Resumption Ordinance, section 10(1).

171. Ibid., section 12(d).

172. For a good illustration of this principle, see *Redhill Properties Ltd. v. Director of Engineering Development* (1984) HKDCLR 1.

173. Taking its name from the Privy Council decision in *Pointe Gourde Quarrying and Transport Co. v. Sub-Intendent of Crown Lands* (1947) AC 565.

174. The *Pointe Gourde* principle has been followed in Hong Kong. See, e.g., *Director of Lands and Survey v. Wong Chung-don* (1977) HKLTLR 43; *Director of Lands and Survey v. Lam Tung-sum* (1977) HKLTLR 148; *Hofei Estates Ltd. v. Secretary for City and New Territories Administration* (1980–82) CPR 486.

175. Lands Resumption Ordinance, section 12(aa).

176. *Director of Lands and Survey v. Wong Chung-don and Ors.* (1997) HKTLR 43 and *Golden Hand Industrial Co. Ltd. v. Director of Lands and Survey* (1979–1980) HKTLR 24.

177. Lands Resumption Ordinance, section 12(a).

178. Ibid., section 10(2)(c).

179. (1991) HKDCLR 33.

180. Although the Lands Resumption Ordinance does not use the word "disturbance," it is commonly agreed that Hong Kong courts can derive assistance from common law decisions dealing with the concept of "disturbance": *Director of Public Works v. Leung Sze* (1977) HKLTLR 158.

181. Lands Resumption Ordinance, section 10(2)(d) and (e).

182. Ibid., section 10(2)(b).

183. See the speech made by the attorney general moving the second reading of the Roads (Works, Uses, and Compensation) Bill in the Legislative Council on March 10, 1982, *Proceedings of the Hong Kong Legislative Council (1981–82 Session),* 547.

184. Cap 370.

185. Cap 519.

186. Roads Ordinance, section 13; Railways Ordinance, section 16.

187. Roads (Works, Uses, and Compensation) Ordinance, Schedule Part II, item 1; Railways Ordinance, Schedule Part II, item 1.

188. Roads Ordinance, section 26; Railways Ordinance, section 31.

189. Roads Ordinance, Schedule Part II, item 2; Railways Ordinance Schedule Part III, item 2.

190. Roads Ordinance, Schedule Part II, item 3; Railways Ordinance Schedule Part III, item 3.

191. Roads Ordinance, Schedule Part II, item 4; Railways Ordinance Schedule Part III, item 4.

192. Roads Ordinance, Schedule Part II, item 5; Railways Ordinance Schedule Part III, item 5.

193. Roads Ordinance, Schedule Part II, item 5; Railways Ordinance Schedule Part III, item 5.

194. Roads (Works, Uses, and Compensation) Ordinance, section 29; Railways Ordinance, section 34.

195. Roads (Works, Uses, and Compensation) Ordinance, section 22; Railways Ordinance, section 27.

196. See Roads (Works, Uses, and Compensation) Ordinance section 23; and Railways Ordinance section 28.

197. See, e.g., R. M. C. Duxbury, *Telling and Duxbury's Planning Law and Procedure,* 11th ed. (London: Butterworths, 1999), chapter 13; Victor Moore, *A Practical Approach to Planning Law,* 7th ed. (London: Blackstone Press Ltd., 2000), 491–495.

198. Cap 301, Long Title.

199. Cap 301, section 3(1AA).

200. Cap 301, section 3(1)(c).

201. Protection of the Harbor Ordinance (Cap S31), section 3.

202. Foreshore and Seabed (Reclamations) Ordinance (Cap 127), Long Title.

203. *Li Ling Shi (No. 2) v. The Government* (1964) HKLR 428.

204. Foreshore and Seabed (Reclamations) Ordinance (Cap 127), section 12.

205. Gordon N. Cruden, *Land Compensation and Valuation Law in Hong Kong,* 2nd ed. (Singapore: Butterworths, 1999), 395. See also *Chan Sik Sheung & Ors. v. Director of Lands* (1995) 3 HKC 199 at 207 (Lands Tribunal).

206. *Sisters of Charity of Rockingham v. R.* (1922) 2 AC 315 (PC).

207. *Re Trustees of the Estate of Tsang Hing Tin, deceased* (1971) HKLR 68 (FC).

208. Foreshore and Seabed (Reclamations) Ordinance (Cap 127), section 13.

209. Country Parks Ordinance (Cap 208), Long Title.

210. Marine Parks Ordinance (Cap 476), Long Title.

211. Country Parks Ordinance, section 10; Marine Parks Ordinance, section 9.

212. Country Parks Ordinance, section 18.

213. Ibid., sections 10, 16.

214. Ibid., section 19.

215. See *Chan Sau Ying v. Director of Lands* (1983–1985) CPR 487.

216. Marine Parks Ordinance (Cap 124), section 17(1).

217. Ibid., section 19(2).

218. "Except in the case of resumption under the Lands Resumption Ordinance no compensation shall be paid by reason of the fact that it lies within or is affected by any zone or district set apart" in a plan: Town Planning Ordinance, section 4(3). Lands Resumption Ordinance, section 12(aa) reflects this rule.

219. Section 19 provides that a person affected by the inclusion of his or her land within a marine park will be entitled to compensation if such is payable for land resumption.

220. Town Planning Ordinance, section 4(2).

221. Marine Parks Ordinance, section 17(1).

222. Case No. CLR 15/94 cited in Cruden, *Land Compensation and Valuation Law in Hong Kong,* 81.

223. Today such zones are known as comprehensive development area zones.

224. Cap 357.

225. See, e.g., Foreshore and Seabed (Reclamations) Ordinance, section 11; Land Resumptions Ordinance, section 9; Country Parks Ordinance, section 18(2); Marine Parks Ordinance, section 19(2).

226. (1995–1996) CPR 547.

227. See Cruden, *Land Compensation and Valuation Law in Hong Kong,* chapter 22, "Valuation Methods."

228. Ibid., 552–553.

229. Ibid., 553–555, and Albet Chen, "The Basic Law and the Protection of Property Rights," *Hong Kong Law Journal* 23 (1933): 31.

230. Land Development Corporation Ordinance (Cap 15), section 15 (3) (6). See *Silver Mountain Investments Ltd. & Anor. v. Attorney General & Anor.* (1994) 2 HKLR 297 (PC).

231. Roads Ordinance, section 5(a); Railways Ordinance, section 4.

232. Roads Ordinance, section 11.3.

233. Town Planning Ordinance, section 13 A.

234. See Anton Cooray, "Recent Developments in Planning Law," in *Law Lectures for Practitioners 1997* (Hong Kong: Hong Kong Law Journal Ltd., 1997), 135–160.

235. For the existing multistage objection procedure, see "Statutory Development Plans," *supra.*

Select Bibliography

Bokhary, Kemal. "Section 16(1)(g) of the Building Ordinance (Cap 123)—A Shooter's Guide." *Hong Kong Law Journal* 19 (1989): 314–330.

Bristow, Roger. *Land-use Planning in Hong Kong: History, Policies and Procedures.* Hong Kong: Oxford University Press, 1984.

Chen, Albert. "The Basic Law and the Protection of Property Rights." *Hong Kong Law Journal* 23 (1993): 31.

Cooray, M. J. A. "Enforcement of Planning Control in Rural Hong Kong: Reflections on Recent Legislative Reforms." *Asia Pacific Law Review* 1, no. 1 (1992): 108–117.

Cooray, M. J. A. "Enforcement of Planning Control in Hong Kong." *The New Gazette,* June 1995, 50–52.

Cooray, M. J. A. "Recent Developments in Planning Law." In *Law Lectures for Practitioners 1997,* 135–160. Hong Kong: Hong Kong Law Journal Ltd., 1997.

Cooray, M. J. A. "Hong Kong in China: The Promise of 'One Country: Two Systems.'" *McGill Law Journal* 42 (1997): 751–760.

Cooray, M. J. A. "International and Domestic Sources of Human Rights in Harmony? The Hong Kong Experience." *Yearbook Law & Legal Practice in East Asia* 4 (1999): 71–94.

Cooray, M. J. A. "Town Planning." In *Halsbury's Law of Hong Kong*, volume 25, 532–782.

Cooray, M. J. A. "The Environment." In *Halsbury's Law of Hong Kong*, volume 11, 273–522.

Cruden, Gordon N. *Land Compensation and Vacation Law in Hong Kong*. 2nd ed. Singapore: Butterworths, 1999.

Ghai, Yashi. *Hong Kong's New Constitutional Order*. 2nd ed. Hong Kong: Hong Kong University Press, 1999.

Hong Kong Planning Department. *Town Planning in Hong Kong: A Quick Reference*. Hong Kong: Government Printer, 1995.

Law, Anthony M. W. "Judicial Review of Government Leases in the Hong Kong Special Administrative Region." *Hong Kong Law Journal* 29 (1999): 240–266.

Wesley-Smith, Peter. *Constitutional and Administrative Law in Hong Kong: Text and Materials*. Hong Kong: China and Hong Kong Law Studies, 1987.

Chapter 4

Japan's Land Use Law

TSUYOSHI KOTAKA

Outline of Land Use Planning and Regulation Law

Public laws related to land use planning and regulation that are carried out with clear precision are not old. Such law began in the Meiji period; however, it did not reach its complete form as a statute until the old City Planning Law and City Building Law were enacted in 1917. Following a rapid increase in population, the concentration of people in urban areas, and the expansion of social economic activities after World War II, the necessities of land use planning, positive land use for the public interest and public projects, comprehensive plans for nationwide development, land acquisition for public projects, charging for public facilities, and so forth, began.

LAND USE PLANNING AND REGULATION LAW SYSTEM

As various laws dealing with these purposes were legislated—and we have many statutes related to land use planning and regulation at present—it became difficult to understand the mutual relationships of these statutes. But laws of land use planning and regulation are roughly classified as follows:[1]

1. Fundamental Laws: Laws providing fundamental policies and comprehensive plans for national land development and land use regulations. Examples are the Comprehensive National Land Devel-

---

Professor, Faculty of Law, Meijo University.

opment Law (1950), the National Land Use Planning Law (1974), and the Land Fundamental Law (1989).

2. Regional Planning Laws: Laws relating to land use planning of a wide area like the Tokyo metropolitan area. Examples are the Tokyo Metropolitan Area Development Law (1956) and the Kinki Area Development Law (1963). A very special example of this type of law is the Hokkaido Development Law (1950).

3. Urban Development Laws: Laws relating to urban development and harmonious land use regulation. Examples are the Readjustment of Town Lots Law (1954), the City Planning Law (1968), the City Redevelopment Law (1969), and the Building Standard Law (1950).

4. Land Acquisition Laws: Laws relating to land acquisition, including taking land for public projects or public use. Examples are the Land Expropriation Law (1951) and the Land Acquisition Special Measures Law (1961). As for just compensation, the cabinet enacted in 1962 the Guideline of Standards for Compensation for Loss Caused by Acquisition of Land for Public Use.

5. Preservation of Natural, Historical, and Cultural Environment Laws: Laws relating to land use regulation to preserve the natural environment and historical or cultural assets. Examples are the Forest Law (1951), the Natural Park Law (1957), the Natural Environment Preservation Law (1972), and the Preservation of Inner City Green Tract Law (1973).

MAIN LAW SYSTEMS RELATED TO LAND USE PLANNING AND REGULATION

Comprehensive National Land Development Law (CNLDL)

The purpose of the Comprehensive National Land Development Law is to take account of natural conditions of national land; to totally use, develop, and preserve the land; to distribute industries properly; and to contribute to the progress of social welfare from the comprehensive standpoint of policies related to economy, society, culture, and so forth (Art. 1).

The law intends to make a framework for a total national land development plan related to the following five subjects:[2]

1. Utilization of land, water, and other natural resources.
2. Protection from flood, storm damage, and other disasters.

3. Adjustment of sizes and locations of cities and villages.
4. Proper location of industries.
5. Volume of electricity, transportation, and other important public facilities, and protection of resources related to culture, public welfare, tourism, and so forth.

Among comprehensive development plans, the most important is the Nationwide Comprehensive Development Plan made by the prime minister (Art. 7, CNLDL), which indicates the fundamental policy of development for a ten-year term. The newest and Fourth Plan was decided in 1987.

National Land Use Planning Law

The National Land Use Planning Law, which was enacted in 1974, has two main purposes: land use planning and land transaction regulation. Under this law, three kinds of National Land Use Plans—nationwide, prefectural, and municipal—are drawn up to indicate administrative measures for land use (Arts. 4–8). The most important land use plan that is made under the National Land Use Plan is the Land Use Fundamental Plan decided by the prefecture (Art. 9). In this plan, urban areas, agriculture areas, forest areas, natural park areas, and natural environment preservation areas are designated. These five areas are expected to function as higher-rank plans to "Zoning-District Regulations" assigned by the City Planning Law, the Agriculture Promotion Area Preparation Law, the Forest Law, the Natural Park Law, and the Natural Environment Preservation Law.[3]

Land Fundamental Law

Recently, after serious experiences with an unprecedented, unusually rapid rise in land prices, the Land Fundamental Law was enacted in 1989. Since this law provides only policies and objectives, and entrusts concrete measures to future legislation, it declared: (1) preference of public welfare over land use (Art. 2); (2) proper land use following land use plans made by government (Art. 3); (3) restraint of speculative transaction of land (Art. 4); and (4) responsibilities of both national and local governments and landowners based on basic doctrine (Art. 6).[4]

City Planning Law

The City Planning Law was enacted in 1968, and completely revised old law as the basic law of comprehensive development of urban areas harmonizing with the surrounding countryside. Under this law, an urban area is designated as mainly two areas, the urbanization area and the urbanization restraint area (Art. 7). In the urbanization restraint area, development activities are restrained in general, unless one has obtained development permission from the governor (Art. 29). In the urbanization area, various kinds of zoning are drawn up and public projects necessary for social and economic activities in cities are carried out. Among zoning-district systems, Yoto-Chiiki zoning is recognized as the most important and is sure to be in the urbanization area. Yoto-Chiiki zoning is the same kind of zoning as the so-called Euclidean zoning in the United States, and includes twelve kinds of zoning from "the first category residential" to "exclusive industry."[5] The effect of these zoning systems is secured by building regulations under the Building Standard Law (sec. 3, sub-sec. 3, Art. 48).

Outline of Land Acquisition Process and Just Compensation

OUTLINE OF LAND ACQUISITION PROCESS

Under Article 29, Paragraph 3 of the constitution, the Land Expropriation Law was enacted in 1951 as a general statute concerning compulsory acquisition of land for public purpose.[6] In addition, the Law of Special Measure for Land Acquisition (1961) provides a procedure for urgent expropriation for projects that are especially needed for the social and economic life of society and are expected to be accomplished urgently. In general, land acquisition for public projects is not done by procedure under the Land Expropriation Law but by mutual negotiation among the project initiator, the landowner, and interested parties.

Projects That May Expropriate Land

The Land Expropriation Law (LEL) enumerates projects that may expropriate or compulsorily use land (Art. 3). Road construction, river improvement, water supply, railway construction, and waste disposal facilities are examples. Public projects that are enumerated in Article 3 of the LEL may have the legal ability to acquire land compulsorily by carrying out procedures provided in the LEL. On the other hand, even a big project that seems to offer almost the same benefits to society cannot expropriate land as long as it does not come under a project enumerated in Article 3 of the LEL.

Parties Appearing in the Expropriation Process

Under the Land Expropriation Law, three main parties appear in the process:

1. Project Initiator: Government organizations and public utilities that undertake a project related to any one of the items enumerated in Article 3 are called "Project Initiators" (Art. 8, Para. 1). In other words, project initiator means condemnation agency.
2. Owner of Land and Interested Party: Owner of land means the owner of such land as is involved in the expropriation (Art. 8, Para. 2). Interested parties are diverse, corresponding to the legal title that is expropriated. For instance, in the case of an expropriation of land, the person who at the time has holds on the land, involving superficies, servitude, quarrying right, pledge, mortgage, rights obtained by loan of use, lease, or other rights excluding ownership, as well as the person who holds ownership of other rights to articles on the land, shall be treated as interested parties in the expropriation process (Art. 8, Para. 3).
3. Administrative Agencies: In the process of the expropriation, two kinds of administrative agencies perform important roles:
   a. The minister of construction shall make dispositions concerning the "Recognition of the Project" that bestow the project initiator with the right of claim to expropriation in a concrete case under the condition to carry out necessary procedures provided in the LEL (Arts. 16, 20). For the project executed within the boundary of the prefecture, the governor shall be charged with recognition of the project.
   b. The Expropriation Committee that is established under the jurisdiction of the respective prefectural governors and has the competence to make rulings of expropriation (Art. 47-2) shall exercise its competence independently (Art. 51).

Recognition of a Project

After the project initiator has finished preparation for the project, the initiator begins to negotiate with the landowner and interested parties as to land acquisition and compensation. If the project initiator suspects it would be difficult to enter into a contract with the landowner and interested parties, the initiator shall submit a written application for recognition of the project.

The recognition of the project decided by the minster of construction or the governor defines the scope of land to be taken into consideration for both public use and harmful influence on environment (Art. 20, LEL). (Tokyo Hi. Ct., July 13, 1973).[7]

The recognition of the project has the following main legal effects:

1. Bestows the competence of expropriation on the project initiator.
2. Fixes the price of land at the date of notification of the recognition (Art. 71).
3. Fixes interested parties. No person who has newly obtained a right after the notification shall be included in the interested parties (Art. 8, Para. 3 proviso).

If the project initiator wants to defer the expropriation procedure to after project recognition, the initiator may apply for "Declaration of Deferment of Expropriation Procedure" by the minister of construction or governor (Arts. 31, 32). In this case, the effect of the project recognition is suspended until "Notification of Starting the Procedure" (Art. 34-5).

Record of Land and Record of Articles

After the recognition of the project, the project initiator must examine and check land and other articles, then draw up a record of land and of articles (Arts. 35, 37). Since these records are basic documents for an expropriation ruling made by the expropriation committee, the project initiator, landowner, and the interested parties have to sign their names to confirm the contents of the record (Arts. 36, 38).

Ruling for Expropriation by the Expropriation Committee

The project initiator may, within one year from the date of the project recognition, apply to the expropriation committee for a ruling concerning expropriation (Art. 39). The ruling for expropriation by the expropriation committee includes "ruling for acquisition of right" and "ruling for evacuation" (Art. 47-2, Para. 2). The project initiator shall acquire the ownership of the land at the time the acquisition of right is fixed in the ruling for acquisition of right (Art. 101). Any person who is dissatisfied with the ruling of the expropriation committee may request that the minister of construction investigate (Art. 129) and may bring a lawsuit concerning the ruling on compensation for a loss (Art. 133).

OUTLINE OF JUST COMPENSATION

Compensation Concerned with Private Property

With respect to compensation under the Land Expropriation Law, in order to put full compensation in practice, the cabinet decided on "The Guideline of Standard for Compensation for Loss Caused by Acquisition of Land for Public Use" (Cabinet Decision, June 29, 1962, revised, December 12, 1967).[8] The purposes of this guideline are to provide comprehensive requisites for compensation and its calculation, thereby ensuring smooth implementation of the public project and appropriate compensation for loss (Art. 1). This guideline is mainly aimed at applications for land acquisition by agreement but, furthermore, compensation in connection with expropriation shall be based on this guideline ("On the Execution of the Guideline of Standard for Compensation for Loss Caused by Acquisition of Land for Public Use" [Cabinet Agreement, June 29, 1962]).

As under this guideline, each ministry and agency was asked to enact or amend the standards of compensation for loss immediately. The Yochi-Taisaku Renrakukai (Public Works Enterprise Association—generally it is called Yotairen) made internal detailed rules, which are called "The Standard for Compensation for Loss Caused by Acquisition of Land for Public Use" (Board of Directors of Yotairen Decision, October 12, 1962) and "The Detailed Standard for Compensation for Loss by Acquisition of Land for Public Use" (Board of Directors of Yotairen Decision, March 7, 1963).

More than thirty years have passed since these guidelines were decided, and with changes in social and economic situations and emerging wide varieties of values, new issues of substance and the extent of compensation for loss have been raised. After three years' revising work, Yotairen, under the guidance of the Ministry of Construction, revised their compensation standard and detailed rules recently to conform to current society (Board of Directors Decision, June 22, 1998).[9]

Compensation Concerned with Public Facilities

Generally, compensation is paid for loss caused by acquisition of land owned by a private person. But in the process of the execution of a public project, the project initiator is obliged to acquire some kind of public facilities, such as school buildings, public road sites, and the like. With respect to these situations, the Land Expropriation Law provides that "No lands which have already been furnished for use of a project which may expropriate or use land in accordance with the provision of this law or any other law can be expropriated or used unless there exists a special need therefor" (Art. 4). Thus, if there exists a special need compared with the function of an existing public facility, the public project initiator can expropriate the facility.

The compensation for loss of a public facility caused by a public project is defined as "Compensation for Public Loss Caused by Execution of a Public Project" (usually this compensation is called "public compensation"), which is distinguished from "Compensation for Loss Caused by Acquisition of Land for Public Use" (usually this compensation is called "general compensation"), which is applied to private property.

The cabinet decided "The Guideline of Standard for Compensation for Public Loss Caused by Execution of Public Project" (Cabinet Decision, February 21, 1967) to provide "for the principal standards for compensation for public loss caused by a public project, thereby to ensure the smooth implementation of the public project and appropriate compensation for public loss" (Art. 1 of the Guideline).

The main point of difference between public compensation and general compensation in appraisal of compensation is that the former adopts "functional recovery" criteria related to functional replacement of the property, while the latter is based on "fair market value" criteria. The Guideline of Public Compensation provides that "Functional Recovery means rationally reproducing or restoring the function of public facilities inside the project site, which the execution of the public project necessarily discontinues or stops" (Art. 3, Para. 4 of the Guideline).[10]

Types and Contents of Compensation

CRITERIA OF JUST COMPENSATION

To examine the criteria of just compensation, I will identify the purpose, substance, and scope of regulations on a case-by-case basis, establishing the following analytical framework by which I decide whether the regulation on property in question prevents the use of the property, not whether it diminishes the value of a property. With respect to the general criteria on the issue of land use regulation and just compensation, not only the Supreme Court's and other court decisions, but also theory has often referred to it as the "limitation in itself" standard, by which they mean that there is no compensation for this type of land use.[11] However, this standard is only a general one, and in each case whether and how much compensation is needed should be considered in a comprehensive manner that takes into account the purpose, substance, and scope of regulation.

Judge Takatsuji's article is the first attempt, beyond the display of general criteria, to analyze the mode of property regulation by making several categories. In deciding whether just compensation should be needed, he stated a balancing approach that weighs the substance of regulation on property rights against social obligation for public welfare in the exercising of rights, and formulated the following categories.[12] When a case is in one of the following categories, regulation does not substantially infringe on the property rights and requires no constitutional compensation. Otherwise, constitutional compensation is required.

1. Although a regulation brings sacrifice on its face,
    a. If it derives from what the property owner did (Art. 30 of the Control of Soil Erosion Law; Art. 12, Para. 1 of the Coastal Law; Art. 21 of the Natural Park Law; Art. 14, Para. 2 of the National Highway Law, etc.); or
    b. If it is accompanied by other kinds of regulation (Art. 12, Para. 4 of the Building Standards Law, Art. 17 of the Development of Housing Site Regulation Law, etc.) there is no compensation.
2. If sacrifice is within the scope of social obligation of the property owner without diminishing the property's substantial value such as
    a. Achieving the obligation of preventing a risk that derives from the property against others' lives, bodies, or property (Art. 18 of DHSRL, Art. 10 of BSL, Art. 18 of the Land Sliding Prevention Law, etc.);
    b. Carrying out the obligation to prevent a disturbance of public safety, which derives from the property (Art. 44, Para. 3 of the Road Law; Art. 49, Para. 1 of the Aviation Law, etc.); or
    c. Carrying out the obligation to assist governmental regulation in preserving public safety and order (Art. 27 of the Fire Law, Art. 12 of the Flood Control Law, etc.) there is no compensation.
3. Sacrifice for preventing the peril to preserve and enhance the public welfare with respect to living conditions such as housing conditions also requires no compensation.

The criteria set up by Judge Takatsuji raise some questions, although they are concrete enough to decide whether regulation requires just compensation. For example, a Special Regulation Area Along the Route provided in Article 14, Paragraph 2 of the National Highway Law is quoted as substantially in the same category as Regulation Area Along the Route provided in Article 44, Paragraph 3 of the Road Law quoted. Rather, the difference is that a Special Area Regulation needs compensation if it is within the meaning of Article 14, Paragraph 3 of the National Highway Law, while a Regular Area Regulation does not.[13]

In this chapter, referring to court decisions and theories set forth in the past, I will try to divide land use regulation into three categories—taking, regulation, and regulatory taking—based on the purpose, substance, scope of land use regulation, and the need for compensation. In each category, I will examine the type of regulation and just compensation based on the particular criteria. "Taking" means compulsory acquisition of a particular property for public use. "Regulation" means a land use regulation that does not require just compensation. Land use regulation is imposed in order to achieve reasonable land use such as development, use, and preservation based on the particular administrative land use planning, to achieve public works, or to secure the importance of the property itself like a national treasure. "Regulatory taking" means such land use regulation that requires just compensation.[14]

TAKING AND COMPENSATION

Statutory Basis of Right for Compensation

The statutory basis of just compensation has been discussed from the following three perspectives:

1. "Constitution as nonbinding statutory guidance theory" (i.e., the issue of constitutionality is not raised even if a particular land use regulatory statute has no just compensation provision);
2. "Void for unconstitutionality theory" (i.e., a particular statute providing land use regulation is unconstitutional if it has no compensation provision, although compensation should be needed); and
3. "Constitution as an authority of just compensation theory" (i.e., taking under a statute without just compensation is valid, and just compensation is provided based on Article 29, Paragraph 3 of the constitution: the property owner can bring suit before the court, claiming compensation under the provision).

The third theory is currently supported by courts and academics.[15]

The Supreme Court mentioned, through dicta, as follows:

Art. 4, Sub-Para. 2 of the River Adjacent Land Regulation Order (repealed) without a just compensation provision does not mean there will be no compensation in any case necessary, and the defendant, through proving his actual loss, could request just compensation based on Art. 29, Para. 3 of the Constitution. (Sup. Ct., November 27, 1968, 22 Keishu 12, 1402 [1968])[16]

Since this decision, the Supreme Court has been following the "Constitution as an authority of just compensation theory" (Sup. Ct. March 13, 1975, 771 Hanrei-Jiho 37 [1975]; Sup. Ct., April 11, 1975, 777 Hanrei-Jiho 35 [1975]).

If a particular statute has a just compensation provision, a plaintiff should claim just compensation under this provision, not under the constitution, because the provision embodies just compensation under the constitution in substance and procedure, although the legal basis to claim just compensation could be found in Article 29, Paragraph 3 of the constitution. The Tokyo High Court also followed this theory in a case of just compensation for refusal of permission under Article 17, Paragraph 3 of the Natural Park Law (Tokyo Hi. Ct., August 28, 1985, 1177 Hanrei Jiho 49 [1985]).

Full Compensation

The law of just compensation is the system for compensating for loss of property in its sacrifice for public use under the idea of equal social burden (Art. 14 of the constitution). In this regard, this is the system of compensation for economic value of property. Thus, "just compensation" provided in Article 29, Paragraph 3 of the constitution should be "full compensation," which means the objective value of the acquired property (fair market value) should be provided for compensation. If compensation is not full and all losses of the acquired property are not compensated, unequal sacrifice to such an extent remains, and it results in an inconsistency with the purpose of the just compensation system.

Satisfying the following three requisites makes compensation just.[17]

1. All actual losses caused by an acquisition of property should be compensated fully. However, as the Land Expropriation Law adopted the "adversary doctrine" (Art. 48, Para. 3; Art. 49, Para. 2), the amount of compensation should be decided based on contentions set forth both by the project initiator, that is, the condemnation agency and landowner, and interested parties. Thus, this amount

is regarded as "just compensation," provided in Article 29, Paragraph 3 of the constitution.

2. Criteria of calculation of loss should be socially objective, that is, by fair market value, and no consideration should be made to either special conditions or the subjective and emotional value of aggrieved persons (Art. 7, Art. 8, Para. 4 of the Guideline of Standard for Compensation for Loss Caused by Acquisition of Land for Public Use). From the standpoint of equal burden for the public, loss of subjective values does not constitute a deprivation that would invoke compensation.

3. The standard date for calculating compensation for land is the date of the notification of the project recognition under the provision of Article 26, Paragraph 1 of the Land Expropriation Law (Art. 71, LEL). On the other hand, when land is acquired through agreement, not condemnation, the date of calculation is the date of conclusion of the contract (Art. 47 of the Guideline).

Under the old Land Expropriation Law of 1889, Daishinin (Great Court of Judicature, the old Supreme Court) stated that the standard date of calculation of acquired property was at the date of condemnation (Gre. Ct., June 4, 1928, 7 Minshu 426 [1928]).

With respect to the meaning of full compensation, in the case where the issue was the amount of compensation for the taking of land that had been regulated under a city plan for a future public project, the Supreme Court held as follows:

> Under the Land Expropriation Law, compensation for loss should be full compensation, that is, the property value of an aggrieved person does not change before and after condemnation, and the amount should be sufficient enough to acquire alternative land nearby which is equivalent to the land taken. (Sup. Ct., October 18, 1973, 27 Minshu 9, 1210 [1973])[18]

Under this rule, the issue is raised whether Article 71 of the Land Expropriation Law is constitutional. Hiroshima District Court held that it is because the fair market value rule for compensation for landowners is secured. The reasoning went as follows:

1. The landowner has the vested right to claim compensation under Article 46-2;
2. Corresponding to this claim to compensation, the project initiator

should pay compensation within two months in an amount fixed by estimation (Art. 46-4);

3. The Expropriation Committee shall, by ruling for expropriation, impose an expensive additional charge or a penalty charge when the project initiator pays unduly low compensation or does not pay by the due date (Art. 90-3); and

4. The amount of compensation for land fixed at the date of the notification of the project recognition should be revised by the revision rate corresponding to the changes of prices during the period between the date and the date when the ruling for the expropriation order is given (Art. 71). (Hiroshima Dist. Ct., May 15, 1974, 762 Hanrei-Jiho 22 [1974]).

Compensation for Ordinary Loss Caused by Land Taking

Compensation for ordinary loss caused by land taking is called "Tsuson Hosho," in general. Compensation for removal expenses and compensation for business loss are the main examples. Among them, the Land Expropriation Law provides only removal expenses (Art. 77) and has a general provision for the rest that "compensation shall be made for separation from farming, for loss in business, loss of rent caused by removal of a building, and for other ordinary losses caused to the owner of land or interested parties by the acquisition or compulsory use of the land" (Art. 88).

With changes of social and economic situations causing the emergence of a wide variety of values, new issues of substance and the extent of compensation for loss caused by the acquisition of land have been raised. One problem is whether compensation should be needed for the loss of cultural value separately from compensation for land acquired under Article 88 of the Land Expropriation Law. In the Gifu Prefecture Waju-Tai (round embankment) case, a landowner claimed compensation for the cultural value of the Waju-Tei besides compensation for land acquired. The Supreme Court held as follows:

Ordinary loss caused by land acquisition provided in Art. 88 of the Land Expropriation Law means economic and property loss which is an unavoidable, socially objective loss that the aggrieved person suffers from compulsory land acquisition, and it does not include non-economic value.

Historic or academic value in the regard through which national history, and the life and culture of ancient times could be understood generally puts no additional value on the economic or property value as real estate and gives no influence on its market value. Cultural value in this regard cannot be calculated into economic value, and loss of its value could not be compensated under the Land Expropriation Law. (Sup. Ct., January 21, 1988, 1270 Hanrei-Jiho 67 [1988])[19]

Thus, the Supreme Court concluded that although Wajo-Te has historic, social, and academic value, its cultural value in this regard cannot be calculated into economic value, and the loss of these values is outside of ordinary loss in Article 88 of the Land Expropriation Law.

A commonly accepted theory of courts, academics, and administrative practice takes compensation for ordinary loss as that for which any landowner who is deprived of rights to land can claim compensation, under usual circumstances, for unavoidable economic loss caused by condemnation, but he or she cannot claim for loss under special circumstances.[20] Whether cultural values can be compensated for depends on how these values influence market values. For example, cultural values such as art or historic values of calligraphy, swords, and industrial arts may influence property market values, while cultural values such as historic or academic values of a Waju-Tei, a shell mound, or a ruin of an old barrier have no influence on property market values. In the case above, the Supreme Court also held with this reasoning.

Compensation for ordinary loss is "the loss usually caused by condemnation" and is not actual loss. However, compensation for the land to be acquired is equivalent to actual loss that is the market value of the land. For example, compensation for removal expenses of a building is "an estimated compensation," which is calculated based on "the estimation of compensation that shall be made to cover expenses required to move the building to a location where it is generally deemed to be reasonable by a generally accepted reasonable method" (Art. 24 of the Guideline).

LAND USE REGULATION FOR PREVENTION OF DISASTER

Police Power

One type of land use regulation specifies a particular area and regulates it in order to prevent disaster. The issue of requirements of just compensation for this kind of land use regulation was raised in the case of the Nara Prefecture regulatory ordinance, which regulated the land use of an embankment of irrigation ponds. In this case, the prefecture ordinance prohibited any actions, such as planting trees or constructing buildings, which might cause the irrigation ponds' collapse. The majority opinion of the Supreme Court was as follows:

> The purpose of this ordinance is to prevent disaster and promote public welfare. Article 4, Sub Paragraph 2 of the ordinance stringently regulates the exercise of property rights, such as prohibition of using the embankment of irrigation ponds. However, this regulation is necessary in social life in order to prevent disaster and to promote public welfare, and any person with property rights on the embankment has to take this burden. Thus, under Article 29, Paragraph 3 of the constitution, compensation is not required. (Sup. Ct., June 6, 1963, 17 Keisyu 521 [1963])[21]

This judicial decision is famous for affirming property regulation by ordinance of the local government. However, it also should be noted that the Court declared that land use regulation for preventing disaster required no compensation.

As the Court held, the regulation is necessary in social life in order to prevent disaster and promote public welfare. This type of land use regulation derives from the exercise of police power of local government to prevent social barriers derived from land use. Examples are some kinds of prohibition in areas designated as Housing Development Areas (Arts. 3 and 9 of the Housing Area Development Regulation Law), and in the area designated as Danger of Collapse Caused by Steep Inclinations (Art. 18 of the Land Sliding Prevention Law). Compensation is not required for this type of land use regulation because the regulation poses some kind of obligation to prevent infringement on others' lives, bodies, or property caused by property owners. The regulation does not infringe upon the substantive value of the property concerned.

The obligation derived from the exercise of police power requires any person not to cause danger against the safety and order of society from his or her actions or property. This is the fundamental principle based on Articles 12 and 13 of the constitution. These articles confirm that civil rights be exercised within their own limitation, and that the obligation derived from the exercise of police power is a type of these limits. By exercise of police power (police power of local government is authorized under Art. 2, Para. 2 of the Local Autonomy Law), the government may regulate a person's action or property in order to redress his or her abuse of property rights on the presupposition that a person has an obligation to society to remove social barriers he or she has brought.

This kind of regulation orders a person merely to exercise his or her property rights within their limitations and does not put another kind of additional obligation on his or her property rights. Thus, land use regulations such as the exercise of police power to prevent abuse of property rights is within the limitation of the rights themselves, and just compensation is not required (Art. 29, Para. 2 of the Fire Law, Art. 9 of the Building Standard Law, etc.).[22]

Regulation on Dangerous Equipment

The Supreme Court has taken strictly the obligation on property rights under the exercise of police power. For example, in one case, the issue of whether compensation for construction cost related to adjacent land was required was raised when an underground gas tank of a gas station had to be moved to allow the construction of an underground crosswalk. The Supreme Court held as follows:

> When a regulatory statute provides scientific standards, such as rules that dangerous equipment shall be kept some distance from certain facilities, and violation against the regulatory standard brought by the construction of a road that made the property owner do something such as remove facilities in order to meet the standards above and he suffered from loss by removing his facilities, compensation for such loss, provided in Art. 70, Para. 1 of the Road Law, is not required simply because the loss by exercise of police power becomes actual. (Sup. Ct., February 18, 1983, 37 Minshu 1, 59 [1983])[23]

Under the Fire Law, regulation on "dangerous equipment" such as a gas tank of a gas station (Art. 10) differs from general "fire-prevention" regulation (Art. 2, Para. 2) in the obligations of facility owners. An owner of dangerous equipment has to make it meet scientific standards provided in Article 10, Paragraph 4, and Article 12, Paragraph 1 of the Fire Law. A newly revised statutory requirement applies to any dangerous equipment to which old standards had been applied hitherto, unless a grace period is provided.

Thus, new standards provided in Article 10, Paragraph 4 of the law are applied to any dangerous equipment, while newly revised standards are generally not applied to common buildings unless otherwise provided, taking into account the obligation and economic burden of the owners. Owners' obligations for dangerous equipment are more stringently required than those on common buildings, because the former have more potential to be a threat to public safety.

It seemed that considering these circumstances under the Fire Law, the Supreme Court decision quoted above did not require compensation. Some questions remain, although the Court's holding on the interpretation of obligations in the Fire Law is appropriate. The obligation of the property owner for the purpose of unavoidable necessities, such as prevention of disaster, is not required a priori, but should be considered in relation to social factors. In the case above, the question is raised whether compensation is not required in any case, including when a reasonable person takes on an obligation she or he could not expect. In other words, in 1952 when a gas station was built, although a gas station owner may predict development nearby, he might not be able to predict an underground crosswalk built in the future.[24]

LAND USE REGULATIONS FOR ZONING AND PUBLIC WORKS

There are two types of land use regulation that do not require just compensation: zoning and regulation for the effective accomplishment of public works or for securing safety in maintaining public facilities.

Zoning (Yoto Chiiki)

Yoto Chiiki zoning is one of the district-area systems under Article 8, Paragraph 1 of the City Planning Law and is zoning that is necessarily decided in the "area designated for urbanization" (Art. 13, Para. 1). Yoto Chiiki zoning is a type of zoning that regulates land use based on priority. For example, housing has priority in the housing area, and land use for enterprises and industrial or commercial purposes is regulated. The practical effect of zoning is ensured by building regulations under the Building Standard Law.

The Supreme Court has not yet ruled whether no compensation for zoning is constitutional. The reason no compensation is necessary for Yoto Chiiki zoning has been explained as adoption of civil law's "action-damages relationship" theory (Sorin-Kankei theory). Land use regulation in zoning does not infringe on the substance of property rights and the obtaining of proper land use. A more comfortable life environment in the area offsets losses that might arise. Besides Yoto Chiiki zoning, the law provides for other kinds of zoning, such as an "area designated for restraining urbanization," which does not require just compensation (Art. 7 of the City Planning Law).

Regulation for Effective Accomplishment of Public Works

Land use regulation on a future-planned public work project area to secure effective accomplishment of work is another type of land use regulation (Arts. 53 and 54 of the City Planning Law, Art. 76 of the Readjustment of Town Lots Law). For example, a person who wants to build in the city planning facilities area or city development area should obtain approval of the governor (Arts. 53 and 54 of the City Planning Law).

The loss derived from this regulation does not constitute deprivation of property, and no person can claim compensation. The Supreme Court held the following:

> Though it cannot be denied that regulation on buildings is regulation on property, . . . it goes without saying that regulation is necessary for public welfare. Thus, though regulation on buildings is some kind of regulation on property, this regulation is constitutional as far as it is necessary for city planning, and it is supposed as regulation for public welfare. (Sup. Ct., April 9, 1958, 12 Minshu 717 [1958])[25]

The Supreme Court also held in the 1973 case quoted before that "No statutory compensation for building regulation simply means no compensation for loss is required independently" (Sup. Ct., October 18, 1973, 27 Minshu 9, 1210 [1973]). These holdings agree with the view described above.

Securing Proper Maintenance of Public Facilities

There are three types of land use regulation for securing the maintenance of public facilities: (1) regulation on public facilities themselves (Art. 4 of the Road Law); (2) regulation on land attached to public facilities (Art. 44 of the Road Law, Art. 54 of the River Law, Art. 7 of the Coast Law, Art. 37 of the Port Law); and (3) regulation on underground (Art. 64 of the Mining Law).

With respect to regulations on public facilities themselves, in the case in which the issue is effectiveness of regulations on private property under Article 4 of the Road Law, the Supreme Court held the following:

> The road site at issue is a part of road as public facilities and subject to regulation under the Road Law, because the road has been open to the public since the agency's legitimate announcement of utilization. Regulation on road sites derives from roads' being open to the public and does not derive from property rights of the land. Thus, even when a road agency

cannot prevail its claim based on its property rights against a party who obtained the ownership of the land, regulation on the road site is not taken away unless the road would be closed. (Sup. Ct., December 4, 1969, 23 Minshu 12 [1969]).[26]

With respect to regulation on land attached to public facilities, the Supreme Court held in a 1968 case the following:

> Regulation under the Article 4, Paragraph 2 of the old River Nearby Land Order is simply to provide a Governor's permission system in order to prevent a hindrance on the preservation of the river. This type of regulation is a general regulation to accomplish public welfare, and any person should bear the regulation. Thus, the provision of Article 4, Paragraph 2 itself does not bring a special sacrifice of property rights and no compensation is required for the regulation to this extent. (Sup. Ct., October 27, 1968, 22 Keishu 12, 402 [1968])

The Supreme Court, I consider, takes regulation to prevent hindrance on the maintenance of public facilities as a regulation on abuse of rights, as well as a land use regulation for preventing disaster.

In the case in which the issue is whether compensation is required for regulation under Article 64 of the Mining Law, the Supreme Court, quoting a 1968 case, held that, under Article 64 of the Mining Law, no person may claim compensation for regulation on mining rights. It stated the following:

> Regulation under the Mining Law simply provides that any person has to obtain the facility owner's approval for mining in order to prevent a hindrance on the maintenance of public facilities and buildings such as railroads, rivers, parks, schools, hospitals, and libraries. This type of regulation is a general minimum regulation for public welfare and does not bring special sacrifice on a particular person, and no person can claim compensation. (Sup. Ct., February 5, 1982, 36 Minshu 2,127 [1982])[27]

REGULATORY TAKING

Meaning of Regulatory Taking

Regulatory taking is a type of land use regulation that requires compensation for loss of property caused by land use regulation. Many issues in regulatory taking have been raised compared with taking or simple land use regulation. For example, under the compensation provision for regulatory taking, there is the issue of how loss should be evaluated and how much compensation should be paid. Also, as a matter of interpretation, there is the issue of whether land use regulation requires compensation (regulatory taking) or does not require compensation (mere land use regulation).

This is because regulatory taking is a regulation on the exercise of rights on land and may decrease future benefits by the exercise of rights, but does not acquire ownership. Nor does a time-limited use of property such as the compulsory use of land necessary in carrying out public works under the Land Expropriation Law. Thus, calculation of compensation cannot be based on a market value like a taking or on a leasing rate like a compulsory use of land.

Typical regulatory taking is a land use regulation that is called "Preservation District Regulation" or "Maintaining Status Quo Regulation." Examples are "Special Preservation District of Historical Climate" (Art. 6, Para. 1 of the Ancient Capital Ruin Preservation Law), "Green Tracts of Land Preservation District" (Art. 3, Para. 1 of the City Green Tracts Preservation Law), "Natural Environment Preservation Special District" (Art. 25 of the Natural Environment Preservation Law), and "Special Area and Special Preservation District of National Park" (Arts. 17, 18 of the Natural Park Law). In these preservation districts a landowner requires an agency's approval if his or her land is located within these districts, and compensation will be required for loss caused by disapproval or conditioned approval (Art. 9 of the Ancient Capital Ruin Preservation Law, Art. 7 of the City Green Tracts Preservation Law, Art. 33 of the Natural Park Law).[28]

This type of regulation impedes inherent use of property in districts, and regulations such as historic climate of ancient capital or preservation of the landscape of a national park have no relationship with inherent use of the property concerned. In this regard, compensation for loss is claimed because this regulation of property is beyond the extent that compensation is not required. Another example of this type of land use regulation is regulation to preserve an important cultural asset. To do this, a certain district in a nearby area is designated as regulated (Arts. 45 and 81 of the Cultural Asset Preservation Law).[29]

Regulatory Taking and Compensation

With respect to compensation for loss caused by a regulatory taking, the concurring opinion by Justice Irie of the Supreme Court in the 1963 case quoted above said the following:

If a person who had cultivated an embankment of irrigation ponds prior to effectiveness of the Ordinance, is prohibited from cultivation after the Ordinance being effective, and obliged to remove or dispose of plants such as bamboos, trees and tea-trees, or if a person is obliged to dispose of young plants which would be planted, compensation for loss caused by the regulation is claimed under Article 29, Paragraph 3 of the Constitution. (Sup. Ct., June 26, 1963, 17 Keishu 5, 521 [1963])

In addition, in the 1968 case quoted above, the Supreme Court declared that, in general, any person should bear the regulation on a river's nearby land to protect damage caused by abuse of his or her execution of property rights, and cannot claim compensation. However, it held as follows:

The defendant had paid for leasing of non-embankment land and employed those who gathered gravel from the land. However, under the River Nearby Order, once the area was designated as river nearby land, he becomes unable to gather gravel without obtaining the Governor's permission. Under these circumstances, there is no small amount of loss caused by the prohibition of doing business by paying for leasing, employing people, and investing no little capital.

Thus, though sacrifice on his property derived from the regulation for public welfare, it seems to go beyond the extent of general sacrifice and may be considered as special sacrifice, . . . the actual loss the defendant suffered from in this case may be compensatory. (Sup. Ct., November 27, 1968, 22 Keishu 12, 1402 [1968])

In this case, the Supreme Court conceded that the defendant who has suffered actual loss might be able to claim compensation caused by a regulatory taking.

With respect to the calculation, there are the following three theories: "Compensation for Actual Loss" theory, "Compensation for Loss Derived from Land-Price Decreasing" theory, and "Compensation for Loss Which Has a Substantial Relationship with Regulation" theory. At present, no theory has prevailed. Supposedly, administrative practice has nearly supported the first theory.[30]

Notes

1. Hide Ara and Tsuyoshi Kotaka, eds., *Outline of Real Estate Law (2)*, 4th ed., 1–24 (Tokyo: Yuhikaku, 1997); Tsuyoshi Kotaka, *Law of Administrative Activities*, 75–162 (Tokyo: Yuhikaku, 1984).

2. Kotaka, *Law of Administrative Activities*, 79–91; Yoriaki Narita, *Land Policy and Law*, 46–74 (Tokyo: Kobundy, 1989).

3. Kotaka, *Law of Administrative Activities*, 84; Narita, *Land Policy and Law*, 111–132.

4. Narita, *Land Policy and Law*, 1–17; The Land Agency, Land Bureau, ed., *Interpretation of the Land Fundamental Law*, 16ff. (Tokyo: Gyosei, 1990).

5. Hide Ara and Tsuyoshi Kotaka, eds., *Outline of the City Planning Law*, 129–168 (Tokyo: Shimzaunsha, 1998). See Hide Ara, Tetsuo Seki, and Shigero Yabuki, *Commentary to the Building Standards Law*, rev., 426–445 (Tokyo: Daiichikoki, 1990).

6. On the land acquisition process, see Tsuyoshi Kotaka, *Research on Just Compensation (Meijo Law Series 4)*, 28–53 (Tokyo: Seibundo, 2000); Tsuyoshi Kotaka, *Commentary to the Land Expropriation Law* (1980); Michikazu Ozawa, *Interpretation of the Land Expropriation Law (1), (2)*, rev. (Tokyo: Gyosai, 1995).

7. Kotaka, *Commentary to the Land Expropriation Law*, 157; Yasutaka Abe, *Administrative Discretion and Administrative Relief*, 116–130 (Tokyo: Samseido, 1987). Among notes on this case, see Yasutaka Abe, 152 Hanrei-Hyoron, 20 (1976); Naohiko Harada, *1973 Term Important Court Decisions (Jurist)* 42–43, (1974); Hiroshi Shiono, 178 Hanrei-Hyoron, 24 (1973); Hidekazu Hama, *Court Decisions on Public Nuisance & Environment (Jurist)*, 2nd ed., 161–163 (1980); Yoshikazu Tamura and Giichi Shibaike, 111, 112 Ritsumeikan L.R. 566 (1973); Mitsuo Kobayakawa, *A Hundred Decisions on Town Planning and National Land Use Planning (Jurist)*, 118 (1989), etc.

8. On the Guideline, see Tadao Kobayashi, *Outline of the Guideline of Standard for Compensation for Loss Caused by Acquisition of Land for Public Purpose* (Tokyo: Kimdaitosho, 1900); Tsuyoshi Kotaka, *Land Acquisition and Compensation*, 2nd ed. (Tokyo: Yukikaku, 1996); Akira Nishino and Aiichi Tanabe, *Law of Compensation* (Tokyo: Shinyusha, 2000).

9. Tsuyoshi Kotaka, *Research on Just Compensation*, 290–303; Tsuyoshi Kotaka, *Revision of Compensation Standard, Administrative Law and Rule of Law, A Collection of Articles for 70 Years Commemoration of Dr. Hiromasa Minami*, 183–202 (Tokyo: Yuhikaku, 1999); Tsuyoshi Kotaka, "Present State of Land Acquisition and Compensation," Kotaka ed., *Theory and Practice of Compensation*, 14–58 (Tokyo: Jutakushimposha, 1997); and Research Team Report of 1999 on Compensation Practice (Tsuyoshi Kotaka, ed.), 51ff. (1999).

10. The Ministry of Construction, Planning Bureau, General Affairs Section, ed., *Interpretation on Public Compensation Standard*, rev., 40–41 (Tokyo: Kimdaitosho, 1999).

11. Kotaka, *Law of Administrative Activities*, 221–223; Hide Ara, *Land*

Use Regulation and Compensation, Contemporary Administrative Law System, vol. 6, 257 (Tokyo: Yuhikaku, 1983); Akira Nishino, *Standard and Contents of Compensation*, 52ff. (Tokyo: Chiryusha, 1991).

12. Masami Takatsuzi, *Study on Property Right*, 38 Jichi-Kenkyu 4, 3 (1962).

13. Professor Imamura and Professor Yasumoto also examined types of regulation and the need for compensation. See Shigekazu Imamura, *Research on System of Compensation*, 19–22 (Tokyo: Yuhikaku, 1968); Norio Yasumoto, *Land Use Regulation and Compensation (1)*, 223, 224 Ritsumeikan L.R. 409 (1992). Also see Hiroshi Shiono, *Administrative Law (2)*, 2nd ed., 282–286 (Tokyo: Yuhikaku, 1994).

14. Tsuyoshi Kotaka, "Land Use Regulation and Supreme Court Decisions," 47 Hoso-Jiho 1, 2ff. (1998). This article is translated into English by Hitoshi Ushijima (associate professor of law, Faculty of Law, Fukuoka University). See Research Team Report of 2000 on Compensation Practice (Tsuyoshi Kotaka, ed.), 55ff. (2000).

15. Shigekazu Imamura, *Law of National Liability of Compensation*, 72 (Tokyo: Yuhikaku, 1957); Ziro Tanaka, *New Edition of Administrative Law* (complete rev., 2nd ed.), 213 (Tokyo: Kobundo, 1978); Naohiko Harada, *The Substance of Administrative Law* (complete rev.), 226 (Tokyo: Gakuyushobo, 1994); Shiono, *Administrative Law*, 280; Hitoshi Kaneko, *General Theory of Administrative Law*, 216–217 (Tokyo: Samseido, 1983); Tsuyoshi Kotaka, *General Theory of Administrative Law*, 2nd ed., 159–160 (Tokyo: Syosei, 2000); Yasutaka Abe, *Law of National Liability of Compensation*, 263ff. (Tokyo: Yuhikaku, 1988); Katsuya Uga, *Law of National Liability of Compensation*, 394 (Tokyo: Yuhikaku, 1997).

16. Renpei Kuwano, Note, Commentary to Supreme Court Criminal Law Decisions of 1968 Term, 263ff. (1968); Shozo Kondo, Note, *A Hundred Court Decisions on Administrative Law* (2), 3rd ed., 332 (1993), etc.

17. Kotaka, *Commentary to the Land Expropriation Law*, 369; Kotaka, Land Use Regulation and Supreme Court Decisions, 7; Kotaka, *General Theory of Administrative Law*, 163.

18. Yasuyuki Shibata, Note, Commentary to Supreme Court Civil Law Decisions of 1973 Term, 147 (1973); Giichi Shibaike, Note, 71 Minshoho-Zasshi 3, 544 (1978), etc.

19. Tsuyoshi Kotaka, "On Compensation for Cultural Loss," Shozo Inui, ed., *Theoretical Development of Land Law*, 331ff. (Tokyo: Haritsubankasha, 1990); and Tsuyoshi Kotaka, *Re-Consideration on Compensation for Cultural Loss, Realization of Policy and Administrative Law, A Collection of Articles for 70 Years Commemoration of Dr. Yoriaki Narita*, 231ff. (Tokyo: Yuhikaku, 1998). As notes on the Supreme Court Decisions, see Tsuyoshi Kotaka, 361 Hanrei-Hyoron 25, (1989); Kazuo Masui, 912 Jurist 65 (1988); Yoshio Miyazaki, 912 Jurist 62 (1988); Rintaro Shiina, *1988 Term*

Important Court Decisions (Jurist), 44 (1988). Akira Nishino, 93 Hogaku-Kyoshitsu, 104 (1988); Shuzo Hayashi, 1326 Tokino-Horei, 83 (1988), etc.

20. Kotaka, Commentary to the Land Expropriation Law, 456–458; Kotaka, Land Acquisition and Compensation, 337; Ozawa, Interpretation of the Land Expropriation Law, 244ff.; Kenzo Takada, Newly Revised Land Expropriation Law, 363 (1963).

21. Kotaka, Land Use Regulation and Supreme Court Decisions, 11. As to the Supreme Court Decision, see Kazuo Fujii, Note, Commentary to Supreme Court Criminal Law Decisions of 1963 Term, 41 (1963); and Shozo Kondo, Note, A Hundred Court Decisions on Administrative Law (2), 3rd ed., 330 (1993).

22. Kotaka, Land Use Regulation and Supreme Court Decisions, 12; Kotaka, Law of Administrative Activities, 7, 21.

23. Katsuya Uga, Note, A Hundred Court Decisions on Administrative Law (2), 3rd ed., 322 (1993); Keiici Murakami, Note, Commentary to Supreme Court Civil Law Decisions of 1983 Term, 41 (1983); Tsuyoshi Kotaka, The So-Called "Mizo-Kaki Compensation," Meijo L.R. Special Edition for 60 Years Commemoration of Professor Hisae Nagao, 13 (1986), etc.

24. Kotaka, Land Use Regulation and Supreme Court Decisions, 14; Abe Yasutaka and Hiroshi Mori, Legal Problems of Fire Administration, 195 (Tokyo: Zemkukajohorei, 1985).

25. Takahiro Mikami, Note, A Hundred Court Decisions on Administrative Law (1), 200 (1993), etc.

26. Tsuyoshi Kotaka, Note, 63 Minshoho-Zasshi, 3, 419 (1970); Eiichiro Uno, Note, Commentary to Supreme Court Civil Law Decisions of 1969 Term, 608 (1969); and Yoshimoto Yanase, Note, 137 Hanrei-Hyoron, 21 (1970).

27. Tsuyoshi Kotaka, Note, 99 Minshoho-Zasshi 1, 106 (1988); Tsutomu Shiozaki, Note, Commentary to Supreme Court Civil Law Decisions of 1982 Term, 2111 (1982).

28. Tsuyoshi Kotaka, "Land Use Regulation and Compensation," Osaka City University L.R. 3-4, 468 (1982); Kotaka, Law of Administrative Activities, 228.

29. Renpei Kuwano, Note, Commentary to Supreme Court Criminal Law Decisions of 1968 Term, 263ff. (1968); Shozo Kondo, Note, A Hundred Court Decisions on Administrative Law (2), 3rd ed., 332 (1993), etc.

30. Kotaka, Land Use Regulation and Supreme Court Decisions, 22–23; Kotaka, ibid., 479, Naohiko Harada, "Compensation Standard of Land Use Regulation," 29 Public L.R. 169–170 (1967).

References

Agriculture Promotion Area Preparation Law (1969)
Ancient Capital Ruins Preservation Law (1966)

Building Standard Law (1950)
City Planning Law (1968)
Comprehensive National Land Development Law (1950)
Constitutional Law (1946), Sec. 29
Forest Law (1951)
Land Expropriation Law (1950)
Land Fundamental Law (1989)
National Land Use Planning Law (1974)
Natural Environment Preservation Law (1972)
Natural Park Law (1957)

Hide Ara and Tsuyoshi Kotaka, *Outline of Real Estate Law* (2), (4th ed.)
    (Yuhikaku, 1997).
Hiroya Endo, *National Compensation Law* (Seirinshoin, 1981).
Shigekazu Imamura, *National Compensation Law* (Yuhikaku, 1957).
Tsuyoshi Kotaka, *Commentary to Land Expropriation Law* (Daiichhoki,
    1980).
Tsuyoshi Kotaka, *Research on Just Compensation* (Seibundo, 2000).

Chapter 5

Land Use Planning and Compensation in Korea

WON WOO SUH

In Korea, the modern land use plan originated from the "Enforcement Decree of Chosun Urban District," promulgated by a Japanese viceroy in 1934. The decree was a combination of the Japanese Urban Planning Act and the Construction Act. Because this decree was invasive and coercive, it has been criticized as serving Japanese interests. Since this decree was concerned with the designation of areas and districts, the restriction of construction, and the land adjustment work, it can be regarded as the first piece of legislation dealing with city planning in Korea. It divided the land into five specific use areas. This decree was in operation until the late 1950s, despite the installment of a new Korean government after Korean independence. In 1962, the city planning system, as outlined in the Urban Planning Act (UPA), succeeded the land use plan that was based on Japanese law. The UPA was Korea's first original land use plan legislation. However, it was merely an imitation of Japanese law, and the similarities in the structure and content can be seen to this day.

Before getting into the specific content of the Korean land use plan system, an overview of some provisions of basic legislation such as the constitution and the civil code is in order. According to Article 23 of the constitution: (1) The right of property of all citizens shall be guaranteed. The contents and limitations thereof shall be determined by Act. (2) The exercise of property rights shall conform to the public welfare. (3) Expropriation, use, and compensation shall be governed by law, provided that in such case, just compensation shall be paid. In addition to the

---

Professor Emeritus, Seoul National University.

above Article, the constitution also provides for the basic socioeconomic principle in Article 119(2). The state may regulate and coordinate economic affairs to maintain the balanced growth and stability of the national economy, to ensure proper distribution of income, to prevent the domination of the market and abuse of economic power, and to democratize the economy through harmony among the economic agents. In Article 120(2), the constitution specifically provides for the land development plan as follows: "The land and natural resources shall be protected by the State, and the State shall establish a plan necessary for their balanced development and utilization."

On the other hand, according to the civil code, the right of ownership includes the right to use, derive benefits from, and dispose of the article owned, within the limits set by law and regulations (Article 211). Article 212 of the code provides that right of land ownership extends both above and below the surface of the land. Of various elements composing the contents of the right of land ownership, the right to use it, and in particular the right to build on it, is very important in Korea given that Korea has a small landmass (approximately 99,000 square kilometers), a very small portion of which can be used as building sites.

In the field of public law, various restrictions are imposed from a variety of directions on right of land ownership as provided for in the civil code. For instance, one can say, if a bit exaggeratedly, that the right to build on land, which constitutes the very core of the right to use land, is subject to general prohibition imposed by legislation such as the UPA and the Act on the Utilization and Management of the National Territory (AUMNT). In other words, according to the Korean public law governing land use planning, one is generally prohibited from exercising the right to use land in connection with building activities as guaranteed in the civil code. Only if and when one satisfies the requirements set by legislation such as the UPA and the Building Act (BA), does the state grant permission to put into effect one's right to use land for building purposes.

Given that the Korean law provides for an extensive restriction on the right to use land for construction and other purposes, the question of compensation for losses incurred by such restriction inevitably arises. In order for the violation of property rights resulting from public necessity to qualify for compensation for loss, according to general scholarly opinion, the loss incurred from such a violation must pertain to specific injury. It should be noted that if the damage is merely a consequence of social limitations inherent in property rights, the owner of that private property must accept it. This is based on the notion that property rights are public in nature, which is suggested by Article 23(2) of the constitution. In practice, however, the distinction between special damage and social limitations inherent in property rights remains, and in many cases it is unclear. The issue appears mainly in cases of public violations involving the restriction of profits or use of private property, rather than in instances of expropriation. The loss suffered by owners of land in designated urban green belts is an example, as we will see in detail later on.

Let us first examine the specific contents of restrictions imposed through the mechanism of the land use planning system regulated by various Korean laws and regulations. Then we will tackle the question of how compensation for the losses incurred by various kinds of land use planning is regulated specifically under Korean laws, after presenting a general picture of compulsory purchase procedures and the compensation system in Korea.

The System of Specific Use Area as Provided for in the UPA

The UPA has as its objectives, inter alia, a sound and balanced development of the urban area and the efficient utilization of urban land. A multitude of urban planning measures are contemplated by the UPA, but the system of specific use area (SUA), according to which an urban area is subdivided into various subareas, is most important. Within respective subareas, restrictions are imposed on the kinds and forms of buildings authorized to be constructed.

Conditions for the issuance of construction permission in urban areas are provided in the BA as well as the UPA. However one should not confuse the objectives and functions of the BA with those of the UPA. Whereas the BA is concerned with the questions of police administration relating to the structure and safety of given buildings, the UPA concerns issues such as the aesthetic compatibility and the surrounding environment of buildings. In dealing with such issues, the UPA employs, inter alia, the system of specific use area. This system purports to prevent a disorderly development of urban areas and dictates that a given building be compatible with the aesthetic and functional requirements of the urban community. In particular, the UPA provides for the concentration of certain kinds of buildings—residential, commercial, or industrial—within a given area (restriction by kind). It also provides for the restriction of the height and area of buildings within a respective SUA (restriction by form with the use of building-to-land ratio [BLR] and floor-to-area ratio [FAT]). The zone in regard to which an urban plan is adopted is called an "urban planning zone." Within such a zone, the person who wants to engage in construction-related activities should obtain permission from the head of the *shi* (city) or *kun* (county). The UPA provides for four SUAs: residential, commercial, industrial, and green areas. In the residential area, only those buildings specifically indicated in the separate list contained in the Enforcement Decree of the BA are allowed. The BLR within this area is up to 90 percent. That is, in this area a given building can occupy up to 90 percent of the surface of the building site. The FAT is limited to seven times the area of the building site. In the commercial area, only those buildings specifically indicated on the separate list contained in the Enforcement Decree of the BA are allowed. The BLR within this area is limited to 90 percent. The FAT is limited to fifteen times the area of the building site. In the industrial area, only those buildings specifically indicated in the separate list contained in the Enforcement Decree of the BA are allowed. The BLR within this area is limited to 70 percent. The FAT is limited to four times the area of the building site. In the green area, a very limited range of buildings, as indicated in the separate list contained in the Enforcement Decree of the BA, are allowed. The BLR within this area is limited to 20 percent. The FAT is limited to double the area of the building site.

Thus, the SUA system establishes various areas within which construction of buildings is allowed in principle. However, the right to construct buildings within these areas is partially restricted in light of their functions and the environment of urban areas.

A similar regulation applies to urban planning facilities such as green belts, playgrounds, amusement parks, markets, and squares. Parking lots and urban parks used to belong to the category of urban planning facilities, but now they are regulated by separate legislation such as the Parking Lot Act and the Urban Park Act. When these facilities are included in urban planning, they are subject to regulation similar to that provided for in the UPA. However, when a certain area is designated as an urban planning facility, restrictions within this area are decided in light of general and indeterminate criteria such as designation purposes. This constitutes a contrast with the SUA system under the UPA, where specific and determinate conditions for the issuance of construction permission are put in place.

Restrictions on Construction under the Zone System

Aside from the SUA, there is an administrative planning measure called the "zone system." Whereas the SUA system imposes restrictions for the purpose of rationalization of land use in urban areas, the zone system purports to prevent excessive concentration of population and facilities in urban areas. If the zone system is determined and given public notice with respect to a specific area, that area is subject to a specific regulation as provided for in the UPA. The Act provides for the following zones:

1. Urbanization Control Zone: This zone can be established by the minister of construction and transportation in order to prevent chaotic and disorderly urbanization of an urban community, and to administer to a planned and staged development thereof. If a certain area is designated as an urbanization control zone, urbanization is suspended with respect to the area for such a period as is prescribed by the presidential decree.
2. Detailed Planning Zone: This zone can be established by the minister of construction and transportation in order to achieve the rational utilization of land and to preserve and efficiently manage the functions, aesthetic view, and environment of the urban community.
3. Metropolitan Planning Zone: The minister of construction and transportation can designate a certain area as this zone for the purpose of systematic readjustment of the metropolitan facilities, a balanced development of the whole metropolitan area, and as an efficient preservation of the metropolitan environment. He or she does this by connecting the functions of the various urban communities of the whole metropolitan area.
4. Development Restriction Zone (DRZ): This zone can be put into place by the minister of construction and transportation in such cases as he or she finds it necessary to restrict development of an urban community to secure a sound living environment for the residents of the urban community. The DRZ prevents a disorderly expansion of the urban community and the preservation of the natural environment surrounding the urban community. The minister can also establish this zone for the purpose of national defense at the request of the minister of national defense.

Of the four zones, we will restrict our consideration to DRZ and the urbanization control zone, both of which are generally considered to encroach upon the right to build most substantially.

RESTRICTIONS ON LAND USE
WITHIN THE DEVELOPMENT RESTRICTION ZONE

With the designation of a DRZ, generally known as a green belt, construction activities are in principle prohibited within the zone. According to Article 21(2) of the UPA, the construction of buildings, the installation of building equipment, the alteration of the shape and quality of the land, the division of the area of the land, and the execution of an urban planning project that is contrary to the purpose of the designation of the zone shall not be allowed. The prohibition does not apply to the person who, at the time the DRZ is designated, already had started a construction work or project relating to the construction of buildings, installation of building equipment, or alteration of the shape and quality of the land after having obtained the necessary permission. He or she may continue with the construction work or project under the conditions prescribed by the presidential decree. Even after the designation of the zone, some construction-related activities are allowed with the authorization of or the report to the head of *shi* or *kun*. These acts are enumerated in Article 20 of the Enforcement Decree of the UPA. According to Article 20(1) of the Enforcement Decree, the following acts are allowed with the permission of the head of *shi* or *kun* (among these acts, insignificant acts prescribed by the ordinance of the minister of construction and transportation can be carried out only with a report to the head of *shi* or *kun*):

1. Construction of structures and installation of constructions that are necessary for the sake of the public good;
2. Construction or installation of such structures and constructions as have been found, in light of their uses, improper to be placed in a population-concentrated area, but proper to be placed in a development restriction zone;
3. Construction of such structures as have been found necessary for the management of such businesses as agriculture, forestry, and fisheries, which will not hinder the fulfillment of the designated purposes of the development zone concerned;
4. Extension, remodeling, and reconstruction of residential building structures that existed at the time the DRZ was designated;
5. Remodeling or reconstruction of nonresidential building structures or other constructions;
6. Reconstruction, in new places, of the buildings or other constructions that were removed due to the installation of village facilities

for the public interest, facilities for common use, and so on, as prescribed by the ordinance of the Ministry of Construction and Transportation, within the DRZ concerned; and

7. Construction or installation of such buildings and constructions, as prescribed by the ordinance of the Ministry of Construction and Transportation, that are necessary for the improvement of the living environment of the residents of the DRZ.

In addition, alteration of the shape and quality of the land within the DRZ that is not accompanied by the excavation of a substantial quantity of earth and sand or does not have the possibility of hindering the designation purposes of the DRZ is allowed. The same Article also indicates as a permitted act within the DRZ the partition of land that is not accompanied by new construction or extension of building structures or that does not have the possibility of hindering the designation purposes of the DRZ concerned. Even when certain construction-related acts are permitted in accordance with the provisions of the UPA and the Enforcement Decree of the UPA, restrictions relating to the minimum building site area (132 square meters), BLR (60 percent), FAT (300 percent), and so on, are imposed.

Thus, restrictions on construction-related acts are stricter in the DRZ than in other zones enumerated in the UPA. If a certain area of land is designated as a DRZ, a strict set of restrictions is applied to the right to build freely on one's own land, which constitutes one of the core components of the right of landownership. It is because of this that there is controversy over whether designation of a certain piece of land as DRZ is an administrative action involving compensation for loss. This question will be addressed in some detail below.

Restrictions on Land Use within the Urbanization Control Zone

Similar to the DRZ, the urbanization control zone is designated in order to restrict certain construction-related acts within specific urban areas in accordance with a special kind of urban planning. With the designation of the urbanization control zone, acts for the development of the urban area concerned, including construction-related acts, are in principle suspended for the purpose of preventing chaotic urbanization and of achieving a planned and staged development of an urban community.

Notwithstanding the general suspension of construction-related acts within the urbanization control zone, the following acts can be carried out with the permission of the head of *shi* or *kun:*

1. Construction of building structures for agriculture, forestry, or fisheries of such categories and sizes as are prescribed by the presidential decree; and
2. Cutting or planting of bamboo and trees, excavation of earth and sand, and such other insignificant acts as are prescribed by the presidential decree.

The person who already started construction work or a project at the time the urbanization control zone was designated may continue with the work or project after reporting it to the head of *shi* or *kun* under the conditions as prescribed by the presidential decree.

Restrictions on Land Use under the Plan for Utilization of National Territory

Planning for the utilization of national territory has as its object of regulation the whole national territory, including urban areas that are regulated by the UPA. The question of whether construction is permitted or not in an area that is not covered by urban planning is generally governed by the AUMNT.

At present the AUMNT provides for five specific use areas: urban, semiurban, agricultural, semiagricultural, and natural environment preservation area. The Act prescribes specific rules restricting certain construction-related activities within respective areas. In addition to these five areas, the Enforcement Decree of the AUMNT further subdivides these areas into various districts and articulates sets of restrictions to be applied within each district. For instance, a semiurban area is subdivided into a community district, an industrial promotion district, a sport and recreational district, a collective cemetery district, and a facility site district. Thus, the AUMNT employs a hierarchical system composed of areas and districts. Provisions of the AUMNT governing restrictions on land use relate generally to restrictions on certain activities, installations of public facilities, developments of idle land, and division of land within the SUAs, and the designation of SUAs, regulation areas, and idle land.

According to the official statistics, urban area occupies 14 percent of the whole national territory; semiurban area, 0.9 percent; agriculture area, approximately 50 percent; semiagricultural area, 27 percent; natural environment preservation area, 6 percent; and the rest (such as sea surface) takes up 3 percent. Thus, agricultural area, together with semi-agricultural area, accounts for slightly more than three-quarters of the whole national territory. As the urban area is regulated by the UPA, we will not discuss that area.

Semiurban Area

Semiurban area means the area corresponding to the urban areas that have been used or are to be used as the collective living base of residents. These areas require the utilization and development of land to be used for sports, tourism, and recreation facilities for the best use of the leisure time of citizens. Semiurban areas also include places for sight-seeing and recreation, agricultural and industrial complexes, collective burial grounds, and land to be used for other various facilities. Building activities or large-scale repair within the semiurban area are subject to permission from the head of *shi, kun* or *ku*.[1]

As the semiurban area is further subdivided into community districts, industrial promotion districts, sports and recreational districts, collective cemetery districts, and facility site districts, construction-related activities compatible with the object and purpose of each district are regarded as permissible. For instance, the question of whether construction-related activities are permitted within a given community district is governed by whether there is subdivision of SUAs in accordance with the AUMNT. Provisions of the AUMNT apply when: (1) there is the subdivision; (2) a development plan is established in regard to the community district; and (3) the development plan regulates the district concerning, inter alia, collective living facilities of the residents. Consequently, the question of whether certain construction-related activities are permitted or not within such a district is governed by the relevant provisions of the development plan. In cases where a development plan is not established, construction of facilities such as the air pollutant emission facilities, as prescribed under the relevant provisions of the Clean Air Preservation Act, or waste discharge facilities, as provided for under the relevant provisions of the Water Quality Conservation Act, are prohibited.

Agricultural Area

An agricultural area includes agriculture promotion areas and reserved forestland. Restrictions on land use, including construction-related activities, within this area are provided for in separate legislation such as the Farmland Act (agriculture promotion area), the Forestry Act (reserved forestland), and the Grassland Act (grassland and complex preparation zone), respectively.

SEMIAGRICULTURAL AREA

A semiagricultural area includes the areas that are used not only for promoting agriculture and forestry and preserving forests, but also for the purpose of development, such as farmland, semireserved forestland, and so on, in areas other than the agriculture promotion areas. In semiagricultural and forest areas, such land use as carries the risk of causing environmental pollution or construction of buildings and other structures in excess of the size and scope as prescribed by the presidential decree shall be forbidden. With regard to the area that the minister of agriculture and forestry deems necessary for the promotion of agriculture or the preservation of the farmland, it is permitted to restrict activities in accordance with the Farmland Act. In this case, attention shall be paid so as to be in equilibrium with the purpose of such restrictions of activities under the Act.

Article 14 of the Enforcement Decree of the AUMNT elaborates on the air pollutant emission facilities and wastewater discharge facilities, which are provided for in the relevant articles of the AUMNT. Article 14(1)(c) prohibits construction or installation of facilities, buildings, and other structures, the site area of which is larger than 30,000 square meters, within the semiagricultural and forest area. However, exemption from this prohibition is provided for certain facilities under specifically prescribed conditions. Notwithstanding such prohibitions of construction-related land use within the semiagricultural and forest area, insignificant activities may be permitted unless they offend the designated purpose of semiagricultural and forest zones (road expansion, etc., within the existing road or its neighboring zone) by the ordinance of the Ministry of Construction and Transportation. In this case, the minister of construction and transportation shall consult with the head of the central government agency concerned in advance.

To sum up, various provisions relating to semiagricultural and forest areas, and buildings and structures, the site areas of which do not exceed 30,000 square meters and do not pose pollution threats, are permitted in principle within the semiagricultural area, which is not incorporated into the farmland preservation area. The area that the minister of agriculture and forestry deems necessary for the promotion of agriculture or the preservation of the farmland (agriculture promotion area) is subject to the restrictions provided for in the Farmland Act.

NATURAL ENVIRONMENT PRESERVATION AREA

Natural environment preservation areas include those areas that are necessary for the preservation of natural landscapes, water resources, seashores, ecosystems, and cultural property, and for the preservation and cultivation of marine resources. In this area, the following activities are forbidden:

1. new construction, reconstruction, or extension of buildings and erection of structures or other facilities;
2. cutting trees and bamboo not incidental to the forest management programs;
3. reclamation, filling, or dredging;
4. alteration of the form and nature of land;
5. grazing animals on pasture;
6. hunting or collecting wild animals and plants (excluding marine animals and plants); and
7. gathering earth, sand, gravel, stones, and the like, and mining minerals.

However, such insignificant activities as prescribed by the presidential decree are permitted. These activities include, inter alia, installation of the facilities, buildings, and other structures within a marine resources preservation district; construction of farmhouses and fishing houses, unless their construction does not significantly damage the surrounding natural environment; and installation of agricultural facilities such as reservoirs, irrigation channels, and the like.

In cases where the area in question is a park zone, park protection zone, water supply source protection zone, historic spot, scenic beauty place, natural monument, and protection zones thereof, the restrictions as prescribed in the Natural Parks Act, the Water Supply and Waterworks Installation Act, or the Protection of Cultural Property Act apply, respectively.

Restrictions on Construction under the Building Act

According to Article 12 of the BA, if the minister of construction and transportation recognizes the necessity for the management of the national land, or if the competent minister recognizes the necessity for national defense, preservation of cultural properties or environment, or national economy, and makes a request, the minister of construction and transportation may restrict the issuance of construction permission under the conditions prescribed by the presidential decree. If the necessity for regional or urban planning is acknowledged, the mayor or *do* (province) governor may impose restrictions on the head of *shi/kun/ku* granting permission in accordance with the presidential decree. In the case where the minister of construction and transportation or mayor/*do* governor intends to restrict granting any construction permission, he or she shall notify the permission granter of such intention, specifying the object, period, and contents of restriction. The permission granter shall, upon receiving such notification, make a public notice thereon without delay.

The Outline of Compulsory Purchase Procedures and Compensation System

THE COMPULSORY PURCHASE PROCEDURE

In Korea, the compulsory purchase of land procedure is, in general, prescribed in the Land Expropriation Act (LEA) and other specific legislation, such as the Urban Planning Act, Mining Industry Act, Agriculture Modernization Promotion Act, and Road Act. The LEA prescribes two kinds of procedures: general and summary. Besides the LEA, there is an Act on Special Cases concerning the Acquisition of Lands for Public Use and Compensation for their Loss. The latter's purpose is to prescribe the criteria and the method pertaining to the acquisition and use of land, and so on, by agreement and to the subsequent compensation for loss, necessary for public projects in order to facilitate smooth execution and to determine the appropriate compensation for loss.

For the general procedure of compulsory purchase, four steps are prescribed: approval of projects, investigation of land and articles, agreement, and adjudication and compromise. In cases where public project operators intend to expropriate or use any land, they shall obtain approval from the minister of construction and transportation (MCT) in accordance with the presidential decree. When the MCT has approved the project, he shall, without delay, notify the public project operator, owners of land, persons concerned, and the mayor/*do* governor concerned. He shall also announce in the official gazette the names or title of the public project operators, the type of projects, the details of the project sites, and the land to be expropriated or used. The approval of the project shall become effective as of the date of announcement of the government gazette. If public project operators do not file request for adjudication within one year after the approval of the project was notified, the approval of such projects shall be canceled from the day following the date when the term expires.

After the announcement of approval of projects is made, public project operators, or persons who are ordered or delegated to do so by the operators, may have access to the land or to structures for survey or investigation in preparation for the projects or to prepare inventory lists. Then public project operators shall prepare land investigation records and article investigation records, and affix their signs and seals thereto, and have owners of land and persons concerned attend and sign the documents. After the approval announcement of projects is made, public project operators shall agree with owners of land and persons concerned in order to acquire or extinguish rights to the land in accordance with the presidential decree. If the agreement is not reached or is impossible, public project operators may file an application for adjudication to the competent land commission within one year after the approval announcement of the project is made in accordance with the presidential decree. If an agreement is reached among project operators, owners of land, and persons concerned, public project operators may request, with the consent of the owners of land and persons concerned, that the competent land commission confirm an agreement has been reached as prescribed by the presidential decree within the period for requesting adjudication regarding the expropriation. The confirmation shall be regarded as confirmed if the commission accepts the request. The confirmation also shall be regarded as the adjudication as prescribed by the provisions of LEA. Public project operators, owners of land, and persons concerned shall not controvert whether or not the agreement is reached or the contents of agreement is reached. On the other hand, if an agreement has not been reached, owners of land and persons concerned may demand in writing that public project operators promptly apply for adjudication. Then, public project operators shall file an application for adjudication to a competent land commission within two months. When it is necessary to urgently carry out public projects for maintaining public safety because of natural disasters or other accidents, public project operators may use others' land immediately by obtaining permission from the head of the *shi/kun/ku* concerned, as prescribed by the presidential decree. The period for use of land under this procedure, however, shall not exceed six months (the summary procedure).

In order to adjudicate matters concerning the expropriation and use of land, the Central Land Commission (CLC) shall be established under the MCT and a local commission shall be established under the special metropolitan city, metropolitan cities, and *dos*. Matters subject to adjudication by each commission shall include: (1) scope of land to be expropriated or used and the method of use; (2) compensation for loss; (3) time and period of expropriation of use; and (4) other matters provided in the Act. Although each commission shall adjudicate cases within the scope for which public project operators, owners of land, or persons concerned have applied, the commission may decide to increase the amount for compensation for loss. A land commission shall adjudicate within two weeks from the date of commencing the deliberation, provided that if there is a special cause, the period may be extended only once for two weeks. A land commission concerned may, at any time before its adjudication, require a subcommittee composed of three members to urge the public project operators, owners of land, and persons concerned to compromise.

THE COMPENSATION SYSTEM

As for compensation, it shall be made in cash unless otherwise provided for by another Act. However, if the public project operator is the state, local government, the Korea Land Corporation, or another government-invested institution or public organization, as prescribed by the presidential decree, which falls under any of the cases prescribed by Article 45, Paragraph 5, compensation shall be made by bonds issued by the public project operators. The amount of loss shall be calculated on the basis of the price at the time agreement is reached, in the case of agreement. It is decided on the basis of the price at the time when expropriation or use of land is approved, in the case of adjudication. The calculation method for the amount of compensation shall be as follows: (1) With respect to the land to be acquired or expropriated after the agreement, agreement shall be reached according to the public announced land price under the Public Notice of Values and Appraisal of Lands Acts. However, the amount of compensation should be estimated from the base date of public announcement to the date of the agreement or judgment. The estimate should take into consideration the utilization plan for the land under the relevant acts and subordinate statutes; the fluctuation rate of land price determined by the presidential decree, with respect to an area where land price shall not be changed due to the relevant public projects; and the rise rate of wholesale prices and other matters, including location, shape, surroundings, and status of usage. (2) With respect to the land to be used, the amount of compensation shall be appropriately estimated in consideration of rent of the relevant land and neighboring land, and so on. Other than the above-mentioned compensation provisions, there are also provisions such as compensation for loss and work expenses of remaining land (Art. 47), request for purchase or expropriation of remaining land (Art. 48), compensation for removal of articles (Art. 49), prohibition of offset (Art. 53), compensation for loss due to survey (Art. 54), compensation for loss due to cancelation or alteration of project (Art. 55), and compensation for expenses (Art. 56).

In cases where public project operators neither pay nor deposit the compensation amount adjudicated by the competent land commission before the expropriation or use is effected, such adjudication shall become invalid. In cases where, after the approval for any public project, all or part of the expropriated land becomes unnecessary due to abolition or alteration of the relevant public projects, or another reason, within ten years from the date of acquisition by agreement or from the date of expropriation, the owner of land or his or her successor at the time of the expropriation may repurchase the land. The person would pay to operators of said public projects the amount equivalent to the compensation paid for both the land and rights other than the ownership thereof, within one year from the date when all or part of the land becomes unnecessary or within ten years from the acquisition date by agreement or from the expropriation date. The provision of this procedure shall apply also to the cases where the entire part of the expropriated land is not utilized after five years have already elapsed from the acquisition date by agreement or from the expropriation date after approval for projects. In cases where the price of the land considerably changed in comparison with the price at the time of expropriation, public project operators or the person who has the repurchase right may request the court to increase or decrease the amount for repurchasing said land.

As for the filing of complaint, persons who are dissatisfied with the adjudication of the CLC may file a complaint to the same committee within one month from the date of service of the original copy of the written adjudication. In cases where an adjudication on any complaint is not satisfactory, an administrative suit may be instituted within one month from the date of service of such written adjudication, provided that the public project operators deposit the compensation amount determined by the adjudication on the complaint before the action is instituted. Finally, in cases where the person concerned does not fulfill her or his duties arising under LEA or from any disposition taken under the same Act, and where such duties are unlikely to be fulfilled within the specified period, or where it is deemed that it might be conspicuously harmful to the public interest to have the person under such duties fulfill the duties, then a mayor/*do* governor or a head of *shi/kun/ku* may, at the request of public project operators, execute the duties vicariously, in accordance with the Administrative Vicarious Execution Act.

In Korea, although LEA prescribes general procedures for expropriation and compensation thereof, it is noted that most land acquisitions are carried out in accordance with the procedures prescribed by the Special Act concerning the Acquisition of Public Land and Compensation for Loss. Other than compensation provisions in general, similar to those of LEA mentioned above, it is particularly noticeable that the Act provides for a relocation plan. According to Article 8, the project operator, on behalf of the person who has lost sources of livelihood because he or she has provided the land necessary for the execution of the public project, shall establish and execute a relocation plan for the person as prescribed by the presidential decree. Then, according to Article 57-2, it is prescribed that, with respect to the issuance of bonds, the method and standard of computation of the compensation amount shall apply mutatis mutandis, except as provided in LEA and Articles 3-2, 4, and 8 of the Special Act concerning the Acquisition of Public Land and Compensation for Loss. Therefore, at least in cases where compensation problems are concerned, this Special Act concerning the Acquisition of Public Land and Compensation for Loss has a significant effect and has played a very important role so far in the compulsory purchase and compensation system in Korea.

In cases other than the expropriation or use of land, compensation for violation of property rights in light of public necessity is provided for in individual Acts as mentioned above. The problem is that in practice, although these laws provide the basis for the violation of property rights through public necessity, many do not have provisions concerning compensation, which raises the question of whether compensation for loss would be possible in such cases as we will discuss in detail in the following sections.[2]

Land Use Planning and Compensation for Loss

Constitutional Principles

Article 23(1) of the constitution provides for and guarantees the right of private property of all citizens, including the right of landownership. Article 23(3) goes on to provide that "Expropriation, use or restriction of private property for public necessity and the compensation therefore shall be governed by law. In such a case, just compensation shall be paid." In accordance with this provision, the LEA prescribes elaborate provisions governing general procedures of land expropriation, including compensation for loss. The LEA was not intended to be a general law governing compensation for loss. As most legislation governing problems of land expropriation (such as the UPA, Urban Redevelopment Act, Housing Site Development Act, Land Compartmentalization and Rearrangement Act) applies mutatis mutandis the provisions of the LEA, the LEA in fact plays the role of general law for the legislation concerning compensation for the losses arising from land expropriation. However, one needs to note that the LEA has some limitations in regard to losses arising from the restriction of the right of land use, in particular, the freedom to build on land, because it presupposes the expropriation of land as the cause for compensation. Perusal of the relevant provisions of the constitution brings to light some problems relating to restrictions on the right of landownership, which includes the right to freely use one's own land.

First, the question, which is at present hotly debated among administrative lawyers in Korea, concerns what kind of restrictions on the right of landownership, in particular the right of land use, entail compensation for loss. According to the general doctrinal opinion, if a certain restriction on the right of property does not fall under the concept of "restriction of private property for public necessity" as provided for in Article 23(3) of the constitution, such a restriction merely represents inherent limitations of the right of ownership and does not entail the question of compensation for loss. In other words, not every restriction imposed on the right of landownership, which includes the right of land use, gives rise to the question of compensation for loss. In order for the question of compensation for loss to be triggered, the restriction in question should be more than a simple restriction. It should approximate or equal the "encroachment upon the right of property," to employ the expression generally used in the field of administrative law. As such, it is similar to expropriation or use for public necessity as prescribed in Article 23 of the constitution in terms of the degree of encroachment upon private property. The present essay focuses on the question of whether some or all restrictions imposed on the right of land use by way of various administrative plans fall within the ambit of "restriction of private property for public necessity" as provided for in Article 23 of the constitution. This question will be addressed in more detail below.

Second, even if one supposes that some restrictions imposed by way of administrative plans represent the case of special sacrifice and that consequently they constitute the causes for compensation for loss, the question arises of whether one should recognize the right to claim the compensation even in the absence of specific provisions providing for compensation. The constitution does not recognize the right to claim compensation in an unmediated manner. It simply provides that "the compensation [for expropriation, use, or restriction of private property for public necessity] shall be governed by law."

At present a heated controversy is being staged in Korea over the question of whether the government should pay compensation to the residents living within the DRZ.[3] This controversy arises because the UPA provides for the application, mutatis mutandis, of relevant provisions of the LEA to the cases of "expropriation or use of land," while it remains silent with regard to the restriction of the right of land use within the DRZ. The failure to prescribe any provision for the case of restrictions on land use can be interpreted as implying the intention of the legislators to consider the imposition of restrictions within the DRZ as reflecting the inherent limitations or social obligation of the right of landownership.

Another possibility is to interpret that designation of a given area as DRZ, and the resultant restriction on the right to use the area falls within the ambit of "restriction of private property for public necessity" as prescribed in Article 23 of the constitution, which necessitates the compensation for loss. Even when one agrees to the proposition that compensation should be paid to the residents of the DRZ in accordance with such an interpretation, the question remains of what should be the proper legal basis of the compensation. According to some scholars, the right to claim compensation is directly grounded in the constitution. Others contend that the right to claim national compensation should be recognized while regarding the UPA as unconstitutional and void in so far as it lacks any specific provisions relating to compensation in cases of restrictions imposed on the right of land use within the DRZ.

NATURE OF THE RESTRICTION IMPOSED ON THE RIGHT OF PROPERTY BY LAND USE PLANNING

If the concept of "public necessity," as provided for in Article 23(3) of the constitution, is interpreted as meaning the same thing as "public interest," all restrictions imposed on the right of property fall under the concept of "restriction of private property for public necessity," as prescribed in Article 23(3). It is obvious that such an interpretation is flawed since "restriction of private property for public necessity" connotes only those restrictions constituting the cause for compensation for loss.

Let us elaborate on this point by way of illustration. The Building Act (BA) prohibits construction of buildings or other structures on the road, or provides that a building site should abut the road, the breadth of which should be at least 2 meters. It is evident that these restrictions do not fall under the concept of "restriction of private property for public necessity" of the constitution since the concept of "public necessity" relates to "specific programs or projects carried out by the Government for public interest." Prohibition of construction-related activities under Articles 33 and 34 of the BA does not have anything to do with specific projects for public interest. Therefore, the absence of any provisions relating to compensation for loss does not give rise to any problems.

The UPA provides for the institution of urban planning, with the main emphasis on the SUA system. Within the area subject to urban planning, only those buildings satisfying the requirements relating to the kind and form of buildings as imposed by the SUA system are eligible for construction permission. Such restrictions on the right to use land as are imposed by the SUA system do not fall under the concept of "restriction of private property for public necessity" as prescribed in Article 23 of the constitution. It is true that some restrictions relating to the kind and form of buildings are imposed. However, such restrictions do not amount to the prohibition of construction-related activities themselves. Designation of SUAs alone does not constitute encroachment upon private property for public necessity, and consequently does not involve the question of compensation for loss. Imposition of restrictions on the right of land use by way of administrative plans has as its objective the prevention of disorderly and irrational construction activities within urban areas. To that extent, it reflects the inherent limitations or social boundaries of the right of landownership and does not entail compensation for loss.

The same consideration applies to the restrictions on construction-related activities within urban planning facilities such as parks and playgrounds, the restrictions within four SUAs provided for under the AUMNT, and the temporary restrictions on construction as prescribed in Article 12 of the BA. In contrast, restrictions within the DRZ or the urbanization control zone are not mere restriction on construction, but they virtually amount to the prohibition of construction within these zones. Therefore, the question arises whether restrictions on construction within the DRZ or the urbanization control zone belong to the category of "restriction of private property for public necessity." Let us restrict our discussion to the DRZ, which is the main focus of attention in connection with the question of land use planning and compensation for loss.

DEVELOPMENT RESTRICTION ZONE AND COMPENSATION FOR LOSS

The question of whether designation of a certain area as a DRZ entails compensation for loss has attracted so much attention, both practical and theoretical, that it cannot be left outside the realm of the law any longer. From 1971 to 1978, there were eight designations of DRZ. As a result, the total area of DRZ occupies 5.4 percent of the whole national territory; 2.2 percent of the total population reside within the zone. If the number of landowners residing outside the zone is added, the number of interested persons will substantially increase.

According to the prevailing scholarly opinion, designation of a DRZ results in special sacrifice and constitutes the cause for compensation for loss.[4] In contrast, the official side, including the Constitutional Court,[5] the Supreme Court,[6] the Ministry of Construction and Transportation,[7] and the Ministry of Justice, supports the view that a DRZ merely represents the inherent limitations or social boundaries of the right of landownership, and that consequently it does not constitute encroachment on private property for public purposes, which entails the issue of compensation for loss.

Even when one admits the view that designation of a DRZ entails compensation for loss, the further question of the extent and content of compensation arises. For instance, if loss results from the designation of the DRZ, is the loss limited to the "present loss" incurred by the designation, or does it include the "relative diminution of exchange value" on a cumulative basis that has resulted from the freezing of the land price in question while the price of neighboring land has risen after the designation? If the former is the case, given that the price level of land within the DRZ is at present very low, the actual amount of compensation to be paid to the residents should also be low.

At a more fundamental level, the question concerns whether the land within the DRZ other than the building site is also eligible for compensation for the losses incurred by the designation of the zone. At present, the proportion of building sites within the DRZ is 2.5 percent and the rest is largely composed of forestland and farmland. Since no restrictions exist on the right of land use with respect to forestland and farmland, other than indirect restrictions relating to the prohibition of the change of the shape and quality of the land, it can be said that the payment of compensation, if existent at all, should be made in connection with the restrictions imposed on the building site only.

According to the recent jurisprudence of the Constitutional Court, designation of the DRZ entails compensation, the extent of which is limited to the loss resulting from the restriction of the present right to land use. The court also held that special sacrifice takes place only with respect to the building site.[8] It is doubtful whether the decision of the Constitutional Court is to be welcomed either by the residents affected or by the government officials. Neither would it be a reasonable solution to interpret special sacrifice as including the relative diminution of exchange value on a cumulative basis.

Under the circumstances, it is suggested that the thorny questions relating to the DRZ cannot be fully addressed only by the discussion of compensation for loss. What the interested parties, including residents within the DRZ, ultimately want is abolition or rational readjustment of the zone, and the government has recently made substantial progress in that direction.[9]

Conclusion

THE PROBLEMS OF THE KOREAN LAND USE PLAN

Korea has a dualistic land use plan system, managing urban and non-urban areas separately. The basic method of land use regulation is to divide the land into specific use areas and to place restrictions on use diversion. There are also supplementary methods such as the district detail plan system. These land use plan systems have various problems.

First, the dualistic system of dividing land into urban and nonurban areas is out of date and lowers the efficiency of land management.

Although the Utilization of National Territory Plan designates specific use areas throughout the whole territory, the land use in urban areas is dealt with primarily by city planning, which ultimately means that urban and nonurban areas are managed differently. It is doubtful whether such dualism is necessary. In other words, is it impossible to utilize and manage the national territory at the present level without the Utilization of the National Territory Plan? The answer can be inferred from the recent case in the urban-rural integration areas, where it was decided that these areas would be regulated as nonurban areas, and not as urban areas. Now that Korea has achieved urbanization, industrialization, and economic growth, managing urban and nonurban areas separately is even less necessary. Moreover, the land use plan in the developed countries manages urban and nonurban areas unitarily. Of course, these arguments are raised from the point of view that the Utilization of National Territory Plan is useless when considering the future of national territory management and utilization. However, it is difficult for Koreans to accept this statement, when Koreans are so accustomed to dividing the land into urban and nonurban areas. However, in an era of localization, Korea should explore a unification system to design a proper land use plan appropriate to the actual local situation.

Second, the land use plan is based on the principle of freedom of construction, and thus the land is restrained only when it is designated as an SUA. This permits the private ownership of developmental profits, which creates the problems of equity among landowners. It also causes civil petitions against the restraints of development in green belt areas. Therefore, the land use system based on the freedom of construction operates to raise land prices and to bring about speculation. While a system based on the freedom of landowners may be said to be good in terms of public welfare, it is not very desirable.

Third, the SUA system regulates how a piece of land should be utilized, so that the landowner may predict how the land may be used. However, the decided SUA sticks to its own use so thoroughly that it does not allow any flexibility to the extent that the aforesaid merit cannot be expected. Furthermore, since the SUAs are divided based on the present situation, the supply for new land demand and the systematic land supply cannot be easily achieved. Because the strict use restraints according to the SUAs apply to the whole national territory, the land use according to the actual situation of the land areas is hardly ever achieved. Therefore, the land use plan policy should change to reflect the local characteristics more flexibly.

Fourth, the reservation areas should be changed into development use areas in order to mitigate the strict use restraints, but this has a serious side-effect: the destruction of the environment and mass development, for the change leads to sudden development demand. It is shown in the pressure for development in subagricultural/forest areas, according to the recent remodeling of the Utilization of the National Territory Plan. The fact that the development is carried on without a particular plan or proper foundation facilities is a serious problem.

Fifth, the detailed planning district system in place to supplement the specific use areas system is grossly insufficient to function as the land use system by planning. We have the detailed planning district system in the UPA and the city planning system in the BA, but both are regarded as the district detail plan system, and they have the same purposes and functions, bringing about dualistic effects. In addition, the application of the detailed planning districts is very limited, and the administrators are not required to designate these districts. Since it is very loosely regulated and the range for freedom of choice is very wide, it is different in substance from the district detail plan. Therefore, the detailed planning district should be developed into the deliberate land use planning system.

Sixth, the SUA system is not appropriate for the prospective method of the land use policy. All of the aforementioned points confirm that current Korean land use policy is neither proper nor reasonable. Designation of the SUAs allots high prices to some land, and low prices to other land, which creates inequality. It also provides landowners with vested interest, which makes it difficult to found the social infrastructure. Furthermore, with the unification of Korea just around the corner, it is undesirable that the present defective land use system be applied to North Korea.[10]

THE PROBLEMS OF THE COMPULSORY ACQUISITION OF LAND AND COMPENSATION SYSTEM

The number of compulsory land acquisitions by the administrative authorities has been on the increase since the Central Land Commission was transformed into a permanent institution in January 1991. The number stood at only ninety-six in 1980; it increased to 2,010 in 1991. The number of adjudication decisions given in 1996 was increased by 1.6 percent compared to 1991. Such an increase can be explained by the heightened interest in the compulsory land acquisition owing, among others, to the rapid economic development, which led to an aggressive pursuit of public projects and to the growth of the Korean people's rights awareness.

In connection with the system of compulsory land acquisition in Korea, an active debate is being conducted on, among other topics, the expropriation procedures or the proposals for improving the procedures for the submission of complaints. However, the point of contention that attracts the most attention is the institution of compensation for loss. In particular, the dual structure of the present system of loss compensation is hotly debated. Namely, with respect to compensation for the compulsory land acquisition, there are, on the one hand, provisions of the Land Expropriation Act, which are of public law nature. On the other hand, there are provisions relating to voluntary consultation in the Act on Special Cases concerning the Acquisition of Land for Public Use and the Compensation for Their Loss, which are of a private law nature. For instance, in case the voluntary consultation as provided for in the latter Act does not succeed, one has to resort to the procedures as stipulated in the former Act. This delays the process of loss compensation, which in its turn causes the delay of commencement of public projects and the increase of the budget for compensation.

However, despite the fact that there exist no essential differences between land acquisition through consultation, as provided for in the Act on Special Cases, and the land acquisition through consultation or compulsory acquisition as stipulated in the Land Expropriation Act, those who voluntarily follow the government policy and accept the option of selling their land through consultation end up receiving less compensation than they would have under the provisions of the Land Expropriation Act. Such a result seems to violate the principle of equity. Because of this, it is persuasively argued that the Act on Special Cases and the Land Expropriation Act should be incorporated into a single act. In addition, the subjects that need further discussion and study in the future include, among others, reducing legislation governing exceptional cases of land acquisition, strengthening professionalism, delegating compensation-related affairs to professional compensation consultants, and reassessing the standards for loss compensation.[11]

Notes

1. According to Article 2 of the Local Autonomy Act, the special metropolitan city (Seoul) and metropolitan cities with populations over a million may have *ku* within their respective jurisdictions, which have an equivalent status of *shi* and *kun*.

2. For a detailed description of the compensation in general, including

the LEA and the Act on Special Cases Concerning the Acquisition of Public Land and Compensation for Loss, see Won Woo Suh, "Government Liability in Korea," in Yong Zhang, ed., *Comparative Studies of Governmental Liability in East and Southeast Asia* (The Hague: Kluwer Law International, 1999), 9–28.

3. For the scholarly discussion on this problem in Korean administrative law writings, see Do Chang Kim, *The General Theory of Administrative Law* (l) (Chung Woon Sa, 1990) 588; Yun Heum Park, *A New Lecture on Administrative Law* (Vol. 1) (Park Young Sa, 1997) 690, etc.

4. Yun Heum Park, ibid., 717; Dong Hee Kim, *The Administrative Law II* (Park Young Sa, 1997) 315; Nam Jin Kim, *The Administrative Law ll,* (Bup Moon Sa, 1995) 526. Also for the opinion that it does not necessarily constitute the cause for compensation, see Won Woo Suh, *Administrative Law Theory in an Age of Transition,* (Park Young Sa, 1997) 863–876.

5. The Constitutional Court Decision of June 3, 1991 (89 Heon ma 46) and Constitutional Decision of September 16, 1991 (89 Heon ma 152).

6. The Supreme Court Decision of August 8, 1990 (89 bu 2).

7. The Ministry of Construction and Transportation, An opinion to the constitutional court decision of November 3, 1991 (89 Heon ma 213); An opinion to the constitutional petition regarding Article 21 of the UPA (November 11, 1993).

8. The Constitutional Court Decision of December 24, 1998 (97 Heon ba 78).

9. For a detailed critical analysis of the 97 Heon ba 78 decision, see Moon Hyon Kim, "Consitutional Petition to Article 21 of the Urban Planning Act," in *Constitutional Norm and Constitutional Reality, Treatises in Memory of Professor Young Sun Kwon's Retirement* (1999), 709–729. Also, for a detailed analysis of the DRZ system and compensation, see Hai Woong Ryu, "A Legal Study on Development Restriction Zone and Compensation, I, II," in *Korean Land Corporation* (ed.), Land Research, vols. 2 and 3 (1999).

10. See Hai Woong Ryu, "Toward a Prospective Development of Land Use Plan System," *Korean Journal of Immovable Property Law,* vol. 4 (1998) 23–49.

11. Ministry of Construction and Transportation, *A Study of the Reform Measures for Public Land Acquisition and Compensation System,* June 2000, 399–419.

References

Act on the Promotion of New Airport for Seoul Metropolitan Area Construction, 1991

Act on Special Cases Concerning the Acquisition of Lands for Public Use and the Compensation for Their Loss, 1975

Aviation Act, 1961, fully amended in 1991
Balanced Regional Development and Support for Local Small and Medium
    Enterprises Act, 1994
Constitution of Korea, 1987
Housing Construction Promotion Act, 1972, fully amended in 1997
Housing Sites and Development Act, 1990
Industrial Sites and Development Act, 1990
Land Expropriation Act, 1962
Mining Industry Act, 1951, fully amended in 1981
Promotion of Distribution Complex Development Act, 1995
Small River Maintenance Act, 1995
Tourism Promotion Act, fully amended in 1986
Urban Planning Act, 1962
Waste Control Act, 1986, fully amended in 1991

Ho-Joung Im, Land Appraisal and Compensation Law (Bulhyonsa: Seoul,
    2000) (Korean).
Nam-Jin Kim and Sang-Hee Park, Public Land Law: Land Appraisal and
    Compensation Laws (Bulhyonsa: Seoul, 1994) (Korean).
Korean Association of Land Expropriation Compensation Law, *Land Expro-
    priation Compensation Law* (Seoul, 2001) (Korean).
Pyoung-Jun Park, A Study on Land Expropriation Law (Kosiyounggusa:
    Seoul, 1999) (Korean).
Hai-Woong Ryu, A New Study on Land Expropriation and Compensation
    Law (Bulhyonsa: Seoul, 2001) (Korean).
Jeoung-Wook Suh, Compensation Law (Hong: Seoul, 2000) (Korean).
Won-Woo Suh, *Government Liability in Korea*, in Young Zhang (ed.),
    Comparative Studies of Government Liability in East and Southeast Asia,
    9–28, (The Hague: Kluer Law International, 1999) (English).

Chapter 6

Land Acquisition in Malaysia

GRACE XAVIER

Malaysia, a country of approximately 20 million people, is situated just above the equator.[1] The weather, therefore, is hot and humid all year, with temperatures ranging between 20 and 30 degrees Celsius. Situated with the Indian Ocean on one side and the South China Sea on the other, and with Singapore at its southernmost tip, Malaysia has long been the meeting place for traders and travelers from both the east and the west. Due to its strategic position, Malaysia was colonized first by the Portuguese, then by the Dutch, and finally by the English. However, although Malaysia gained independence in 1957, it has maintained its continual interaction with foreign powers and influences.

A land of cultural and geographic diversity, Malaysia is made up of thirteen states and four main races. The population is made up of Malays, Chinese, Indians, and other indigenous peoples, and the melting pot of different cultures contributes toward a rich cultural heritage. The capital city of Kuala Lumpur is inhabited by 1.2 million of the approximately 20 million persons. The rest of the population is concentrated mainly on the west coast of Peninsular Malaysia and in the two states that make up East Malaysia.[2] The population is expected to increase at a rate of 2.4 percent, and accordingly it is estimated that this will see an increase in the per capita gross national product (GNP) by 1.9 percent to RM 12,369 (U.S. $3,255) in 1999 as against RM 12,134 (U.S. $3,093) in 1998.[3]

The Malaysian economy recovered in 1999 from the financial crisis that hit Southeast Asia in 1997. The gross domestic product (GDP) of Malaysia that registered an unprecedented 10.3 percent growth in the

---

Lecturer, Faculty of Law, University of Malaya.

fourth quarter of 1998, registered a growth of 1.3 percent in the first quarter of 1999 before recovering to 4.1 percent in the second quarter of 1999. The GDP growth was projected to accelerate to a rate of 7.2 percent during the second half of 1999 against the 1.4 percent real growth in the first half.[4] The annual rate of inflation has decelerated from an average of 5.3 percent in 1998 to an average of 3 percent during the first nine months of 1999.

The higher per capita income is a reflection of an improvement in the employment sector. The recovery of this sector depends on the better financial performance of the business sector, in particular, the recovery of the manufacturing and services sector. However, the growth in the construction sector remains subdued due to the fact that there was already a surplus of completed projects even before the economic recession in 1997. Large areas of unoccupied office space and hotel rooms, as well as unsold up-market condominiums, flooded the market in 1997, and it will take some time for the construction industry to pick up in these specific sectors. However, activities in relation to medium and low-cost housing as well as civil engineering projects related to the public sector have seen a positive forward movement since 1999. These projects have cushioned the drop in the construction sector's contribution to the GDP to a certain extent. However, the projected growth in the year 2000 augurs well for the construction industry. It is expected that the construction sector will record a growth rate of 5 percent in 2000 as compared with a 3.7 percent in 1999 and a 4 percent growth rate in 1998. The government, in its 2000 budget, has made a higher budgetary allocation for the construction and upgrading of roads, bridges, ports and airports, drainage and irrigation, schools, industrial training institutions, hospitals, and other health facilities.[5] These construction projects are projects that serve the community and may therefore result in an increase in land being acquired from private owners.

Landownership and Related Issues

LANDOWNERSHIP

Land is a state matter.[6] Under the provisions of the National Land Code of 1965 (the Code) and the federal constitution, all property[7] in land is vested in the state.[8] The state is the only governing body that can vest and divest title to land[9] and property. A citizen, therefore, virtually has the land "on long-term loan." This is not to be confused with the concept of leasehold lands in the United Kingdom.[10] What is meant is that a person, although in law may be declared the owner of the land, holds and uses the land subject to the needs of the state. In Malaysia, this "temporary ownership" is enshrined in the constitution,[11] which provides for the acquisition of land from a person according to "due process of law" and upon the payment of "adequate compensation" for the deprivation of his or her land and house, if there is one on the land.

DISPOSAL OF LAND AND DEALINGS IN LAND[12]

In Malaysia, disposal of land takes place when state land is bestowed by the state on an individual or a corporation. Disposal of land by the state includes alienation, granting of temporary occupation licenses, reservation of land, and granting of permits.[13] Alienation by the state is a more permanent form of disposal of land by the state to an individual. Land may be alienated in perpetuity or for a term of years.[14] Once alienation is approved, however, the person does not become the lawful owner of the land until it is registered in accordance with the provisions of the Code.[15] The Torrens system of conveyancing, which originated in Australia[16] and is practiced in New Zealand and Malaysia, provides for a system of title by registration. Title by registration means that title to land, or legal ownership, may only be acquired by the process of registration. It is an act by the state and not any other act—for instance, the signing of a contract or an agreement for sale and purchase of land that can vest and divest title to the land. The effective date of ownership or proprietorship begins on the date the registration takes place.

A dealing in land, on the other hand, occurs when a registered proprietor of land deals with her or his land, either by way of transfer or any of the other forms of dealing[17] permitted under the code, with another individual or corporation.[18] Whether a transaction is a disposal of state land by way of alienation, or is a transfer between two private individuals or organizations, the transaction must be registered. In other words, transfer of land must be carried out in accordance with the Torrens system of registration of title.

LAND USE

When land is alienated by the state, it is not an alienation that is free from restrictions. The state has the power to impose conditions on title and restrictions on land use.[19] This power is primarily enshrined in statute to ensure that development and use of land is consonant with the state's development plans and policies. Alienation of a particular piece of land may be refused if the said alienation would have an adverse effect on the subsequent potential development of the lands surrounding it.[20] Therefore, land use is controlled by the state and any subsequent alienation of land in a particular location will be subject to the development plans and projected growth of the location and area. The local authorities and the city council in collaboration with the state government carry out development of land.[21]

Land use is classified into three categories: agriculture, building, and industry.[22] Upon approval of an application for alienation of land, the particular category of land use will be stated on the title. The control of state power can be seen from the fact that should an owner of land develop his or her land, or occupy or use the said piece of land contrary to the stated use on the title, then the land will be subject to forfeiture by the state authority for breach of a condition.[23] Once land is subject to forfeiture by the state authority, an appeal by a landowner is restricted to statutory grounds[24] and, if those grounds are not available, the land will revert to the state authority and become state land.[25]

Although the state may impose a particular category of land use on the title, a registered proprietor of land may, under the provisions of the Code, apply for a change in the category of land use.[26] The state authority may approve the application, or it may not. The registered proprietor would then have to adjust plans to deal with or develop his or her land accordingly. Any dealing with or development of land contrary to the land use specified on the document of title may result in land being forfeited to the state authority.[27]

STATE CONTROL

The state authority has the power to control use of land by a registered proprietor. The various forms of control are provided for by statute. A registered proprietor of land has only a limited right to use the land— that is, to use and enjoy the land so far as is reasonable for him to do so. He has a limited right to enjoy the air space above his land[28] and a limited right to support of land.[29] Although a registered proprietor has the right to support of his land, the right to support is restricted to support of land in its natural state. This means that A is not supposed to do anything to his own land that would, as a consequence, result in A's land becoming weakened so that when his neighbor, B, does something on B's land, then as a result of B's work on his land, A's land collapses due to its originally weakened state. However, if A had not done any work on his land that had weakened his land, then B would be liable to A if B's actions on his land had caused A's land to collapse.

Apart from the restricted use of land by a registered proprietor, the state has the power to acquire land if the land is needed for a public purpose. The power of the state to acquire land from an individual is contained in the constitution, and land acquisition procedures are provided in the Land Acquisition Act of 1960 (the Act).

Land Policies

The Code and the Land Conservation Act of 1960 primarily govern matters concerning land policies in Malaysia. The Sabah Land Ordinance of 1930 and the Sarawak Land Ordinance of 1948 govern Sabah and Sarawak, respectively. Land policies are formulated and drafted, to a large extent, toward eradicating poverty and providing land to the landless. However, the government can achieve the above objectives but only with due consideration being paid to each individual state's political, economic, and social realities. For instance, Malaysia is made up of thirteen states. Not all thirteen states would support a uniform framework of land policy guidelines. Land policy considerations need to take into account the physical aspects of the land, the economic and fiscal aspects, the social aspects, and the political climate. Planning controls must therefore be formulated along these guidelines. This therefore calls for a close integration between the state authority and the people in planning and land use issues.

The local authorities working closely with the consumers carry out planning of townships. A draft structure plan is formulated and put up for inspection by the public. After a considerable time given for any objections, only then is the draft structure plan put into action.[30] When the development plans are finalized and the land of an individual is required in order to accommodate these development plans, one of the ways by which land is taken back from an individual is by way of land acquisition procedures.

However, a recent development may result in fewer lands being subject to acquisition proceedings. The government is looking toward the introduction of land readjustment (LR)[31] programs for identified lands. The concept of LR is different from acquisition of land for the purposes of assisting in development of the country. In LR, the land is not acquired.

Instead, the land is exchanged. The state takes the land of a landowner and gives him or her an equal portion of land in a different part of the same project that is being developed. The landowner is part of the development process; land is developed with the original owner still being present on the same land. The landowner gets to remain in the same land area after development has taken place. There is no necessity for the owners to be relocated to another part of the country, town, or district. Since this particular mode of land development is still in the discussion stage, and there is no doubt that land will still be needed for projects, especially those projects that are considered important for the economic development of the nation, it is only appropriate to consider the law governing acquisition of land in Malaysia.

Land Acquisition—Practice and Procedure

The right to property is a fundamental right entrenched in the constitution.[32] As long as a person has the financial means to buy land, a Malaysian citizen is entitled to purchase and own land. However, the right to own land is not an absolute right. As already mentioned above, in Malaysia, land is a state matter. Under the Code,[33] land may only be disposed[34] of by the state. Although the Code deals with the power of the state to dispose of state land, acquisition of owned land may only be carried out under the machinery provided for under the constitution. Under Article 13 of the constitution, land may be acquired by the state under due process of law and provided that adequate compensation is paid. The article provides as follows:

> Article 13: Rights to property
> (1) No person shall be deprived of property save in accordance with law.
> (2) No law shall provide for the compulsory acquisition or use of property without adequate compensation.

Due process of law is provided for under the Act.[35] The Act came into force on October 13, 1960. The purpose of the enactment was to provide a clear, unambiguous, and simple system of acquisition supported by a uniform procedure of essential forms. Uniformity of procedure is essential to ensure that each acquisition is carried out without any prejudice. Since its inception, the principal Act has undergone a number of amendments. One amendment was, however, not well received and became the subject of much debate and argument. This was the Land Acquisition (Amendment) Act of 1991.

THE LAND ACQUISITION ACT OF 1960 — SCOPE AND EFFECT

Under section 3 of the Act, the state was empowered to acquire land for, inter alia, any public purpose, or for any person or corporation undertaking work that concerned public utility or industrial purposes.[36] This provision was consistent with the taking of land in other jurisdictions, for example, the United States, India, and Singapore.[37] Under the Act, the state was the sole authority to decide what amounted to an undertaking of public utility[38] and a civil court could not question the opinion of the state authority.[39] A challenge to any land acquisition proceeding was, therefore, a virtual impossibility as can be seen from the said provisions. Once the state authority made a declaration, it was conclusive evidence that the land was needed for the purpose that was specified in the said declaration.[40] A party attempting to challenge a land acquisition faced an uphill task. The only avenue that was open was for the party to allege and adduce evidence to show that the state authority had acted with mala fides when it exercised its discretion in the said acquisition proceedings. Again, proving mala fides was a serious matter and concrete evidence had to be adduced. Merely stating that other properties were available in the said area and why a particular property was acquired when similar properties were available and yet not acquired, was held to be insufficient evidence to prove mala fides.[41]

One particular safeguard for all parties concerned is that natural justice is given due recognition in all matters concerning the state and the individual. An owner of land is required to be given the due notice that her or his land is the subject of acquisition proceedings. Although an owner of land is unable to question the issue of the acquisition, she or he is to be given an opportunity to be present at the proceedings and to negotiate the compensation to be awarded. The state authority, therefore, has to ensure that the owner and occupier, if a person other than the owner occupies the land, are served with notice of the acquisition proceedings.[42]

The assessment of the compensation amount is to be made in accordance with the provisions of the Act. The factors to be taken into consideration are the market value of the land and other matters (these are set out in Paragraph 2 of the First Schedule to the Act). The valuation method is also set out in the said paragraph, and it is clear from decided case law that no other consideration should be taken into account when computing the award, apart from what is provided in the Act and the Schedule to the Act.[43]

JUSTICIABILITY OF PUBLIC PURPOSE

Section 8(3) of the Act provides that the declaration issued under this provision shall be conclusive evidence that the lands proposed to be acquired are needed for a particular purpose as specified therein. As already stated earlier, the Act makes it a virtual impossibility to challenge any acquisition except on the question of mala fides of the state authority in the exercise of its powers in the acquisition proceedings.[44] There is no provision in the Act for an owner of land to object to the intended acquisition. He or she may, however, have a say in respect of the quantum of compensation payable. The only avenues available for a landowner to challenge an acquisition already made is to show that the state authority had abused its powers, or that the purpose of acquisition does not come under any of those described in section 3 of the Act, or that the state authority has acted with mala fides. What, then, is mala fides?

MALA FIDES

Mala fides or bad faith is not something that can be proved easily. Mere negligence does not amount to bad faith. Mere suspicion of bad faith on the part of the state authority is, similarly, insufficient. The court needs hard evidence, which must be adduced by the party alleging mala fides, that there indeed was a clear instance of bad faith present.[45]

A recent example of what constituted bad faith arose for discussion in *Honan Plantations Sdn Bhd v. Kerajaan Negeri Johor (Government of the State of Johor) & Ors.*[46] The State Authority of Johor had acquired the plaintiff's land in 1993. The plaintiff had decided to develop the land in 1990 and had accordingly applied to the state authority for approval of the proposed development. However, there was no reply to the application. Subsequently, the land was acquired by the state and the plaintiff was awarded a compensation of approximately 80 sen per square foot.[47] The plaintiff subsequently discovered that his acquired land had been sold to a corporation, which was planning to develop the land in a similar manner as was earlier proposed by the plaintiff.[48] The said corporation was now offering the land for sale to the public at RM 17 per square foot.[49]

The plaintiff alleged that the decision to acquire the land had been taken in bad faith, especially as the plaintiff had informed the relevant government departments and state authority of his intention to develop the land as far back as 1990. According to the plaintiff, the *Menteri Besar*[50] had verbally approved the proposal of the plaintiff to develop the land. In disregarding the application of the plaintiff, the state authority had acted without considering the desire of the landowner to develop his land.[51] However, the court did not consider this point.

The High Court judge, Mohd Ghazali, in his judgment, agreed that the amendment had indeed widened the powers of the state authority to acquire any land that was needed for the economic development of the country. The provisions of the Act ostensibly excluded judicial review of the state's action. The only matters that could be litigated by the court were limited to those prescribed in Part V of the Act. The plaintiff's proposal, which had been approved in principle by the *Menteri Besar,* could not be relied upon because the plaintiff ought to have applied to the Executive Council (Exco), which had the authority to approve or reject such applications. The *Menteri Besar* only presided over the Exco, and any approval given by him while acting alone could not bind the Exco.

The judge apparently held the view that the amendment under section 3(b) may allow land to be acquired for the purpose of economic development, and such economic development would encompass a host of activities not merely restricted to undertakings of works, which are public utilities.[52] As long as the proposed development was in the opinion of the state authority beneficial to the economic development of the country or to the state concerned, or to the public or any class of the public, then the state authority was authorized to acquire such land.

In this case, the plaintiff's land had been acquired for the creation of a new township. This was a purpose that is beneficial to the economic development of that part of the state of Johor. Industries situated within the township would create more jobs and result in more commercial activities. The cumulative effect would enhance the economic development of that part of the state of Johor. There was no problem here. But, the observation of the judge needs further clarification. It is not accurate to state that the section allows for acquisition of land for "a host of activities not merely restricted to undertakings of works which are public utilities."[53] It is possible that the land may not actually be used for the provision of public utilities, but whatever development planned on any acquired land ought to be for a public purpose.[54] The said public purpose ought to contribute to the economic development of the nation. The reason for this contention follows.

The underlying purpose of the Act of 1960 was to consolidate the law relating to the acquisition of land, the assessment of compensation to be made on account of such acquisition, and other matters incidental thereto. Under Article 13(1) of the constitution, constitutional protection is provided to a landowner regarding the right to own property. As already outlined in the introduction section, right to property is not an absolute right. The state may acquire an individual person's property in accordance with due process of law and provided adequate compensation is paid to such a landowner.

To acquire land from a property owner, it must be done in accordance with the provisions of any law that is in force in relation to such acquisitions. There is such a law and that is the Land Acquisition Act of 1960. Such an Act must be read in the light of all the surrounding circumstances governing the acquisition.[55] In the present case, the Exco did not consider the landowner's application because an individual had given the approval in principle. That was not a formal approval.

The plaintiff alleged that his constitutional right to land had been infringed. However, the court held that when a state authority acquired any alienated land, the result was that the owner was deprived of his land. But, on the other hand, the state was empowered to do so under the provisions of the Act. The judge held that there was nothing in the Act that imposed any obligation for a preacquisition hearing. The landowner was only to be informed of the date of the inquiry and hearing in respect of the quantum of compensation payable.[56]

With all due respect to the judge, the case of *S. Kulasingam & Anor v. Commissioner of Lands, Federal Territory & Ors,*[57]did not abrogate the rights of a landowner to be given a preacquisition hearing. Abdoolcader J (as he then was), when delivering the judgment of the federal court, said:

> The conclusive evidence clause in s 8(3) which we have mentioned in effect provides that the decision of the State Authority that the land is needed for the purpose specified under s 8(1) is final and conclusive and cannot be questioned (*Wijeysekera v Festing* AIR 1919 PC 155). The Privy Council however held in *Syed Omar Alsagoff & Anor v Government of the State of Johore* [1979] 1 MLJ 49 (at p. 50) that it may be possible to treat a declaration under s.8 as a nullity if it be shown that the acquiring authority has misconstrued its statutory powers or that the purpose stated therein does not come within s 3 or if bad faith can be established. The purpose of the acquisition can therefore be questioned but only to this extent.[58]

A landowner therefore has a right to question the acquisition proceedings to the extent of proving mala fides on the part of the state authority. The state authority may not rely upon a statutory provision and hold that the conclusiveness of the provision allowed it to defeat the claim of a litigant who was alleging that the state authority had acted unconscionably or had carried out an act that bespoke its unmeritorious conduct.

As observed by Gopal Sri Ram JCA in the case of *Sia Siew Hong & Ors v. Lim Gim Chian & Anor*[59] regarding the doctrine of estoppel:

> Another way of stating the doctrine when applying it to written law is comprised in the maxim "equity will not permit statute to be used as an engine of fraud". It is a doctrine of wide operation. . . . The doctrine, when invoked, has the effect of precluding a litigant who is guilty of unconscionable or unmeritorious conduct from relying upon a statutory provision that would defeat his opponent's case. An application of the doctrine requires a meticulous examination of the facts and circumstances of the particular case to determine whether there has been any inequitable conduct. The doctrine has been applied to several statutes, including those governing contracts, wills, trusts and assignments. The categories of statutes to which the doctrine may be applied are not closed and I am certainly unable to find any serious impediment in applying it to bar a litigant from raising and relying upon the provisions of the Limitation Act 1953.

The Court of Appeal, in *Stamford Holdings Sdn Bhd v. Kerajaan Negeri Johor*,[60] held that in land acquisition cases, if the acquisition proceedings had deprived a landowner of his legitimate expectation of profit from the development of the said land, then it may be held that the acquisition proceedings may be challenged on the ground of mala fides or bad faith.

The appellant in the case of *Stamford* had applied to the government of Johor for development of his land. The application had not been approved even after four years had passed since his application. Subsequently, the land was approved for development. However, the respondents (government of Johor) wanted 70 percent equity in the proposed development plans. The respondents also proposed that the land should be sold to them for a certain sum. The appellant disagreed and the respondents began proceedings for the compulsory acquisition of the said land.

The appellant contended that the acquisition was unconstitutional and outside the ambit of section 3 of the Act. The Court of Appeal held that the acquisition proceedings were mala fide since the proceedings had resulted in the appellant being deprived of his legitimate expectation of profit from the land. The respondents were unconscionable and unmeritorious in the conduct of the whole acquisition proceedings, and if the facts alleged by the appellant were to be proven, the appellant had a good cause of action against the respondents.

THE LAND ACQUISITION (AMENDMENT) ACT OF 1991

On September 13, 1991, the Land Acquisition (Amendment) Act of 1991 (the 1991 Amendment Act) came into force. Two provisions caught the attention of the public and landowners. The original section 3 of the Act was amended and a new section, section 68A, was inserted. Section 3(b) of the 1991 Amendment Act provided for land to be acquired by the state authority as follows:

> (b) by any person or corporation for any purpose which in the opinion of the State Authority is beneficial to the economic development of Malaysia or any part thereof or to the public generally or any class of the public.

Under the original provisions in section 3, the state was empowered to acquire land for, inter alia, any public purpose or by any person or corporation undertaking work that concerned public utility industrial purposes.[61] Under the 1991 Amendment Act, however, acquisitions for public purposes or for undertaking work concerning public utility was no longer the sole reason. Land could now be acquired for another purpose, that of economic development of the nation.[62] Where the state authority was of the opinion[63] that land was needed for the sake of economic development of the country, a landowner could have her or his land acquired. The 1991 Amendment Act extended the power of acquisition of private land to purposes including the taking of such lands for the benefit of the nation. Public purpose is of course beneficial to the nation.

The difference in the wording of the 1991 Amendment Act, section 3(b), cannot be overlooked. The land could be acquired for the purposes of the economic development of Malaysia, or any part thereof, or to the public generally, or to any class of the public. The difference is subtle but cannot be ignored. Land that could hitherto be acquired for public purpose or for purposes of work concerning public utility could now be acquired not just for a new category, that is, economic development, but again without the requirement that the land was needed for public purpose. It could be acquired for the public generally, or even for a class of the public.[64] Apart from the addition of a new category for the acquisition of land, a new section was added. Under section 68A, the subsequent disposal, or use of, or dealing with, the acquired land, by the party on whose behalf it was acquired, would not invalidate the acquisition.

The main dissatisfaction expressed about the 1991 Amendment Act was the lack of substantive or procedural safeguards regulating the power of the state authority in land acquisition proceedings.[65] Subsequently, due to the furor caused by the acquisitions carried out under the 1991 Amendment Act, another amendment was made in 1997, the Land Acquisition (Amendment) Act of 1997 (Act A999) (the 1997 Amendment Act). The 1997 Amendment Act came into force on July 31, 1997, and provides for tighter control and more transparent procedures for land acquisition. The Amendment Act was enacted with the hope of curbing unhealthy practices by decision makers as well as to prevent indiscriminate acquisition of land.[66]

Of even greater importance, and the cause of much dissatisfaction to many landowners, was the addition of a new provision, section 68A. The section read as follows:

> Where any land has been acquired under this Act, whether before or after the commencement of this section, no subsequent disposal or use of, or dealing with, the land, whether by the State Authority or by the Government, person or corporation on whose behalf the land was acquired, shall invalidate the acquisition of the land.

The section provides that any subsequent disposal of, or use of, or dealing with, the acquired land, by the party on whose behalf it was acquired, shall not invalidate the acquisition. What is suggested by this section is that any subsequent disposal of, use of, or dealing with the acquired land, whether or not in compliance with the original purpose for which the land was acquired, would not invalidate the acquisition. In one respect, the new section 68A allows the acquiring body to release any acquired land that, for some reason or other, is not or is no longer suitable for the purpose for which it was originally acquired. However, the lack of any substantive or procedural safeguards as to when the power thereunder can be exercised may render the section open to abuse. The section appeared to remove the access to justice of a landowner who was aggrieved by the decision of the state authority.[67]

THE LAND ACQUISITION (AMENDMENT) ACT OF 1997

The 1997 Amendment Act, contrary to hopes that acquisition proceedings would be curbed, appeared to extend the powers of the state even further. The 1997 Amendment Act added an additional purpose for the acquisition of land. Land could now be acquired for recreational purposes.[68] However, there are detailed provisions concerning how applications for land acquisition are to be considered. These include taking into account public interest and feasibility of the proposed project.[69] A committee, the *Jawatankuasa Khas Pengambilan Tanah*,[70] would be established. The committee was comprised of the state secretary, the state director of lands and mines, the director of the state economic planning unit, the state director of town and country planning, and representatives of other related government departments or agencies. The duties of the committee include evaluating the appropriateness of the applications that came in for acquisition of land and then forwarding the applications to the state authority with the recommendations as the committee saw fit.

One important aspect of the 1997 Amendment Act is that it has amended the First Schedule to the Act, which provides for the assessment of compensation awards. Information on whether the land to be acquired was within a local planning area or whether the said land was subject to any development plan and the land use to which the land was subjected, were matters to be considered.[71] Computation of compensation would also include consideration of recent sales of similar land with the same characteristics[72] and specific land use of the scheduled land.[73] However, value of any building already on the land was not to be considered if the building was not one that was permitted under the category of land use to which the scheduled land had been subjected to.[74] Where a landowner was dissatisfied with the award, he or she could appeal to the court, where the case would be heard by a judge and two assessors.[75] However, the decision of the court was final, and there was no further right of appeal to a higher court.[76]

PROCEDURE FOR LAND ACQUISITIONS: THE HEARING AND INQUIRY

The hearing or inquiry relating to land acquisition proceedings must be conducted in accordance with the principles of natural justice. Where an aggrieved party adduced evidence to show that the acquisition proceedings had taken place contrary to the provisions of the Act and in breach of the rules of natural justice, then the applicant will be entitled to ask for a declaratory remedy.[77] Some of the procedural rules are set out in the following paragraph.

The same collector has to make full inquiry into the value of all the scheduled lands and to assess the amount of appropriate compensation.[78] Where different collectors are involved, for instance, one collector holds the inquiry and another computes compensation, the proceedings will be declared to be invalid.[79] The acquisition must be completed within two years after the declaration stating that the lands had been gazetted for acquisition by the state authority. If it takes more than two years, the said acquisition will lapse.[80] An unreasonable delay in holding an inquiry and in making an award may cause grave or serious injustice to the land-owner when land value and land prices escalate.[81] A long-delayed award would, therefore, not reflect a truly adequate compensation as provided for in Article 13 of the constitution. For example, a delay of seven years between the publication of a section 8 declaration and the notice of inquiry would actually be contrary to the provisions of the statute. Any resultant award by the collector would be ultra vires the powers of the collector, would be declared null and void, and would, accordingly, be set aside.[82] However, a delay in the payment of compensation itself would not be a factor to quash the award of the land administrator.[83] But again, it must be emphasized, that the delay shall not be unreasonably long as it would then deprive a landowner not just of his or her land, but also access to the money that was rightfully his or hers.

ADEQUATE COMPENSATION

Adequate compensation is not defined in the Act. It may be defined as the basic principle governing compensation, that is, that the sum awarded should as far as practicable place the person in the same financial position as she or he would have been had there been no compulsory acquisition of her or his land.[84] The principles relating to the computation and determination of compensation are provided in the Act.[85] But what is adequate compensation for a person who has been deprived of his property? To own a property is every man's dream. Once he owns a piece of property, it becomes a nightmare when he has to face reality. Reality here is that there is always the possibility that he may have his land taken away from him under the guise of economic development. Community interest and the interest of the nation cry out for development. But somewhere, a pendulum swings between the two "rights"—that of the nation builder and that of a property owner. Just as a pendulum swings back and forth, so must the apportionment of needs and wants of private individuals be balanced with that of the nation's economic development.

PRINCIPLES GOVERNING COMPENSATION

The First Schedule to the Act lists three criteria for determining the amount of compensation to be awarded. Briefly, first is the process of determining the market value of the land; second is any contemplated increase in the value of the land likely to accrue from the use to which the land acquired is to be put and any damages that are likely to be sustained through the process of acquisition; and third, a list enumerates the factors that ought to be neglected in determining the award.

Market Value

In the First Schedule, market value[86] of the land is stated as the market value of the land at the date of publication in the gazette of the notification of proposed acquisition or of a declaration of such an acquisition.[87] The market value of the land need not be calculated with mathematical accuracy and precision; what is meant is a fair market value or something that is close to the prevailing market value of similar lands. The safest method to use is to compare sales of similar lands in the same neighborhood as the scheduled land is situated. The potential value of the land may also be appraised when computing the market value of the land. However, the court shall have the final say as to whether potential value shall be a consideration or whether it is too remote to be considered.[88]

The effect of any express or implied condition of title restricting the use to which the scheduled land may be put shall also be considered in assessing the market value of the land.[89] In some cases, buildings on the land may be taken into account when valuation is being computed. However, a building that was built without the required planning permission from the relevant authorities may not qualify to be considered. This is because such a building would have been constructed illegally and would, therefore, be governed by Paragraph 1(3) of the First Schedule and properly excluded from consideration.[90] In the event that a conflict occurs in the valuation process, the court will take into consideration various factors, including the potential development of the scheduled lands, to resolve the conflict.[91]

Willing Vendor and Willing Purchaser Criteria

Market value of the land has also been described as the price that an owner willing and not obliged to sell might reasonably expect to obtain from a willing purchaser with whom he or she was bargaining for sale and purchase of the land. Three recognized methods for arriving at this price are: (1) the opinion of experts; (2) the price paid, within a reasonable time, in bona fide transactions of purchases of lands acquired, or of the lands adjacent to the land acquired and possessing similar advantages; and (3) a number of years' purchase of the actual, or immediately prospective, profit from the lands acquired.[92]

A similar view was held in a 1991 case. In *Ko Rubber Plantations Pte Ltd. v. Pemungut Hasil Tanah, Batu Pahat*[93] there was a dispute over the amount of compensation paid for land acquisition. K was the owner of a piece of property, X. Part of the estate was Lot A. On September 13, 1979, part of Lot A was acquired under the Land Acquisition Act of 1960 for the purpose of constructing a road from the main road to a village. The acquired land was a strip cutting across Lot A which divided the lot in half. At the date of acquisition, R and members of the public were using the acquired land. K had no objection to this. The dispute was in relation to the amount of compensation, which K asserted was below market value at the date of acquisition. Details of previous awards of compensation in the neighboring and said area were submitted.

It was held by the court that an acquisition award previously made was relevant in determining the market value, but this was subject to adjustments as to size, time factor, and other dissimilarities between the land previously acquired and the subject land. Richard Talalla JC referred to Syed Agil Barakbah FJ's judgment in *Ng Tiou Hong v. Collector of Land Revenue, Gombak*,[94] where five main principles were set out relating to the determination of compensation payable as follows:

First, market value means the compensation that must be determined by reference to the price which a willing vendor might reasonably expect to obtain from a willing purchaser. The elements of unwillingness or sentimental value on the part of the vendor to part with the land and the urgent necessity of the purchaser to buy have to be disregarded and cannot be made a basis for increasing the market value. It must be treated on the willingness of both the vendor to sell and the purchaser to buy at the market price without any element of compulsion.

Secondly, the market price can be measured by a consideration of the prices of sales of similar lands in the neighborhood or locality and of similar quality and positions.

Thirdly, its potentialities must be taken into account. The nature of the land and the use to which it is being put at the time of acquisition have to be taken into account together with the likelihood to which it is reasonably capable of being put to use in the future e.g. the possibility of it being used for building or other developments.

Fourthly, in considering the nature of the land regard must be given as to whether its locality is within or near a developed area, its distance to or from a town, availability of access road to and within it or presence of a road reserve indicating a likelihood of access to be constructed in the near future, expenses that would likely be incurred in levelling the surface and the like.

Fifthly, estimates of value by experts are undoubtedly some evidence but too much weight should not be given unless it is supported by, or coincides with, other evidence.

It was thus the opinion of the court that after a careful consideration of all the factors and the evidence adduced, a prospective buyer who was ready, willing, and able and who had surveyed the market at the time of acquisition would have paid RM 12,000 per acre for the acquired land, bearing in mind all the factors. The respondent had in fact been awarded compensation at the rate of RM 7,000 per acre. The court adjusted the award accordingly.

Comparable and Similar Lots

Cases have held that in relation to the determination of compensation as spelled out in the First Schedule to the Act, the most reliable guide in determining fair market value is evidence of sales of the same or similar land in the neighborhood, due allowance being made for the particular circumstances of each case.[95] Comparable and similar lots must resemble each other in distinctive features. Where there was little information about the characteristics of the land or obvious dissimilarities existed between the lands to be compared, then such lands could not be used as comparable or similar lots for the purposes of assessing compensation.[96] Where a considerable time had lapsed since the transactions had taken place, the courts will reconsider whether such lands could indeed be used as comparable lands for the purposes of assessing compensation.[97]

The issues discussed above were tested in the case of *Pentadbir Tanah*

Daerah Petaling v. Glenmarie Estate Ltd.[98] In determining the market value of certain portions of land acquired in the 1980s, the learned judge had solely relied on an earlier award made by the High Court concerning a portion of the same estate made in 1979. For the purpose of assessing the value of the lands, the learned judge doubled the award per acre but in some cases gave due allowances for the location of the lands, and the size and time of acquisition.

The Supreme Court held that the learned judge had not applied the correct principle in making the award. Although it was not wrong for the learned judge to accept the evidence of a previous acquisition award of the same estate as relevant consideration indicative of the market value of the property, it would be more reliable to follow the normal and accepted guide in determining the fair market value of the lands by considering the sales of similar lands in the neighborhood after making due allowances for all circumstances, when such evidence is available.

Bona Fide Transactions

Where the court is using similar pieces of land or property that have been acquired or sold earlier as a comparison, it must be satisfied that the transactions were bona fide. The sale must be a genuine sale and the price paid must be a realistic figure when all the circumstances of the case and the current market value of property are taken into account.

This was discussed in the case of *Che Pa bin Hashim & 3 Ors. v. The Collector of Revenue, Kedah.*[99] The applicants, who were the former landowners, disputed the amount of award for the acquisition of a parcel of land. The allegation was that on the relevant date, the market value of the land was RM 18,000 per relong[100] and the market value of the house was RM 40,000. These amounts were a lot more than what had been offered.

A further contention was that the collector should have used a similar lot of land, Lot 756—an adjacent lot that had been sold just four months earlier—as a comparable lot, rather than the properties that had been taken into account.

Although it was agreed that Lot 756 was a comparable lot because it was very similar in size to the land that was acquired, the sale price was much higher when compared with a valuation report that had been done on the same plot four years earlier. The price that was paid for the lot was 116 percent higher than that quoted on the said valuation report. The Land Office had prepared such a report when they wanted to acquire the lot in 1980.

Such an escalating increase in the price of the land did not reflect the true market value of property prices during the years 1980–1984. In fact, there was a drop in property prices during the year the sale took place. Other neighboring properties were transacted at lower prices. Furthermore, the purported sale was not reflected on the title. There was no endorsement of transfer on the said title. The government valuer therefore took into account a sales transaction, which had taken place earlier, and the current market value of neighboring lots.

The court, considering the circumstances of the case and current property values, concluded that the purported sales transaction of Lot 756 was not bona fide. It was reasonable to infer that a high price had been paid for Lot 756 to artificially boost the compensation award that was to be made. There was no reason for any purchaser to pay such a high price for a lot when he knew that it was going to be acquired. Lot 756 was eventually acquired by the government.

It was held that the applicants had failed to adduce evidence to show that the sales transaction of Lot 756, the comparable lot, was a bona fide transaction. The government valuer was not wrong in considering the earlier valuation report of Lot 756 and the current market value of neighboring lots in assessing the market value of the land, which was acquired.

Potential Development

Potential development of the land in question is not to be taken into consideration.[101] Therefore, any increase in value due to improvement made by the owner within two years before the declaration of the acquisition should not be taken into consideration unless it can be proved that the improvement was made bona fide and not in contemplation of proceedings for the acquisition of the land.[102] An increase in the value of the land by reason of the use of the land where it is shown that the use was contrary to law, or was detrimental to the health of the residents of the premises or to the public health generally should not be taken into consideration when assessing compensation.[103]

However, cases have taken potential development into account when determining the amount of compensation to be awarded. The court recognizes that the value of the land must be considered as it stands in its actual condition at the material date with all its existing advantages due to the carrying out of any scheme by the government for which the land is compulsorily acquired. In this regard, the fairest and most favorable manner to consider compensation is to take into account the most lucrative and advantageous way in which the owner could dispose of the land with reference to its future utility.[104] An additional factor to be considered was the element of accessibility to the land. This factor had to be considered in the light of the potential development of the land.[105]

In *Er Boon Yan & Ors v. The Collector of Land Revenue, Port Dickson*,[106] the collector was held to have erred when he valued the land solely upon the value of the rubber on the land and not upon the land itself. The court held that he should have taken account of the potentialities of the land for other purposes.

In *Kwang Hap Siang Ltd. v. Pentadbir Tanah Daerah Gombak*,[107] the land was acquired for the proposed construction of the Kuala Lumpur-Karak Highway. The acquisition was gazetted in 1977. However, in 1967–1968, when the owner proposed development, the planning department had proposed that the land could be used to house two petrol stations. Whether the proposed development would in fact take place depended on the detailed submissions of the landowner and the confirmed written approvals of some ten other government departments. Based on the suggested proposals of the planning department, the plaintiff contended that the true basis for the valuation of the acquired portion was that at the material date it was potential petrol station land and that compensation should be awarded accordingly. After a due consideration of all evidence put before it, the court was of the opinion that valuation of the subject property should be on the basis of the highest and best use to which the property could be put. It would thus be fair to accept the owner's proposal to incorporate the two petrol station sites, which did have the potential for such use.

Before potential development is taken into consideration, it should not be too remote. This was reiterated in the case of *Siah Brothers Plantation Sdn Bhd v. Pentadbir Tanah dan Daerah Kuantan*[108] that came on appeal[109] from an oral decision of the High Court. The High Court had decided that the compensation for 18.58 acres from Lot No. 2685 C.T.1048 Mukim Kuala Kuantan, Daerah Kuantan, Pahang, was RM 8,900 an acre. The court had agreed with and accepted the estimated compensation figure given by the Pentadbir Tanah Daerah Kuantan.

The appellant appealed against this award on two grounds. First, the appellant alleged that the judge had made a mistake in fact and in law by rejecting the evidence of the appellant's valuer regarding the market value of the land. The second ground was that in fixing the amount of compensation, the judge had not given any consideration to the damages suffered as a result of the partitioning of the land and the adverse consequences that followed.

The appellant's counsel contended that the market value was RM 25,000 per acre based on comparative sale basis and not on actual sale. The comparison was made with three other lots after having considered time, size, and infrastructure development as well as the provisions of section 214A[110] of the Code. The appellant also contended that the potential development of the land was not taken into account and that the value of the land was reduced by 20 percent because of severance of the said land from other land due to the laying of some gas pipes.

The Supreme Court, in dismissing the appeal, held that the learned judge, in rejecting the valuation of the appellant and by accepting the respondent's basis of valuation, had followed the guidelines normally used by the Court in the assessment of compensation and market value. The comparative lots were not suitable as a basis for comparison because the area of the lots was too small and the lands did not possess the same characteristics as the land that was valued. Furthermore, the comparative lots were sold two or three years before the said land was acquired.

Potential development of the land was too remote to be taken into account, and it was not encouraging because of the size and the location of the land. Regarding damages, the court held that the appellant did not suffer damages because Petronas Gas (the corporation for whom the land was acquired) had promised to build access roads together with culverts across the gas pipes. There was no severance of the land from the other lands, no problem of access, and, therefore, no damages. Where potential development was not taken into account, the court may increase the amount awarded to a more accurate figure to reflect the development potential of the lands.[111]

Recent Sales of Land in the Vicinity

Where a large area of land was to be acquired, recent sales in the vicinity were only guides for ascertaining the valuation. Prices that had been paid in the past for similar land in the neighborhood could be used as a guide.[112] In fact, it may be said that the best guide to determine the fair market value of land to be acquired is to use evidence of sales of similar land in the neighborhood.[113]

Objection as to the Award

Under section 37 of the Act, any person[114] affected by the acquisition may object, inter alia, as to the measurement of the land or the amount of compensation. An objection may not be brought if the total amount awarded to any land did not exceed RM 13,000. However, the objector must first make a claim to the land administrator for the amount expected and inform the land administrator that she or he did not accept the award given and was making an objection as to the award.[115] If a person does not make a claim against the award, the court cannot award any sum exceeding that which was originally awarded by the collector.[116] Once she or he accepts an award, she or he cannot subsequently make an objection merely because there was a delay in the payment of the award[117] or make an objection after the period of time allowed for the objection is past.[118] The burden is on the person making the objection to make out a prima facie case that the award is inadequate.[119] When reviewing an objection brought by a landowner, the court may take into account factors such as a rise in property market prices, or whether there was damage on account of severance and injurious affection.[120]

Conclusion

The Act was enacted to consolidate the law relating to acquisition of land. This Act was the due process of law as mentioned in the constitution. When affecting the constitutional rights of the individual, due process of law must be administered in accordance with the fundamental principles of natural justice and fairness. Economic development is necessary for any nation or country, but so is the right of property to an individual. Balancing these two considerations requires sensitivity and discretion that is exercised with judicial clarity. If necessary, the exercise of any discretion or power by the state authority ought to be done in such a manner as to preserve an individual's right to property as enshrined in the constitution.

Notes

1. Malaysia has a land area of 329,750 square kilometers and is made up of the Peninsula Malaya or West Malaysia and the two states of Sabah and Sarawak (East Malaysia). Singapore was initially part of the coalition of Malaysia but withdrew in 1965, leaving Malaysia with thirteen states presently.

2. The two states in East Malaysia are Sarawak and Sabah. Sarawak was under British rule from 1841, and in 1888 Sarawak and Sabah became British protectorates. Following the independence of the Federation of Malaya (Peninsular Malaysia) in 1957, the confederation of Malaysia, including these two states, was formed in 1963. Singapore, too, was initially part of the confederation but withdrew two years later.

3. RM = Ringgit Malaysia (the Malaysian currency). The information in

relation to the Malaysian economy was extracted from "The Performance of the Malaysian Economy in 1999 and Prospects for 2000," 2000 Budget Report on the Malaysian Government: website: http:// www.treasury.gov.my accessed on November 10, 2000.

4. See "The Performance of the Malaysian Economy in 1999 and Prospects for 2000," 2000 Budget Report on the Malaysian Government: website: http:// www.treasury.gov.my accessed on November 10, 2000.

5. Ibid.

6. Section 40 of the National Land Code of 1965 (the Code).

7. The word "property," whenever used, refers to either land or buildings, or both.

8. This concept of land being vested in the state is not peculiar to land in Malaysia. In England, for instance, theoretically, all land is vested in the Crown or the king. The only person who is capable of owning land is the monarch.

9. Land includes buildings pursuant to the definition of land: "land includes all things attached to the earth." Section 5 of the Code.

10. In the United Kingdom, there are two estates and interests in land that may be conveyed or created in law—the first is an estate in fee simple absolute in possession, and the second type of estate is the one known as "for a term of years absolute." The fee simple is of greater duration while land that is conveyed for a term of years absolute means usually for a period of ninety-nine years.

11. Article 13 of the constitution.

12. Under the provisions of the Code, dealings in land are covered in Parts Fourteen to Seventeen. The recognized dealings in land are transfers, leases (including tenancies exempt from registration), charges (including liens), and easements. Transfers, leases, charges, and easements must be registered before they are recognized as dealings under the Code. Tenancies exempt from registration are protected by the entry of an endorsement on the Register Document of Title (section 213(3)) and liens are protected by the entry of a lienholder's caveat (section 281(2)). For the purposes of this chapter, only the dealing of transfer is discussed.

13. Permits that may be issued include permits to remove rock material from the land but not removing the same for the purpose of obtaining metal or mineral therefrom: section 42 of the Code.

14. This is similar to the fee simple in absolute possession and for a term of years absolute in the United Kingdom.

15. Section 78(3) of the Code. This is consistent with the Torrens system of conveyancing, which only recognizes the transfer of title upon the act of registration by the state authority.

16. A system of conveyancing as was propagated by Sir Robert Torrens, therefore carrying his name "Torrens system." Under the Torrens system of

conveyancing, title to property can only be vested and divested by the state pursuant to an act of registration. Only the act of registration can vest and divest title. The position is different in the United Kingdom, where there are two interests in land—legal and beneficial interests—and beneficial interest in land may pass to a purchaser upon the execution of a sale and purchase agreement. Under the Torrens system of conveyancing, only one interest in land is recognized and that is "title by registration": section 89 of the Code.

17. See note 12, *supra,* regarding what can constitute other forms of dealing in the land.

18. See section 5 of the Code for a definition of disposal of land and dealing of land.

19. Section 103 of the Code; refer also to section 5 of the Code.

20. For instance, if the state had plans for a particular area of land to be developed into a commercial or business center, then an application for alienation of a piece of land for the purposes of erecting residential accommodation may be refused unless the accommodation was part of business or office premises.

21. Development plans, structure plans, and projected townships are governed by the provisions of the Town and Country Planning Act of 1976 (Act 172); the Federal Territory (Planning) Act of 1982 (Act 267); and the Town Planners Act of 1995 (Act 538).

22. Section 52(1) of the Code.

23. Alienated land may be forfeited by the state authority for two reasons: for nonpayment of rates and taxes and assessment fees or for breach of a condition stipulated on the title. Provisions regulating forfeiture of land are contained in the Code: see sections 99–130 of the Code.

24. Section 134 of the Code.

25. "State land" is defined in section 5 of the Code as land that is still vested in the state; that is, land that has not yet been disposed of, or land that has been disposed of but has reverted to the state by virtue of forfeiture provisions.

26. Section 124(1) of the Code.

27. See note 23, *supra.*

28. Section 44(1)(a) of the Code. In *Lacroix v. The Queen,* 4 DLR 470 (1954), Fournier J held as follows: "It seems to me that the owner of the land has a limited right in the air space over his property; it is limited by what he can possess or occupy for the use and enjoyment of his land. By putting up buildings or other constructions, the owner does not take possession of the air but unites or incorporates something to the surface of his land. This which is annexed or incorporated to his land becomes part and parcel of the property." See also section 19, Civil Aviation Act of 1969, in relation to right of action of trespass into another person's air space.

29. Section 44(1)(b) of the Code. The case of *Madam Chah Siam v. Chop Choy Kong Kongsi,* MLJ Rep 187 (1939) applied the common law principle of England relating to the right of support of land. The court decided that land in its natural state had an absolute right of support from the adjoining land.

30. Development of land and planning of townships is governed by the Town and Country Planning Act of 1976.

31. LR has been successfully carried out in Japan. However, in Malaysia, such programs are still very much in the discussion stages. Potential development areas have been identified, but the workability and economic viability of such programs are being explored currently. Since the matter is still in the discussion stages, the author is unable to provide further details in relation to the said areas that have been identified as LR Project Areas.

32. See Article 13 of the constitution.

33. Section 40 of the Code provides that the entire property in all state land shall be vested in the state.

34. Section 42 of the Code provides for the powers of disposal of state land by the state authority.

35. The Land Acquisition Act of 1960. The Act has already been mentioned earlier and abbreviated accordingly. However, for purposes of easy reading, the title of the Act is reproduced in this note.

36. Section 3 reads as follows: "The State Authority may acquire any land which is needed—(a) for any public purpose; (b) by any person or corporation undertaking a work which in the opinion of the State Authority is of public utility; or (c) for the purpose of mining or for residential, agricultural, commercial or industrial purposes."

37. The Fifth Amendment to the U.S. constitution provides that it is a sovereign right to acquire private property at a fair price for a public use; Article 31 of the constitution of India provides for the taking of private land for public use; and the Land Acquisition Act, Cap 272, provides for acquisition of land for public and other purposes in Singapore.

38. Section 37(3) of the Act.

39. *United Malacca Rubber Estates Bhd v. Pentadbir Tanah Daerah (District Land Administrator) Johor Bahru,* 4 MLJ 1 (1997).

40. Section 8(3) of the Act.

41. *Yeap Seok Pen v. Government of the State of Kelantan,* 2 MLJ 202 (1982), a decision of the Federal Court of Malaysia.

42. *Lai Tai v. The Collector of Land Revenue,* MLJ 82 (1960).

43. *Lembaga Amanah Sekolah Semangat Malaysia v. Collector of Land Revenue, Dindings,* 1 MLJ 34 (1978).

44. The conclusiveness of a section 8(3) declaration was clarified and reiterated in *S. Kulasingam & Anor v. Commissioner of Land, Federal Territory, & Ors,* 1 MLJ 204 (1982), a decision of the Federal Court.

45. *Yeap Seok Pen v. Government of the State of Kelantan,* 1 MLJ 449 (1986), a decision of the Privy Council.

46. 5 MLJ 129 (1998).

47. Sen is the Malaysian currency for coins. 100 sen = RM 1 (Ringgit Malaysia).

48. The plaintiff had sent in his development plans in 1990 but had not received any reply from the state authority either approving his application or otherwise.

49. The plaintiff had been awarded RM 0.80 per square foot, and the same land was now being offered for sale to the public at a price of RM 17 per square foot.

50. Chief minister.

51. See the "Dewan Rakyat" (House of Commons) Reports dated July 30, 1991, at pages 162–163. The Act underwent a major amendment in 1991. On September 13, 1991, the Land Acquisition (Amendment) Act (the 1991 Amendment Act) came into force. For a discussion of the impact of the amendments brought about by the 1991 Amendment Act, refer to "The Land Acquisition (Amendment) Act of 1991" section in this essay. The plaintiff raised the argument that when the 1991 Amendment Act was discussed in parliament, one of the members had suggested that if a landowner had indicated a desire to develop his land, then the state authority should consider his request and approve the development plans forwarded by the landowner.

52. *Honan Plantations Sdn Bhd v. Kerajaan Negeri Johor (Government of the State of Johor) & Ors,* 5 MLJ 129, at 146 (1998).

53. Ibid.

54. Section 3(1)(a) of the Act.

55. See the "Dewan Rakyat" (House of Commons) Reports dated July 30, 1991, at 162–163, especially in relation to the paragraph as to what should be done when a landowner had already proposed plans for development.

56. The judge referred to the case of *S. Kulasingam & Anor v. Commissioner of Lands, Federal Territory & Ors,* 1 MLJ 204 (1982) to support his view on this matter.

57. 1 MLJ 204 (1982).

58. At page 11 of the judgment.

59. 3 MLJ 141, at 155 (1995).

60. 1 MLJ 607 (1998).

61. Section 3 of the Act prior to the amendment read as follows: "The State Authority may acquire any land which is needed—(a) for any public purpose; (b) by any person or corporation undertaking a work which in the opinion of the State Authority is of public utility; or (c) for the purpose of mining or for residential, agricultural, commercial or industrial purposes."

62. Economic development, however, was not defined in the 1991 Amendment Act.

63. The state authority was conferred with a power and discretion to determine the purpose of the acquisition, that is, to determine what was economic development for the nation.

64. Could it then be that land could be acquired for the purpose of building a recreation park (for the public generally) or for a golf course (for a class of the public)?

65. According to the Land Use and Cover Change (LUCC) Case Study in Malaysia, land acquisition pursuant to the 1991 Amendment Act was suspended until a proposed amendment had been carried out. This was because under the 1991 Amendment Act, the state authority had acquired extensive land areas in the states, including forestlands. Land use was then changed to commercial land uses, resulting in severe environmental damage as well as cases of abuse. Source: http://www.start.or.th/LUCC/Malaysia_Conclusion.htm. Accessed website on November 13, 2000.

66. When the 1991 Amendment Act was debated in parliament, a number of fears were voiced by members of parliament. These fears included the fact that there were no clear guidelines for the determination of the award of compensation in view of the new category of land acquisition that was proposed. The state authority could, therefore, acquire land for any purpose, in its opinion, that was beneficial to the economic development of Malaysia. But the provisions for computing award of compensation remained the same as when the state authority could acquire for public purposes. Another fear that was voiced was that the amendment gave the state authority a discretion to acquire land. This power would be subject to abuse. The state authority could acquire lands for economic development, and later the acquired lands could be disposed of to individuals or groups of persons or corporations who had considerable ties or influence with the state authority. Refer to the "Dewan Rakyat" (House of Commons) Reports dated July 30, 1991.

67. The state authority, although vested with power and discretion, may not operate as if the power and discretion were unfettered. In the case of *Pengarah Tanah dan Galian, Wilayah Persekutuan v. Sri Lempah Enterprise Sdn Bhd*, 1 MLJ 135 (1979), the late Tun Suffian (lord president then) referred to a number of English decisions regarding the powers of the local authorities. He came to the conclusion that whatever powers were given to the state or local authorities, these powers had to be exercised fairly and reasonably. The authorities were not at liberty to use their powers for an ulterior object, however desirable that object may seem to them to be in the public interest.

68. Section 3(1)(c) of the 1997 Amendment Act. Prior to the amendment, land could only be acquired for industrial purposes.

69. Sections 3(2) and 3A of the 1997 Amendment Act.

70. Special Land Acquisition Committee.

71. Section 30 of the Act.

72. Paragraph 1A of the First Schedule.

73. Paragraph 2BA of the First Schedule.

74. Paragraph 3A of the First Schedule.

75. Section 40A of the 1997 Amendment Act. Formerly, only a judge would hear the case.

76. Section 40D of the 1997 Amendment Act.

77. *Goh Seng Peow & Sons Realty Sdn Bhd v. The Collector of Land Revenue, Wilayah Persekutuan*, 2 MLJ 395 (1986).

78. Section 12(1) of the Act.

79. *Oliver Young v. Collector of Land Revenue, Batu Pahat*, 2 MLJ 208 (1972).

80. Section 8(4) of the Act. See the case of *Straits Credit Sdn Bhd v. Pentadbir Tanah Daerah, Wilayah Persekutuan Kuala Lumpur,* Originating Summons No. R1-24-59-93, High Court, Kuala Lumpur (Wan Adnan J), May 23, 1994. See also *Oriental Rubber and Palm Oil Sdn Bhd v. Pemungut Hasil Tanah, Kuantan,* 1 MLJ 315 (1983), where a delay of six years between the section 8 notification and the holding of the section 10 inquiry caused the section 8 notice to be exhausted and of no effect. The award of the collector was quashed. However, on appeal to the Supreme Court, it was held that the respondent had failed to prove that he had suffered a grave injustice as a result of the unreasonable delay. As a result, the order of the learned judge was set aside.

81. However, refer to note 80, *supra*. A party, therefore, bears the burden of proving that he has suffered grave injustice as a result of the long and unreasonable delay in the acquisition proceedings.

82. *Pemungut Hasil Tanah Deaerah Barat Daya, Penang v. Kam Gin Paik & Ors*, 1 MLJ 362 (1986).

83. *Dato' Fong Chow & Ors v. Pentadbir Tanah Daerah Jerantut & Anor*, 3 MLJ 325 (1988).

84. *Pentadbir Tanah Daerah Gombak v. Huat Heng (Lim Low & Sons) Sdn Bhd*, 3 MLJ 282 (1990), a decision of the Supreme Court.

85. Sections 12, 35, 46, and 47 of the Act. See also the First Schedule that sets out the factors to be considered and ignored when determining the amount of compensation to be awarded.

86. Market value of land may be defined as "the price which an owner willing but not obliged to sell might reasonably expect to obtain from a willing purchaser with whom he was bargaining for the sale and purchase of the said land." *Kho Choon Jee v. Superintendent of Lands and Surveys, Third Division*, 1 MLJ 265 (1972), a decision of the Federal Court.

87. Section 1 of the First Schedule.

88. *Chua Ah Hu & Anor v. Pemungut Hasil Tanah Kuala Terengganu,* Land Reference Nos. 15-50-1983 and 15-51-1983, High Court, Kuala Terengganu (Ahmad Fairuz J), November 27, 1991.

89. Section 1(2) of the First Schedule.

90. *Pentadbir Tanah Daerah Petaling v. Swee Lin Sdn Bhd*, 3 MLJ 489 (1993).

91. *Bertram Consolidated Rubber Co. Ltd. v. Deputy Collector of Land Revenue, Butterworth*, 1 MLJ 171 (1965). See also *Superintendent of Lands & Surveys, Sarawak v. Aik Hoe & Co. Ltd.*, 1 MLJ 243 (1966), a decision of the Federal Court.

92. See *Nanyang Manufacturing Co. v. Collector of Land Revenue, Johor*, MLJ 69 (1954). See also *Industrial Oxygen Incorporated Bhd. Ins. v. Pentadbir Tanah Daerah Jempol*, RT No. 15-49-91, High Court, Seremban (Faiza Tamby Chik J), November 12, 1993.

93. 1 CLJ 179 (1991).

94. 2 MLJ 35, at 37 (1984])

95. *Bertram Consolidated Rubber Co Ltd v. Pemungut Hasil Tanah, Seberang Perai Utara, Butterworth*, 2 MLJ 178 (1989). See also *Ng Tiou Hong v. Collector of Land Revenue Gombak*, 1 CLJ 350 (1984).

96. *Boon Siew Sdn Bhd v. Collector of Land Revenue*, Kedah Land Reference No. 15-15-86, High Court, Alor Setar (K. C. Vohrah J), August 10, 1993.

97. *Selangor Coconuts Bhd v. Pemungut Hasil Tanah, Kedah*, 2 MLJ 433 (1999).

98. 1 MLJ 331 (1992), 2 SCR 29 (1992).

99. 1 CLJ 193 (1993).

100. Local unit of land measurement approximately equal to 0.71 acre or 0.29 hectare.

101. Section 1(2B) of the First Schedule.

102. Section 1(3)(a) of the First Schedule.

103. Section 1(3)(b) of the First Schedule.

104. See *Khoo Peng Loong & Ors v. Superintendent of Lands and Surveys, Third Division*, 2 MLJ 156 (1966). In this particular case, the court increased the award. See also *Bukit Rajah Rubber Co. Ltd. v. Collector of Land Revenue, Klang*, 1 MLJ 176 (1968), where the court held that the property must be valued not only with reference to its condition at the time of acquisition but also its potential development value.

105. *Petaling Rubber Estate Ltd. v. Collector of Land Revenue, Kedah*, 3 MLJ 438 (1989).

106. MLJ 133 (1955).

107. 1 CLJ 146 (1992).

108. 3 CLJ 435 (1993). The judgment is in Bahasa Malaysia (the national language of Malaysia) but there is an English translation of the headnotes.

109. This was an appeal under section 49 of the Land Acquisition Act of 1960, where an appeal may be brought from a decision of the court to the Federal Court (now the Supreme Court) when a party is dissatisfied with the

amount of compensation awarded. Before an appeal may be brought under this section, the amount awarded by the court must exceed 5,000 ringgit.

110. Section 214A controls transfer of estate land. Estate land may not be transferred to two or more persons without prior approval from the Estate Land Board.

111. *Harrisons & Crosfields (M) Sdn Bhd v. Pemungut Hasil Tanah Wilayah Persekutuan,* 2 MLJ 299 (1988), a decision of the Supreme Court.

112. *Chuah Say Hai & Ors v. Collector of Land Revenue, Kuala Lumpur,* 2 MLJ 99 (1967).

113. *London Asiatic Rubber & Produce Co. Ltd. v. Pemungut Hasil Tanah Seremban,* Land Reference No. 12 of 1985, High Court, Seremban, July 9, 1993. See also *Hock Lim Estate Sdn Bhd v. Collector of Land Revenue Johor Bahru,* 1 MLJ 210 (1980), a decision of the Federal Court. However, where prices that had been paid for similar lands were on the high side and they were not normal prices, then these should be disregarded. *Draman bin Kassim v. Pentadbir Tanah Daerah, Hulu Terengganu,* 3 MLJ 284 (1990), a decision of the Supreme Court.

114. A party for whom the land had been acquired was entitled to object to the amount of compensation paid to the landowner. *Ng Kam Loon & Ors v. Director of Public Works Department, Johore & Anor,* 2 MLJ 229 (1990).

115. Re Yeap Char Ee, SSLR 94 (1932).

116. *Woo Chee Meng & Ors v. Collector of Land Revenue,* MLJ 262 (1950).

117. *Tan Boon Bak & Sons Ltd. v. Government of the State of Perak & Anor,* 1 MLJ 117 (1983).

118. *Mohd Saperi Mohd Nasir lwn Pentadbir Tanah Daerah Alor Gajah,* 5 MLJ 800 (1997). (lwn is the Bahasa Malaysia version of v.).

119. *Ong Yan & Anor v. Collector of Land Revenue, Alor Gajah, Malacca,* 1 MLJ 405 (1986). In this case, the findings of an expert valuer were insufficient to constitute a prima facie case.

120. Paragraph 2(d) of the First Schedule. *Siah Bros Plantation Sdn Bhd v. Pentadbir Tanah dan Daerah Kuantan,* 3 MLJ 51 (1993).

References

Federal Constitution of Malaysia
Land Acquisition Act, 1960

Gan Ching Chuan, "Section 68A, Land Acquisition Act 1960: A Stumbling Block to Judicial Review?" *Journal of Malaysian and Comparative Law* 203 (1993).

Clarence Edwin, "The Ambivalent Mind in Compulsory Acquisition—Amending a Section 8 Declaration?" *Current Law Journal* 12 (1998).

M. P. Jain and Grace Xavier, "Compulsory Acquisition of Land in Malaysia," *Malaysian Law Journal* 29 (May 2, 1996, Part I); 49 (June 2, 1996, Part II). (This article was published in two parts.)

Alam Panji, "The Land Acquisition Act: Making the Law Humane," *Malaysian Law Journal* 7 (January 1996).

Grace Xavier, "Compulsory Acquisition of Land in Malaysia—Recent Developments," *Journal of Valuation and Property Services* 97, no. 2 (1999).

Grace Xavier, "The Land Acquisition (Amendment) Act 1991," *Malaysian Law Journal* 81, no. 1 (April 1, 1995).

Chapter 7

Compulsory Land Acquisition and Compensation in New Zealand

Glenys Godlovitch

New Zealand Land System: An Overview

Location and Physical Geography[1]

Located 1,600 kilometers from its closest neighbor, Australia, New Zealand is in the South Pacific, and runs primarily in a NNE-SSW direction between 34–47S, 166–179E. It comprises two main islands, currently called the North Island and the South Island,[2] and a number of smaller islands, most significant among which are Stewart Island, off the southern tip of the South Island, and the Chatham Islands group, situated 800 kilometers east of the South Island. The main landmass of New Zealand is long and narrow: 1,600 kilometers in length and 400 kilometers at its maximum breadth. It sits astride an ever-shifting seam between two plates: the Indian-Australian plate and the Pacific plate. This location explains both the shape and instabilities within the land. It has a tectonic ridge running up the west side, with heights up to 3,764 meters. It is prone to both volcanic and seismic activity. It is reminiscent of the geomorphology of California, with a major alpine fault akin to the San Andreas faultline. New Zealand also has active glaciers, and its land bears the marks and scars of glacial history, with broad alluvial plains and terminal moraines. However, the climates and soils of the islands make it an eminently suitable country for agriculture and horticulture, with a total landmass of 267,500 square kilometers.

Lecturer in law and in philosophy, Lincoln University.

SETTLEMENT AND POPULATION

As with so many islands in the South Pacific, New Zealand was settled by waves of seafarers. According to Maori legend, settlement occurred toward the end of the 10th century. However, radiocarbon dating of the legendary earliest sites indicates a later date of approximately 1480. There is some evidence of the presence of previous people in New Zealand, but little or nothing is known of those people.

European exploration and settlement began in earnest in the 17th century. First to map the west coast of New Zealand was the Dutch explorer, Abel Tasman, in 1642. However, he did not land. The country's name reflects the Dutch connection. It was left to Cook and the *Endeavour* expedition of 1767–1769 to explore fully and chart—remarkably accurately—the North and South Islands. Whaling posts and sealers' settlements were established shortly afterward, and British colonization began in earnest in the 1820s–1840s. New Zealand was annexed as a separate British colony in 1840, having previously been largely under the jurisdiction of New South Wales. Extensive organized settlement companies brought large populations to New Zealand from the 1850s on in a steady stream, which reached its heyday in the 1950s as post–World War II resettlement reached new heights.

New Zealand currently has a population of approximately 3.8 million, with recent years exhibiting a marginal loss of population as emigration exceeds immigration and the birth rate drops. Approximately 800,000 New Zealanders are self-identifying Maori. Until recent decades, the rest were traditionally of predominantly British extraction, with other North European nationals making a new home in New Zealand to a lesser extent. Settlers of Dutch heritage form a significant proportion of non-U.K. settlers. Modern immigration reflects a much more mixed ethnic basis, with greater influx of peoples of ethnic Chinese and Indian background, irrespective of their country of departure. The focus on and attention to things English is in marked retreat as New Zealand establishes its autonomy and distinctiveness in the Pacific setting and also acknowledges the undeniable international significance of the Asian-Pacific connections.

LEGAL SYSTEM IN NEW ZEALAND[3]

As a former British colony and dominion, New Zealand is now an independent state, a democratic monarchy with three branches of government: executive, legislative, and judicial. The head of state is the Crown (currently Queen Elizabeth II), represented by the governor general, a role occupied nowadays by a New Zealander rather than a colonial administrator as in former times. New Zealand is a member of the British Commonwealth. Its legislative body is unicameral by direct and proportional representation. The term of each parliament is three years. Historically, the British settlers brought and implanted the English common law legal system with the doctrines of precedent and stare decisis. Whether the British acquired sovereignty by cession is moot. Certainly it would not have been by conquest, since the British troops never won a final and decisive confrontation with the Maori, who were concurrently engaged in extended internecine wars and raids against each other.

In 1840 two versions of an extremely short but extremely significant constitutional document, circulated in English and in Te Reo Maori, consisting of only a short preamble and three articles, totaling fewer than 1,000 words, was signed by some, but not all, Maori leaders. The document was drafted in English, translated into Maori, and also presented orally by Maori interpreters for signature by Maori chiefs. It is called the Treaty of Waitangi, or, to give it its Maori name, Te Tiriti o Waitangi. As a legal document of constitutional status, it is extremely fraught. The equivalence of the English version and the Maori translation has been frequently challenged. It is a puzzling constitutional instrument if only because it seems to acknowledge complete Maori home rule and also British sovereignty. In essence it seems to establish a protectorate as part of the British Empire, acknowledging the supreme authority of the British sovereign, her majesty Queen Victoria, with equal acknowledgment of Maori traditions, social entities, and political structures.

The treaty has special significance for land law, especially for land taking and compensation, by virtue of the provisions of Article 2. In this context there is major divergence between the English and the Maori formulations of the provision. The English version guarantees Maori signatories' tribes "full, exclusive and undisturbed possession" of their lands, forests, and fisheries in exchange for Crown's "exclusive right of Preemption over such lands as the [Maori] proprietors thereof may be disposed to alienate [sic] at such prices as may be agreed upon." In contrast, the retranslation into English of the Maori states: "The Queen of England agrees to protect the chiefs, the subtribes and all the people of New Zealand in the unqualified exercise of their chieftainship over their lands, villages and their treasures. But on the other hand . . . all the Chiefs will sell [sic] land to the Queen at a price agreed to."

At first English public, private, and administrative law applied in issues pertaining to the colonial settlers, and Maori traditional process applied to matters involving only Maori. In criminal law, English law applied to all settlers and to Maori where the alleged offense was more than just a summary matter. Needless to say, this legislative and political meld has been fraught with problems, some of which are directly relevant to New Zealand land law and to the compulsory acquisition and expropriation of land. Current emphasis lies on Maori dissatisfaction with the common law system of land holding and with the historical treatment of Maori land. Thus, as elsewhere, aboriginal land claims and land claim settlements against the Crown are at the forefront of New Zealand land law.

The judicial structure of New Zealand is hierarchical. The final court, that is, the court of last appeal, remains the Privy Council in Westminster. Decisions from that court are binding on all lower courts. Those are, in descending order: the Court of Appeal, the High Court, and the District Courts. There are a number of specialist courts, some as divisions of the District Courts (the Family and Youth Courts and the Disputes Tribunals) and some as separate statutory courts, such as the Employment Court, the Environment Court, and the Maori Land Court. The Employment Court is at the same level as the High Court in the hierarchy. The Environment Court is at the same level as the District Courts.

The Maori Land Court is also at the District Courts' level. It is the locus for registration of Maori land held specifically as Maori land[4] and has jurisdiction over disputes concerning Maori land. Appeals from findings of the Maori Land Court are taken initially to the Maori Land Appellate Court, with appeals on matters of law alone being taken to the High Court.

The Court of Appeal, as the highest appellate court within New Zealand, hears no trials. But by statute it is accorded the otherwise inherent jurisdiction of the High Court and the jurisdiction to hear appeals from the High Court. Below it is the High Court, which holds sessions throughout the judicial seats in New Zealand and is the court of inherent jurisdiction to conduct jury trials, issue warrants and orders, and hear appeals from lower courts. In addition to the courts, there is another very politically significant body, the Waitangi Tribunal, which hears and makes nonbinding but politically influential recommendations on matters concerning the Treaty of Waitangi.

LANDHOLDING

Maori Landholding

Maori oral tradition tells that Maori tribes and subtribes held land by occupation and use. The traditional relationship between Maori and land was thus usufructuary rather than proprietary in the English sense. There is no suggestion of tenure and estates as legal notions prior to the colonial period. Land could be acquired in a number of ways: by ancestral claim (*take tupuna*), by occupation (*take ahi ka*), by gift (*taka tuku*), or by conquest (*taka raupatu*). Once established, claimed land could be held by either actual occupation or by nominal occupation signified by maintenance of fires (*ahi*: fire; *ka*: lighting or burning) at selected sites within the claimed area while members of the tribe were off hunting, on war parties, or traveling. Needless to say, landholding during absence could be very tenuous, especially during the Maori wars and the expansion of some tribes such as the Ngai Tahu into the South Island.

Conventions about boundary markers and fires did not always and automatically command respect. The boundaries were typically identified by prominent landmarks or waterways, or could be marked by erecting cairns. Land was not an individual's property; rather, it was a collective interest, partly in terms of which a particular tribe would identify itself. Maori landholding to a large extent remains collective rather than individual. Maori land is registered with the Maori Land Court and is held in trust for a tribe, subtribe, or an extended family (an *iwi*, a *hapu*, or a *whanau*).

With the arrival of British colonial settlers, literacy, and English commercial law in the 19th century, culminating in the Treaty of Waitangi, official British Crown agents entered into contracts with individual Maori and with groups of Maori to acquire rights to land. It appears to have been British policy to take land only on a consensual basis. But in addition to some unscrupulous, opportunist Crown agents as purchasers, and possibly some equally unscrupulous and opportunist Maori as vendors, insufficient account was paid to the collective aspect of landholding in the Maori tradition.

In itself this has been the source of many current grievances before the Waitangi Tribunal and the courts in general, with the Maori claim based on original lack of power to alienate the land. Many New Zealanders of European heritage now count themselves as sixth-generation New Zealanders. In many cases they still work the same land that was acquired over a century ago by their forefathers. Hence, there is considerable objection to the settlement of Maori land claims going back to the 1850s, when an individual Maori might have bartered or sold what the Crown agent took to be his land rights; the Crown agent was then authorized to sell the land to a settler.

Colonial Landholding

Pre-Torrens System: Deeds, Doctrines of Tenure, and Estates

Deeds. Until the introduction of the Torrens system of land registration and title by registration in 1870,[5] the English system was the traditional common law land system embodying the doctrines of tenure and estates, with all land held by the Crown as the ultimate owner of everything. Ownership by anyone else was a revocable privilege held only at the pleasure of the Crown. Prima facie ownership of an estate in land was evidenced by the conveyancing documents and the previous deeds behind any current conveyancing deed. The principle of *Nemo dat quod non habet* (you can't give away what isn't yours to give), while given a key role in conveyancing, was often very hard to maintain as a principle of law. This was because of the problems intrinsic in any unguaranteed, paper-based recording system. The land as written might be misdescribed, the boundaries described could have shifted or have been removed or destroyed, the prior document could have been a complete fraud, or lost or destroyed. Deeds could have been duplicated, leading to divergent and competing innocent claims on the same land.

Although deed registration schemes were legislated,[6] registration was typically voluntary and even then did not amount to a verification of the contents of the deed, but merely confirmed that the deed had been sighted and entered in the records. Whereas this would help a conveyancing solicitor to a certain measure with backtracking through the historical documents, it provided no certainty and no guarantee of title.

But within all this confusion was the legal requirement dating back to the Statute of Frauds (1677) that, to be recognized in a court of law, all dealings in land must be in writing. By itself, the lack of writing in the Maori setting made the exploitation of New Zealand land both easy to perpetrate (no title without written deed could be used as legal justification to disestablish many Maori) and more open to contentious profiteering by avaricious or fraudulent land-baggers.

The deeds and registered deeds system the British settlers brought with them in the mid- to late nineteenth century was largely superseded by the introduction of the Torrens system of title by registration. Nonetheless that system preserved the doctrines of tenure and estate.

The Doctrines of Tenure and Estate. What was especially important about deeds was their role within the common law system of tenure and estates. Deeds purport to establish both elements, which are at the heart of the English common law on land ownership.

Derived from the Norman feudal system landholding in the English common law system involves two distinct legal components: first, the relation between grantor and grantee (Who did you get it from?); and, second, the relation between a grantee and the land (What did you get?). The first element is called tenure; the second is called the estate. Tenure establishes the chain of acquisition, tracing back to the (feudal) Crown that granted privileges of landholding. Estates define the extent and nature of the privilege granted. A freehold estate is the largest estate that is recognized in modern English common law. Lesser estates include such things as leaseholds and rights of way. As conveyancing instruments, deeds set out the transfer of tenure from one party to another. By their content, they identify the estate that is acquired.

Because conceptually all tenure and estates derive ultimately from Crown largesse, all of them could be extinguished by the revocation of the Crown grant of tenure. This is the traditional resumption by the Crown of its full ownership. Technically the Crown could rescind its grant of tenure and claim back the land, taking full possession free and clear of all lesser estates. Historically, land was neither automatically alienable to third parties nor transmissible on death to one's heirs.

Viewed thus, New Zealand law on land taking is closely tied politically and historically to the idea of eminent sovereign domain and resumption. Land use regulation and planning laws are seen as delimitations of the nature of the estate a person has, not as a restriction of it or as a divestment of an estate akin to the withdrawal of a privilege rather than the breach of a right. Although the phrase "an Englishman's home is his castle!" is bantered around, it is neither literally nor figuratively true, unless one remembers the extremely precarious tenure that a lord of the realm has on his castle. As a result, planning that requires land taking is seen as a matter of determination of public planning policy that just happens to have (typically adverse) effects on one's interest in land.

Practical problems about the authenticity, uniqueness, and preservation of any given deed, and the accuracy and precision of the estates defined in it, led to much confusion and dissatisfaction. The matter was improved immensely by the introduction of the Torrens system.

Torrens System of Title by Registration

The Torrens system, introduced in 1870 with its core notions of inde-feasibility of legal title and legal title by registration, wrought major changes in New Zealand land law, while maintaining the key concepts of tenure and estate.

At first registration was voluntary, but 1924 saw registration made compulsory.[7] Registration is maintained by the Land Information Services (a state-owned entity) and is regulated chiefly by the provisions of the Land Transfer Act of 1952, as amended. Registration creates two interchangeable certificates of title,[8] both of which the registrar must have present if a transfer of an existing estate or the creation of a new estate is to be registered.[9] One certificate of title never leaves the Registration Offices for the region. The other certificate is called the Duplicate Certificate of Title or, simply, the DCT. It may be given to the registered proprietor with a clear title (that is, with no charges registered against the estate) or to the mortgagee as security to prevent registration of most kinds of further instruments without prior notice.

At the time of writing, New Zealand is in transition to an elec-tronic system of registration of land titles, but completion is still a few years off.

The only land that is not required to be registered is Crown land and Maori land. From time to time surveys turn up little areas of registrable land that have been accidentally left out, but those occasions are now quite rare. Title to those parcels may be claimed by prescription,[10] but absent a successful application for prescription, the omitted parcels are Crown land. Maori land is recorded with the Maori Land Court, and Crown land is recorded as a separate folder.

In theory, the certificate of title shows and establishes each and every interest in any given parcel of land. Title to any interest in land is created immediately upon and by registration.[11] Mistakes are remedied by mon-etary compensation. In this way the Torrens system is said to embody three key principles. They are:

1. The "mirror" principle—the register accurately and completely mir-rors the state of title;
2. The "curtain" principle—purchasers of land should not concern themselves with trusts and other interests lying behind the curtain of the register, rendering redundant the need for historical and equi-table searches; and

3. The "insurance" principle—if the mirror is flawed and gives an incorrect image of title, then compensation is available to a person who suffers loss as a result of reliance on the title.[12]

Any claim of an unregistered interest will be entertained only as an equitable claim, ranking in priority behind registered claims. A bona fide purchaser for value of a registered interest where that interest itself was created through prior fraud or error will normally be immune from divestment. The victim of the fraud or error will be compensated by the assurance fund raised in part through the registration fees.[13]

However, in combination with other statutes—in particular, the Public Works Act of 1981—the Torrens system perpetuates the defeasibility of tenure and the power of the Crown to restrict, reduce, or extinguish any estate held. Legal room exists for a bona fide proprietor to be dispossessed or to have her or his estate curtailed where a Crown agency lays claim to the land under the doctrine of eminent domain and right of resumption. Over the years, the legal framework for land taking has imposed restrictions on the rights of the Crown to resume and entitles a dispossessed or reduced owner to compensation for the loss. Even before New Zealand was colonized by settlers from Britain, Blackstone had indicated the restricted nature of the power of compulsory land taking in his *Commentaries* as early as 1765.[14] The restrictions he spoke of have been extended even further by later legislation.

Legislative Types of Compulsory Acquisition

SUMMARY OF THE PROCESS LEADING TO LAND TAKING

The following brief synopsis on land taking is intended to help the reader with a thumbnail sketch at this stage before getting into details.

Q: Who may take land?
A: A *requiring authority,* as defined.

Q: What may be taken?
A: Any estate in land.

Q: Why may it be taken?
A: As required for *public work,* as defined, or as incidental to public work.

Q: How may it be taken?
A: In any of the following ways:
private contractual agreement;
statutory consensual *acquisition by agreement,* as defined;
statutory *compulsory acquisition,* as defined; and
Environment Court judicial order to acquire, as defined.

Q: When must the acquisition occur?
A: Within five years, if the public works use approval is acquired by designation, or within two years where it is by way of a resource consent. Time periods may be renewed on application to the appropriate authority.

It is helpful to bear in mind that a requiring authority may acquire interests in land by the same method as does any other purchaser. It can simply offer to buy out the existing owner, and if the offer is rejected, nothing further happens. By contrast, land taking is typically nonconsensual and involves making an offer to purchase, which, ultimately, the existing proprietor cannot refuse, assuming the legal validity of the purpose for which the land is requisitioned. The only matter for resolution is the level or form of compensation. The acquisition or taking may be challenged in the Environment Court.

The Environment Court is a specialist court of record with broad adjudicative and procedural powers in relation to planning, resource management, development, and conservation and preservation matters. The Resource Management Act is at the forefront of legislation within the mandate of the Environment Court.[15] By operation of the Resource Management Act with its cross-references to the Public Works Act, determinations of the court impinge upon the operation of the Public Works Act, which is the primary legislation for land taking procedures. In exercising its jurisdiction, the court may subpoena parties and documents, as well as issue warrants and other orders to facilitate decision making on the best available evidence. To that end, the rules of evidence are more flexible than those in a High Court criminal trial. With respect to land takings, the court has the power to ratify or disallow a taking in whole or in part and even to require a taking (for example, on the application of parties who would be adversely affected by public works, but whose property is not actually sought for the works). However, the Environment Court does not have the power to determine the nature or quantum of compensation.[16] Applications may be granted in whole or in part.

Among the judicial desiderata that must inform any decision of the court, some are specific to the role of the Environment Court as a specialist court. Of special importance are the principles set out in the Resource Management Act for sustainable management[17] as well as the principles enunciated in the same Act for determining whether a designation should be confirmed and clearance given for the proprietors to be expropriated to make way for public works.[18] The court must also regard the principles for decision making under the Public Works Act, that any taking be "fair, sound and reasonably necessary for achieving the objectives of the Minister or local authority"[19] in the light of all the circumstances and other possible alternatives. When the Environment Court determines an application under the Resource Management Act and orders a taking, the order expressly has the same force and effect as would an order granted at the conclusion of a contested hearing under the Public Works Act.[20] This is to preclude the prospect of relitigation of the same issues under different legislation.

Even assuming that the Crown has or acquires the ownership of the land, that by itself is not sufficient for the public work to proceed. The work must still be shown to comply with the applicable planning and development standards or else must gain clearance under the Resource Management Act.

Who May Engage in Public Works Activities

There are three principal categories of "requiring authorities," that may undertake public works.[21] They do not have to be public civic bodies. They can be private companies. This is a result of the commercial privatization over the past decade and a half of many of the functions formerly thought to be within the mandate only of civic local or national government bodies. Now defined in the Resource Management Act of 1991, a requiring authority is any of these: (a) a minister of the Crown; (b) a local authority; or (c) a network utility operator.[22]

A "network utility operator" is any agency—typically a private organization—gazetted as such for standard types of utilities: water and sewerage, natural gas or petroleum, electricity, roads, railroads, airports, and telecommunications. The categories can be extended by executive declaration.[23]

Status as a network utility operator is sought by application under the Resource Management Act for an executive declaration. If successful, the accreditation is promulgated through public notice in the gazette.

Thus, the third category includes individual companies listed by name, for example, private electricity, gas, telephone, telecommunication, and railway companies. The list may be extended by regulation.

In addition to the works contemplated for network utility operators, the other kinds of requiring authorities may designate land for things such as roads, schools, hospitals, museums, ports, harbors, water supply and flood control, historic and cultural sites, national parks and reserves, civil defense, and military facilities.

For requiring authorities to undertake public works, other parties may have to be divested against their will of their estates in land and compensated for the loss. This is done by the Crown or local authority through compulsory acquisition under the Public Works Act. The land is then vested in the requiring agency, be it the Crown, the local authority, or the network utility operator.

Using Land for a Public Purpose

The Crown is not at liberty to ignore the regulatory mechanisms and is not entirely free to act in an unfettered exercise of Crown prerogative even in respect of land that is exclusively its own. This is because planning and resource management law in New Zealand is expressly binding on the Crown. Thus, for example, the Resource Management Act provides that the Act binds the Crown.[24] So, even where the Crown is the outright owner of land, it is still obliged to comply with the Resource Management Act in order to carry out any public work.

The Resource Management Act requires territorial authorities[25] to develop planning instruments for the relevant jurisdiction. These are called district plans. In most cases of land taking, the territorial authorities involved will be either district councils or city councils, each as bodies directly elected by the local population. Any party seeking to pursue a new activity within that jurisdiction must consult the plan to assess the legality of the proposed activity. Whether the activity may proceed is a reflection largely of the provisions set out in the plan. This is the case with public works as much as for any other kind of activity. Obviously though, the procedure is less complicated where a contemplated public work is to be undertaken on exclusively Crown-owned land than where the work is to be undertaken on land involving other registered proprietors of estates in the land in question. What makes it less complicated is that landowner's consent and compensation for loss are not issues.

The plan is reviewed to determine whether the proposed activity or use is already built into the permitted or permissible uses for that land. The plan developed by the local authority indicates various types of activity as: permitted, non-complying, discretionary, or prohibited.

Where a plan shows a public works activity as permitted in that particular zone or parcel, public works are relatively straightforward, assuming the land belongs exclusively to the Crown. They do not require resource consents[26] as a precondition for their exercise, but again they do require certification and compliance with the appropriate building design and construction standards. So, if the proposed public work is already countenanced as a permitted activity, no consent is required, just permits for the development to commence and inspection certificates to ensure compliance with the building and development standards under the building code provisions of the Building Act regulations. These matters are chiefly architectural, structural, and engineering standards that must be met.

Where the plan provides for a discretionary or noncomplying use of land, a resource consent will always be required before development or any change from the existing use may proceed. However, where the proposed activity is a public works or a network utility, the same result may be obtained by way of a *designation* instead of a resource consent. The difference between a resource consent and a designation lies in the procedures to be followed and the effect of a determination. Whereas designation can be sought only by a requiring authority (a minister of the Crown, a local authority, or a network utility operator), any interested person may seek a resource consent.[27] Normally the application for a resource consent would be from the registered owner of the land, a leaseholder, or a licensee or the agent of any such person, but there is no express limit in the legislation, and indeed a nonowner may apply.

A resource consent lapses if not put into effect within two years, but may be extended on application at least three months after lapsing. The three months is a sunset period outside the two-year limit.[28] Renewal is contingent on evidence of attempts to give effect to the consent and the reasonableness of the request overall.

The plan may also record specific parcels as designated as required for some specific public work.[29] Legally, a "designation" is defined as "a provision made in a district plan to give effect to a requirement made by a requiring authority."

The plan itself and the designation are under the Resource Management Act.[30] The designation is not the acquisition process. It is a preliminary to it. It simply starts a five-year time frame during which the acquisition must be achieved and the work must commence; the designation will lapse unless renewed prior to the last three months of the five-year period.

Designation indicates some public works project yet to be undertaken, ongoing, or pending completion. It may be used to cover existing public works, such as the transportation infrastructure. Designation may occur at the initial stages of evolution of the plan itself, or it may be incorporated after the plan has been adopted. Policy reasons foster designations at the formulation stages for the plan, at a time when public input is sought and interested parties may make submissions on the proposed plan as a whole or on any aspect of it. For example, proposals for future roadways, power lines, railroad tracks, oil pipelines, and so on are normally taken into consideration in evolving the plan. Submissions are invited and public hearings may be held. If matters are resolved without recourse to court by aggrieved parties, then the project is adopted and the affected lands designated for the particular contemplated use. The designation then forms part of the plan and the relevant certificates of title are annotated to disclose the designation.

Where the designation is sought after the plan has been adopted, the same procedures are followed with the same results. Again, the net effect is that the designation starts the clock for a five-year period during which the land must be acquired and the public works project must be commenced. Before the last three months of the five-year period, the designation may be renewed provided there has been "substantial progress or effort toward giving effect to the designation."[31] In general, interested parties may challenge a proposed designation at the initial hearing stages or through mediation stages (if any) and may pursue the matter on appeal to the Environment Court.

Once land is designated as being required, it precludes the land's being used for any purposes inconsistent with the designation.[32] In effect it puts a stop on any other development of that parcel while the designation is in force. If, during the term of the designation, the requiring authority does in fact decide to go ahead with the project, it must then actually seek to acquire the ownership of the land if it does not belong to the requiring authority. So the next step is for the registered owner(s) and the requiring authority to attempt to negotiate an amicable settlement for appropriate and adequate compensation prior to the acquisition of the land.[33]

One aspect militating in favor of the designation approach rather than the resource consent approach is the five-year time frame. Another is that expansive public works projects are assessed as a whole package. By contrast, applications for resource consents are dealt with on a piece-by-piece basis with each parcel of land. The duration of a resource consent is also a significant factor in determining whether to proceed by way of designation or by way of resource consent. If granted, the resource consent lapses where the project is not commenced within a two-year period or where the consent is not renewed by three months after the two-year limitation.[34]

Because resource consents are designed to apply on a parcel-by-parcel basis rather than as an entire project covering potentially many parcels of land, there is a potential for a multiplicity of separate applications (which would need to be consolidated to be dealt with as a single proposal) and thus even for inconsistent handling and, more remotely, of inconsistent decisions. A resource consent application would be an appropriate measure for some unitary public works projects, such as the erection of a statue or of a single, stand-alone telecommunications microwave tower to be situated on land registered in a single certificate of title.

What Interests in Land May Be Acquired

Land taking may be effected on any or all estates, in whole or in part, whether below, on, or above the surface.[35] "Land" is defined in the Resource Management Act as follows: "'Land' includes land covered by water and the air space above land."[36] The Public Works Act defines "land" as "any estate or interest in land."[37] It is noteworthy that both these definitions do not claim to be exhaustive, but only inclusive.[38]

Since the Public Works Act acquisition process applies to registered land, it incorporates by implication definitions found in other legislation addressing the registration of land. Most important are the definitions in the Land Transfer Act of 1952; the Land Act of 1948; and Te Ture Whenua Maori (Maori Land Act) of 1993. The first is important because it establishes and regulates the Torrens land registration system. The second statute is important because it identifies the Crown land and provides for it to be recorded. Finally, the Maori Land Act is important as it establishes and regulates the Maori Land registration scheme and the Maori Land Court. It thus serves to bring Maori land under the purview of the Public Works Act. The general tenor of all the variant definitions is for an expansive conception of land as including all estates and interests in real property, corporeal and incorporeal interests, fixtures, and emblements.

The scope of land taking is therefore extremely broad. It may take the form of disestablishing a previous estate, such as fee simple, or it may constitute the imposition of an estate, such as an easement, without the removal and extinction of the fee simple estate. However, the acquisition of any estate extinguishes all lesser estates unless the acquiring authority stipulates otherwise. That is to say, land taking takes a free and clear title.[39] Thus all estate holders have to be dealt with and appropriately compensated for their loss. The types of interest that may be extinguished cover all kinds of estate, fee simple and less than fee simple, freehold and less than freehold, present and future estates, easements, leases, licenses, profits a prendre, charges, and encumbrances such as mortgages. However, the acquiring authority may elect to preserve any interest and acquire the land subject to such interests. Thus, for example, the acquiring authority may acquire an easement (e.g., for overhead or underground workings) but leave the fee simple estate otherwise unaffected.[40]

Cases from the late nineteenth century on have established the overarching requirement that the taking be "fair, sound, and reasonably necessary."[41] Exercise of such a dramatic power must be in good faith and for a proper purpose. It must be neither for personal vendetta or gain, nor for frivolous or vexatious purposes. It must be in accordance with the express statutory purposes. Anything else would be likely to be a breach of natural justice and would be an ultra vires action.

GROUNDS FOR LAND TAKING

What is common to all procedures under the Public Works Act is that the acquisition by the requiring authority must be for a "public purpose." Any other purpose will not suffice for compulsory land taking measures to be invoked by the requiring authority. It is this feature that distinguishes the Act and its legal mechanisms from voluntary transfers to the Crown. The reference to "public work" in the Public Works Act of 1981 is a change that was introduced by an amendment that came into force in March 1987.[42] When originally passed, the Act specified that land could be taken only if it was "for an essential work." The change is clearly significant. What is needed for a public purpose might not be essential. Examples of the monumental kind spring to mind. Monuments are scarcely essential, but are frequently thought to be important public works.

"Public work" is defined in the Public Works Act to refer very broadly to work pursued on behalf of the government or on behalf of a local authority. The definition includes construction, maintenance, and management of a wide spectrum of activities that might be thought to be generally for the public good. The provisions, standing by themselves, do not expressly cover the third type of requiring authority works, namely, network utility operators. These are incorporated by operation of the Resource Management Act: land required for work conducted by a network utility operator as a requiring authority is treated pari passu government work, but paid for by the network utility operator and with the land ultimately vesting in that party, not the Crown.[43]

The definition of public work in the Resource Management Act extends further the definition in the Public Works Act by expressly including public reserves or proposed public reserves under the Reserves Act of 1977 and any national park purposes under the National Parks Act of 1980.[44] One must also look to the Resource Management Act for the extended definition of public work, where it is broadened further to include ancillary activities to any primary public work.

How Land Taking Is Effected

The following time line is provided as an aid to understanding the procedures for obtaining a designation or resource consent as prerequisites to land taking. Both are done under the Resource Management Act, and the rules governing the procedure for resource consents are adapted mutatis mutandis for designation applications. Reference to "days" is to "working days" as defined in the Resource Management Act and excludes weekends, public statutory holidays, and a period covering Christmas and New Year.

There are a variety of steps to be met before the holding of a hearing, if any, and a number of steps following the decision, or "recommendation" as it is properly called. Public notice and hearing are not required in every case (unless the requiring authority is also the territorial authority). The presumption is that such will happen, but the local authority may determine that there is no need for that.

Prehearing steps:
1. Requiring authority serves a notice of requirement on the territorial authority.
2. Within ten days, the territorial authority must ensure all relevant parties have been served and call for submissions.
3. Time for submissions closes twenty days thereafter.
4. Prehearing meetings, if any, are held to identify issues and attempt to obviate a need for formal hearings. If matters are resolved and

formal hearings are dispensed with, proceed to step 7. Otherwise all further briefings must be exchanged between the parties and formal hearings conducted.

5. Within twenty-five days of notice of hearings, hearings must commence.

Hearings:

Applicant, all submitters, and all expert witnesses and reports are considered in public hearings conducted under the Resource Management Act. The hearings are to be "public and without unnecessary formality."[45] The strict rules of examination in chief, cross-examination, and the hearsay rules do not apply. In fact, there is no right of cross-examination at all. Such matters were supposed to have been addressed through the exchange of submissions and reports ahead of the hearing. The hearings may be conducted in discontinuous adjourned sessions. The territorial authority then deliberates, concluding in a written recommendation with reasons conveyed to the requiring authority.[46]

Posthearing steps:

6. Within thirty days of notification of the recommendation, the requiring authority must respond in writing to the recommendation (accept or reject in whole or part). The response is its decision.

7. Within fifteen days of the decision, the territorial authority must notify all parties of the response.

8. Within fifteen days of the notification, any party, including the territorial authority, may appeal from the decision of the requiring authority to the Environment Court. When this happens, the requiring authority is always the respondent in the action.

The requiring authority, which intends to undertake a public work, by way of obtaining a designation first indicates the land as required by serving a notice of requirement on the territorial authority under section 168 of the Resource Management Act. This is given to the relevant territorial planning authority and asks to have the land designated (as required land) on the relevant plans. Concurrently, the requiring authority may initiate preliminary informal negotiations with potentially affected landowners. This is to assess the potential opposition and the reluctance to be bought out. The requiring authority must weigh possible alternative sites and routes in determining its response to the notice of requirement and the application for designation. It must also consider whether the land can be acquired by agreement or whether compulsory acquisition would be necessary.

The notice of requirement must provide reasons in sufficient detail and justification to show prima facie that the land is required. It must indicate what alternatives have been considered and what mitigation will be provided. In essence, it must make out a good case in writing why the land should be taken, showing the taking to be reasonably necessary. Next, the territorial authority ensures that all relevant parties are served with the notice, publicly notifies through the public notices section of the local newspapers, and calls for submissions on the requirement decision. These procedural steps are normally tasks delegated to officers in the planning department and legal department of the territorial authority, which also advises on whether a public hearing needs to be held.

Ultimately, the territorial authority evaluates the application for designation and provides its evaluation to the requiring authority. The evaluation is technically called a recommendation.

In deciding whether public hearings should be held, the format will normally be that the district council or city council delegates its preliminary reviews of the notice of requirement to its Planning Department. Planning officers then provide an initial internal assessment and advise council whether the application should be publicly notified or not. The requiring authority, in providing its notice of requirement, would have indicated whether it sought publicly notified evaluation. The territorial authority would normally adopt the internal report and advice of its planning officers, but clearly is not bound to do so. Where the territorial authority is itself seeking to designate the land, the matter must be publicly notified, and in practice is normally dealt with by an impartial accredited commissioner who is appointed by the territorial authority but not as its advocate or agent.

The evaluation must be given in writing and with reasons. It may be acceptance, conditional acceptance, or rejection in toto. The result is provided in the form of a recommendation to the requiring authority that it confirm the requirement with or without conditions attached, or withdraw its requirement. This is done under section 171 of the Resource Management Act. It is next up to the requiring authority to react to the planning authority's recommendation. If the requiring authority accedes to any conditions, or if the planning authority's acceptance is unconditional, the requiring authority asks the authority to proceed to designate the relevant land as being required by the requiring authority. Then if the preliminary informal negotiations with the landowners are not progressing well, the designation usually leads in practice to formal steps under the Public Works Act for the minister of lands or the local authority to activate the acquisition procedures. The minister must determine whether to try to acquire by agreement with the registered owner, or to acquire by the compulsory mechanisms under the Public Works Act. Use of the former does not preclude subsequent use of the latter if the former is unsuccessful. On the other hand, even if the informal negotiations do proceed well and settlement seems likely, the requiring authority will protect its interest in acquiring the land by a notice of desire to acquire under section 18 of the Public Works Act.

Compulsory Acquisition of Land under the Public Works Act

The current legislation that provides the legal mechanism for land taking is the Public Works Act of 1981. It came into force on February 1, 1982. As is evident, however, it must be read in conjunction with the Resource Management Act to get the full picture of land taking. When conducted in a prudent and proper fashion, the compulsory acquisition process moves from the Resource Management Act through to the Public Works Act by means of an order under section 185 of the former to acquire under the latter.

THE MINISTER OF LANDS

Broadly speaking, the Public Works Act is both substantive and facilitative. It establishes the permitted purpose and the mechanisms for compulsory acquisition of land, for settlement of compensation, and for the divestment of land by the Crown if the land is no longer required for a public purpose. Under section 4A of the Act, the minister of lands is the primary minister of state responsible for land taking. The minister of lands is expressly empowered to acquire and dispose of property in land, to settle the terms of acquisition, and to administer the acquired property.[47]

The minister acts on behalf of other ministers or network utility operators, as requiring authorities, in obtaining title to land that is needed for public works. Other ministers are empowered to enter into contracts for public works and may delegate their authority in this regard.[48] The minister of lands is not permitted to do so for the acquisition of land.[49] All dealings relating to a government work under the Act are entered into in the name of the Crown. But, as noted, the minister of lands also acts on behalf of private utility operators seeking expropriation of land. In those cases, the acquired land vests in the name of the private utility operator, not that of the Crown.

Two Procedures for Land Taking

The Public Works Act establishes two major approaches to such land taking. They are "Acquisition by Agreement" and "Compulsory Acquisition of Land." The first approach, namely consensual alienation, is a transaction involving a willing vendor and a willing purchaser. However, it is conceptually problematic, raising issues of duress. The state seeks to acquire the land for a public purpose for which it is allowed to acquire the land by compulsory land taking. Hence, if the proprietor declines to sell and the court authorizes the acquisition, the requiring authority is able to force the proprietor to sell. The second approach is then available as a "backup" approach to be used if and only if the taking is duly authorized and the registered owner is unwilling to sell.

For each of the two approaches, procedures are set out in the Act that must be followed in order to acquire title and extinguish the claim of the proprietor or proprietors of an estate or estates in a parcel of land. The procedural requirements depend upon the extent to which the transaction is voluntary or forced. The requirements also vary somewhat depending on whether the land to be taken is Maori land.[50]

Acquisition by Agreement

Acquisition by agreement as a statutory transfer of land is different from private contract law conveyance of property only in that:

- the purchaser is invariably a requiring authority,
- the transfer occurs within the context of public works,
- the official valuer general's office may assist in determining quantum for the appropriate consideration,
- official notices of various kinds will be given to the vendor, and
- the imminent transfer will be protected by registration of an instrument on the certificate of title to the property, equivalent to a caveat.

The process leading to acquisition by agreement is under sections 17–21 of the Public Works Act. The process starts legally with a notice of the desire to acquire.[51] This is a formal notice given by the minister of lands or the local authority to the registered proprietor(s) of the land in question.

As indicated above, the minister of lands has the legal capacity to pursue acquisitions on behalf of (any minister of) the Crown and also on behalf of network utility operators as requiring authorities. A local authority as the third of the three kinds of requiring authority may acquire land directly where the public work is within its local jurisdiction and its financial mandate and control. The notice of the desire to acquire is also registered against the certificate of title to the property to act as a warning to anyone dealing with the property of the prospective acquisition. As part of the notice served on the property owner is an invitation to the registered proprietor to open negotiations with the requiring authority.

After service and registration of the notice of desire to acquire, there follows a mandatory waiting period of three months during which the requiring authority may not take further legal action to acquire the land. The three-month period is precisely to enable the registered owners to respond to the invitation to negotiate. If during that initial three months there is no response or there is a response in the form of a refusal to negotiate, then the requiring authority may proceed at any time in the following nine months to begin the compulsory acquisition process. That is, by the end of one year from the time of service of the notice of the desire to acquire, either the parties take active measures to assess terms and compensation, or the requiring agency commences the aggressive route to acquire the land by compulsion. If the one-year period expires without either, then the notice of desire is deemed to have been withdrawn. The minister or the local authority may of course actively withdraw the notice at any stage.

If the parties successfully negotiate a buyout of the owner, the agreement is protected by registering a compensation certificate against the title pending the actual conveyance of the property into the name of the Crown or the other requiring authority.[52] As set out more fully below,[53] the registered owner may be compensated in kind, and the requiring authority is granted the discretionary power to acquire and convey alternative land complete with improvements, if that would bring the acquisition to an amicable and fair settlement.[54]

A somewhat anomalous acquisition by agreement is the result of a contested designation application through the Environment Court. As mentioned earlier, the Environment Court may order the acquisition of land under section 185 of the Resource Management Act. When it does so, statute law deems the parties to have agreed to the acquisition subject only to the determination of compensation.[55] The requiring authority does not have to start from scratch after an acquisition order and serve a notice of desire to acquire, wait three months, then commence the compulsory acquisition process.[56]

Compulsory Acquisition

Where the registered proprietors refuse to negotiate a settlement or negotiations stall, the requiring authority may elect to pursue the more aggressive route to acquire the land and expropriate the landowners. This is the compulsory acquisition of land procedure under sections 23–27 of the Public Works Act.

In this scenario, the registered owner is served with a notice of intention to take, which is also published in the gazette and publicly notified twice. Public notice is given by being published twice in local newspapers, or if there is no local newspaper, then by being posted at the site. The notice is also registered against the title to the land as notice to parties dealing with the land.[57] The notice must set out the particulars called for under the Act in sufficient detail to provide a prima facie justification for the taking.[58] The notice is valid for a one-year period from the date it was gazetted.[59] It automatically expires at that point in time unless one of three things has happened: proclamation, confirmation, or Environment Court action. The first, that a proclamation has issued,[60] is the penultimate step to the actual conveyance of the land and divestment of the owners. The second form of continuance is a confirmation of intention to take, which stretches the period out a further two years for obtaining the proclamation.[61] In brief, it amounts to a declaration by the minister or local authority that it is still proceeding with its intention to take. There can be no further extension or reconfirmation.[62] No further legal steps to acquire the land under the Public Works Act may be undertaken for a period of six months. The third form of continuance is in effect abeyance pending judicial decision of the Environment Court.[63]

Anyone objecting to the proposed taking may be heard in the Environment Court,[64] which will determine whether the taking is warranted in whole or in part, and will make the corresponding order. The objector makes a formal written objection under section 23 of the Public Works Act. The court's jurisdiction, process, and effect are pursuant to section 24 of the Public Works Act. It is an extremely important provision in the contested compulsory taking of land, providing the Environment Court with a broad power of inquiry. The process calls for a formal response within one month to the objection (much like the ordinary civil proceedings of Statement of Claim, or Writ, and Statement of Defense), followed by a hearing in the Environment Court on fifteen days' notice. The parties may be represented by counsel, and the hearings may be held in closed session, at the discretion of the court.

The process itself and the jurisdictional powers were recently reviewed most clearly in *Daroux v. Minister of Lands*.[65] Whiting EJ in that case reviewed an objection to a compulsory taking. In brief, a gazetted network utility operator applied to the minister of lands under section 186 of the Resource Management Act for the compulsory acquisition of land (easements) required for overhead power lines. After lengthy negotiations over approximately six years, four of the property owners continued to oppose the acquisition and filed the appropriate notices of objection under section 23(4) of the Public Works Act. Thus the matter returned to court for determination of the validity of the requirement and the proposed compulsory land taking. The court reviewed the legislation, its jurisdiction, the history of the privatization of the electricity industry, and the particular events leading up to the hearing. Judge Whiting stated that:

> Electricity still remains and will continue to remain in the foreseeable future an important public utility. The shift to privatization does not in any way diminish the importance of electricity as a commodity necessary for many facets of modern day living. . . . No doubt it is for this reason that Parliament prescribed the right for a network utility operator to apply to the Minister of Lands to take land under Party II of the PWA. *What is required is a proper and fair sense of balance between the two interests.* (Paragraph 57 of the Report and Findings, emphasis added)

The court held that the case was made out in support of the grant of the easement for an indeterminate period of time.[66]

In reaching its decision, the Environment Court must have regard to the statutory provisions in 24(7) of the Public Works Act. These specify, inter alia, that the court must:

(a) Ascertain the objectives of the minister or local authority;
(b) Inquire into the adequacy of the consideration of alternatives to the contested taking as ways of achieving the objectives;
(c) Remit the matter for such further consideration, if appropriate; and
(d) "Decide whether, in its opinion, it would be fair, sound, and reasonably necessary for achieving the objectives . . . for the land of the objector to be taken."

The court then prepares a written report and its findings. The report and findings on the merits are binding, although the question of appeal on points of law go only to the High Court.[67] Clearly (a)–(d) above impose a limited discretion on the court. Paragraph (d) is especially significant: it is conjunctive ("and"), not disjunctive ("or"); thus the proposed taking must be each and all of "fair," "sound," and "reasonably necessary."

Hence, for example, if the taking is not found to be reasonably necessary for the objectives as determined on evidence by the court, the court may not confirm the taking, even if there are other property owners who have not objected and have gone along with the acquisition of their land. The other property owners would have ceded their land unnecessarily, but might not be able to get it back once it has been transferred to the requiring authority. It would all depend upon whether the requiring authority wants to divest itself of the acquired land.

Relinquishing Crown Ownership of Acquired Land

Compulsory acquisition is reversible under the legislation. If the land is no longer required for public work it must be disposed of by trying to reverse the acquisition unless it would be impracticable or inequitable to do so. Where it was acquired from a private proprietor, the land is offered for sale back to the person from whom it was acquired, or her or his legal successor, at a maximum price of the current market value.[68] By parity, when the acquired land was Maori land, it is offered back to the former trustees or pursuant to order by the Maori Land Court.[69] In any case, if such transfers back are not possible or not accepted within forty working days, then the land is to be offered for sale to the adjoining landowners or by auction to the public.[70] Alternatively, if the transfer back is "impracticable, unreasonable or unfair,"[71] the minister may declare and officially gazette the land to be Crown land.[72] Land rights acquired by compulsory land taking under the Act are subject to avoidance if the substance of the original compulsory acquisition evaporates.[73] It is not open to the minister to leave in abeyance formerly required land that was not put to the use for which it was acquired.

In *Attorney General v. Horton*,[74] land had been acquired originally for coal mining works, a proper public purpose. Years later, Coal Corp no longer wanted the land for its mining operations and was prepared to relinquish its interest in the land. The minister of lands at that point could have dealt with the property pursuant to section 40 of the Public Works Act by offering it back to the registered owners from whom title was taken. However, this was not done; instead, the minister in effect "banked" the land to have it available to offer in possible settlement for Maori grievance settlements and compensation. In the meantime, the land remained in Crown ownership although the substratum of its original acquisition had gone.

Privy Council ruled that the actions of the minister were improper: as soon as the Crown or a state-owned enterprise determines that land it has acquired is no longer required for a public purpose, it must forthwith offer the land back to the former owner or the successor.

The meaning of "successor" in section 40(1), above, has been clarified by the New Zealand Court of Appeal recently in *Gisborne Ltd. v. Smiler.*[75] Arguably, in obiter dicta, the court discounted Maori claims of an improper land taking from an individual Maori in 1881. That transfer, according to Maori advocates, should never have stood. It led to a chain of acquisition that should, to the Maori way of thinking, have reverted back to the proper tribal ownership. But through the court's interpretation of "successor" in section 40, the Court of Appeal effectively created a one-generation rule, thereby excluding historical Maori claims from the meaning in section 40 of the phrase "the person from whom [the land] was acquired or . . . the successor of that person." The net effect would seem to be that of precluding Maori from raising historical wrongful taking arguments.

Case law seems to confirm that the offer-back provision is a right of first refusal and not an equitable estate in land.[76] Most recently this was confirmed in *Brothers Inn Ltd. v. Southland Regional Council.*[77] There are many cases dealing with the time according to which current market value is to be gauged. Each case is to be taken on its facts in setting the time for determining current market value. Ordinary contract law rules of offer and acceptance and invitations to treat will apply in deciding what constitutes an offer and whether it was accepted, countered, or rejected without countering.

If the previous owner or the successor does not accept the offer then, as set out above, the property may be offered to owners of adjoining properties. Failing any contract being entered into with any of them, the property may be offered to the public by auction. In exceptional circumstances, if it would be impractical or inequitable to do otherwise, then the minister may declare the land to be Crown land simpliciter.

Compensation

Compensation is covered under Parts V and VI of the Public Works Act. The function of Part VI is to provide a legal means to compensate by way of grants of other land in lieu of compensation. It empowers the minister to acquire and, if appropriate, improve other land to be swapped for the land taken. In a strong sense, there is an intention of replacing land with land, a home with a home, and money is paid where that cannot be done or cannot be done in full and complete satisfaction of the value taken.

The Public Works Act provides a general rubric to indicate both the scope and principles for setting compensation awards. The underlying ideology is that a person who has been forced to surrender an interest in land or who has been otherwise adversely affected by the land taking should receive fair compensation. In the case of an owner who has had land taken, compensation is to be largely commensurate with the ordinary principles of valuation—what a willing vendor would accept and a willing purchaser would pay for the interest.[78]

Compensation is available not only to all those with damage or loss of an interest in land that has been taken[79] but also to those who have suffered injurious affection where no land was taken.[80] Thus it is available, to various extents, to registered owners, charge holders, occupants, holders of future estates, and adversely affected neighbors. This is set out in sections 60 and 63 of the Act.

Each party alleging expropriation, loss, or damage must bring a separate claim within two years of the vesting of title in the Crown or local authority. This applies to holders of all affected estates, including those affected by the taking of adjoining land. On application, each deprived party is "entitled to full compensation" assessed in accordance with the provisions of section 62. That section directs the valuation to be determined as if it were between a willing vendor and willing purchaser.

Valuing the lost land is treated counterfactually, as if there were no compulsion and as though the value of the land were not impinged upon either positively or negatively by the imminent public works activity.[81] It treats compensation as between a willing vendor and a willing purchaser. It does, however, include the loss of potential value.[82] For example, the owner might have been intending to subdivide the land or convert it to a commercial use. To ascertain the credibility of a claim of lost potential value, regard will need to be had again to the appropriate plan to see whether, for example, the potential use or subdivision is permitted by the plan on the date when compensation is to be assessed. The applicable date, called the specified date,[83] is the date of vesting of title in the Crown or local authority. That is the date of proclamation of acquisition, when all that remains to be done is the proof of formal registration of the transfer. Compensation is set as representing the highest and best use at the specified date. Thus, if the land is classified as rural agricultural land, compensation is gauged not only on the agricultural basis, but also on the basis of its being sold to be a farm in production.

The starting point is that compensation is payable by the requiring authority under the auspices and purview of the Land Valuation Tribunal. The Land Valuation Tribunal is established as a specialist forum under the Land Valuation Proceedings Act of 1948. It reflects an expertise in property development, appraisal, and marketing, but is an administrative tribunal with adjudicative powers; thus it may set the value of expropriated property.

Where the compensation is for substantial injurious effect to neighboring property owners, rather than for land taking, the compensation is set in accordance with section 63, which is predicated upon a common law right of action for damages. However, the scope of coverage excludes anything that is not "substantial" and such things as change in traffic flow. Thus neither a home owner who has more traffic passing his or her property, nor a business that suffers a drop-off in trade as a result of the construction of a bypass is eligible for compensation.

The hearings under which compensation may be paid are the following:[84]

- Loss of land;
- Substantial injurious affection caused by construction (not maintenance or operation) of the public work;
- Disturbance arising through the land taking, including reasonable removal costs, valuation, appraisal, and legal fees or costs;
- Actual and reasonable transportation costs for goods and chattels where land is swapped;
- Loss of improvements allowance;
- Loss on repayment of a mortgage;
- Business loss including loss of goodwill, where the business is forced to move; and
- Solatium of $2,000 to the occupant owner or occupant leaseholder where the land taken was the principal private residence at the time of giving vacant possession.

The structure of the award is particularized to the circumstances and the parties involved. For example, compensation may be paid, at the discretion of the requiring authority, to a holder of a weekly or monthly tenancy of residential or business premises, where such tenancies do not fall under the rubric of registrable leases.[85] Assistance may also be provided in the purchase of alternative accommodations, or alternative farm or industrial location. However, the assistance is only by way of a loan and constitutes a due debt. There is no discretion in the legislation for an extension of time to bring an application for compensation; thus the onus to claim compensation is decidedly on the displaced owner, and the claim for the compensation must be made within two years of the taking.[86] If a land taking is abandoned prior to vesting, but the notice of desire to acquire or of intention to take had been given, prospective displaced owners are entitled to recover their actual costs and other expenses incurred prior to the abandonment. The claim must be made within six months of the notice of abandonment of the taking.[87]

Summary

Land taking in New Zealand is a stringently regulated activity, with many checks and balances intended to guard the interests of registered landowners in the event that the land is required for a public purpose. However, once it has been established that the land is required, all proprietors can be legally divested of their interests against their will and despite their objections. The measures are provided as alternative procedures: voluntary alienation of one's interest in land pursuant to the acquisition by agreement process, and compulsory alienation pursuant to the compulsory acquisition process. The taking of land is not viewed in New Zealand as an invasion of a person's rights so much as a regulation of land use meriting compensation to those who are deprived in the interests of the broader society. The Environment Court is the main forum for determining the validity of any taking, but it is powerless to set quantum for compensation.

Compensation is as a result of a negotiated settlement between the parties or by decision of the Land Valuation Tribunal. Compensation is intended to provide "a home for a home, a farm for a farm," either by way of monetary compensation or by transfer of other property to the displaced parties. It is also intended to cover the costs incurred in the process as well as to provide a small sum for loss of enjoyment. The levels of compensation are geared to the fair market value on the date of proclamation of transfer, but without regard to the imminent public works. The compensation for loss of enjoyment is purely nominal, in a set amount, and is far from any equivalent to the types of punitive damages that might be awarded were a person to bring a successful action in torts.

Notes

I would like to acknowledge my indebtedness to colleagues at Lincoln University and to Mr. Russell Crowther, who read earlier drafts of this material. Special thanks are due to Professor Peter Skelton, who recently retired from the bench of the Environment Court, for his extremely helpful comments and patient clarification of the workings of the court. The law is as stated at June 1, 2000.

1. The following paragraph is drawn from material in *The New Zealand Official Year Book 1998* (Wellington: GP Publications, 1998); Statistics New Zealand Website (www.stats.govt.nz); and D.W. McKenzie (ed.), *Reed New Zealand Atlas* (Reed Publishing [NZ] Ltd. in association with the Department of Survey and Land Information) (Auckland: Heinemann, 1995).

2. The South Island is also commonly referred to as the Mainland. There is ongoing discussion whether to officially adopt the older Maori names for the islands. These names appear on Cook's map of the islands from 1767–1769. One problem would be that North Island would become Maui, which of course is already better known as an island in the Hawaii group. In contrast, South Island would be called Te Wai Pounamu (meaning Greenstone Waters), which does not roll easily off European tongues.

3. An excellent general survey of New Zealand legal history is provided by Spiller, Finn, and Boast, *A New Zealand Legal History* (Wellington: Brooker's, 1995).

4. Contingent Maori ownership of non-Maori land is dealt with in the ordinary way through the Land Information New Zealand (Torrens system) registry at the regional Land Transfer Offices.

5. The Land Transfer Act of 1870.

6. The Deeds Registration Ordinance of 1841, and later, The Land Registry Act of 1860.

7. The Land Transfer (Compulsory Registration of Titles) Act of 1924. However, such registration only occurs when the deed is dealt with in some fashion. Thus there are significant tracts of land, particularly lands that were granted to the church or to schools, where there has been no action on title since 1924. These parcels remain unregistered, but tend to be well-known historical institutions in the older parts of the original settlers' cities.

8. There is a shift in other Torrens system jurisdictions to move away from two equivalent certificates of title as a key element in the registration

system. This is explained by the move to electronic records and registration, which render the need to cross-check two hard copies otiose. Alberta, for instance, abandoned the need for issued Duplicate Certificates of Title (DCTs) in 1999. New Zealand is still some way off from achieving independence from two hard copies. The Land Transfer (Automation) Amendment Act of 1998 has yet to be brought into full effect. Until all the Land Registry Offices are fully automated and their existing record banks transferred into electronic form, the need for DCTs will continue to be core to the New Zealand version of the Torrens system.

9. Sometimes, of course, a DCT is misplaced, lost, or destroyed so as to make it impossible for the registrar to deal with both documents. When that occurs, a court order must be obtained to dispense with the missing DCT and to generate a new one. This is done under the Land Transfer Act of 1952, section 87.

10. Open, notorious, and exclusive possession adverse to legal ownership for a continuous period of not less than twenty years. This is regulated by the Land Transfer Amendment Act of 1963. Prior to that date it was not possible in New Zealand to gain title by adverse possession.

11. *Gibbs v. Messer* (1891) AC 248; *Fels v. Knowles* (1906) 26 NZLR 604; *Frazer v. Walker* (1967) NZLR 1069 (PC).

12. These three principles are extrapolations from the legislation, not explicit within it. They were first postulated and discussed by Theodore Ruoff in his work *An Englishman Looks at the Torrens System* (Sydney: Law Book Company, 1957). The relevant provisions of the legislation are found in sections 62, 63, 64, 75, 182, and185 of the Land Transfer Act of 1952.

13. *Frazer v. Walker* (1967) NZLR 1069 (PC).

14. "So great . . . is the regard of the law for private property, that it will not authorise the least violation of it . . . even for the general good of the whole community. . . . [T]he law permits no man, or set of men, to do this without the consent of the owner of the land. . . . In this and similar cases the legislature alone can, and frequently does, interpose, and compel the individual to acquiesce. But how does it interpose and compel? Not by absolutely stripping the subject of his property in an arbitrary manner; but by giving him full indemnification and equivalent for the injury thereby sustained. . . . All that the legislature does is to oblige the owner to alienate his possessions for a reasonable price, and even this is an exertion of power, which the legislature indulges with caution and which nothing but the legislature can perform." Blackstone, *Commentaries,* 1, 139.

15. Mining, ore, mineral, and subterraneous extraction are excluded from the Resource Management Act of 1991, because these activities clearly are not compatible with the resource being sustainable—they are the deliberate depletion of a supply without possibility of human replacement. Nonetheless, all the surface workings connected with the mining process are regulated by

the Resource Management Act of 1991. Hence, even these destructive activities are tangentially under the Act.

16. *Queenstown Airport Corp Ltd v. Skipworth* (1999) HC Dunedin, Chisholm J (AP 19/99) on appeal from a determination of the Environment Court purporting to set compensation. Held: it is ultra vires the Environment Court to do so. The matter of nature and quantum referred back to the Public Works Act process, mediation, or Land Valuation Tribunal assessment.

17. Resource Management Act of 1991, Part II, sections 5–8 inclusive. Section 5 is particularly instructive. It puts the emphasis on "sustainable management," not just "sustainable development." It provides:

(1) The purpose of this Act is to promote the sustainable management of natural and physical resources.

(2) In this Act, 'sustainable management' means managing the use, development, and protection of natural and physical resources in a way, or at a rate, which enables people and communities to provide for their social, economic, and cultural wellbeing and for their health and safety while—

(a) Sustaining the potential of natural and physical resources (excluding minerals) to meet the reasonably foreseeable needs of future generations; and

(b) Safeguarding the life-supporting capacity of air, water, soil, and ecosystems; and

(c) Avoiding, remedying, or mitigating any adverse effects of activities on the environment.

18. Resource Management Act, section 171, provides that in considering any application, the court must have regard to various items that can be summed up as a requirement that the designation be "reasonably necessary for achieving the objectives of the public work or project or work for which the designation is sought" (Section 171(1)(a)).

19. Public Works Act 1981, section 23.

20. Resource Management Act 1991, sections 185, 186; Public Works Act 1981, sections 17, 40, 41.

21. Resource Management Act 1991, section 166; Public Works Act 1981, section 16.

22. Resource Management Act 1991, section 166.

23. Ibid., section 167.

24. Ibid., section 4.

25. Territorial authorities are any local or municipal council or, if there is no relevant council for the district, the minister of local government.

26. A "resource consent" is defined in section 87 of the Resource Management Act to legitimate land that would otherwise contravene the Act. There are different types of resource consent: (a) a "land use consent"; (b) a "subdivision consent"; (c) a "coastal permit"; (d) a "water permit"; and (e) a "discharge permit."

27. Resource Management Act 1991, section 88.

28. Ibid., section 125.

29. This is done by a requiring authority. See *supra,* 235.

30. Resource Management Act 1991, section 166.

31. Ibid., section 184.

32. Ibid., section 176.

33. See *infra,* 246–251, for more details on the acquisition of title under the Public Works Act.

34. Resource Management Act 1991, section 125. It is of note that the three-month renewal period for resource consents follows the expiry of the full term, whereas for designations the three-month renewal period is the last three months before expiry. In itself this raises some legal question as to the status of a resource consent during the immediate post-expiry three months.

35. Public Works Act 1981, section 4A, and definition of "land" in section 2.

36. Resource Management Act 1991, section 2.

37. Public Works Act 1981, section 2.

38. Other relevant definitions of "land" are to be found in the Land Transfer Act of 1952, section 2; the Property Law Act of 1952, section 2; the Land Act of 1948, section 2; Te Ture Whenua Maori (Maori Land Act) of 1993, section 2; and the High Court Rules, R.3.

39. On the general principles, see P. Salmond, *The Compulsory Acquisition of Land in New Zealand* (Wellington: Butterworths, 1992), 1–30. However, the book is seriously dated in other regards and should not be relied on as a statement of the current law. D. Brown, *Land Acquisition,* 4th ed., (Sydney: Butterworths, 1996), considers the principles of compulsory acquisition in Australia and New Zealand; however, the author neglects to cover the significance of the Resource Management Act in relation to land taking in New Zealand, which makes the work unreliable on the processes as they apply to New Zealand.

40. *Daroux v. The Minister of Lands* (unreported), September 1, 1999, Environment Court, Whiting EJ (EC Decision A88/99), confirming the right of the Crown to acquire land by way of an easement for a power corridor in favor of a power company as a network utility operator requiring authority. The plaintiff was one of four objectors who sought relief from the Environment Court at least to limit the duration of the easement to a fifty-year period. The application was denied.

41. The phrase has been incorporated into the Public Works Act 1981, section 24.

42. Public Works Amendment Act (No. 2) 1987 (1987 No. 67), section 2(1).

43. Resource Management Act 1991, section 168.

44. Ibid., section 2.

45. Ibid., section 39.

46. The rules of procedure and evidence are set out in the Resource Management Act 1991, section 39.

47. Public Works Act 1981, section 4A.

48. Ibid., section 4B.

49. Ibid., section 4C(1)–(8).

50. It should be recalled that in light of Article 2 of the Treaty of Waitangi, only the Crown may acquire Maori land, and then only by virtue of a right of preemption, not eminent domain or resumption. See *supra,* 229.

51. Public Works Act 1981, section 18.

52. Ibid., section 19.

53. See *infra,* 253–255 (forms of compensation).

54. Public Works Act 1981, section 19.

55. Resource Management Act 1991, section 185.

56. Public Works Act 1981, sections 17 and 20.

57. Ibid., section 23.

58. Ibid., section 23(1)(b).

59. Ibid., section 23(4).

60. Ibid., section 23(4)(a).

61. Ibid., section 23(4)(b).

62. Ibid., section 23(5).

63. Ibid., section 23(4)(c).

64. Ibid., section 23(3).

65. *Daroux v. Minister of Lands,* Environment Court, Decision No. A88/99, Report and Findings dated September 1, 1999, Whiting EJ.

66. In an earlier judgment of the court, Skelton EJ set out the process succinctly but without the complication of a network utility operator as the requiring authority. See *Jones v. Southland District Council,* Planning Tribunal (the immediate legal predecessor of the Environment Court), Decision C049/96, findings and decision dated June 28, 1996.

67. Resource Management Act 1991, section 299. Further appeal to the Court of Appeal is by leave of that court only, pusuant to section 308.

68. Public Works Act 1981, section 40.

69. Ibid., section 41.

70. Ibid., section 42.

71. Ibid., section 40(2).

72. Ibid., section 42(3).

73. Recent development in case law has established that a change of purpose will not sustain the acquisition by the Crown. The land once acquired is available to the Crown only for the purpose for which it was taken, unless the minister has expressly declared it to be required for some other public work. *Attorney General v. Horton* (1999) BCL 441 (PC).

74. *Attorney General v. Horton* (1999) BCL 441 (PC).

75. *Gisborne Ltd. v. Smiler* (Court of Appeal) CA No 182/98, April 26, 1999.

76. A good discussion of the section 40 offer-back provisions is provided by J. E. Toomey, "The Offer-back Provisions in the Public Works Act 1981—A Fair Deal to the Parties?" *Canterbury Law Review* (1996): 272–290. However, there have been developments in the interim, in particular, the series of High Court judgments involving the Papakura Military Camp and the McLennan family as successors to the parties from whom title was acquired. See *McLennan v. Attorney General* (1/12/99, Paterson J, High Court, Auckland) M267/98 for a review of the myriad issues in the case, which will probably wend its way next to the Court of Appeal.

77. *Brothers Inn Ltd. v. Southland Regional Council* (7/4/99, Chisholm J, High Court, Invercargill) CP 19/97. See also, *Glucina v. Auckland CC* (28/2/96, Baragwanath J, High Court, Auckland M931/95).

78. This is referred to as the "Spencer Principle" following the decision in *Spencer v. Commonwealth* (1907) 5 CLR 418. In the case of Maori land, where there would be several sellers and buyers in the hypothetical model, the Spencer Principle has been modified to the "Maori Trustee Principle" on the basis of *Maori Trustee v. Minister of Works* (1958) 3 All E R 336 (PC).

79. Public Works Act 1981, section 60(1).

80. Ibid., section 63.

81. This is referred to as the "Pointe Gourde Principle" on the basis of *Point Gourde Quarrying & Transport Co. v. Sub-Intendent of Crown Lands (Trinidad)* (1947) AC 565 (PC).

82. Following *In re Whareroa 2E Block Maori Trustee v. Ministry of Works* (1959) NZLR 7 (PC).

83. Public Works Act 1981, section 62(2).

84. Ibid., sections 62–68 (compensation), 72–74 (financial assistance).

85. Ibid., section 75.

86. Ibid., section 78.

87. Ibid., section 76.

References

Interpretation Act, 1999
Land Transfer Act, 1952
Property Law Act, 1952
Public Works Act, 1981
Resource Management Act, 1991
Te Ture Whenua Maori, 1993 (also called Maori Land Act, 1993)

Bibliography

Brown, D. 1996. *Land Acquisition*. 4th ed. Sydney: Butterworths.

Farman, P. 1983. *Compulsory Acquisition and Compensation*. Wellington: Butterworths "Laws of New Zealand."

Salmond, P. 1982. *The Compulsory Acquisition of Land in New Zealand*. Wellington: Butterworths.

Toomey, J. E. 1996. "The Offer-back Provisions in the Public Works Act 1981—A Fair Deal for the Parties?" *Canterbury Law Review* 7 (1996): 272–291.

Williams, D. 1999. "Public Works Takings and Treaty Settlements." *New Zealand Law Journal* (July 1999): 262–263.

Chapter 8

Compulsory Purchase in Singapore

WILLIAM J. M. RICQUIER

The emergence of Singapore as a tiny but audible voice on the world stage has been one of the most remarkable features of the history of Asia since the end of World War II. After independence from Britain and separation from Malaysia in 1965, Singapore was still a scruffy seaport harboring apparently justifiable doubts about her ability to "go it alone." Thirty years or so later, Singapore has emerged as a significant economic power, renowned for competitiveness and efficiency, and with a voice in the world belying her physical size.

Appearances can be deceptive, but more often than not they provide a telling impression of the reality that lies below the surface. The impression presented by Singapore is modernity tempered by tradition and a sophisticated cityscape tinged with tropical greenery. The physical transformation of postcolonial Singapore has been as startling as its economic and political development. Gleaming skyscrapers tower over lovingly restored shophouses in the business district located near the historic waterfront, while outside the city center serried ranks of public housing blocks provide good-quality, affordable housing for roughly 85 percent of the city-state's population. Elsewhere, industrial estates and technology parks testify to the continued growth—notwithstanding the "Asian financial crisis"—of one of Asia's legendary "tiger" economies.

While it would be misguided to attribute Singapore's progress solely or even primarily to the existence of a developed system of compulsory land acquisition, it would be naive to downplay its significance. Singapore's progress has not been haphazard or accidental, in physical and

---

Partner, Tan Rajah & Cheah.

urban planning or in anything else. The existence of compulsory acquisition legislation has been a vital link in the chain of regeneration and progress.

Land Law in Singapore

It is sensible to begin with a brief introduction to Singapore land law. The starting point for any discussion of Singapore law must be the Second Charter of Justice,[1] by virtue of which English law as it existed on November 26, 1826, and subject to modifications due to local custom and the like, was received in Singapore.[2] The question of precisely what was received, and subject to what modifications, is a complex one, on which it would be profitless to dwell at length here, but it should be pointed out that in the context of real property, all the basic common law and equitable rules were received, together with those statutes that were not held to be of "purely local" (English) significance.[3] Thus, the Statute of Frauds 1677[4] became part of the law of Singapore and remained so (in part)[5] despite its repeal in England, until the passage of the Application of English Law Act[6] in 1993.

The questions of what English law has been received in Singapore since 1826 is one of infinite complexity. Again confining the discussion to land law, the common law (as opposed to statute) has generally continued to be applied. This was historically by virtue of the Charter and is now enshrined in the provisions of the Application of English Law Act. Whatever the theory, the fact is that post-1826 common law developments, such as restrictive covenants and the various types of license, have taken root in Singapore.[7] There is no doubt that post-1826 English statutes do not generally apply (subject to the Application of English Law Act). In 1878, the Civil Law Ordinance[8] of the Straits Settlements (still in force in Singapore as the Civil Law Act),[9] in a section the precise ambit of which was the subject of much speculation,[10] provided for the continuing reception of English "mercantile law." Section 6(2) of the Ordinance[11] provided as follows: "Nothing therein shall be taken to introduce into Singapore any part of the law of England relating to the tenure or conveyance or assurance of or succession to, any immovable property, or any estate, right or interest therein."

Hence, the 1925 property legislation does not apply in Singapore. Transfers of land must be drafted so as to comply with the rule against perpetuities, unaffected by the Perpetuities and Accumulations Act.[12] Thelluson's Act[13] was received, but the Prescription Act was not.[14] (Section 5 of the Civil Law Act was repealed by the Application of English Law Act.)

Of course, even by the time of the Civil Law Ordinance, Singapore was acquiring its own land law. In the first years of colonial rule, Singapore, Penang, and Malacca were administered as a part of British India, and "Indian acts" were the relevant legislation.[15] A number of these acts dealt with land law.[16] From 1867, however, the three Straits Settlements came to be governed directly from London as a separate colony.[17] Most of the existing property legislation in Singapore dates from this period and is very similar to provisions found in the English Vendors and Purchasers Act[18] and Conveyancing Acts[19] of the 1880s. In their details, these provisions do not differ drastically from their counterparts in the English property legislation of 1925 (leaving aside the major reforms brought about by that legislation). It should be noted that Singapore has a Registration of Deeds Act[20] based loosely on the Yorkshire Registries Act of 1884,[21] but no system for the registration of "charges" on unregistered land as such. Singapore also has a Land Titles Act[22] (first enacted in 1956), which established a form of land registration based on the Australian Torrens system.[23]

One act that originated in the 1880s but is not similar to any contemporaneous English provision is the State Lands Act.[24] This merits some comment. The Act, according to its short title, is "an Act to regulate the alienation and occupation of State land." Because of the application of the doctrine of tenure to Singapore, all land is subject to the statute. The statute (and the rules made thereunder)[25] specify four modes of alienation from the state to private individuals: the fee simple (but only in very limited circumstances);[26] the estate in perpetuity; the lease; and the temporary occupation license.[27] The estate in perpetuity is a statutory creation,[28] similar in duration to the fee simple, but automatically subject (like state leases) to a variety of conditions and covenants in favor of the state.[29] In these circumstances, section 8[30] is noteworthy in providing as follows:

An assignee of, or any person who becomes a proprietor of any land in Singapore, shall be bound by such exceptions, reservations, or covenants (restrictive or otherwise) contained in the Crown grant or lease, or State grant or lease, irrespective of whether he has notice (actual or constructive) of such exceptions, reservations or covenants.

This is, to say the least, a somewhat sweeping provision, eradicating in a single sentence the force behind the distinction between the enforceability of positive and negative covenants, and the doctrine of notice, insofar as they relate to alienation from the state.[31] A final provision to note is rule 10 of the State Lands Rules,[32] which provides that "The title ordinarily to be issued shall be a lease for a term not exceeding ninety-nine years."

It might be thought that the amount of land which the state had available to alienate in the years since 1968 would be relatively small. This is not the case. Indeed, the amount of state land (as opposed to land in private ownership) rose from 49 percent in 1969 to approximately 65 percent in 1975, and there is no reason to believe that this trend has altered.[33] There are various possible reasons for this phenomenon,[34] but there is little doubt about the principal one: the provisions of the Land Acquisition Act.[35]

The Urban Redevelopment Authority

Before looking at the Land Acquisition Act in detail, it might be useful to make a few general remarks about the most important body with general town planning functions in Singapore, namely, the Urban Redevelopment Authority (URA). The URA is the body primarily responsible for the transformation that has taken place in Singapore over the past thirty years. The URA was established in 1973 by the Urban Redevelopment Authority Act[36] of that year and replaced the Urban Renewal Department, which had been a branch of the Housing and Development Board. The URA's powers were considerably extended in 1989.[37]

The broad sweep of the URA's significance is revealed by considering its functions and duties, laid down in section 6. It has to:

(a) prepare or execute or prepare and execute proposals, plans and projects for [inter alia]:
    (i) the clearance, development, and redevelopment of such land as the Authority may think fit for the purpose of resettling persons displaced by the Authority and other resettlement projects approved by the minister or for any other purposes;
    (ii) the erection, conversion, improvement, and extension of any building for sale, lease, rental, or other purpose;
    (iii) the provision and improvement of services and facilities for the promotion of public safety, recreation and welfare.

The URA must also sell, lease, or grant licenses to use or occupy such land belonging to it for the purpose of development and redevelopment as it thinks fit, and manage such lands, buildings, or other property as it thinks fit. The URA has a number of other functions, including making proposals regarding the preservation of monuments and land of historical or traditional interest, providing information to the government about urban redevelopment, collecting and analyzing information about building and land use, and providing and managing car-parking facilities.[38]

The following sections provide the URA with its teeth. By virtue of section 7 it can carry on such activities as appear to it to be "advantageous, necessary or convenient for it to carry on or in connection with its duties," and exercise the various powers granted by the Second Schedule to the Act (e.g., the power to carry out or assist in carrying out [with the approval of the minister] any project in connection with "urban redevelopment"[39] and to "acquire, hire, procure, construct, erect, manufacture, provide, operate, maintain, or repair, anything, whether movable or immovable required by the Authority for the purposes of this Act)." In particular, under section 8 of the URA Act, with the approval of the minister (for national development) the URA may declare an area to be an urban redevelopment area, with the result that the area may be acquired by the government within three years. The URA may, by its employees, agents, or contractors, enter a building or land at all reasonable times to survey, inspect, or carry out any authorized work without being liable to any legal proceedings whatsoever.[40]

It is the powers of the URA, and in particular its power of declaring land to be an urban redevelopment area and setting the acquisition procedure in motion and carrying on objects of urban redevelopment, coupled with its power to hold "land sales," which has been at the heart of Singapore's development since 1973.

Compulsory Acquisition

The first point to note is that the Republic of Singapore has a written constitution.[41] Many of the provisions of that constitution are also to be found in the constitution of Malaysia, of which Singapore was a constituent part between 1963 and 1965.[42] Article 13 of the constitution of Malaysia provides as follows:

13(1) No person shall be deprived of property save in accordance with law.
   (2) No law shall provide for compulsory acquisition of property without adequate compensation.

Upon the separation of Singapore from Malaysia, the question arose of whether to retain this constitutional guarantee. In any event, section 6 of the Republic of Singapore Independence Act of 1965[43] provides that "Article 13 [of the constitution] shall cease to have effect." The prime minister left parliament in no doubt of the government's main objection to the existence of the constitutional guarantee. It would "leave open the door for litigation and ultimately for adjudication by the Courts as to what is or is not to be adequate compensation."[44] One particular matter was of concern, and was referred to by both the prime minister and the minister for law in the parliamentary debate.[45] Cases were occurring where the government was carrying out development and improvements to land as a result of which adjacent land rose appreciably in value. Under the law as it then stood, the government, were it to acquire that land, would have to pay a sum reflecting an improvement that owed nothing to the owner's efforts. It was preferable for benefits arising from land to be shared by all, and not restricted to the fortunate few. In 1966 a Constitutional Commission recommended the reintroduction of Article 13 in a modified form, but the recommendation was rejected.[46] This paved the way for the Land Acquisition Act of 1966[47] (the Act), which remains at the heart of Singapore's transformation into an ultramodern metropolis.

By section 3 of the Act, the president of the Republic of Singapore is authorized to enter a notification in the *Singapore Government Gazette* that land in a locality is likely to be useful for a purpose specified in section 5. Public notices must be put up, and services can be done at this stage. Section 5 in turn provides the government with wide discretion in determining land requirements. Wherever any particular land is needed for any public purpose—or by any person, corporation, or statutory board—for any work or undertaking which, in the opinion of the minister, is of public benefit, of public utility, or in the public interest; or for any residential, commercial, or industrial purposes, the president may declare a notification in the government gazette. That is deemed to be conclusive evidence that the land is needed for the specified purpose. This is a very broad power, and the provision relating to the evidential effect of the notification leaves little scope for judicial review.[48] As was said in one of the few reported cases:

> The Government is the proper authority for deciding what a public purpose is. When the Government declares that a certain purpose is a public purpose, it must be presumed that the Government is in possession of facts which include the Government to declare that the purpose is a public purpose.[49]

Basco Enterprises Pte. Ltd. v. Soh Siang Wai[50] provides an interesting example of an attempt to challenge an acquisition by way of judicial review. In this case, the appellants had been the owners of Stamford House, a splendid colonial building in the heart of Singapore that had been acquired in 1984 (at the prevailing 1973 market value). This acquisition was challenged. (The instant case was actually an appeal against a decision in the High Court in a summons brought against the former owners for trespassing on state land.) One argument was that there was an improper motive or bad faith on the part of the acquiring authority (the URA and the Ministry of National Development), and that they acted improperly and for an improper purpose. The alleged purpose was to acquire the property at the 1973 market value and resell it by open tender at the current market value, thereby making a substantial profit. On this point, the Court of Appeal concurred with the finding of the court below that there was no evidence that the purpose of the acquisition was the making of a profit.

The appellants' second argument related to the use ultimately made of the building: being in a historic part of the city, its façade was preserved while the interior was used for retail outlets. The appellants contended that this was ultra vires the acquisition legislation for two reasons: first, "preservation" was within the exclusive bailiwick of the Preservation of Monuments Board under its governing legislation, the Preservation of Monuments Act.[51] Second, in any event, "preservation" was simply not "urban redevelopment" for the purposes of the URA Act.[52]

On the first of these contentions, the Court of Appeal held that there was no issue regarding the Preservation of Monuments Act; Stamford House, however elegant, was not a "monument." On the broader issue, Chan Sek Keong J (as he then was), delivering the judgment of the Court of Appeal, stated as follows:[53]

> The acquisition of Stamford House must not be considered in isolation as if the public purpose of redevelopment was concerned only with that building. Stamford House was acquired together with other buildings in the area for the purpose of urban redevelopment, and just because, as one aspect only of the redevelopment, its façade is to be preserved or because the whole of the existing building is to be preserved, does not, in our view, mean that it is not within the ambit of urban redevelopment. It is not necessary for us to decide the narrower point whether, if Stamford House had been acquired alone for urban redevelopment, it would have been *ultra vires* the function or power of the URA to carry out that purpose by merely

preserving it. But, having regard to the definition of "urban redevelopment" (which includes reconstruction and repair), it is arguable that the URA is entitled to carry out redevelopment of dilapidated buildings by merely reconstructing and/or repairing them to their original state and condition.

The law of procedural ultra vires is fully applicable to the compulsory acquisition process. Subsection (2) of section 5 lays down requirements that must be included in a notification, namely, the town subdivision or mukim in which the land is located, the lot number and other relevant details of the land, and details of where any plan of the land can be inspected. These requirements are conditions precedent to any acquisition.

The gazette notification is the trigger that gets the acquisition procedure moving. Significantly, it is provided in section 33(6) (section 33 is the principal section on compensation) that "[f]or the purposes of this section, the date of acquisition of any land shall be the date of the publication of the notification under section 5(1) declaring that that land is needed for the purpose specified in the declarations."

After publication of the gazette notification, the minister for national development directs the collector of land revenue to take proceedings to acquire the land, which he commences by notifying "interested persons" that the government intends to acquire the land and that claims for compensation may be made to him. He also has to issue a general notice to be posted in the locality.

It is therefore important to know the "interested persons" because they are the only people who can claim compensation. They are defined in section 2 of the Act as "*including . . .* every person claiming an interest in compensation" but not including a statutory tenant under the Control of Rent Act.[54] This is a circular and somewhat unhelpful definition, but it clearly means that anyone with a legal or beneficial interest in the land to be acquired will be entitled to compensation and therefore to be notified by the collector. The notice to the "interested persons" must contain certain specific information regarding the land to be acquired and requires all persons interested to appear before the collector not earlier than twenty-one days from the date of the notice. The notice also gives details of the information that has to be provided by an interested person intending to claim compensation.

On receipt of claims from interested persons, the collector is to hold an inquiry into the said claims and make awards of compensation accordingly.[55] There is no specific procedure laid down for the inquiry. The resultant award made by the collector to the person or persons interested is in effect an offer that can be accepted or rejected. If rejected, there will be an appeal to the Appeals Board (under section 23 of the Act), a quasi-judicial body that may confirm, reduce, increase, or annul the collector's award, or make such order thereon as it thinks fit. The board's decision is final, but there is a right of appeal to the Court of Appeal on a point of law,[56] and the board itself may state a case on a question of law to the Court of Appeal. (It is not proposed to deal in detail here with the law on appeals.)[57]

In the absence of an appeal, the award becomes final and the collector takes possession of the land under section 16 of the Act after payment of the award. Section 16 requires the collector to post a notice on the subject land and serve a copy on the persons interested. It has been held that it is the serving of this notice, rather than the physical taking of possession, which constitutes "taking possession" for the purposes of the Act.[58]

One supplementary point to be made is that there is a "fast track" method of acquisition under section 17 of the Act. The collector, in cases of urgency and where so directed by the minister, is authorized to take possession of the subject land within seven days of the section 8 notice. Under subsection (2), the minister can direct the collector to take possession of land without the publication of a section 5 notification, provided that such a notification is published not later than seven days after the collector takes possession.

A second supplementary point relates to compulsory acquisition in accordance with the provisions of other statutes (albeit ultimately under the Act). There is a plethora of "statutory boards" in Singapore, quasi-governmental bodies carrying out various functions, such as the provision and management of public housing.[59] Each such body, as the generic descriptive name implies, has been established by statute. A standard provision for the acquisition of land is used to appeal in such statutes. A typical example is what used to be section 21(1) of the Port of Singapore Authority Act,[60] which provided as follows:

21(1)—Where any immovable property, not being state land, is needed for the purposes of the Authority *and cannot be acquired by agreement,* the Authority may request, and the President may, if he thinks fit, direct the acquisition of such property and in such case, such property may be acquired in accordance with the provisions of any written law relating to the acquisition of land for a public purpose and any declaration under any such written law that such land is so needed may be made notwithstanding that compensation is to be paid out of the funds of the Authority, and such declaration shall have effect as if it were a declaration that such land is needed for a public purpose made in accordance with such written law. (Emphasis added).

In *United Engineers Ltd. v. Collector of Land Revenue & Anor, Straits Trading Ltd. v. Collector of Land Revenue & Anor,*[61] each of the plaintiffs contended that the compulsory acquisition of its land by the Authority under section 5 of the Land Acquisition Act was invalid on the ground that the Authority had made no attempt to acquire the land by negotiated agreement, as was allegedly required by section 21. The contention was rejected by the High Court, with Lai J stating, "to accept the construction contended would do violence to the scheme of compulsory acquisition in Singapore."[62] The court held that the words of section 21(1) were inapt, being too oblique to constitute a condition precedent for the operation of section 5. The words emphasized were said to be purely "descriptive." According to Lai J, the Authority had to satisfy the president that the land was not available for acquisition by private treaty. If the president thought fit, compulsory acquisition would be ordered, but this was exclusively a matter between the Authority and the president. This was, in some respects, a curious construction of the words emphasized, but it certainly preserved the integrity of the acquisition system. To remove any doubt, the offending words were taken out of a number of statutes by the Statutes of the Republic of Singapore (Miscellaneous Amendments) Act of 1983, and now the acquisition power has been removed from such statutes.[63]

Reference should be made to the Street Works Act,[64] formerly the Local Government Integration Act.[65] This gives wide powers to the Land Transport Authority for the construction of roads and road-related facilities. The Authority has the right, under section 9, to enter upon and take possession of the land in question after giving the occupier and any person interested not less than two months' notice. Under section 12, an owner of land served with a notice under section 9 can, within two years of the date of the notice, request the president to direct the acquisition of the affected land under the Land Acquisition Act.

The broad powers to acquire land for public purposes have excited little or no controversy in Singapore. This is not so with regard to the basis for assessing compensation. For many years the level of compensation was fixed at no higher than the market value of the acquired property on November 30, 1973. As the property boom of the 1980s saw prices and values escalating, this basis for assessing compensation became increasingly inappropriate, and a system of ex gratie compensatory payments was introduced. The Act has since been amended, however,[66] and section 33(1) lays down the factors that an appeals board (and the collector, by virtue of section 15) will consider in assessing compensation. These are:

(a) (i) the market value (A) as at 1st January 1986 in respect of land acquired on or after 30th November 1987 but before 18th January 1993, (B) as at 1st January 1992 in respect of land acquired on or after 18th January 1993 but before 27th September 1995, and (C) as at 1st January 1995 in respect of land acquired on or after 27th September 1995; and (ii) the market value at the date of the section 3 notification if it is followed within six months by a section 5 declaration in respect of the same land; or (iii) the market value as at the date of the section 5 declaration; *whichever is the lowest;*[67]

(b) any increase in the value of any other land of the person interested likely to accrue from the use to which the land acquired will be put;

(c) any damage sustained by the severance of the acquired land from other land;

(d) any damage sustained by the acquisition injuriously affecting other property, whether movable or immovable;

(e) expenses due to any enforced changes of business or residence; and

(f) fees and costs due to any necessary re-issue and registration of title.[68]

It can be seen that although the law has been amended, the principle of assessing compensation retrospectively has been retained.[69] There is no statutory definition of "market value," so this has to be assessed from first principles, but the Act offers plenty of guidance as to what is to be taken into account and as to what must be disregarded.

Of the matters listed above that are to be taken into account in assessing compensation, item (b) enables the acquiring authority to set off any betterment value accruing to their landowner, while items (c) (severance), (d) (injuries affection), and (e) (disturbance) are clearly matters to which any developed system of compulsory acquisition would look in compensating a dispossessed landowner. Matters (a) and (e) are to be disregarded if the acquired land has been devastated or affected, directly or indirectly, by fire, earthquake, flood, and so on, and if the acquisition takes place within six months of the disaster. Instead, the board is to consider the market value of the land immediately before the disaster, taking into account the fact that the land, being subject to encumbrance, tenants, squatters, and so on, could not have been sold with vacant possession and disregarding the value of any building or other structure. The value of compensation in such a case shall not exceed (a) one-third of the value of such land had it been vacant and not subject to encumbrances, unless the minister specifies otherwise; or (b) the market value as on the various alternative dates referred to above, whichever is the lower.[70] In these circumstances, the owner or occupier may well, of course, have insurance claims in respect of the disaster; such claims are unaffected by the acquisition.[71]

Section 33(5) makes further modifications to the basic principle of assessment set out above as matter (a). These can be briefly disposed of. They all provide grounds for restricting the notional "market value" of the land. For example, any increase in value as a result of improvement during the two years prior to the commencement of the acquisition process is to be disregarded (unless it was made in bona fide and not in contemplation of the acquisition), as is any increase in value due to the use of land in a manner that could be restrained by law, or, within the seven years preceding the instigation of the acquisition procedure to the provision of roads, drains, and other facilities. Similarly, the value of the land is not to exceed the value stated, by or with the knowledge of the owner, in any affidavit, return, or other public document,[72] or the price that a bona fide purchaser might be expected to pay for the land on the basis of its existing use or the use designated in the Master Plan, whichever is the lower, after taking into account zoning and density requirements and other restrictions imposed under the Planning Act.[73] This last provision is particularly significant, as it effectively negates the notion of "potential value" as an aspect of market value, thus depriving the landowner of much of the development value of the acquired land (although he would have to pay tax, in the form of a development charge, if he were to develop the land to its full potential himself).[74]

To ensure that there is absolutely no doubt about the scope of the board's inquiries, section 34 provides a list of factors which the board is *not* to take into account. These include (there are eight in all): the urgency of the acquisition; any disinclination of the person interested to part with the land acquired; any damage likely to be caused to the land in consequence of the use to which it will be put; any increase in value likely to result from such; and evidence of sales of comparable properties, unless the Appeals Board is satisfied that the sales are made for bona fide purposes and not for speculative purposes. The onus of proving the latter is on the appellant.

Town Planning[75]

THE MASTER PLAN

The legal aspects of planning in Singapore are dealt with by the Planning Act.[76] In the planning process, public authorities have both a direct and an indirect role to play. This dichotomy is reflected in Parts II and III of the Planning Act. Part II (sections 6–11) concerns the "Master Plan" (and conservation areas) (which is, in fact, a series of maps but also technically includes the written statement submitted to and approved by the governor in council in 1958 and the rules thereunder and including all alterations), which is to be reviewed every five years by "the competent authority," who is to report to the minister, although the authority can submit proposals for altering the plan at any time.[77] The Master Plan contains the government's general ideas on zoning and other relevant matters and provides the framework in which the URA and private developers operate. The Act makes provision for the amendment of the Master Plan.[78]

PLANNING CONTROL

Part III of the Planning Act (sections 12–24) deals with the development and subdivision of land. No person may "develop" land outside a conservation area without planning permission.[79] "Develop" is defined as to carry out any building, engineering, mining earthworks, or other operations in, on, over, or under land, or the making of any other material change in the use of any building or land.[80] There is, however, a proviso to this, various types of operation being deemed not to constitute development. These include alterations or improvements to a building that do not materially affect its external appearance or floor area; road maintenance by a public authority; and the use of any existing building or land within the curtilage of a dwelling house as such.[81] Such operations, therefore, can be done without permission. Section 3(3) gives examples of "material changes of use"[82] that constitute development and require permission: for example, the use as two or more dwelling-houses of any building previously used as a single dwelling-house; the use as a dwelling-house of any building not originally constructed as one, and vice versa, and the use for the display of advertisements of any external part of a building not normally used for the purpose. It is also provided that the demolition or reconstruction of or addition to a building constitutes development.[83]

No person can subdivide land without first having obtained subdivision approval pursuant to section 12(3) of the Planning Act.[84] Subdivision is defined in section 4(1) as the conveyance, assignment, demise, or disposal, by any deed or instrument of any part of the land in such a manner that the part so disposed of becomes capable of being registered under the Registration of Debtor Act[85] or having a separate folio under the Land Titles Act[86] but excluding in respect of certain types of residential development the grant of a lease in any unit therein for a term not exceeding an aggregate of fourteen years, in respect of certain types of commercial development the grant of any lease for a building or any part of a building comprised in the development for a term not exceeding an aggregate of fourteen years, and in respect of any other land the grant of a lease of the whole or part of the land for a term not exceeding an aggregate of seven years.[87]

Works within a conservation area[88] are not to be carried out without conservation permission.[89] "Conservation areas" are designated by the minister under sections 7, 8, and 9 of the Planning Act. Such an "area, district or premises must be of special architectural, historic, traditional or aesthetic interest" and may comprise an area, a group of buildings, or a single building (section 9(2)).

Section 14 provides for how the competent authority is to deal with applications for the various types of permission. Essentially, save in relation to specified instances, such as the land being required for a public purpose, the competent authority must act in conformity with the Master Plan.[90] It must deal with applications within three months (section 13(2)). It may grant permission, either conditional or unconditional, or refuse it (section 14(4)). When the application is refused, or granted conditionally, reasons must be given. The minister may direct that any application be referred to him instead, and his decision is final (section 21). Any conditions may limit the period for which permission is granted and may provide, for example, inter alia for the commencement or completion of any work before the expiration for a specific period, for requiring 30 percent of the floor area of any development to be under the ownership of one person for a period of ten years from the date of the latest grant of a temporary occupation license before the grant of the certificate of fitness in respect of the development;[91] or restrictions as to height and the prohibition of subdivision.[92]

Any permission granted lapses if the development is not completed within two years of the date of grant or of the determination of any appeal,[93] but the competent authority can renew the permission for any period it considers necessary.

If it appears to the competent authority that there has been a breach of planning control in respect of any land, it may serve an information notice on the owner or occupier of such land or on any person carrying out operation on such land requiring them to provide certain information regarding the planning status of the land and/or the operations being conducted.[94] It is a criminal offense not to comply with the terms of an information notice.[95]

The competent authority in the event of development being carried out without permission or in breach of any condition imposed thereunder may serve[96] an enforcement notice requiring the steps therein directed to be taken, to the owner or occupier of the land, or to anyone responsible, in the authority's view, for the contravention. Noncompliance with an enforcement notice is a criminal offense.[97] Any applicant aggrieved by a refusal of permission to develop or subdivide, or by a conditional grant, may appeal to the minister within twenty-eight days of the notification of the decision; his decision is final (section 22(1)).

The competent authority may apply for an injunction to restrain any apprehended breach of planning control.[98] The competent authority is given various powers to facilitate the exercise of its functions and the recovery of any money due, for example, by attaching and selling a person's land.[99] Section 61 empowers the minister to make rules regarding every aspect of the planning process, from the development of land to the procedure for the handling of applications and appeals.

DEVELOPMENT CHARGE

The owner (or the developer) in effect pays for the permission granted by the competent authority by way of a development charge levied on any planning or conservation permission.[100]

The development charge is the difference between the Development Baseline[101] and the Development Ceiling[102] and is determined by the competent authority in accordance with the provision of section 38. The competent authority may first make an interim (estimated) order in respect of any proposed development. Where an interim order is issued, the competent authority shall, within twelve months from the date of the grant of planning or conservation permission, determine the actual amount of the development charge and issue a final order.[103] If no final award is made at the end of the twelve-month period, the interim order is deemed to be the final order.[104]

Any person dissatisfied with an interim order may make a written request for the competent authority to determine the development charge in accordance with section 39,[105] subsection (3) of which provides that the development charge payable for any planning or conservation permission in respect of the proposed development shall be a prescribed percentage of any appreciation in the value of the land arising from the grant of the relevant permission to develop the land. For the purposes of subsection (3), the chief valuer or such other person as the minister may appoint shall determine the amount of appreciation, if any, in the value of the land.[106] The competent authority may by interim order require the payment of an estimated amount of development charge to be determined with similar consequences to where the determination is made pursuant to section 38.[107] If a person liable to pay any development charge under this section is dissatisfied with any interim order or any final order, she or he can appeal to the minister, whose decision shall be final. The minister is specifically authorized to make rules with regard to development charge.[108]

Conclusion

Compulsory purchase is a necessary process, but inevitably a painful one for its "victims." That one is making a contribution to the common cause may be a limited consolation. Money can soften the blow, and it is important that in these circumstances reasonable compensation is paid. Ironically, perhaps, the current dip in Singapore property prices may well bring about an absolutely fair compensation system. The artificially weighted compensation system has not always worked fairly but it has *worked*. Singapore has managed to become a planned city that has not lost its heart or soul. The compulsory acquisition system has had a part to play in this. In the future, it will be possible to say of the unsung planners of Singapore something similar to what is said of Sir Christopher Wren on his otherwise unmarked grave in St. Paul's Cathedral, London: "If you seek this monument, look around you."

Notes

1. Letters Patent Establishing the Court of Judicature at the Prince of Wales' Island (Penang), Singapore, and Malacca in the East Indies. The First Charter of Justice, issued in 1807 and couched in virtually identical terms, applied solely in Penang. There was a Third Charter of Justice, promulgated in 1855, but this had no relevance to the importation of English law. See R. S. Braddell, *The Law of the Straits Settlements, A Commentary* (Kuala Lumpur: Oxford University Press, reprint 1982), 34.

2. See ibid., 14–20, where some of the leading cases (actually dealing with the effect of the First Charter) are discussed. A good general account of the reception of English law in what is now the state of Singapore is G. W. Bartholomew's "Introduction" to the *Tables of the Written Laws of the Republic of Singapore 1819–1971* (Singapore: Maloya L. Reu., 1972).

3. See generally W. J. M. Ricquier, *Land Law* (Singapore: Butterworths, 1995), 2nd ed., vol. 7. On this basis, *Choa Choon Neoh v. Spottiswood*, the English Statutes of Mortmain have been assumed to be inapplicable in Singapore: 2 Ky. 216 (1869).

4. 29 Car. 2, chapter 3.

5. Section 4 (enforceability of contracts) remained in force while section 3 (assignments of leases) was arguably repealed by section 53 of Conveyancing and Law of Property Act (Cap 61, 1994 rev. ed.)

6. Cap 7A, 1994 rev. ed.

7. See Ricquier, *Land Law*, 6 and *passim*. See also Ricquier, "Land Law and the Common Law in Singapore," in *The Common Law in Singapore and Malaysia*, ed. Harding (Singapore: Butterworths, 1965).

8. Ordinance No. IV of 1878.

9. Cap 43, 1994, rev. ed.

10. See, e.g., Bartholomew, "Introduction," *passim*; Hickling, "Civil Law (Amendment No. 2) Act 1979 (No. 24), Section 5 of the Civil Law Act: Snark or Boojum?", 21 *Mal. L. Rev.* 351; Soon and Phang, "Reception of English Commercial Law in Singapore—a Century of Uncertainty," in *The Common Law in Singapore and Malaysia*, 33.

11. Subsequently section 5 of the Act: see *supra*, note 9.

12. 1964, chapter 55.

13. Accumulations Act 1800 (39 & 40, Geo. 3, ch. 98); see *In the Matter of the Estate of Tan Kim Seng* (1897) 4 S.S.L.R. 148.

14. The doctrine of the lost modern grant has been held applicable: *China Mohamed v. The Yan Poh* (1914) 13 S.S.L.R. 39.

15. See Bartholomew, "The Singapore Statute Book," *Mal. L. Rev.* 26 (1984): 1, 5–11.

16. Indian Act No. XX of 1837 (real property to be regarded as chattels real for purposes of devolution on death): Act No. XXXI of 1854 (abolishing the real actions).

17. See Braddel, *The Law of the Straits Settlements*, 38.

18. (1874) 37 & 38, Vict., chapter 78.

19. (1881) 44 & 45, Vict., chapter 41; (1882) 45 & 46. Vict., chapter 39.

20. Cap 269, 1989, rev. ed.

21. (1884) 47 & 48, Vict., chapter 54.

22. Cap 157, 1994, rev. ed.

23. See generally R. Baalman, *The Singapore Torrens System* (Singapore: The Government of the State of Singapore, 1961). There is also legislation governing "strata title."

24. Cap 314, 1985, rev. ed. See generally Ricquier, *Land Law*, 11–14.

25. In particular, the State Lands Rules 1968, section 290/93.

26. See sections 14–18 of the Act.

27. These are governed by the State Lands Rules, *supra* note 25, rules 19–25.

28. See Sheridan, *Malaya and Singapore, The Borneo Territories* (London: Stevens, 1961), 14–21, chapter 13.

29. These reserve mineral rights, rights of access, rights to collect ground rent, and so on, and are collectively quite sweeping; see sections 4–6 of the Act, and generally Ricquier, *Land Law*, 12–13.

30. Inserted by the State Lands (Amendment) Act, Act No. 33 of 1980.

31. The amendment was passed in response to a Privy Council decision on the enforceability of covenants in Crown grants, *Collector of Land Revenue v. Hoalim* (1977) 1 M.L.J. 88. In regard to leases, this might be a case of ex-abundante cautela, but an estate in perpetuity seems more like a freehold than a leasehold estate.

32. *Supra* note 25.

33. See Motha, *Singapore Real Property Guide* (Singapore: Guins Pty Ltd., 2nd ed., 1982), 7–13.

34. These are, for example, the provisions for forfeiture by the state in the State Lands Act; land that is "abandoned" becomes state land: State Lands Encroachments Act, Cap 315, sections 9–11; land belonging to someone who dies intestate with no one entitled to his or her property reverts to the state: Intestate Succession Act Cap 46, section 7, rule 9; even before adverse possession was abolished there could be no adverse possession of state land: State Lands Encroachments Act, section 12; and reclaimed land becomes state land: Foreshores Act, Cap 113.

35. Cap 152, 1985 rev. ed. See Khublall, *Compulsory Land Acquisition—Singapore and Malaysia* (Singapore: Butterworths, 1994) ("Khublall"); and Koh, "The Law of Compulsory Acquisition in Singapore" 2 *M.L.J.* 2 (1967): ix.

36. No. 65 of 1973.

37. The current Act is the Urban Redevelopment Authority Act, Cap 340, 1990, rev. ed. This Act effected a merger between the old URA and the Planning Department of the Ministry of National Development.

38. See Planning (Provision of Car Parks) Rules, Cap 232, R. 4, 1990 ed.

39. Defined in section 2 as involving "the construction, reconstruction, extension, repair, alteration, change of use, aggregation and subdivision of a building and change of uses, aggregation and subdivision of land."

40. Section 16.

41. Constitution of the Republic of Singapore (1992 rev. ed.).

42. See generally Jayakumar, *Constitutional Law* (Singapore: Malaya L. Rev., 1976).

43. No. 9 of 1965.

44. Singapore Parliamentary Debates, vol. 25, col. 1051.

45. Ibid.

46. See Jayakumar, *Constitutional Law*, 4.

47. No. 41 of 1966.

48. See Chinkin, "Abuse of Discretion in Malaysia and Singapore," in *The Common Law in Singapore and Malaysia*, 259.

49. *Galstaun v. Attorney-General* (1981) 1 M.L.J. 9, at 10, per Chua J.

50. (1990) 1 M.L.J. 193.

51. Cap 239, 1985 rev. ed.

52. Cap 390, 1990 rev. ed.

53. (1990) 1 M.L.J. 193, at 199.

54. Cap 58, 1985 rev. ed.

55. Section 9.

56. Section 29.

57. See Khublall, *Compulsory Land Acquisition*, chapter 5.

58. *Singapore Woodcraft Manufacturing Co. (Pte) Ltd. v. Mok Ah Sai* (1979) 2 M.L.J. 16C.

59. Housing and Development Act (Cap 129, 1985 rev. ed.). This Act contains its own unique scheme of "compulsory acquisition." Section 56 enables the Housing and Development Board (HDB) to acquire flats compulsorily from their owners (long lessees of the HDB). Causes (fourteen in all) triggering this power of acquisition include the owner and his spouse ceasing to occupy the premises; the premises being used, in the opinion of the HDB, otherwise than for the purpose permitted by the lease; breach or nonobservance of condition if the HDB is of the opinion that he or she is likely to continue to do the same if he or she remains in possession; the making of a misleading or false statement in the owner's application for the premises; the making of a misrepresentation of a material fact, whether innocently or otherwise, in the owner's application; assignment, subletting, or parting with possession without the HDB's prior consent; the fact that, in the opinion of the HDB, the premises are not being occupied by such minimum number of persons as the HDB may require; conviction for an immigration offense; and conviction for a so-called killer-litter offense (involving the ejection of articles from the windows and balconies of upper-story flats). The

HDB must serve a notice stating its intention to acquire and the amount of compensation (to be determined by the HDB) for the owner and any "interested persons," and they have twenty-eight days in which to object "to the acquisition and compensation offered by the HDB." The HDB must consider the objection and may either disallow it or allow it in part or in whole, its decision being subject to an appeal to the minister, whose decision is final.

60. Cap 209 (1985 rev. ed.).

61. (1982) 2 M.L.J. 152.

62. Ibid., at 155.

63. Indeed, section 21(1) of the Port of Singapore Authority Act (Cap 236) provides that "No compulsory acquisition of any immovable property before 15th April 1983 shall be called in question in any court on the ground that the acquisition was not in compliance with section 20 as in force before that date."

64. Cap 320A.

65. Cap 210.

66. By Act No. 2 of 1988 and Act No. 9 of 1993 and Act No. 40 of 1995.

67. This reflects the various dates with effect from which the compensation provision of principal Act have been amended, most recently by the Land Acquisition (Amendment) by Act No. 2 of 1988 and Act No. 40 of 1995.

68. Land Acquisition Act, Cap 152, section 33(1).

69. See *Collector of Land Revenue v. Ang Thian Soo* (1990) 1 M.L.J. 327 on the construction of "as at." The Appeals Board has to put a value on the land in its developed state (it being developed after the specified and relevant valuation date) but reflecting the market value at the earlier relevant valuation date, e.g., January 1, 1992.

70. Section 33(3).

71. Section 33(4).

72. Section 33(5)(d).

73. Section 33(5)(e).

74. See generally Khublall *Compulsory Land Acquisition*, 127ff.

75. See N. Khublall and B. Yuen, *Development Control and Planning Law in Singapore* (1991).

76. Cap 232, 1998 rev. ed.

77. The competent authority can also prepare and certify as a "Certified Interpretation Plan" any plan on a scale larger than the Master Plan: Planning Act, section 7.

78. Ibid., section 8. See also Planning (Master Plan) Rules, Cap 232, R. 1, 2000 ed.

79. Planning Act, Cap 232, section 12(1).

80. Ibid., section 3(1). See *Public Prosecutor v. Khoon Eng Seng* (1994) 2 SLR 71 (HC).

81. Ibid., section 3(2).

82. See further Planning (Use Classes) Rules, Cap 232, R. 2, 1990 ed., providing that changes of use within certain defined classes do not constitute development.

83. Planning Act, Cap 232, section 3(3)(d).

84. Subdivision approval is required for the partition of land among co-owners according to *Abu Bakar v. Jawahir & Ors* (1993) 2 SLR 738 (HC) 742 per Rajendran J.

85. Cap 269, 1989 rev. ed. The wording suggests, misleadingly, that title is registered under the Registration of Deeds Act.

86. Cap 157, 1994 rev. ed.

87. Planning Act, Cap 232, section 4(2) and Schedule 2. In computing the duration of a lease for these purposes, an option for renewal is taken into consideration but not a provision for early termination: section 3(4).

88. The phrase is defined in section 2 to include "any development of land within a conservation area and decorative, painting, renovation or other works (whether internal or external) which may affect the character or appearance, of any building, within a conservation area."

89. Ibid., section 12(2).

90. For details of planning application regulations, see the Planning (Development) Rules, Cap 232, R. 3, 1990 ed.

91. This provision is designed to involve developers in the maintenance of condominium blocks prior to the issue of a strata title under the Land Titles (Strata) Act, Cap 158, 1999 rev. ed.

92. Planning Act, Cap 232, section 15.

93. Ibid., section 20(1).

94. Ibid., section 25.

95. Ibid., section 26.

96. See *Public Prosecutor v. Abdul Razak Valibhoy* (1993) 3 SLR 902 (HC) on requirements for valid service and policy considerations.

97. Planning Act, Cap 232, section 30. See *Chuan Hoe Engineering Pte. Ltd. v. Public Prosecutor* (1996) 3 SLR 544 (HC). It is also an offense to develop land without permission: section 12(4).

98. Planning Act, Cap 232, section 33.

99. Ibid., section 43.

100. Planning Act, section 35ff. Indeed the competent authority will not grant planning or conservation permission until the amount of development charge estimated pursuant to section 38 has been secured or paid: Ibid. section 37(3). The charge is levied on the owner or on the person who applied for the relevant planning permission, section 37(1).

101. Defined as "the value of one of the following developments which, when calculated in accordance with the prescribed method and rates, gives the highest figure:

(a) any development for which that land was allocated in the Master Plan as approved by the Governor in Council on 5th August 1958 under the provisions of Part IV of the Singapore Improvement Ordinance (Cap 259, 1995 ed.);

(b) any development for which that land was allocated in the Master Plan as the result of any alteration or addition made under section 6(1) of the former (repealed) Planning Act prior to 24th April 1982; or

(c) any development of that land in respect of which:
   (i) development charge, where payable, has been paid;
   (ii) no development charge is payable by reason of any exemption under this Act or the repealed Act; and
   (iii) development charge is not payable under the written law in force when written permission was granted for the development of that land or any part thereof.

(But where the value of any development referred to in (a) or (b) above cannot be ascertained, the Development Baseline is determined without reference to any such development and any development of land, being a development in respect of which no development charge is payable by reason of any exemption under the Act or the former Planning Act, is to be disregarded for the purposes of determining the Development Baseline for the land if any term of the exemption provides that the development must be disregarded for that purpose or has ceased to be or is not complied with.) Any development of the land before the current zoning (i.e., the most recent zoning at the material date—the date of the application for permission) and previous zoning of the land took effect is to be disregarded. Where the Development Baseline for any land cannot be ascertained according to this formula, it is deemed to be the value of the last development of the land before the material date, being a development which was duly authorised by written permission. Where the Development Baseline can still not be ascertained in the competent authority may, with the prior approval of the Minister, assign the Development Baseline for that lands. Ibid., section 36(1)-(6).

102. Defined as the total of the following when calculated in accordance with the prescribed method and rates:

(a) the value of the development of the land previously authorized and to be retained; and

(b) the value of the development of the land to be authorized by the written permission: section 36(7).

103. Ibid., section 38(4).
104. Ibid., section 38(5).
105. Ibid., section 39(2).
106. Ibid., section 38(4).
107. Ibid., section 38(5) & (6).
108. Ibid., section 40. See the Planning (Development Charges) Rules,

Cap 232, 2000 ed., R. 5 of which set out detailed formulas for determining the Development Baseline and the Development Ceiling with reference to quantifiable characteristics such as plot ratio, and method of controlling development by reference to the maximum density permitted by reference to floor area and site area. Originally it was applicable only to commercial developments, residential developments being governed originally in the Master Plan by "residential density," but since 1989 the "residential density" has been converted to an "equivalent plot ratio" by a calculation set out in the Planning (Development Charges) Rules. Also see the Planning Development Charge—Exemption Rules Cap 232, R. 6, 1997 ed.

References

Constitution of the Republic of Singapore (1999 reprint)

Housing and Development Act, Cap 129, 1997 rev. ed.

Land Acquisition Act, Cap 152, 1998 rev. ed.

Planning Act, Cap 232, 1998 rev. ed.

Republic of Singapore Independence Act, No. 9 of 1965

Street Works Act, Cap 320A, 1998 rev. ed.

Urban Redevelopment Authority Act, Cap 340, 1990 rev. ed.

S. Angel, R.W. Arger, S. Tamphiphat & E. A. Wegelin (eds.), *Land for Housing the Poor* (Singapore: Selec Books, 1983)

S. Jayakumar, *Constitutional Law* (Singapore: Malaya L. Reu., 1976)

N. Khublall, *Compulsory Land Acquisition—Singapore and Malaysia* (Singapore: Butterworths, 1994)

N. Khublall B. Yuen, *Development Control and Planning Law in Singapore* (Singapore: Longmans, 1991)

T. T. B. Koh, *The Law of Compulsory Acquisition in Singapore*, 2 M.L.J. ix (1967)

Tan Sook Yee, *Principles of Singapore Land Law* (Singapore: Butterworths, 1994)

Chapter 9

The Land Use Zoning Control and the Land Expropriation System in Taiwan

The System of Land Use Planning in Taiwan

Taiwan is approximately 36,000 square kilometers in size. As far as the system of current land use planning is concerned, it can be classified into three tiers: the highest tier is "Land General Development Planning," the middle tier is "Regional Planning," and the lowest tier is "Urban Planning" and "Nonurban Land Use Planning." Among the land use planning of these tiers, higher planning guides lower planning.

Land General Development Planning aims at formulating the long-term policies and concepts with respect to the future space allocation of population, land, industry activities, material public facilities, nature resources, and so on in Taiwan. Basically, it is the guiding principle involving policies and concepts. Although Land General Development Planning is the highest guiding principle of Taiwan's land use, its formulating procedure and effect do not have any legal foundation.

Regional Planning with the region as its planning sphere was promulgated according to the provisions of the Regional Planning Law (enacted in 1974) and under the goals and the development ideas of Land General Development Planning. Its content mainly regulates the urban development pattern within the region, regional public facilities, industry zoning, the development and preservation of natural resources, and nonurban

Associate professor, National Chengchi University.

286

land use planning. At present, Regional Planning covers Northern, Central, Southern, and Eastern Taiwan.

Urban Planning concretely and in detail regulates the use of the land within an urban area or the use of land planned to be developed as an urban area under the guideline of Regional Planning and according to the provisions of the Urban Planning Law (enacted in 1939). At present, there are an estimated 444 Urban Planning areas with the total size of approximately 4,584 square kilometers.

To realize the goal and content of the above-mentioned land use planning, the administrative governing authorities carry out land use zoning control according to the laws and often adopt the appropriation methods to acquire such land for public works or urban development as regulated under Land Use Planning. This essay explains the system of land use zoning control and the land expropriation system in Taiwan, and provides a brief review of such systems.

Land Use Zoning Control

Land use zoning control in Taiwan can be classified into two categories: urban land and nonurban land with the application of different laws and regulations. Urban land, that is, the land within the area of Urban Planning promulgated according to the laws, is mainly controlled according to the Urban Planning Law. Nonurban land means land outside the area of Urban Planning. Its use is controlled according to the Regional Planning Law, and Rules for the Nonurban Land Use Control, which is authorized to be enacted by the Ministry of the Interior.[1]

URBAN LAND USE CONTROL

According to the Urban Planning Law, Urban Planning can divide the land into such land use zones as the residential zone, the commercial zone, the industrial zone, the agricultural zone, the conservation zone, the administration zone, the culture and education zone, the scenic zone, and the specified use zone (Art. 32). It also zones such public facility land as parks, roads, schools, and markets (Art. 42). After Urban Planning is put into effect, the purpose of the land and building of each classified zone, the size of the building base, the Construction Shelter Ratio, the Floor Area Ratio, the building height, and such relevant matters as traffic, landscape, and fire prevention all are controlled by the provisions of the Urban Planning Law. In addition, the land, after classified as land for public facilities, and before being used for public facilities, can be used only temporarily in addition to its continued original use.

Where the use of the land or the building within the area of Urban Planning violates the provisions of the Urban Planning Law, the owner of such land or building is fined between NT $60,000 and NT $300,000, and ordered to remove, amend, or cease to use the building. The owner or the user of the land or the building who does not remove, amend, or cease to use the building may be successively punished, water and electricity will cease to be supplied, and the building will be sealed or forcefully removed (Art. 79, the Urban Planning Law).

Also, after Urban Planning is put into effect, in principle every zone classified may not be changed at will. The governmental authority regulating Urban Planning, however, should conduct a comprehensive review every five years, and make the necessary changes on the basis of the condition of the urban development and the suggestion of the city residents. Furthermore, land for unnecessary public facilities should be canceled and rezoned (Art. 26, the Urban Planning Law). In case of the occurrence of any major disasters, or to serve the national cause such as the construction of the nation's major infrastructure, Urban Planning may be changed according to the legal procedure, depending on the actual need (Art. 27, the Urban Planning Law).

Nonurban Land Use Control

According to the provision of Article 15, the Regional Planning Law, for nonurban land, on the basis of the "Nonurban Land Zoning Use Plan," drafted in accordance with Regional Planning, the municipal or competent city/county government[2] enacts a "Nonurban Land Use Zoning Map," codifies the variety of "Land Uses," and then promulgates them as well as enforces their control. According to the provision of Article 2, the Rules for the Nonurban Land Control, nonurban land can be classified into one of ten zones: the specified agricultural zone, the general agricultural zone, the industrial zone, the village zone, the forestry zone, the slope preservation zone, the scenic zone, the river zone, the national park zone, and the specified special zone. According to the nature of every zone, eighteen land use categories are codified, such as A-grade construction land, B-grade construction land, C-grade construction land, D-grade construction land, arable and pastoral land, forestland, fish culture land, salt industry land, mining industry land, pottery industry land, transportation and communications land, irrigation and drainage land, recreation land, historical site land, ecological conservation land, protection and conservation land, cemetery land, and land for special purposes.

After nonurban land has been zoned and categorized, its use is only limited to the items of use allowed in Rules for the Nonurban Land Control. For example, the A-grade construction land is limited to the building use of the farmhouse, D-grade construction land is limited to the building use of the industry facility, and arable and pastoral land is limited to the use of the agriculture and ranching production (Art. 6, Rules for the Nonurban Land Use Control). When the land is for building use, its Construction Shelter Ratio and Floor Area Ratio should also be controlled and not exceed the legal standard (Art. 9, Rules for the Nonurban Land Use Control).

When the use of nonurban land violates the provisions of use control, the municipal or competent city/county government fines the owner or the user of the land or the structure on the land between NT $60,000 and NT $300,000, and may order the change of use, the cease of use, or the removal of the structure on the land within the specified deadline. Those who do not comply with the order within such a deadline to change the use, cease the use, or remove the structure on the land may be successively punished, water and electricity will cease to be supplied, and the building will be sealed or be forcefully removed (Art. 21, the Regional Planning Law).

In principle, nonurban land should be used according to its category. To respond to the need of the industrial activities, however, the landowner can submit such documents as the plan to establish the undertaking, and apply to the municipal or competent city/county government, where the land is located, for a change of the land category. After being legally reviewed by the municipal or competent city/county government, along with other relevant governmental authorities, to meet the qualification of permit, the category of the land is permitted to change (Art. 12, Rules for the Nonurban Land Use Control). Upon the application of the land category change, under certain circumstances, the landowner has the obligation to donate land or money. For example, upon the application of the land category change into recreation land, the landowner should set up the green land for the environmental protection and the public facilities within the extent required of the plan. The green land set up should not be less than 30 percent of the total size of the undertaken plan to be established and is donated to the municipal or competent city/county government. If the land applied for category change is arable and pastoral land, forestland, fish culture land, or irrigation and drainage land, 12 percent of the total value of the land that is permitted to change into recreation land should be donated (Art. 23, Rules for the Nonurban Land Use Control). The purpose of such land or money donation is to lower the impact on the surrounding environment as a result of the category change and to absorb into the public property some profits created as a result of such land category change.

Issues of Land Use Control in Taiwan

In the system of land use planning in Taiwan at present, due to the lack of a legal foundation, the content of the highest tier, Land General Development Planning, is not enforceable, and it is difficult to provide the effective guidance and coordination to land use planning of the lower tier. Therefore, usually the situation arises that the content of urban planning or the category coding of nonurban land does not match the goal of land development planning so that the land cannot be systematically and reasonably used.

Land use zoning control is divided into two categories of urban land and nonurban land to be controlled. Land use zoning control is closely related to the rights of the landowner. Therefore, from the standpoint of protecting the property of the people, it is necessary and important that in the decision-making process of land use zoning, the relevant owners should have an opportunity to participate or voice their opinion. In the decision-making process of land use zoning in Taiwan, however, only for urban land, during the formulation period of urban planning, will the planning draft be exhibited in public for thirty days and can the public present their opinion letters. In the case of nonurban land, during the period of land use zoning and land category coding, the relevant owners have no chance to issue their opinion. In addition, those relevant owners who are not satisfied with the outcome of nonurban land use zoning and land category coding do not have any chance to seek restitution. Therefore, in view of the due process of law, the system of nonurban land use control is not reasonable.

Land use zoning control has been legally enforced for urban land and nonurban land in Taiwan. Furthermore, there is punishment and forcible execution in the law against the violators of such provisions. But, in fact, because the municipal or competent city/county government does not seriously crack down on violators of land use zoning control, situations with respect to the illegal use of the land or buildings, and illegal land development can be seen everywhere.

Besides, as previously mentioned, when the use category of nonurban land is applied for coding change, the landowner has to set up green land for the environmental protection and donate land or money to the government. Although this measure finds its basis in Rules for the Nonurban Land Use Control, the Regional Planning Law only authorizes the Ministry of the Interior to enact such rules (executive order) to enforce nonurban land use control. It is the general belief that the authorization extent of such law does not include the request of the landowner to donate land or money. Its validity is highly questionable.

Legal Authority of Land Expropriation in Taiwan

In line with public interest, the government will inevitably expropriate people's property rights, which are protected by the constitution, but only through lawful procedures as necessary. As expressly set forth in Article 15 of the constitution of the Republic of China on Taiwan (enacted in 1946), "the right of property shall be guaranteed to the people." The constitution, nevertheless, does not provide prerequisites and procedures regarding expropriation.

The Land Law (enacted in 1930) contains a specific chapter, "Land Expropriation," providing such prerequisites and procedures. In addition to the Land Law, the Equalization of Land Rights Act, the Urban Planning Law, the Encouragement of the Upgrading of Industry Act, the Science-Based Industrial Park Establishment and Management Act, and the Public Housing Act, among others, have specifically provided clauses regarding land expropriation. Regarding the criteria of compensation for expropriated land, quite significant discrepancies have been seen in these laws. As a remedy, the Land Expropriation Act was enacted and officially enforced in February 2000, with a specific clause that the Land Expropriation Act shall be preferentially applicable. To put it in more understandable terms, the Land Expropriation Act has become an ex facto special law on land expropriation.

Taiwan's Land Expropriation System in Summary

CATEGORIES OF LAND EXPROPRIATION

According to current laws in Taiwan, the land expropriation system is further classified into general land expropriation, political land expropriation, and zone expropriation.

General Land Expropriation

The term "general land expropriation" as used herein denotes government actions to compulsorily acquire private land through lawful procedures to meet the needs of specific public interests. As expressly set forth in Article 3 of the Land Expropriation Act, such public interest related undertakings include:

- National defense;
- Transportation infrastructure projects;
- Public utilities;
- Water conservancy facilities;
- Public sanitation and environmental protection installation;
- Construction for government authorities, local self-government agencies and other public needs;
- Education, academic, and cultural undertakings;
- Social welfare institutions;
- National enterprise; and
- Other undertakings for which the land may be duly expropriated according to law.

In Taiwan, private land may be expropriated to meet the needs of public interests. However, such public interest undertakings must be those operated by government. To put it in more understandable terms, a public interest-related undertaking operated by a nongovernment entity is not entitled to apply for land expropriation. As expressly set forth in Article 56 of the Land Expropriation Act, nevertheless, a government agency, when applying for land expropriation, may expressly provide in the expropriation plans that the land so expropriated may be provided to a nongovernment organization to operate through investment, by means of trusted, consigned operation, joint venture, creation of superficies, leasehold, or otherwise.

Land Expropriation Based on Policy

The term "land expropriation based on policy" as used herein denotes the ban on private ownership of land and compulsory acquirement of private land. As expressly set forth in Article 14 of the Land Law, land within certain specified areas of the coast shall not be privately owned and shall be duly expropriated according to law if already owned privately. Further, as expressly set forth in Articles 28 and 29 of the Land Law, as the local situations may justify, the special municipal government, or the local competent city/county government, may restrict the maximum of areas of private land owned by a private individual or organization based on the categories and attributes of the land. When private land exceeds the specified maximum, the municipal or local city/county government orders the partitioning and sale of the land within the specified time limit, and otherwise expropriates such land according to law. The land expropriation in such a case is not intended to promote public interest undertakings but, instead, to safeguard the land policy of the country to prevent private individuals or organizations from monopolization of land at the price of public interest. In fact, nevertheless, such policy expropriation of land has been seen only in law but never in actual practice.

Zone Expropriation

The term "zone expropriation" as used herein denotes that the government mandatorily expropriates private land within the specified zone in full to reconsolidate for development on an overall basis. After such land is used for public facilities and development, the government permits the original landowners to retrieve certain areas of land at the specified ratio and sells the remaining land suitable for construction through transfer or auctions.

Zone expropriation is primarily intended to develop a specified zone and is thus considered a means of land development. As expressly set forth in Article 4 of the Land Expropriation Act, land meeting any of the following is subject to zone expropriation:

- Land in a newly developed urban area in whole or in part, being used for development and construction;
- Land in an old urban area that must be redeveloped for public safety, sanitation, transportation, or reasonable land use;
- An agricultural zone, a conservation zone in an urban area being reclassified for the zone suitable for construction use (e.g., commercial or residential zone), or an industrial zone being reclassified into a residential zone or commercial zone;
- Land in a nonurban area being developed for construction purposes;
- An agricultural community being redeveloped for better public facilities, improvement in public sanitation, or coordination of agricultural development; and
- Land in other cases that is subject to zone expropriation according to law.

PROCEDURES FOR GENERAL LAND EXPROPRIATION

In general, as set forth in the Land Expropriation Act (LEA), land expropriation (general land expropriation) in Taiwan is conducted through the following procedures.

Pre-expropriation Phase: Permit on Undertaking Plans and Agreement to Acquire the Land

The promoter of an undertaking for public interest shall, prior to application for land expropriation, submit the prospectus of the projected undertakings to the competent authorities of the government for approval. The competent authorities of the government shall, prior to granting the permit, hold public hearings to listen to landowners and interested parties, provided that such public hearings or presentations may be dispensed with in case of national defense undertakings subject to confidentiality or if such hearings have been held according to other laws (Art. 10, LEA).

Besides, the promoter of the undertaking shall approach the landowners to reach an agreement to acquire the land through purchase or otherwise, except for undertakings for national defense, transportation, water conservancy, public sanitation, or environmental protection, and for those undertakings in emergency needs for which negotiation with landowners proves impossible. The land may be expropriated according to law only when such efforts fail to reach an agreement (Art. 11, LEA). To put it in more understandable terms, in principle, purchase through negotiation is a prerequisite for application for land expropriation. Only in a case related to national defense, water conservancy, and the like, or a case in emergency needs for which negotiation with landowners proves impossible, can the application for land expropriation be directly filed.

The prerequisite to negotiation for purchasing before land expropriation is a clause provided in the Land Expropriation Act enacted in February 2000. Until then, land expropriation even without such prior negotiation procedures had not been construed as unlawful.[3]

Preparation of Expropriation Documents

Improvements on land (e.g., constructions and crops) shall be expropriated along with the land in a package, unless the owner of the land's improvements takes the initiative to relocate or retrieve them (Art. 5, LEA). The promoter of the undertaking shall, when applying for land expropriation, work out an expropriation plan in detail and apply to the competent authorities (Ministry of the Interior) for approval of the expropriation with such plan along with cadastral transcripts and land use drawings, with copies served to the municipal or competent city/county government in the place where the subject land is located (Art. 13 and 14, LEA).

As required for document preparation, the promoter of the undertaking may apply to the municipal or competent city/county government in the place where the subject land is located to enter the subject land, or for survey or measuring (Art. 12, LEA). In the event that the works on the land must be removed or relocated to meet the needs of survey or to measure the damage, appropriate compensation shall be provided at prices that shall be duly negotiated.

Examination and Approval

Applications for land expropriation shall be subject to examination by the Land Expropriation Examination Commission established by the Ministry of the Interior (Art. 16, LEA). The Ministry of the Interior will authorize the final decision after an application passes the examination process. The laws currently in force do not expressly provide clauses for criteria to approve of an application. Judging from the Land Law and Land Expropriation Act, nevertheless, one can tell that the Land Expropriation Examination Commission shall take into account only the following facts when examining an application:

1. Whether or not the proposed undertaking is entitled to application according to law and has been approved by the competent authorities of the government;
2. Whether or not the land subject to expropriation is indispensable to the proposed undertaking; and
3. Whether or not the expropriation causes the minimum possible damage.

Enforcement

1. *Public announcement and notice.* The Ministry of the Interior shall, after coming to a final decision on land expropriation, hand the case and documents to the municipal or competent city/county government in the place where the subject land is located for thirty days of public notice and shall, meanwhile, keep the land's or improvement's owners and other rights holders informed (Arts. 17 and 18, LEA).

2. *Legal effect of public announcement on expropriation.* The land or

improvement subject to expropriation shall not be subdivided, consolidated, transferred, or mortgaged from the first day of public announcement. Besides, the landowner or land user shall not make new constructions, additions, and modifications on the land or quarry, change terrain, or increase crops (Art. 23, LEA).

The ownership or other rights of the land or construction improvements subject to expropriation shall be on grounds of registered entries having been made in the land or construction improvement registration as of the first day of public announcement (Art. 24, LEA). Accordingly, the public announcement of land expropriation provides the legal effect to ascertain the objects entitled to receive compensations (i.e., the parties entitled to receive expropriation compensation).

3. *Payment of compensation.* The compensation for land expropriation shall be borne by the promoter of the undertaking and shall be paid to the expropriate through the municipal or competent city/county government in the place where the subject land is located within fifteen days from expiry of the public announcement (Arts. 17, 19, 20, LEA). Otherwise, the land expropriation shall become null and void unless the recipients refuse or delay to accept the compensation. In the event a recipient refuses or delays to accept the compensation, such compensation shall be deposited into the account earmarked for land expropriation compensation opened in the national treasury as a means of lodgment where the compensation is construed as having been received (Art. 26, LEA).

The land expropriation compensation shall be duly calculated on grounds of the latest official land price promulgated by the local government.[4] The prices for land reserved for public facilities within urban planning shall be determined based on the latest official land price promulgated by the local government for the neighboring plots. Moreover, the official land price shall be subject to an additional percentage as necessary. Such a percentage shall be proposed by the municipal or competent city/county government on grounds of normal trading rates, and the Land Price Evaluation Commission shall make the final decision (Art. 30, LEA). The compensation for improvements on the land shall be determined at the replacement costs in the case of construction, and determined on grounds of planting costs with reference to the current values (Art. 31, LEA). Other than compensation for land and improvements, the expropriation compensation shall include relocation fees and compensation for loss of business (Art. 33, 34, LEA).

4. *Completion of expropriation.* The rights and obligations for a landowner or land improvement owner cease to exist as soon as the expro-

priation compensation is paid (Art. 21, LEA), while the promoter of the undertaking obtains the ownership of land or improvements simultaneously (Art. 759, Civil Code). After the compensation is paid, the municipal or competent city/county government shall request that the landowner and land user complete relocation within the specified time limit (Art. 28, LEA).

In Case of an Objection

In the event an interested party (i.e., landowner or holder of other rights) of the land subject to expropriation objects to the expropriation within the public announcement period, such a party may bring the objection to the municipal or competent city/county government in the place where the subject land is located. The municipal or competent city/county government shall investigate and clarify the case as soon as the objection is entertained and shall serve the results of clarification to such interested parties in writing. In the case of an objection to the price of compensation, the municipal or competent city/county government may refer the objection to the Land Price Evaluation Commission for a recheck (Art. 22, LEA). Besides, in addition to the aforementioned procedures, an objection also may be solved through Administrative Appeal Law and Administrative Litigation Law.

ZONE EXPROPRIATION IN SUMMARY

Zone expropriation is regarded as an extraordinary land expropriation system because of its unique purposes and terms of compensation, which differ from those of general land expropriation. In line with the causes set forth above, the promoter of an undertaking in a zone expropriation case shall survey and determine the scope of expropriation before submitting the zone expropriation plan, and then report to the Ministry of the Interior for approval (Art. 38, LEA). After the zone expropriation plan passes examination, the municipal or competent city/county government in the subject land's location shall launch a public announcement for thirty days and shall pay compensation to the recipients within fifteen days from expiry of the public announcement. The criteria to determine the zone expropriation compensation are the same as those for general land expropriation.

A landowner, if unwilling to receive cash compensation for zone expropriation, may apply to the municipal or competent city/county government, during the period of public announcement, for offset land instead of cash (Art. 40, LEA). The term "offset land" as used herein means that the land after development that is ready for construction is used to off-set the compensation payable to the recipients. The total area of the offset land shall be 50 percent of the total land expropriated except in an extraordinary consideration, as approved by Ministry of the Interior, but cannot fall below a 40 percent minimum in any case (Art. 33, LEA).

After land in a zone expropriation is obtained through expropriation (where the landownership becomes totally public) and after public facil-ities are completed as planned, the cadastral status will be reclassified, and then the offset land will be allocated and retrieved for the original landowners. The area of the offset land shall be calculated on grounds of the ratio between the compensation payable to the original land-owner and the total compensation for land in zone expropriation, to be duly converted at the unit of the offset land actually provided to her or him.

Except for the offset land, which shall be retrieved by the original landowners, the remaining land in zone expropriation shall be disposed of according to the following (Art. 44, LEA):

1. Land for roads, drainages, parks, green areas, children's amusement lands, plazas, parking lots, athletic grounds, primary schools, and such public facilities shall be registered to the ownership of the municipality, county (city), or village (township)[5] on a gratuitous basis.
2. Land for public facilities other than those set forth in the preced-ing paragraph, land for public housing or specific undertakings ad hoc approved by the Executive Yuan (government organization) shall be sold to the user organizations.
3. Other land suitable for construction use shall be disposed of by means of sales, leasehold in public tenders, or created superficies.

Summing up the above, as a result of land development by means of zone expropriation, the landowners may retain 40 to 50 percent of their land through retrieval of the offset land, while the government could obtain 50 to 60 percent of the land for public facilities or specific under-takings, and for disposition. In other words, through such a system, the subject zone can be well developed, or a specific undertaking can be built while the landowners can enjoy the benefit of land development by retriev-ing the offset land. These are the top characteristics of zone expropriation.

Shortcomings of Land Expropriation in Taiwan

The most notable problem of Taiwan's land expropriation system is over-dependence on expropriation as a means of obtaining land required for public interest undertakings, leading to many cases of land expropriation.[6] While land expropriation is approved through a simplified process, private property rights have not been reasonably safeguarded.

OVERDEPENDENCE ON LAND EXPROPRIATION AS A MEANS OF OBTAINING LAND FOR PUBLIC INTEREST UNDERTAKINGS

In Taiwan, land expropriation is virtually a normal means of obtaining land for public interest undertakings. There are insignificant efforts to obtain land through negotiation and purchase—primarily as a result of unreasonable laws. As mentioned earlier, only government-operated public interest-oriented undertakings are entitled to apply for private land expropriation. Until the Land Expropriation Act was enacted and enforced in February 2000, land price compensation had been on grounds of government-promulgated land prices of the current term in accordance with the Equalization of Land Rights Act. As a matter of fact, such government-promulgated land prices are very often below market prices. If the land is obtained by means of negotiation and purchase, the land can hardly be obtained at government-promulgated land prices. The Criminal Code, nevertheless, punishes the offense of seeking profit.[7]

The public officials in charge of public interest-related undertakings very often bear in mind that land should be expropriated at government-promulgated official prices. They would run against the Criminal Code if they purchased land through negotiation at prices higher than the government-promulgated official prices. As a natural result, when private land is required for public interest undertakings, they simply apply for land expropriation. Besides, until the Land Expropriation Act came into being, the laws had not required that purchase through negotiation be a prerequisite. A land expropriation application is approved through very simplified procedures.[8] Unfortunately, as a result, land expropriation has been taken as the preferential means, or even the sole means, for acquiring private land to promote public interest-related undertakings.

The newly enacted Land Expropriation Act expressly provides that purchase through negotiation be the prerequisite of land expropriation, well embodying the sound concept that the country honors the constitutional human rights of nationals. Nevertheless, as this act is not well backed by other supporting laws, the negotiation becomes virtually worthless. The Land Expropriation Act does not require compensation at market rates or appropriate prices. Instead, it provides that

> For expropriated land, compensation shall be paid at the government-promulgated official prices of the current term. . . . As necessary, an additional percentage may be provided. The additional percentage shall be proposed by the municipal or competent city/county government, in line with prices of normal trading, to the Land Price Evaluation Commission, which will come to a final decision on the grounds of the government-promulgated official prices of the current term. (Art. 30, LEA)

The government's official prices and the criteria for additional percentages are promulgated regularly on July 1 every year. The promoter of the undertaking would be fully aware of the prices for compensation when proceeding with the negotiation. Under such situations, the promoters of the undertaking would find it virtually impossible to purchase land at prices above the legally specified rates. Otherwise, they would rather obtain land through expropriation to defend themselves from being accused of seeking to profit the landowners. To put it in more understandable terms, the negotiation procedures have become a nominal formality, and land required for a public undertaking is still totally acquired by means of expropriation.

Oversimplified Procedures to Approve of Land Expropriation

The harshness of administrative procedures should be in direct proportion with the seriousness of attitude. In other words, for major events vitally related to the nationals' interests, the administrative procedures must be extremely serious. It is true that land expropriation is intended to promote public interests. On the other hand, it is an administrative method to compulsorily deprive nationals of the private property rights protected by the constitution. There must be harsh and just procedures to assure landowners' rights and interests.

Article 208 of Land Law provides that "The land expropriation shall be limited to the scope only as indispensable to promotion of the undertaking." And Article 49 of Enforcement Rules of Land Law provides that "Land expropriation shall be carried out within the scope, not against the expropriation objectives at the least possible damage." Judgment on these issues calls for discerning consideration on concrete facts and objective situations. The laws currently in force do not provide concrete clauses regarding criteria of examination. Throughout the examination process, the interested parties (including landowners, other rights holders, as well as the local government agencies in the place where the subject land is located) are given no chance to speak, leaving extremely large power with the Ministry of the Interior—the competent authorities to approve land expropriation cases—and leading to shortcomings of subjective examination. In particular, until the Land Expropriation Act was enforced, there had been only one official in the Ministry of the Interior doing paperwork to examine and come to decisions, substantially ignoring the landowners' interests. As a result, all land expropriation applications have been virtually 100 percent approved. In turn, the promoters of undertakings have taken land expropriation to be the sole means of acquiring private land.

Since the Land Expropriation Act was enacted and enforced, the land expropriation cases have been examined by the Land Expropriation Examination Commission (made up of eight representatives from government authorities, and five experts or scholars) in the Ministry of the Interior. The problem is the laws lack concrete clauses governing the mechanism required in the land expropriation examination procedures: for example, an open-door policy, chances for interested parties to speak up, and criteria to judge public and private interests. Amid numerous land expropriation cases, the presence and examination procedures by the Land Expropriation Examination Commission are becoming nominal shows. The land expropriation cases are still approved through an oversimplified process, and the landowners' rights and interests are not reasonably protected.

Current Tasks: As a Conclusion

The Grand Justice Conference—the constitution interpreter of the Republic of China on Taiwan—came to Interpretation No. 409 in July 1996, expressly pointing out that

> Land expropriation is vitally linked to nationals' property rights. The laws regarding prerequisites in expropriation and the enforcement procedures shall be provided in as detailed form as possible. The objectives and purposes of expropriation shall be definite and concrete, with express clauses governing the criteria of public interests and urgency in expropriation so

that the competent authorities of the government as well as the judicial authorities will get firm grounds for legal review. Until the expropriation plan becomes final, voices particularly from landowners and interested parties, must be fully heard so as to take care of both public and private interests, and to assure a full-disclosure practice. The Land Law is occasionally ambiguous, and the expropriation procedures are not comprehensive. All competent authorities of the government are advised to review and take required amendment.[9]

Regrettably, the Land Expropriation Act promulgated in February 2000 fails to provide corrective measures in response to the key points made by the Grand Justice Interpretation. The Land Expropriation Act still contains significant problems and inadequacies.

Overall, a sound and reasonable land expropriation system should come to discerning and appropriate judgment on respective public interest-oriented undertakings without total reliance on land expropriation and compulsory deprivation of private property rights. The extent of expropriation must also accord with the principle of proportionality. Only by such serious efforts can private rights and interests be protected while promoting public interest. Still, the land expropriation system enforced in Taiwan is oversimplified, in particular, lacking mechanisms to enable interested parties to speak up.

How does one intensify sound expropriation procedures? This is the first lesson lying ahead in terms of a land expropriation system in Taiwan. Other than sound land expropriation procedures, there must also be mechanisms to purchase land through negotiation. In other words, as a sound practice, land required for public interest undertakings should be obtained by means of negotiation as far as possible, with the least possible applications for land expropriation. Only by helping promoters of undertakings to correct their misleading concept that land expropriation is the only means of obtaining land, and by minimizing the number of land expropriation cases, can we help the Land Expropriation Examination Commission live up to its supposed function, and can landowners get their rights and interests firmly secured.

Notes

1. In Taiwan, the Ministry of the Interior is one of the branches of the central government, and under the jurisdiction of the Executive Yuan (government organization).

2. In Taiwan, a municipality or county (city) is a local self-government body. A municipality (e.g., Taipei City) is a special city directly under the jurisdiction of the Executive Yuan.

3. Pan-Tze No. 241 (1965), Judicial precedent of the Administrative Court.

4. As expressly set forth in Article 46 of the Equalization of Land Rights Act, the municipal or competent city/county government shall, for land within their precincts, survey the updates of land prices and evaluate the land prices from time to time and promulgate them on July 1 every year. The land prices so promulgated by the municipal or competent city/county government are "official land prices latest promulgated by the government."

5. Village (hissing) and township are units of local self-government bodies in Taiwan, under the jurisdiction of the county.

6. Statistics disclosed by the Ministry of the Interior indicate that during 1997–1999, the general land expropriation showed the following results:

Year	Number of expropriation cases	Number of lots expropriated	Land area (in hectares)
1997	1,203	35,780	2,275.3124
1998	1,043	21,508	1,443.4054
1999	1,122	35,675	5,892.4875

7. Article 131 of the Criminal Code: "A public official who, either directly or indirectly, seeks to profit from a function under his control or supervision shall be punished with imprisonment for not less than one and not more than seven years; in addition thereto, a fine of not more than 7,000 Silver Dollars may be imposed."

8. About fifty years ago, Shih Shang-kuan, a well-known law expert in Taiwan, had already pointed to the shortcomings of Taiwan's land expropriation procedures: "Very seldom can one find throughout legislation the expropriation procedures as oversimplified as the Land Law of our country." (cf. Shih Shang-kuan, *The Theory of Land Law* [Cheng-Chung Bookstore, 1951], 522). Until now, the land expropriation procedures in Taiwan were not changed, albeit only by a little even now.

9. *Judicial Yuan Gazette*, vol. 38, issue 8 (August 1996), 37.

References

Constitution of the Republic of China, 1947

Encouragement of the Upgrading of Industry Act, 1990

Encouragement of Private Participation in Transportation Infrastructure Projects Act, 1994

Equalization of Land Rights Act, 1954
Land Expropriation Act, 2000
Land Law, 1930
Public Housing Act, 1975
Urban Planning Law, 1939

Li-Fu Chen, "A General Review on the Land Law," *Taiwan Law Journal* 16 (2000):1

Li-Fu Chen, "A Study on the Wiederkaufsrecht," in *The Contemporary Theory of Land Administration,* 479–512 (Taiwan, 1999)

Li-Fu Chen, "The Concept of Promoter of Understanding," in *On Constitutionalism and Rule of Law,* Vol. III, 241–272 (Taiwan, 1998)

Li-Fu Chen, "A General Review on the Land Expropriation Act," *Taiwan Law Review* 42 (1998): 97

Song-Ling Yang, "A Comparative Study of the Compulsory Purchase System Between Republic of China and Korea," *National Chengchi University Journal* 67 (1993): 329

Song-Ling Yang, "Property Right and Compensation of Eminent Domain," 9 *Socioeconomic Law and Institution Review* 9 (1992): 259

Chapter 10

Land Planning Law System, Land Acquisition, and Compulsory Purchase Law: The Case of Thailand

EATHIPOL SRISAWALUCK

The Profile of Thailand

Thailand is situated in Southeast Asia, and covers an area of 513,115 square kilometers. The country borders Myanmar on the west, and Lao PDR on the east, north, and west. On the southwest it has a common border with Cambodia and the Gulf of Thailand and Malaysia to the south. There are four regions: the mountainous north, central, north-eastern, and southern regions. The population of Thailand is 61.47 million, of which 30.59 million are male and 30.87 million are female.[1] Around 60 percent are currently employed in the agricultural sector. Bangkok is the capital city.

The king of Thailand is the ruling monarch under a constitutional monarchy political system. Parliament is comprised of the House of Representatives presided over by elected members of parliament and the House of Senate, which, under the constitution of Thailand of 1997, is also manned by elected members. The prime minister is the head of the government, with the executive branch divided into central, regional, and local governments.

The central government is comprised of ministries and departments and their regional branches, namely, the provinces, districts, subdistricts, and villages. There are several levels of local governments, namely, the

Faculty of Law, Chulalongkorn University.

provincial administration, municipalities, and Tambon Administration Organization. There are also special types of local governments, such as the Bangkok Administration and the City of Pattaya.

The Legal System of Thailand

The legal system of Thailand is the civil law system. There are several hierarchies of legislation, which are related to the source of authorization, the highest being those drafted by the legislature, followed by the executive and the local governments. The hierarchy of the legislation is as follows:[2]

The Constitution of Thailand, 1997
The Royal Act[3]
The Emergency Decree
The Royal Decree
Ministerial Orders
Provincial Regulation, Bangkok Metropolitan Regulation, etc.
Municipality Ordinance
Sanitary District Regulation[4]
Tambon Regulation

The systems of the Court of Justice are divided into three tiers, namely:

1. The Court of First Instance, which includes the Civil Court, the Criminal Court, the Central Juvenile and Family Court, the Central Labor Court, the Central Tax Court, the Central Traffic Court, the Intellectual Property and International Trade Court, the Provincial Court, and the Kwaeng Courts;
2. The Court of Appeal and the Regional Courts of Appeal; and
3. The Supreme Court.

Land Tenure and Land Utilization

Of the total area of 513,115 square kilometers, 41.31 percent or 211,968 square kilometers is agricultural land. Land utilized for various nonagricultural activities takes up 169,739 square kilometers or 33 percent of the total area, that is, industrial areas, commercial and service activities, residential areas, land belonging to various public agencies, state enterprises, religious establishments, and common areas such as roads, canals, and beaches. Approximately 25.63 percent of the total area is still under forest coverage.[5]

Within the present legal framework, land can be classified into two major categories, namely, public and private land.

PUBLIC LAND

Public land refers to land that has not been claimed for private ownership according to the Land Code. Public land can be classified into three categories:

1. Public domain refers to land reserved for common use by the people, such as common grazing ground, cemeteries, riverbanks, waterways, public highways, and lakes;
2. Public domain reserved exclusively for the state interest or retained for official purposes such as state army areas, state railways, and the like; and
3. Public domain reserved for common usage, but the people have discontinued utilizing the land that results in the return of the land to the ownership of the state.

Apart from the above-mentioned categories, there are also parcels of land that are covered under specific pieces of legislation, such as Crown land belonging to religious establishments according to the law, or land belonging to the Temples Roman Catholic Churches, Christian Foundations, or Islamic Religious Organizations.

Section 2 of the Land Code, 1954, stipulates that "Any parcels of land that have not been claimed by individuals, in effect belong to the state." The Land Code thus clearly distinguishes public from private land by stating that any parcels of land not claimed by private individuals, are, by definition, owned by the state and therefore considered public land.

It is possible that private individuals can arbitrarily occupy public land, or that the state may allow private individuals to utilize the land in one form or another. For example, occupants may be granted usufruct rights such as *Sor. Kor. 1*[6] or may be issued ALRO 4-01,[7] which acknowledge their status as land reform beneficiaries in land reform areas according to the stipulation of the Agricultural Land Reform Act. But the state does not allow private individuals to make legal claims over assets or land parcels or public domain that belong to the state.[8] This means, in effect, that occupants of land classified as public domain will not be granted any legal rights of claimants, no matter how long the period of occupancy.

PRIVATE LAND

Private land refers to land of which private individuals or corporate bodies claim full legal ownership according to the provisions of the Land Code. The legal rights are endorsed by the constitution of Thailand 1997, section 48, which stipulates that "The rights of the individuals over their property shall be protected. The boundaries of such rights and the limitations which may be imposed on the exercise of rights over [the land] will be in accordance with the law." This means that individuals may utilize land that is privately owned, freely and without restraint, if there is no legislation that places conditions on the manner of land utilization.

The Department of Lands (DOL) is authorized by the Land Code to issue rights to utilize land accordingly. There are three types of legal documents issued by the DOL:

- "Title deed" means a document showing ownership of land and shall include title deed map, certificate of ownership in lieu of title deed, preoccupation certificate stamped "Already put to use." (A Title Deed shall be in Form *Nor. Sor. 4 Jor.*)
- "Certificate of Utilization" means a document issued by the competent official certifying that the land has already been put to use. (There are three forms of Certificate of Utilization: Form *Nor. Sor. 3, Nor. Sor. 3 Kor.,* and *Nor. Sor. 3 Khor.*)[9]
- "Preemptive certificate" *(bai chong)* means a document showing authorization of temporary occupation. (There are two forms of preemptive certificate : Form *Nor. Sor. 2* and *Nor. Sor. 2 Kor.*)[10]

Up to 1998, the DOL issued 26,151,260 documents covering an area of 202,254.71 square kilometers (Table 1).

Private land utilization can be classified, according to the types of usage, into agricultural, commercial and service, industrial, and residential land. Utilization of land in some areas may be covered by specific pieces of legislation, which, in some situations, may impose restraints on the nature of land utilization.

Agricultural Land. In general, there are no restrictions on utilization of agricultural land, even in the urban fringe areas. There are exceptions in the case of land utilized for livestock raising, however, such as prohi-

TABLE 1   Number of land documents issued by the DOL from 1901 to
September 1998

Document Type	No. of Documents	Area (sq. km.)
Title Deed	15,652,263	95,647.79
Nor. Sor. 3 Kor.	8,070,834	71,358.78
Nor. Sor. 3	2,040,954	28,766.87
Pre-emptive certificate	387,209	6,481.27
Total	26,151,260	202,254.71

Source: Department of Lands, 1998 Annual Report.

bition of raising swine in or near community areas. In this case, the local
authority may draw upon the Public Health Act of 1992 to prohibit this
type of land use.

Commercial and Services Areas. This refers primarily to land use in
urban areas. Given the fast expansion of the road network, land around
the urban fringes or the suburb is rapidly being transformed into commercial buildings. Again, there are no restrictions except in cases where
activities involve construction works, in which case the ruling legislation
is the Building Act of 1979 and the Highway Act of 1992. The use of hazardous substances such as cooking gas and fuel come under the Hazardous
Substances Act of 1992 or the Fuel Act of 1978.

Industrial Areas. The use of land for industrial activities falls under
several pieces of legislation, namely, the Factory Act of 1992 and the Real
Estate Act of 1979, the Enhancement and Conservation of National
Environmental Quality Act of 1992, and the Public Health Act of 1992.
In addition, there is legislation that falls within the power of local govern-
ments, such as the Bangkok Administration Act of 1985, the Municipal-
ity Act of 1953, and the Tambon Council and the Tambon Administration
Act of 1994.

Residential Areas. Pieces of legislation related to the use of land for
residential purposes include the Building Act of 1979, the Condominium
Act of 1979, the Housing Act of 1964, the Public Health Act of 1992,
and the Public Cleanliness Act of 1992. The latter is concerned with public amenities, and solid waste and wastewater disposal.

Land Planning Law System in Thailand

Land use planning is a measure to systematize the use of land as well as
to control density of land use to ensure consistency with the existing basic

service infrastructures and amenities, such as the telecommunication system that supports effective linkages of activities. In Thailand, land use planning can be divided into many levels. The national and macro policy framework is set within the five-year national economic and social development plan. Presently, Thailand is in the eighth National Social and Economic Development Plan Period (1998–2001). The national plan provides the overall framework for the formulation of regional-, provincial-, and district-level planning by the central and regional branches of the government so as to ensure consistency of approach at all levels.

The comprehensive town plans guide land use development and the development of a network of hierarchies of urban centers as stipulated in the Town Planning Act of 1975 and the Plan for the Development of Sanitary Districts. Similar to the Comprehensive Plan, the purpose of the Plan for the Development of Sanitary Districts is to provide an overall guideline for land use development. The local plans should be consistent with the development concept of the provincial and the district town plans. They should contain details that correspond to the existing problems, the development potential, and the prevailing constraints of the local areas. In some cases, a Special Development Plan is also formulated in fulfillment of the area-specific policy directives, measures, and development projects.

In general, the main piece of legislation on land use planning in Thailand is the Town Planning Act of 1975. It covers the formulation of the town plan and ensures that land use development follows the guidelines of the Comprehensive Plan and the Specific Plan. Details of the Town Planning Act of 1975 and other pieces of legislation concerning land use planning follow.

THE TOWN PLANNING ACT OF 1975

Legislation on town planning dates back to 1952. At the time, it was known as the Town and Rural Land Use Plan. In 1975, the Town Planning Act replaced this Act. This latter Act has been amended twice, in 1982 and 1992. The objective of the Town Planning Act is management of urban land, to develop and renew parts of the urban areas to increase orderliness, improve landscaping, enhance safety, improve urban environment, and upgrade the welfare of the residents. It may also involve the rehabilitation of buildings or locations of historical interest, and extend to the conservation and preservation of areas of natural and scenic beauty.

There are two types of town plans: Comprehensive Plans and Specific Plans. The Comprehensive Plan contains the overall plan, policy, and projects, including measures that will ensure that development progresses in the planned direction. The objective is to preserve the town and improve the landscaping and environs, while at the same time improving the utility of the assets, the transport and communication network, and the development and improvement of amenities. The Department of Town Planning, attached to the Ministry of Interior, is responsible for seeing that other concerned public agencies adhere to the town plans. In addition to the town plans, there are also Specific Plans, which are designed for specific areas within the town and its environs, or in the rural areas that are located within the boundary defined by the comprehensive town plans.

The Act calls for the establishment of a Town Planning Committee. The committee will be responsible for setting the criteria, the approach, and the conditions that will require landowners to comply by changing or adjusting the nature of land use. In some cases, it may even prohibit the landowner from utilizing land if the proposed nature of the usage conflicts with the types of land use specified by the plan, either on grounds of safety requirements or welfare to the local residents.

OTHER PIECES OF LEGISLATION CONCERNING LAND USE

These are laws concerning the use of forestland and land for various economic activities, such as agricultural production; commercial, industrial, and residential areas; and road construction and installation of environmental infrastructures. There are also pieces of legislation that may restrict the usage of private land.

Land Development Act, 1983

This Act covers aspects of soil survey, soil classification, and developing an inventory of soil fertility and land capability. The Act also covers aspects of land use planning and zoning, as well as measures for land and water conservation.

Forestry Act, 1938

This Act covers aspects of utilization of forest resources such as logging and collection of forest products, collection of fees on timber and on forest products, movement of logs and forest products, control over timber processing, forest clearance, and any other activities that may result in the destruction of forest resources. The Act also prohibits the occupation of any parts of the forest areas. Penalties include fines and confiscation of goods and all types of equipment such as tools and machineries, including animals or any other tools used for logging, poaching, or any activities in forest areas prohibited by the Act.

National Park Act, 1961

The main purpose of this Act is to protect natural resources such as flora, forest products, and wild animals to ensure the sustainability of natural resources and of the natural landscape. The Act prohibits the occupation of any part of the national parks, clearance of areas, collection of forest products, hunting wild animals, and collection of any rocks, sand, or stones. The Act does allow entry into the national park areas for educational and recreational purposes. Violators are subject to fines or imprisonment as well as confiscation of weapons, tools and vehicles used in committing the crimes.

The National Forest Reserve Act, 1963

The purpose of declaring any part of the forest areas as a national forest is to ensure the sustainability of the resources. The Act prohibits entry into the declared forest reserve areas and occupation of land inside the boundary of the forest reserve. It also prohibits any types of construction, clearance of forest areas, or activities that may result in destruction and depletion of forest resources. The responsible agency is authorized to evict the violator from the forest reserve areas and to pull down any construction works. In case of degraded forest areas, it is within the authority of the director general of the Royal Forestry Department to allow occupants to remain within the degraded forest area and to utilize the land. Violators are subject to fines or imprisonment and confiscation of tools used to engage in the violation, regardless of whether the possessions belong to the violators.

The Commercial Forestry Act, 1992

The purpose of this Act is to promote forest plantation for commercial purposes, on both public and private lands, to generate employment, and to generate supplies of timber and wood-based products. The principle of the Act is also to provide the investor with assurance of rights to utilize the land and entitlement to the benefit, such as exemptions from the duties and from various clauses of the Forestry Act of 1938.

The Wildlife Preservation and Protection Act, 1992

The purpose of the Act is to support breeding of wildlife species, and to help protect and conserve wildlife species. The principle is also to ensure that Thailand undertakes measures that reflect willingness to cooperate with international communities in protection and conservation of wildlife and endangered species by declaring designated areas as wildlife sanctuaries and no-hunting zones.

Revolutionary Announcement No. 286

Issued on November 24, 1972, its purpose was to impose control on private land transactions. This announcement is based on observations that there are a number of entrepreneurs in the land and real estate sector but no clear legal codes of conduct that may underlie many cases of dispute over land. Moreover, in many incidences, land allocation subdivision procedures do not technically follow the concept of town planning. There is therefore a need for a law to regulate land use by developers to protect the interests of the buyer, as well as to ensure the maximum benefit from land transactions when taking into consideration social and economic objectives.

The Building Control Act, 1979

This Act was enacted to replace the Building Control Act of 1936 and the Building Control in the Fire Area Act of 1933. The details of the two fore-running acts were amended and combined into a single act. The changes were deemed necessary to ensure consistency of the Act and to increase effectiveness in enforcing building regulations to ensure durability and safety aspects as well as fire precaution measures, sanitation, environmental elements, architectural style, traffic flow considerations, and conformity to town plans.

The Highway Act, 1992

This Act replaced the outdated Revolutionary Decree No. 295 dated November 28, 1972. Contents of the Act cover construction, expansion, and maintenance aspects over six categories of highway, namely: motorways, provincial highways, rural roads, municipal roads, sanitary district roads, and concession roads.

The Public Health Act, 1992

This Act replaces the original Public Health Act of 1941. The purpose of this Act is to increase sanitary conditions and oversee provision of public health services. Details of the Act cover aspects of community participation in waste management, maintenance of buildings in old and decaying conditions, regulation of population density, control over public nuisances, keeping of animals, setting up fresh or open markets, putting up vending stalls in public areas, and so on.

The Factory Act, 1992

This Act replaces the previous Factory Act of 1969. The purpose of this Act is to control and regulate the operations of industries. Industries are classified into three categories according to the degree of control and supervision needed to ensure against industrial accidents and restriction of areas of operations that might pose an environmental threat or are likely to become health hazards. The cabinet is authorized by the law to determine the number, size, and location of industries. The expansion of industrial operations in any location is also subject to cabinet approval (section 32(1)).

The Environmental Quality Promotion Act, 1992

This Act covers the formulation of the policy, programs, and action plans to protect and enhance the environmental quality, and to set the environmental standards, monetary and fiscal measures, and investment promotion that lead to the achievement of the objectives of the policy, programs, and plans. This Act also covers aspects of prevention and protection against the spread of pollutants. The Act specifies standards of pollution control at sources, and measures for mobilizing participation and cooperation among public agencies, state enterprises, and the private sector in protecting and preserving environmental quality, as well as monitoring and reporting environmental conditions to the general public.

The Land Consolidation Act, 1974

This Act applies to selected areas targeted for land consolidation measures to ensure that each parcel of land can benefit from irrigation and supporting amenities, thereby ensuring the beneficiaries' ability to upgrade production efficiency and increase levels of income.

The Agricultural Land Reform Act, 1975

The purpose of this Act is to improve rights and agricultural land tenure. The state undertakes the task by reallocating public land or lands that have been appropriated from owners who are not utilizing their land, or who own land exceeding the specified ceiling. The beneficiaries of land reform include the landless, small farmers who have insufficient land to generate adequate income from agricultural production, and farmers' institutions. The beneficiaries can rent or hire-purchase, or they may simply be allowed to occupy and utilize land with assistance from the state in production improvement and in marketing.

The Agricultural Land Reform Act does not cover the whole country but is only enforced in specific locations declared as land reform areas. It is therefore necessary for land use planning in any particular location to take into account the prevailing laws applying to that particular area. For example, revision of existing 'Town Plans' that involve expansion of urban boundaries will need to take into account conditions or standing control measures that specify the nature in which land in those locations can be used.

Current Issues or Most Critical Issues with Respect to Land Use Planning and Development

One of the basic underlying reasons for the inefficiency of land use planning and development in Thailand is the rapid increase in the size of the population. The depletion of forest resources for agricultural land, and the increasing population density and congestion of economic activities in the urban areas, are among the consequences of increasing pressure for land. Presently, there are no laws that impose a ceiling on private landholdings, nor does the existing land taxation system discourage land concentration. The economic boom of the 1970s and the 1980s was, to a great extent, stimulated by wealth from land speculation. Existing land use plans and town plans have no practical impacts on enforcing desirable land use patterns or preventing undesirable land use patterns.

THE POPULATION FACTOR

Between the first and the third National Economic and Social Development Plans, the rate of population increase was around 3 percent per annum. From the third plan on, the rate has gradually reduced to the present rate of around one percent. Between 1960 and 1998, the size of the population has increased from 26 million to 61.5 million (Table 2).

One facet of the population increase is the expansion in the size of the agricultural population and the agricultural labor force that increased demand for land and intensified competition for land resources. Details in Table 3 illustrate that the average landholding size has steadily declined

TABLE 2   Changes in the size of the population in Thailand between 1909 and 1998

Year	Population
1909	8,149,487
1919	9,207,355
1929	11,506,207
1937	14,464,105
1947	17,442,689
1960	26,257,916
1970	34,397,374
1980	44,824,540
1990	54,548,530
1998	61,466,178

Source: Population Census, Ministry of Interior, 1909, 1919, 1929, 1937, and 1947. National Statistical Office 1960, 1970, 1980, and 1990.

over the years. Moreover, the continued depletion of soil nutrients, combined with inadequate land and soil conservation measures, resulted in stagnation of productivity. The observation that farmers became increasingly more dependent on income from nonfarm sources is a clear reflection that they were unable to meet household needs solely from income generated from agricultural production. The land supply situation becomes closely linked to the issue of poverty, constantly an urgent agenda, and a condition that the state must pay full consideration when formulating land use plans.

Currently, there are no laws that prohibit land subdivisions. There are various pieces of legislation on allocation of land to the poor, namely,

TABLE 3   Number of agricultural households and average farm size between 1981 and 1995

Year	Number of agricultural households	Average Farm Siz (rai)[11]
1981	4,532,351	26.8
1991	5,130,531	25.9
1992	5,148,815	25.6
1993	5,173,826	25.4
1994	5,209,299	25.3
1995	5,248,815	25.2

Source: Office of Agricultural Economics.

Land for the Livelihood Act of 1968, and Agricultural Land Reform Act of 1975, which specifies that land parcels should not exceed 50 rai and also prohibits subdivision of agricultural land into parcels that are too small for agricultural production.

LAWS CONCERNING CONSERVATION ISSUES NOT STRICTLY ENFORCED

This is clearly reflected in the steadily declining forest coverage. Increasing competition for land can be traced to a range of reasons, including the expanding population and the market opportunities for exports of agricultural products. The rising demand for land for noncompetitive usage, particularly for industrial and service activities, is also a major underlying cause of land speculation. Agricultural producers who sell land to contending buyers generally encroach on forest areas, seeking new parcels of land for cultivation. The magnitude of the problem is significant, with around one million households that have encroached on forest areas to bring land under cultivation, and that are, in the eyes of the law, illegal encroachers. The state is caught between environmental and equity considerations, with pressures from below demanding rights over land occupied.

There are a number of legislative acts that provide legal protection for forest areas, such as the Forest Act of 1944; the National Park Act of 1961; the National Forest Reserve Act of 1964; and the Wildlife Preservation and Protection Act of 1992. Various exemption clauses are indicators that the control measures introduced by the acts cannot be fully enforced, and constitute a critical constraint to the protection and management of natural resources.

ENVIRONMENTAL PROBLEMS OF URBAN AREAS

One of the major problems of urban areas stems from the stream of rural to urban migration. The compositions of migrant populations are diverse. Some are landless farmers in search of permanent employment in the industrial or service sectors in the cities, while others are seasonal migrants. The number of migrants creates a bottleneck in supplies of housing and urban services and constitutes one of the obstacles to land use planning and enforcement as well as the cause for deterioration of urban environment and quality of life, particularly of the lower-income groups.

No Limits on Landholdings

There are no land laws that put a ceiling on the size of private land owner-ship. Given that land supply is limited, equitable land distribution (assumed to be a prerequisite for efficient management of land resources) to ensure ability to maximize utility of land resources is therefore of critical impor-tance. In Part 3 of the Land Code, sections 34 to 55 of the Act specify that agricultural holdings should not exceed 50 rai in size, while land for industrial activities should not exceed 10 rai. Land for commercial and residential usages, on the other hand, should not exceed 5 rai. The sections in the Land Code however, were overruled by the Revolutionary Decree No. 49 dated April 13, 1959, under the justification that placing restric-tions on the size of landholdings can infringe upon the development potential of the agricultural, industrial, and service sectors. Putting a ceil-ing on the private landholdings may not be in the economic interest of the country. Since the sections in the Land Code have been overruled, no attempts have been made to reintroduce the imposition on the size of private landholdings in the Land Code.

When the Agricultural Land Reform Act was enacted in 1975, the purpose of the law was to introduce a ceiling on land ownership in declared land reform areas. The Act stipulated that land parcels for crop production should not exceed 50 rai, while the ceiling for land used for livestock raising was 100 rai. Exceptions can be made, however, for land parcels exceeding the specified ceiling that were already utilized for those crop productions or livestock raising at the time the Agricultural Land Reform Act was declared. The occupants can submit a request for exemption.

Those who acquired land exceeding the ceiling have been able solely by process of negotiation to obtain voluntary agreements to transfer the area exceeding the ceiling. To date, the Agricultural Land Reform Office has not utilized the law to expropriate land from the landowners. The Agricultural Land Reform Act has therefore been said to have a limited impact on reducing land concentration and ensuring equitable distribu-tion of land in land reform areas.

Misuse of Land

One of the reasons for misuse of land is the large number of land trans-actions during the period of the economic boom, which resulted in large-scale transfers of land formerly used for agricultural production to nonagricultural usages or speculative purposes. This is reflected in the significant reduction in agricultural land and tenanted land. As reported by the Office of Agricultural Economics of the Ministry of Agriculture and Cooperatives, between 1986 and 1988, agricultural land in the Central Region, which is suitable for rice production, has been reduced by around 600,000 rai. Part of the land has been transformed into residential areas, commercial areas, and industrial areas.

The farmers' response to increasing export potential for shrimp has also created market incentives for transfer of land formerly for rice into shrimp farms, which enabled landowners to reap a higher return to land than rice farming. The adverse environmental impacts from the expansion of shrimp farms into areas suitable for rice cultivation, however, necessitated state intervention to prohibit this type of land use.

TAX SYSTEM

The current land tax system does not discourage concentration of land-ownership. Collection of land tax is authorized by the Local Development Tax Act of 1965 and the Land and Building Tax of 1932. Local development tax is a flat rate, and there are exemption clauses, which resulted in large landowners paying proportionally less tax. There have been efforts to introduce measures to restrict concentrations of land-ownership, such as Town Plans and the introduction of progressive land tax. There were such proposals in the Land Policy of 1997. However, to date, recommendations proposed by the Land Policy have not been translated into concrete measures or actions.

A Draft Land Building and Housing Bill was subsequently introduced that would replace the existing Local Development Tax Act of 1965, the Land and Building Tax of 1932; and the Act on Land Valuation Price used as a base for the Local Development Tax of 1986. The approval of the principle of the bill by the cabinet in September 1998 raised a number of issues concerning the appropriateness of the new tax system, and the rates and the capacity of the local authorities. The Act is presently being reviewed and finalized.

FAST-GROWING ECONOMY

Between 1987 and 1996, the Thai economy expanded at a steady rate, partly due to inflow of capital from abroad. The economic boom generated a marked increase in demand for land both for speculative purposes as well as increasing competition for commercial, industrial, and residential purposes.

INEFFECTIVE TOWN PLANNING ACT

The purpose of the Town Planning Act of 1975 is to control land use patterns by specifying land use zones for varying purposes. In practice, however, the Town Planning Act has proved to be ineffective in directing the pattern of land use. One of the main reasons is that land developers try to find land that is low in market price, which is mostly agricultural land. The consequence has been conversion of agricultural land for nonagricultural uses, reduction of green areas, and the evolving unsystematic pattern of land use. This means that in practice there are no effective means to control the physical dimension of urban development. This constraint underlies the problems of inadequacy of expansion of urban services, the loss of green areas around the urban fringe, and various facets of environmental problems. The expansion of urban centers and the appropriate distribution of urban centers around the regions therefore require a range of other inputs beyond planning efforts.

Land readjustment is one of those means to increase use value and market value of "blind" land parcels[12] to ensure that all land parcels can be serviced. Furthermore, land readjustment is an approach that can reduce the financial burdens of the state in purchasing land for construction of amenities. To date, land readjustment is implemented on a trial basis and there is no supporting piece of legislation specifically on land readjustment.

Land Acquisition and Compulsory Purchase Law

The provision of urban services and amenities all create demand for land. In the past, land was considered to be abundant and there were many parcels of vacant land that could be developed. Even where parcels of land were privately owned, landowners were generally cooperative. In that context, procurement of land by the state has been usually made by negotiations and voluntary agreements to sell. Therefore, there has been no perceived need to draft a bill for land acquisition.

With an increase in population coupled with rising competition for land, negotiations between the state and private landowners became increasingly difficult and, in a number of cases, the state could not meet the price demands for land. It has therefore been necessary to expropriate land.

The constitution of Thailand of 1997 specifies rights in private property and the conditions for land acquisition.

Section 48. Clause 1: The property right of a person is protected. The extent and the restriction of such right shall be in accordance with the provisions of the law.

This means that, if a law is to be introduced to place restriction on legal rights of the private property, the power to draft such a law must come from the people.

Section 49. The expropriation of immovable property shall not be made except by virtue of the law specifically enacted for the purpose of public utilities, necessary national defense, exploitation of national resources, town and country planning, promotion and preservation of the quality of the environment, agricultural or industrial development, land reform, or other public interests, and fair compensation shall be paid in due time to the owner thereof as well as to all persons having the rights thereto, who suffer loss by such expropriation, as provided by law.

The amount of compensation under paragraph one shall be fairly assessed with due regard to the normal purchase price, mode of acquisition, nature and situation of the immovable property, and loss of the person whose property or right thereto is expropriated.

The law on expropriation of immovable property shall specify the purpose of the expropriation and shall clearly determine the period of time to fulfill that purpose. If the immovable property is not used to fulfill such purpose within such period of time, it shall be returned to the original owner or his or her heir.

The return of immovable property to the original owner or his or her heir under paragraph three and the claim of compensation paid shall be in accordance with the provisions of the law.

The conclusion that can be drawn from the above is that acquisition of private property can only be undertaken within the framework of the constitution. There has to be a specific law on acquisition. Land acquisition can be justified, namely, for the public good, and if compensation is fair to the lawful owner of the property and paid within a reasonable period of time.

The Act that authorizes the state to expropriate real estate property is the Immovable Property Acquisition Act of 1987 and other acts that relate to the provision of basic infrastructure services and other services for the benefit of the general public. The constitution also specifies the authorized public agencies and the procedure for acquisition. In some cases, acquisition is merely authorized by a specific piece of legislation without specifying the procedures, and it is to be assumed in these cases that the executing agency will follow the steps specified in the Immovable Property Acquisition Act of 1987. Details follow.

IMMOVABLE PROPERTY ACQUISITION ACT, 1987

The present Immovable Property Acquisition Act of 1987 was developed from the initial version enacted in 1934, which was amended twenty years later in 1954. There are altogether thirty-six sections covering the following details:

General Section—the meaning of acquisition and the 'local council.'

Section 1—acquisition of immovable property. Details of this section cover the justification for the state to expropriate immovable properties, the issuing of the decree publicly announcing the area to be covered, the authority of the officials to enter the property to conduct surveys, the appointment of the committee to set the initial price of the property, the procedure for negotiation with the property owners, and the power to expropriate the property in situations of urgency. This section also covers the demolition of the property and the process of the acquisition act.

Section 2—compensation. This section deals with the parties who are entitled to compensation, the acquisition of parts of the property, or the land. This section also specifies the authority of the minister to review the value of compensation, or to appoint a new committee.

Section 3—procedure for acquisition. This section specifies the steps to be followed by the executing agency once a decree has been declared in any particular location. Actions include putting up announcements and notification of property owners who are entitled to compensation. The section provides information on measures to take in incidences where the owner does not come to claim or collect compensation, procedures to follow should disputes arise over shares of compensation among property owners entitled to the compensation, and the rights of the parties who own the mortgage of the property or other types of assets that are subject to acquisition. The section also covers the issue of alterations in registration documents on ownership of the property subject to acquisition.

Section 4—specifics of how to calculate the interests of those entitled to compensation in the situation where payment of compensation is delayed due to actions of the officials. The section specifies the time allowed for collection of compensation as well as the penalties for obstructing the work of officials.

The Immovable Property Acquisition Act of 1987 was amended by the Announcement of the National Peacekeeping Council No. 44, February 28, 1991. The reason for amending is that the old system was perceived to be unfair and that other factors should be taken into consideration. Under the old system the initial price for land can either be based on the valuation price used as the base for calculation of Local Development Tax or the valuation price of the property used as the base for calculating the registration fee for transactions of immovable properties. Whichever of the two base prices are higher will be adopted. Moreover, given the rapid change in the economic situation of the country that also contributed to a rise in land prices, landowners may feel that the value of compensation is not fair.

LAWS THAT AUTHORIZE PUBLIC AGENCIES TO UNDERTAKE ACQUISITION

In addition to the Immovable Property Acquisition Act of 1987, which can be used as the general law on the acquisition of immovable property by public agencies, there are other pieces of legislation that may authorize the responsible agencies to acquire property. In many cases procedures may only be partially laid out while others may not specify any procedures at all, in which case executing agencies are required to follow the procedures from the Immovable Property Acquisition Act of 1987.

These pieces of legislation include the Private Irrigation System Act of 1939, section 23; the Public Irrigation System Act of 1942, section 10; the National Energy Authority Act of 1953, section 21; the Provincial Electricity Authority Act of 1960, section 35; the Electricity Generating Authority of Thailand Act of 1960, section 36; the Town Planning Act of 1975, section 48; the Agricultural Land Reform Act of 1975, section 34; the Airport Authority of Thailand Act of 1979, section 32; the Industrial

Estate Authority of Thailand Act of 1979, section 38; and the State Railway of Thailand Act of 1981, section 37 ff. The Highways Act of 1992, section 68, states that if it is necessary to take acquisition of immovable properties for the purpose of constructing or expanding highways, unless otherwise stated, the executing agency should follow the procedures specified by the Immovable Property Acquisition Act and the Revolutionary Decree No. 290, of November 27, 1972.

The main contents of these acts are stipulations that authorize executing agencies, if it is necessary, to acquire property for the purpose of constructing or expanding facilities such as irrigation systems, power plants, highways, airports, and railway lines, or installing systems for service distribution, the executing agency should follow the procedures specified by the Immovable Property Acquisition Act.

REGULATIONS RELATING TO THE PURCHASE OR ACQUISITION OF IMMOVABLE PROPERTY

Apart from the Immovable Property Acquisition Act of 1987 and the various acts that authorize public agencies to take over property by acquisition, there are also a number of regulations that need to be taken into account, including:

Office of the Prime Minister Regulation on Procurement, 1992. This regulation is used in the stage where public agencies start the normal procurement process by negotiation. A successful outcome of negotiation means that property owners are willing to sell to the public agencies on a voluntary basis.

The Royal Decree on the Criteria and the Methods of Calculating Changes in Price of Property Left over from Acquisition, 1994, issued according to section 21, clause 4 of the Immovable Property Acquisition Act of 1987. This decree deals specifically with methods of calculating the changes in prices of parcels of land that have not been taken over, the value of which has to be deducted or added to the value of compensation to the landowner.

Office of the Prime Minister Regulation on Criteria and Procedures for Depositing Compensation Money with the Courts or the Deposit Office or the Government Savings Bank. This regulation has been drafted based on the stipulation of the Immovable Property Acquisition Act of 1987, section 1, clause 3.

Procurement and Acquisition of Immovable Property[13]

The steps that public agencies should follow in procurement or acquisition of immovable property can be summarized as follows:

Requesting the donation of the property to the public agencies. In some locations where the public agencies need to use private land for the general good of the public, such as building a road that may need to pass through a private land parcel, they may have to request that the private landowners donate that particular parcel of land.

Negotiation with landowners to solicit voluntary agreement to sell the privately owned land. If negotiation proves successful according to the conditions laid out by the Office of the Prime Minister Regulation on Procurement of 1992, the public agency can take over the land for use in the planned projects. The Immovable Property Acquisition Act of 1987 will not apply to this situation even if the agreed-upon price may be lower than the compensation price if acquisition measures were used. Landowners will not be able to claim for compensation money at a later stage.[14]

In situations where agreement cannot be reached on the value of compensation, and if the target project site covers a large area that belongs to several private owners, two approaches can be undertaken: (1) issuing a Royal Decree announcing the target project area as the area where acquisition procedures will be undertaken, and (2) announcing the Immovable Property Acquisition Act to specifically cover the target project area.

The announcement of the Immovable Property Acquisition Act in any specific target project area will have the effect of freezing the price of land in that particular area. After this step has been undertaken, then the value of compensation can be set and the negotiation process with the private landowners can take place. If agreements can be reached, compensation can be paid, and the public agencies will take over the land for development in the planned project.

In cases where negotiations cannot be reached, the public agency will have to draw upon the authority of the Immovable Property Acquisition Act in order to forcefully take over the property by paying the landowner the price set by the public sector (see chart). The acquisition of property according to the Immovable Property Acquisition Act of 1987 is therefore

Procurement and Acquisition of Immovable Property

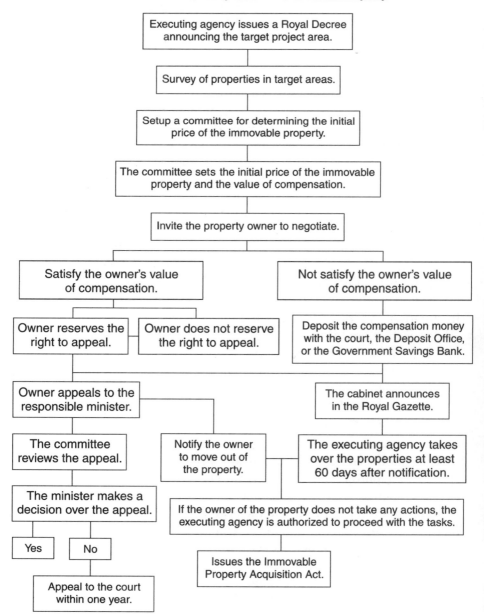

the last step to be undertaken in situations where other preceding steps have failed. In some cases, it may also be possible for the executing agency to bypass the stage of issuing the Royal Decree by drawing directly upon the authority of the Immovable Property Acquisition Act of 1987.

Issuing a Royal Decree Announcing the Target Project Area as the Area Where Acquisition Procedures Will Be Undertaken

Section 6 of the Act states that in declaring the target project area as the area where acquisition procedures will be undertaken, the following details must be provided:

- The purpose of acquisition,
- The executing agency, and
- The limitation of the area for land acquisition in so far as possible.

A map or a land use plan of the area where acquisition measures will be adopted should be attached at the end of the Royal Decree and is also considered part of the Royal Decree.

The Decree will be effective for a period of two years or according to the time frame specified in the Decree based on the estimate of the time requirement for survey and tasks to be undertaken. In principle, the period of decree should not exceed four years.

The normal procedure for issuing the Royal Decree is as follows:

The preparation of the map scale 1:4,000, 1:50,000, or 1:250,000, whichever is appropriate, is to be attached to the Royal Decree indicating the location where acquisition procedures will take place. This should be submitted to the concerned ministry.

The minister of the executing ministry reviews the justifications for land acquisition and the authority provided by the law, from which the agency draws its authority, and submits it to the cabinet for approval.

If the cabinet approves the justification of the draft decree, the draft will be sent to the Office of the Council of State of Thailand to prepare as a legal document according to the standard procedure. Upon completion, the Office of the Council of State of Thailand will send the document back to the cabinet for approval.

Upon the approval of the cabinet, approximately 7,500 copies will be printed.

The Secretary of the Cabinet will submit the decree for the royal signature and it will be publicly announced as a legal document.

The decree and the attached map will be posted in the areas specified by the decree, such as the office of the executing agency, the BMA court, the Provincial Court, the Branch Offices, the District Offices, the Designated District Offices, the Tambon and the villages offices, and the Land Offices (section 7).

THE SURVEY OF PROPERTIES IN TARGET AREAS FOR ACQUISITION

Once the Royal Decree, issued according to section 6 of the Immovable Property Acquisition Act of 1987, is publicly announced, the officials will survey the areas to find out information about the immovable properties subject to acquisition within 180 days. If the purpose of land acquisition is expanding highways, railways, expressways, irrigation canals, or similar purposes, the survey must be completed within two years of the date when the decree was announced. The survey steps are as follows:

The preparation of the names of the land and property owners and indication of the location of the property on the map will be attached to the Decree.

The official will check on the location of the parcels, the building, the trees, and other assets located in the declared area for acquisition, and prepare a map and layout plan indicating the site of the land, and the drawing of the property and buildings. The officials will also verify the legal documents on landownership rights and legal ownership of properties in the target areas.

There will be an estimation of land price, buildings, trees, and other assets in the declared area according to the criteria for determining compensation prices for immovable properties and other assets. Details of calculation of compensation value will be reported to the Committee for Setting Initial Compensation Price or the committee responsible for determining compensation value, who will call a meeting to discuss the procedure for land valuation, and the valuation of immovable properties such as buildings, trees, and so on. Factors to take into consideration are as follows: compensation for damages for properties, the demolition cost (as a percentage of the materials), the labor costs (as a percentage of the materials), the cost of transporting the materials demolished by truck per trip by the number of estimated trips, the cost of removing the equipment divided by the number of estimated trips, the management costs (as a percentage of the materials and labor costs), profit (as a percentage of the materials and labor costs), and taxes and costs (as a percentage of the materials and labor costs, management, and profit).

The items listed above are information that the committee has to take into consideration in determining the compensation price of immovable properties and other assets. The valuation is based on the prices of the materials and wage rates of the date of the valuation.

THE APPOINTMENT OF THE COMMITTEE FOR DETERMINING THE INITIAL PRICE OF THE IMMOVABLE PROPERTY

Once the survey of the area in which acquisition will take place has been partly or fully completed, the executing agency will submit the results to the minister according to the stipulation of the decree. A Committee for Determining the Initial Price of the Immovable Property will be appointed within thirty days of the completion of the survey. A representative of the executing agency will sit on this committee. Other members include a representative of the Department of Lands, a representative of one other public agency, and one representative from each concerned local organization. The committee sets the initial price of the immovable properties, which are subject to acquisition, and the value of the compensation.

For example, if an area in the Bangkok Metropolitan Area (BMA) is the target area, the committee members will consist of the MP of the BMA constituency, a representative of the Department of Lands, a representative of one other concerned public agency, a representative of the Bangkok Council, and one representative from each of the district councils where land acquisition will apply. The head of the Land and Property Registration Division will be the secretariat of this committee.

The responsibility of the committee will be to set the initial price of the immovable property and the value of compensation by following the criteria laid out in sections 18, 21, 22, and 24. The valuation price will be posted in public areas according to section 7 within 180 days after the appointment of the committee.

In situations where it is not possible to complete the tasks within the time allowed, the committee will submit a request to the minister authorized by the decrees for an extension. The extension should not, however, exceed 180 days.

The Setting of the Initial Price

This step involves valuation of the price of land and properties according to the criteria laid out in section 21. The following factors need to be taken into consideration to ensure fair treatment to the property owners and the society at large:

- The market price for land and property in the target area where acquisition of properties will take place at the date the decree is publicly announced according to section 6,
- The valuation price of the property used as the base for calculating the local development tax rate,
- The valuation price of the property used as the base for calculating the registration fee for transactions of immovable properties,
- The condition and the location of the immovable properties, and
- The justification and objectives for the acquisition.

The committee will consider all factors and set the criteria for calculation of the value of compensation for the land, buildings, and construction.

The Upward and Downward Adjustment of the Initial Set Price

To adjust the initial prices upward or downward, the criteria specified in the Decree on The Royal Decree on the Criteria and the Methods of Calculating Changes in Price of Property Left over from Acquisition of 1994 are to be followed. Should acquisition measures result in an increase of prices of remaining properties not subject to acquisition, the rise in price will be deducted from the initial value of compensation. Should acquisition measures result in a reduction of prices of remaining properties not subject to acquisition, the value of the reduction in price of the remaining property will be added to the initial value of compensation.

In some cases, the committee might allow for the increase in the value of compensation according to section 21. Where the owners of the target property are living on the property or using the property for commercial purposes or for other activities and have to move off the property, the owners will be compensated for the inconveniences caused. For example, if the owner of the house or the commercial property has not more than one rai of land, the initial value of compensation for land and property will be increased by 10 percent.

Once the committee has announced the initial prices for part of or for the entire area subject to acquisition, if this results in a steady rise in land price and if the executing agency has already paid compensation for land or immovable properties according to the valuation price of the committee, the situation may appear unfair to the property owner. It may be possible for the minister authorized by the cabinet to request that the committee or the newly appointed committee adjust the initial valuation prices according to the justifications and conditions acceptable by the cabinet. The new valuation prices will be used as the basis for negotiation instead of the initial prices (section 10 ff.)

If the minister sees that the new valuation price for the property subject to acquisition and the compensation value are too high and have not followed the criteria laid out in section 9 or section 21, it is within his powers to:

- request that the committee review the new valuation price and the value of compensation, and to
- appoint a new committee, according to section 23, to assume the responsibilities instead of the old committee.

It is also within the power of the minister to disallow the payment of higher compensation prices for land and property under the following conditions:

The building or property has been newly expanded or renovated, land development, cultivation, or leasing arrangements were made after the day that the decree was announced, according to section 6, without permission by the executing agency, with the exception of the continuation of use of land for rice production, upland crop production, and orchard farming; or

Buildings or properties were newly constructed or expanded, farming activity, or land development or land leasing agreements were made prior to the announcement of the decree, according to section 6, with the intention of collecting compensation money.

Reaching Agreement

This is the stage after the committee has set the valuation price for the land, building, and properties. The property owner will be invited to negotiate the price of his or her property. If an agreement can be reached, a contract will be based on the price agreed.

Where the owner agrees to sell the property but is not satisfied with the value of compensation, she or he is permitted to sign a contract based on the initial prices but stating in the contract that she or he reserves the right to appeal to the minister according to section 25. The right to appeal must be utilized within sixty days after having received a letter from the executing agency requesting the property owner to come forward to collect the compensation money.

The Entitlement to Collection of Compensation

The following persons are entitled to compensation:

The rightful owner or the occupier of the property subject to acquisition.

The owner of the property, or of immovable assets located on the property, subject to acquisition at the dates, that cannot be demolished when the decree was announced, according to section 6, or that have been constructed after the announcement of the decree with the approval of the executing agency.

The tenant of the building or property subject to acquisition who has a legal document to certify status of lease prior to the date when the Acquisition Decree was announced or a leasing arrangement that was concluded after the announcement of the decree, with the approval of the executing agency. Compensation to the tenant for the termination of the contract must be based on credible evidence that the tenant suffers loss from lack of access to the land, the building, or the property prior to the date of the expiration of the leasing contract.

The owners of trees on the land on the date when the Acquisition Decree was announced, according to section 6.

The owner of the property or of immovable assets that can be removed from the land subject to acquisition on the date when the decree was announced, according to section 6. The owner will be compensated for the cost of removing the property and for the cost of construction in the new location.

The person who loses legal rights to use right of way, or the ability to install drainage pipes, power lines, or other similar types of facilities on the land subject to acquisition, according to section 1349 or 1352 of the Civil and Commercial Code, and who paid the landowner for that right of way.

THE PAYMENT OF COMPENSATION

There are two ways in which payment can be made: the full payment or the deposit of compensation payment in specified establishments. In the cases where the owner agrees to sell the property and to accept compensation money, or agrees to sell the property while remaining unsatisfied with the value of compensation but nevertheless agrees to sign a contract based on the initial valuation price, the law stipulates that payment must be made within 120 days from the date the contract was signed and that transfer of property to the executing agency should be concluded.

If the owner of the property does not come forward to collect the compensation money within that period, or if payment cannot be made because of the questionability of the legal status of ownership or problems emerging from inability to divide the compensation money among the legal claimants, section 31 stipulates that the executing agency is to deposit the compensation money with the court, the Deposit Office, or the Government Savings Bank in the name of the owner. Interests generated are to be accredited to the person legally entitled to the compensation money.

APPEAL OVER THE VALUE OF COMPENSATION

The person entitled to compensation who is not satisfied with the value of compensation set by the committee by the authority of sections 9, 10, 23, or 28 has the right to appeal to the responsible minister authorized by the decree or the minister authorized by the Immovable Property Acquisition Act within sixty days of receiving notification from the executing agency, or the representative of the executing agency will come forward to collect the compensation money.

In considering the appeal, the minister will appoint a committee of not more than five members comprised of legal specialists and professional property valuers. This committee will review the appeal and make recommendations to the minister. The minister is to reach a decision over the appeal within sixty days from the date the appeal was submitted.

In situations where the owners are still not satisfied with the decision of the minister over the appeal, or in cases where the minister cannot reach a decision within the specified period, according to section 25, clause 2, the owner has the right to appeal to the court within one year from the date the decision over the appeal was declared.

While the owner of the property appeals to the minister or to the court, the executing agency can take over the property or utilize the property subject to acquisition, or it can remove the construction, move the assets, or proceed with the acquisition of the property.

If the minister or the Court of Law decides to increase the value of the compensation, the owner of the property is entitled to the compensation supplemented by the interest on the difference between the original and the final value of compensation. The interest is to be calculated based on the highest rate of interest for an account in the Government Savings Bank dating back to the day when payment was made or the compensation money was deposited.

The Adjustment of Land Registration Records

In making the contract, if the owner of the property has legal documents, the executing agency should notify the responsible agency, the Department of Lands, to adjust registration records. Transactions undertaken in these circumstances are not subject to the payment of duties or stamps. Transfer of ownership is effective as of the date of the payment.

If, on the other hand, the owner of the property does not have supporting legal documents, the executing agency should appoint a committee. The committee will be comprised of the district officer, the deputy district officer in charge in the location where properties are subject to acquisition, the officer of the Department of Lands at the district level in the designated district, or the representative of the village headman in the location and a representative of the executing agency. The committee is responsible for cross-examination of land rights. Once the claim of ownership is validated, then further acquisition procedures can be taken.

Passing the Immovable Property Acquisition Act

Once all information on property within the area subject to acquisition has been collected and validated, the executing agency can proceed to request the issuance of the Immovable Property Acquisition Act according to the standard legal procedures. This means passing through the House of Representative hearings and the Senate prior to submitting the bill for the royal signature.

Attached to the Act will be details of the land parcels and the immovable properties subject to acquisition, together with the list of owners and the maps or layout plan clearly indicating the location of the property. The maps and the layout plans are to be considered part of the Act. Cadastres have to be placed before the Act is publicly announced.

In some cases, it may be possible to pass an Immovable Property Acquisition Act without first issuing and announcing a Royal Decree.

The Outcomes of the Immovable Property Acquisition Act

The ownership of the immovable property is transferred to the executing agency from the date the Immovable Property Acquisition Act (section 15) is enforced. The executing agency can only take over the properties once the compensation has been paid in full, or has been deposited.

In cases where the subject property is mortgaged, or preferential rights on the property or rights other than ownership rights are also subject to acquisition, all legal obligations tied to those conditions are to be considered terminated. These people are still entitled to compensation for their properties. They are, however, subject to come forward to request the compensation within sixty days from the date they were notified by the executing agency, according to either section 28 or section 29.

Once the Immovable Property Acquisition Act has been enforced, should the owner of the property have transferred the properties to another party, the beneficiary of the transfer is entitled to demand only the compensation money.

In situations where there are temples or religious sanctuaries in the areas where properties are subject to acquisition, the stipulations of the Immovable Property Acquisition Act will also apply to these establishments without exemption.

The Acquisition of the Remaining Parts of the Property

In situations where only parts of the properties are subject to acquisition, the owner can request the executing agency to expropriate the remaining part of the properties that is no longer valuable for other usage (section 19). If the executing agency does not comply with the request, the owner has the right to appeal to the responsible minister authorized by the Royal Decree, section 6, or the Immovable Property Acquisition Act within sixty days from the date notified by the executing agency or representatives of that agency. The minister should consider the appeal within sixty days; otherwise it will be taken as indication of the minister's decision to have the executing agency comply with the wishes of the property owners. The decision of the minister is to be considered final.

Where the remainder of the parcel of land subject to acquisition is less than 100 square meters, or either side of the parcel is less than 10 meters, and if the remaining area does not adjoin other parcels of land belonging to the same owner, upon the request of the owner, the executing agency should take over the remaining piece of land according to the stipulation of section 20.

The Announcement of Acquisition in Cases of Emergencies

The cabinet has the authority to make the announcement in the royal gazette specifying that the acquisition procedures declared by the Royal Decree is an urgent agenda. The cabinet will take this action if it feels that delays in acquisition procedures can be obstacles to economic and social development or other development goals of the country (section 13).

Once the announcement has been made, the executing agency has the authority to take over the properties before the acquisition procedures are launched, provided that compensation money has been paid. The property owners will be notified at least sixty days beforehand.

If agreements can be reached for sale of the property subject to acquisition, compensation will be paid according to the value agreed upon but should not exceed the initial valuation price set by the committee. If agreements cannot be reached, once the compensation money has been deposited, the executing agency is legally authorized to take over the property.

The Removal of the Property

Where it is necessary to demolish the property, move assets, or undertake any actions as part of the acquisition procedures, once the compensation money has been deposited, the executing agency is legally authorized to proceed within the specified period not less than sixty days from the issuing of the letter of notification.

If the owner of the property does not take any actions within the time specified, the executing agency is authorized to proceed with the tasks, and the owner of the property will be responsible for the costs incurred. If any damages should result from the transfer of the properties, the executing agency must provide fair compensation to the owner for the damages.

According to section 7, in a situation where it is not possible to send notification to the owner, announcements will be posted on the premises of the property indicating the date when properties will be removed from the premises, not less than seventy-five days after the date the announcements were posted.

THE STORAGE OF PROPERTIES REMOVED FROM THE PREMISES

The executing agency can store properties that have been removed from the site, and the owner of the property is responsible for the storage costs. If the property can be easily damaged or can deteriorate if kept for too long, or if the storage costs will exceed the value of the assets, the executing agency is authorized to sell the items immediately by methods deemed appropriate. The executing agency will keep the leftover sum after deduction of operating costs.

If the owner does not claim the property's assets or the money within a period of five years from the date of the removal, the mentioned subjects will be considered to belong to the state.

Current Issues with Respect to Land Acquisition

Problems over land acquisition generally emerge in most cases, as property owners are unwilling to let go of the property and transfer ownership to the state. Additionally, problems emerge from the implementation process. Common problems relating to acquisition of immovable properties fall into the following areas:

- Problems relating to the issuing of the Acquisition Act,
- Problems relating to the performance of the executing agency,
- Problems from the people affected by acquisition, and
- Problems relating to cases of appeal.

Problems Relating to the Issuing of the Acquisition Act

Problems occur where the purpose of acquisition contradicts the intentions of the law and is not geared for the benefit of the general public. The enactment of the Immovable Property Acquisition Act to construct the Bangkok Port of 1937, the Immovable Property Acquisition Act to construct the Bangkok Port of 1939, and the Immovable Property Acquisition Act to expand the Port of 1943 were to benefit the commercial slaughterhouse. Because this contradicts the intention of the law, the law was never enforced, and the land was not transferred to the executing agency.[15]

Problems also can relate to the performance of the executing agency. An example of this type of problem is when the Acquisition Act was enacted for one public agency but ended up benefiting another public agency. This happened when the Expressway Authority of Thailand appropriated land for construction of expressways, but upon the establishment of the Metropolitan Rapid Transit Authority, land was transferred from the former to the MRTA for the purpose of constructing underground railways.

In some cases, the cabinet authorized the BMA to appropriate land, which was subsequently used by the Expressway Authority of Thailand or vice versa. There are also cases where land was appropriated for constructing highways but ended up being used for construction of expressways.[16]

Problems have existed when lands acquired were never utilized for the purpose intended, or were only partially used. The land acquisition for construction of the Nong Ngu Hao International Airport, for example, was never used due to a change in government. The cabinet of the new government commanded that the land be used instead for construction of a large pond and public parks. The former landowners therefore appealed to the court to demand fair treatment according to the constitution B.E. 2521 (1978), section 33, clause 5. The Supreme Court, however, ruled that although the constitution does specify such rights, because there was no supporting legislation, it was therefore not possible to redeem the rights of the landowners over their former properties.[17]

There are incidences where land acquired was not all utilized. This occurs where public agencies acquire more land than is actually needed, or where a limited budget prevents the executing agency from implementing the full scale of the intended project. For example, after the acquisition of land for constructing the Mitraparp Road, approximately forty years ago, many parcels of land were never utilized or were only partially utilized. The owners, or the heirs of the owners, therefore appealed to have the land returned, which led to the issuance of the Act authorizing the return of land to the former owners or their heirs on a case by case basis, which proved to be time-consuming and cumbersome.

PROBLEMS RELATING TO THE PERFORMANCE OF THE EXECUTING AGENCY[18]

Delays in implementation are caused by the following reasons:

Lack of cooperation from the people or obstruction of the executing agency from undertaking its tasks due to perceptions that the purpose for which the properties were acquired might create pollution. When the Expressway Authority wanted to acquire land in the Ban Krua community for construction of expressways, the communities protested and obstructed the operations of the executing agency even though compensation payment had been made.

The slow progress of implementation. The Immovable Property Acquisition Act to acquire land for construction of expressways, for example, extends over a period of five years. Since there is a large area to acquire, the executing agency could not complete their work within the set time frame. A number of Acquisition Acts have to be announced to expand the initial period, which finally took as long as twenty years. During that time, there were periods when the duration of the time specified by the Acquisition Act expired before a new Act came into effect, which meant that there were periods when the continuation of land acquisition by the executing agency was in fact undertaken with no supporting legislation. This means that any transfer of land from private landowners to the executing agency during that period has not been concluded within the framework of the Acquisition Law.[19]

The low value of compensation. This generally happens when the committee for determining the initial valuation price adopts either the valuation of the property used as the tax base for calculating the Local Development Tax or the property value used as the base for calculating the fees for property registration or duties for transactions of immovable properties, whichever is higher. The valuation prices for these two purposes are generally much lower than the market value, even though the National Peacekeeping Council has issued an Announcement No. 44, dated February 28, 1991,[20] stating that "in some cases land acquisition is for commercial or profit making purposes, but the Government does not take this into consideration. Acquisition of land for road construction which involves collecting toll charges, or for constructing industrial estates which is commercially leased out."[21]

There are no clear-cut methods for determining the value of compensation. Among the shortcomings are that in practice, there may not be officials dispatched to survey the conditions of land use in the areas subject to land acquisition, random methods have been used, or no data can be obtained under normal circumstances from the banks, financial institutions, or the market on transaction values. It is therefore common for the committee to adopt as the base for determining the market value the valuation price that the Department of Lands adopts as the base for calculating the fees for property registration or duties for transactions of immovable properties. Valuation prices given by zones or by blocks are used as the base price and marked up as deemed appropriate. For example, if the valuation price was 20,000 baht/square wah, the committee may mark up this price by 5,000 baht/square wah.[22] If there were protests, the committee might agree to a further increase of 3,000 baht/square wah.

Delayed payment of compensation may be due to the following reasons:

Budgetary problems. The executing agency may not have an adequate budget but is nevertheless required to go ahead with acquisition procedures. This problem could also occur if the executing agency has prepared the budget for the project on a year-by-year basis and did not estimate the cost for the whole project. For example, land that was acquired for the purpose of constructing a road was hit by a fire, and to this day, the BMA, the implementing agency, has not paid all the compensations. Similarly the Expressway Authority of Thailand has not paid all the compensations for land taken over since 1987. There are a number of court cases over these delayed payments.

The executing agency cannot contact the owners of the properties to ask them to come forward to collect compensation. This often happens where the owners are no longer residents of those areas, have traveled abroad, or have died, and the heir to the property cannot be contacted. In other cases, there is joint ownership, and the executing agency cannot contact all the owners. In other cases, the subject parcel of land may not have legal documents to support the claim.

The executing agency cannot identify the party who should collect the compensation money. This generally happens when the property is jointly owned by a number of people who cannot agree on the share of compensation. For example, it may be difficult to determine the share among the landowner, the owner of the building, and the tenant, or between landowner and the occupier. In these cases, there are disputes over claims that demand time to reach a compromise, during which period the value of the compensation is deposited with the authorized institutions as specified by the law.

Errors on the part of the executing agencies can occur in the following situations:

Failure to notify all the property owners or the concerned agencies, or to demarcate the area subject to acquisition, which could result in the transfer of property to other parties.[23] In some cases, when the executing agency may fail to notify the property owner of the right to appeal and sixty days from the date of notification have passed, the owners will have lost their rights to appeal.[24]

Coverage of cadastral surveys and transfer of properties that exceed the need for land acquisition and utilization outside the declared area.[25] It is also common for errors to occur when sending out notification to property owners or misreporting the size of the land parcels. For example, the subject property may be located on a parcel of 110 square wah, but the executing agency notifies the landowner to come forward to collect compensation money for a land parcel of 100 square wah.[26]

Payment of compensation to the person who has no legal claim. For example, the owner might have already donated the property to the BMA but may not have concluded the legal transfer; the owner's name is therefore still listed in the land registration records.[27] In other cases, compensation is paid to a tenant whose leasing contract has already expired.[28]

Acquisition Acts may differ in criteria and methods of approach, which is why the executing agency should carefully study the details of the Act prior to implementation, in order to avoid mistakes. The Revolutionary Decree No. 295, for example, states that the executing agency can take over the property without having to pay compensation first.[29]

PROBLEMS OF THE PEOPLE AFFECTED BY ACQUISITION

Delays resulting in deferred payment of compensation. This is unfair to the owners since they cannot use the compensation to purchase new houses or move to new areas. Extreme cases of delays and changes in economic circumstances often justify increases in the value of compensation.[30]

Low compensation value. The value of compensation can be markedly below market prices.[31] The limitation is that property owners themselves do not have information on the market prices of their properties. Valuation price is generally below market prices, and the properties, which utilize expensive building materials, trees, and damages, cannot be directly translated into market price. For example, a parcel of land bought for 1 million baht may only receive 500,000 baht compensation, and the owner cannot claim the loss of 500,000 baht.[32]

The land parcel left over after acquisition that can no longer be utilized, which necessitates the owner to find other parcels of land farther away from original location. There are cases where the court concludes that compensation must be paid to the property owner whose land has been acquired for construction of expressways for the loss of habitat and the inconveniences caused by air or noise pollution.[33] There are also cases where the court's decision is that the property owner cannot be paid full compensation, for example, for the construction of high voltage power lines over private property. This was based on the argument that the owner still maintains the ownership over those parcels of land, but is only partially restrained from full utilization.[34]

Inconveniences caused by varying forms of disturbances that prevent the owners from exercising their full legal rights over their properties. For example, the case where the Department of Highways constructed 'elevated' highways to avoid problems of flooding involved putting up constructions that may prevent owners from using the original access to their houses, or owners of commercial properties may complain that their volume of business has been reduced. In cases of this nature, the court often rules that the executing agency does not have to pay compensation to the owners.[35]

PROBLEMS OF CASES ON APPEAL

In a number of cases, the property owners do not make their cases of appeal to the court of law, which means that they forego the rights to receive additional compensation. Others may not wish to appeal because they do not have the money to cover the lawsuits, fees, and lawyers. The higher the value of the subject property, the higher the fees that can usually be anticipated. In many cases, the owners of the property do not make their appeals within the specified sixty days after receiving the notification, which means that they lose their rights of appeal.[36]

In many cases also, the owners of the properties submit the appeals to the wrong executing agency or fail to provide adequate supporting evidence for the appeals. For example, if their properties have been acquired for the purpose of constructing highways, then the appeal should be submitted to the minister of transport and communication, but if the owner appeals to the minister of interior, the prime minister, or other agencies apart from the executing agency, the appeals would be invalidated. In other cases, the property owners bypass the stages of appeal and submit the appeal prior to receiving the notification, which means, in practice, that at the time of appeal, the owners do not have the legal right to appeal.[37] There are also cases where the owners make an appeal over the value of land compensation and do not include the value of the property. In this situation, the court will only review the appeal over land compensation.[38]

In situations where the owner fails to submit an appeal and receives the decision by the responsible minister, and he does not file a case to the court within one year after having received the decision of the minister, then the case is categorically considered terminated.

The court's decision over the value of compensation is based solely on the evidence produced in court. Since the court does not have the means to collect supporting or counterevidence from other sources, the court therefore has to consider the arguments put forward by the executing agency that determination of compensation value has been technically determined against the protests of the property owners who are dissatisfied with the compensation value.

Appendix

HIERARCHIES OF THE LEGAL SYSTEM IN THAILAND

The Constitution
The Royal Act
The Emergency Decree
The Royal Decree

Ministerial Orders
Provincial Regulation, Bangkok Metropolitan Regulation, etc.
Municipality Ordinance
Sanitary District Regulation
Tambon Regulation

The Constitution: Is the highest law of the country. There are clauses concerning the rights and the freedoms of Thai citizens, the national policy guidelines, the legislature, the executive branch, the judiciary, and the local governments. Other legislation cannot contradict the constitution.

The Royal Act: Refers to legislation that has been officially proclaimed by the ruling monarch after being drafted and reviewed through the parliamentary process. The Royal Act is the second highest order of the legislation after the constitution. They are drafted by members of the cabinet or the members of parliament. Upon approval of the draft in parliamentary sessions, the draft is reviewed by the Upper House. With the latter's approval, the draft bill is submitted for endorsement by the ruling monarch with whose signature the bill can then be officially proclaimed in the government gazette, thereby confirming its enactment.

The Emergency Decree: Is a decree proclaimed by the monarch with the advice of the cabinet. Emergency Decrees are considered of the same order as the Royal Act, the difference being that the latter is drafted to address problems or matters of urgency concerning the safety of the country and the welfare of the general public emanating from perceivable natural, economic, or social crises that require immediate action and cannot pass through normal parliamentary processes.

There are two types of Emergency Decrees: general decrees and those that relate to fiscal and monetary issues. In the latter case, it is conditional that the issuance of the Emergency Decree fall within the period of parliamentary sessions on the justification that the issuance is urgently required to protect the country's interest. In this case, the concerned minister will be responsible for presenting the draft to the cabinet. Upon the approval of the cabinet, the Emergency Decree will be submitted for endorsement by the ruling monarch. With the king's signature, the decree is officially proclaimed in the government gazette, thereby sealing its official enactment.

It is stated in the constitution that the Emergency Decrees must be submitted for approval by parliament in the following parliamentary session. Where the decree concerns fiscal and monetary issues, it must be reviewed by parliament within three days following its official proclamation in the government gazette. Should parliament not agree with the Emergency Decrees, the stipulations therein will no longer be enforced, although the termination will not have any backdated effects on any actions undertaken during the time when the Decree was in use.

Royal Decrees: Proclaimed by the monarch with the advice of the cabinet according to the provisions of the constitution, the Act, or the Emergency Decrees, which authorize the executive power to expand details of a particular law. The concerned minister will be responsible for drafting the decree for approval by the cabinet. Upon the latter's approval, the Royal Decree will be submitted for endorsement by the ruling monarch. With the king's signature, the Royal Decree is officially proclaimed in the government gazette.

Ministerial Orders: Refer to details that translate the intentions of the law into implementable (working) measures by the concerned ministers. The concerned minister is responsible for presenting the order for approval by the cabinet. Upon the cabinet's approval, the Ministerial Order is then published in the royal gazette.

Provincial Administration Regulations: Are the local bylaws that the Provincial Administration is responsible for drafting by the authorization of the Provincial Administrative Act or other relevant legislation. The local bylaw is enforced in areas falling within the jurisdiction of the Provincial Administration, which excludes Municipal Areas, Sanitary Districts, and any Tambons that are already under the jurisdiction of the Tambon Administration. The provincial governor or members of the provincial council are authorized to draft Provincial Administration Regurations and submit them for approval by the provincial council. With the latter's approval, they are proclaimed at the Provincial Government Office for a period of fifteen days, after which they can be enforced. In cases of urgency, the Act can be enforced as law the day following its proclamation.

Tambon Regulations: Are bylaws drafted by Tambon Administration by the authorization of the Tambon Council and the Tambon Administration Act of 1994 to be enforced in areas falling within their jurisdiction. The administrative committee members are responsible for drafting the bill for approval by the Tambon Administration Council and the district officer. With their approval, it is enforced as a local bylaw. Contents of these bylaws may cover a collection of various duties and specifications of fines of not more than 500 baht for violations.

Notes

I would like to acknowledge the contribution of Dr. Orapan Nabangchang for her comments and contribution to the drafting of this essay and to Mr. Prapant Subsaeng, judge in the Supreme Court, for his assistance in providing me with the information and insight on the problems of land acquisition.

1. Data on December 31, 1998, Department of Local Administration.
2. See Appendix, *infra,* 343–345.
3. The Revolutionary Decrees, the Announcements of the National Reform Committee, and the Announcements of the National Peace Keeping Council are legally equivalent to the Royal Acts.
4. Presently the sanitary district is no longer a form of local organization. Under the constitution of Thailand of 1997, all sanitary districts have been elevated to the status of municipality.
5. Agricultural Statistics of Thailand, Crop Year 1996–1997, Center for Agricultural Information, Office of Agricultural Economics.
6. *Sor. Kor. 1* is a document issued by the district officer to acknowledge that the holder of the document has laid claim on a parcel of land. Literal translation of this document is the "right" to occupy.
7. ALRO stands for the Agricultural Land Reform Office, while 4-01 is a code number of the legal document issued by this agency.
8. The Civil and Commercial Code, section 1306.
9. *Nor. Sor.* are abbreviations of Thai words meaning the written document certifying the right of the holder to use the land. *Nor. Sor. 3* are issued by ground survey. *Nor. Sor. 3 Kor.* and *Nor. Sor. 3 Khor* are issued by the support of aerial photographs.
10. *Nor. Sor. 2* and *Nor. Sor. 2 Kor* are documents certifying that the holder has been granted occupancy rights by public agencies under land allocation programs.
11. 625 rai = 1 square kilometer.
12. A "blind" land parcel is a parcel of land that has no access to road frontage and is locked in by other land parcels.
13. Information in this section is for Immovable Property Acquisition of the Bangkok Metropolitan Area (BMA) and Express Ways Authority of Thailand.
14. Supreme Court Case No. 4175/1198.
15. Supreme Court Case Nos. 1081/1951, 558/1953, 2214/1974.
16. Supreme Court Case No. 8224/1997.
17. Supreme Court Case No. 6/1983.
18. Parts of information from Prapant Subsaeng, judge in the Supreme Court.
19. Supreme Court Case No. 5778/1996.
20. Supreme Court Case No. 8437/1995.

21. Supreme Court Case No. 1697/1993, 6556/1994.

22. The baht is the unit of Thai money; about 40 baht = 1 U.S. $. One square wah = 4 square meters.

23. Supreme Court Case Nos. 3628/1988, 373/1995.

24. Supreme Court Case No. 4274-4275/1997.

25. Supreme Court Case Nos. 4124/1997, 6521/1998.

26. Supreme Court Case No. 2691/1997.

27. Supreme Court Case No. 665/1939.

28. Supreme Court Case No. 1119/1969.

29. Supreme Court Case Nos. 1334/1974, 4809/1990.

30. Supreme Court Case Nos. 1050/1995, 5301/1996, 334-336/1997.

31. Supreme Court Case No. 2107/1997.

32. Supreme Court Case No. 589/1997.

33. Supreme Court Case No. 7712/1997.

34. Supreme Court Case No. 2364/1992.

35. Supreme Court Case No. 4634/1993.

36. Supreme Court Case Nos. 3535/1993, 6185/1994.

37. Supreme Court Case No. 7102/1996.

38. Supreme Court Case No. 1497/1997.

References

Agricultural Land Reform Act, 1975.

Agricultural Statistics of Thailand, Crop Year 1996–1997, Agricultural Statistics No. 18/1998, Center for Agricultural Information, Office of Agricultural Economics.

Airport Authority of Thailand Act, 1979.

Banyat Uyamwong, Bangkok Metropolitan Immovable Property Acquisition Process, training document, 1997.

Constitution of Thailand, 1997.

Electricity Generating Authority of Thailand Act, 1960.

Highways Act, 1992.

Immovable Property Acquisition Act, 1987.

Industrial Estate Authority of Thailand Act, 1979.

National Energy Authority Act, 1953.

Office of the Prime Minister Regulation on Criteria and Procedures for Depositing Compensation Money with the Courts or the Deposit Office or the Government Savings Bank, 1989.

Office of the Prime Minister Regulation on Procurement, 1992.

Prapant Subsaeng, Laws on Immovable Property Acquisition and Compensation, training document, 1994.

Private Irrigation System Act, 1939.

Provincial Electricity Authority Act, 1960.

Public Irrigation System Act, 1942.
Revolutionary Decree No. 290, November 27, 1972.
Royal Decree on the Criteria and the Methods of Calculating Changes in
    Price of Property Left Over from Acquisition, 1994.
State Railway of Thailand Act, 1981.
Supreme Court Case No. 665/1939.
Supreme Court Case No. 1081/1951.
Supreme Court Case No. 558/1953.
Supreme Court Case No. 1119/1969.
Supreme Court Case No. 1334/1974.
Supreme Court Case No. 2214/1974.
Supreme Court Case No. 6/1983.
Supreme Court Case No. 3628/1988.
Supreme Court Case No. 4809/1990.
Supreme Court Case No. 2364/1992.
Supreme Court Case No. 1697/1993.
Supreme Court Case No. 3535/1993.
Supreme Court Case No. 4634/1993.
Supreme Court Case No. 6185/1994.
Supreme Court Case No. 6556/1994.
Supreme Court Case No. 373/1995.
Supreme Court Case No. 1050/1995.
Supreme Court Case No. 8437/1995.
Supreme Court Case No. 5301/1996.
Supreme Court Case No. 5778/1996.
Supreme Court Case No. 7102/1996.
Supreme Court Case No. 334-336/1997.
Supreme Court Case No. 589/1997.
Supreme Court Case No. 1497/1997.
Supreme Court Case No. 2107/1997.
Supreme Court Case No. 2691/1997.
Supreme Court Case No. 4124/1997.
Supreme Court Case No. 4274-4275/1997.
Supreme Court Case No. 7712/1997.
Supreme Court Case No. 8224/1997.
Supreme Court Case No. 6521/1998.
Town Planning Act, 1975.

Chapter 11

The Compulsory Purchase
of Private Land in the United States

David L. Callies

The use of compulsory purchase of private land is common throughout national, state, and local government jurisdictions in the United States. The use of compulsory purchase is for a variety of public purposes, including providing facilities such as streets and highways, wastewater treatment plants, water distribution systems, schools, and national, state, and local parks, all joint development projects with the private sector, all in part at public cost. What follows is an overview of land use regulations generally in the United States, in order to provide a context or framework for compulsory purchase law and practice in the United States.

Overview of Land Use Controls

THE FEDERAL NATURE OF GOVERNMENT IN THE UNITED STATES AND THE BASIS FOR LAND USE CONTROLS

The national government of the United States is characterized principally by its federal constitutional nature. The fifty states have all the power not granted to the federal government in the federal constitution of 1787.[1] It is this fragmented governmental responsibility that is one of the principal characteristics of the American system of land use control. The regulation of land use is regarded as an exercise of the police power to protect the health, safety, and welfare of the people. Since the exercise

Benjamin A. Kudo Professor of Law, The William S. Richardson School of Law, The University of Hawai'i at Mānoa.

of the police power is one of the powers reserved to state government in the federal constitution, land use controls also remain largely a prerogative of the state, rather than federal government. The states, in turn, have delegated by statute most of that power to their local governments (cities, counties, villages, towns), although several states have recently reserved some broad controls for the state or region.[2] By contrast, the power of eminent domain or compulsory purchase is regarded as an inherent power of government at all three levels: federal, state, and local.

LOCAL CONTROLS

Zoning

Zoning is the most effective and prevalent of local government land use controls. The power to zone is delegated from the state—the repository of police power—to units of local government through a zoning enabling statute. That statute is usually roughly based upon a model Standard Zoning Enabling Act drafted and circulated in 1923 by the U.S. Department of Commerce. Such statutes *permit* (but do not *require*) local governments to divide the land area in their jurisdiction into districts or zones, and to list permitted uses, their permitted height and density ("bulk" regulation), and conditional uses in each. The map upon which the districts are drawn is called the "zoning map," and the lists of uses, bulk regulations, definitions, and so forth, are collectively called the "text." Also in the text are administrative regulations setting forth how the zoning ordinance restrictions on a particular piece of property may be changed. There is also usually a section in the text dealing with uses that were permitted at some past date, but now fail to conform to the existing land use regulations for the district, called collectively "nonconformities."

Subdivision Controls

Subdivision Process

The regulation of land and the dedication of public improvements through the local subdivision process is a relatively modern local land use control technique. A landowner presents properly zoned land to a local government for "development approval" through a series of plans or plats: scaled drawings of the parcel showing the divisions or lots into which it has been divided. Generally there are three such plats:

1. a "sketch" plat showing generally where the land is located and what kind of development is generally proposed;

2. a detailed "preliminary plat" showing the number of lots or divisions, street setbacks, location and width, utilities, and so forth, to be approved by a local government after public hearing; and
3. a more detailed "final" plat, for recording upon local government final approval.

Aside from the above process of plat approval, subdivision ordinances require landowner compliance with so-called design standards: width and composition of streets and sidewalks, perimeter linkage, uniformity of building setbacks, and the like. Local governments approve subdivisions upon the condition that owner-developers also dedicate land for, and construct or help pay the costs of constructing, streets, sewers, water mains, sidewalks, schools, and other public facilities.[3]

Impact Fees

Construction of public facilities (and dedication of land for them) within proposed developments have recently been eclipsed by impact fees for public facilities extrinsic to the development. Land developments often generate a need for off-site improvements and facilities, such as wastewater treatment plants. Typically, an impact fee is levied on a development to pay for public facilities the need for which is generated, at least in part, by that development.[4] In assessing the validity of such fees and other off-site exactions, courts usually address the relationship between the development upon which the fee was levied and the amount and use planned for the fee, requiring that the fee (or land dedication) be rationally and proportionally connected to the proposed development. In other words, the particular development must create a "need," to which the amount of the exaction bears some roughly proportional relationship. Also, the local government must demonstrate that the fees levied will actually be used for the purpose collected, by proper "earmarking" and timely expenditure of the funds.[5]

Building Codes

The building code refers generally to the body of rules prescribing the "materials, minimum requirements, and methods" to be used in the construction, rehabilitation, maintenance, repair, and demolition of buildings. It is nearly always applied prospectively, in contrast to a housing code, which also deals with structural and building matters. The coverage of a basic building code embraces many matters, including minimum standards for light and ventilation; means of egress; structural and foundation loads and stresses; the use of various types of materials; fire safety; electric wiring and equipment; elevator, dumbwaiter, and conveyor equipment; plumbing, drainage, and gas piping; heating, ventilating, cooling, and refrigeration systems; signs and outdoor display structures; and energy conservation. In addition, there are specialized codes that provide more detailed standards with respect to plumbing; fire prevention; electricity; air conditioning, refrigeration and mechanical ventilation systems; or the demolition of buildings. The power to prescribe building code regulations arises out of either state enabling legislation or a general grant of powers. As a practical matter, however, the content of most local building codes is derived from the adoption by reference of one of four model building codes developed by building trade organizations.

Housing Codes

A housing code is an application of state police power put into effect by a local ordinance setting the minimum standards for safety, health, and welfare of the occupants. Housing codes are unique in the panoply of local land use regulations in that they are applied to *existing* structures and so can be said to apply "retroactively," which application has rarely troubled courts in upholding them against claims of taking property without compensation.

STATE LAND USE CONTROLS

While traditional zoning and other local land regulatory ordinances continue to be the primary method of controlling the use of land, a "quiet revolution" in land use controls in the 1960s and 1970s moved much of the broad policy decision making to the states in many developing regions.[6] Essentially, the states took back some of the powers delegated to their local governments by zoning and planning enabling legislation to exercise a variety of state and regional land use controls themselves.

There are several such systems of state control of land today. Among the most prominent—largely due to their unique but disparate features, the frequent challenges thereto, and their considerable impact on growing populations—are those from Hawaii, Florida, Vermont, and Oregon. They are tied together by several common threads, among the most common of which is reliance on statewide planning of some sort as an initial or later addition to the basis for exercising land use controls. All systems supersede, in some fashion, the local land use regulatory function. All attempt to preserve certain identified critical natural resources, and to control developments with regional impact.[7]

REGIONAL LAND USE CONTROLS

Regional—as opposed to statewide—land use controls, which partially or entirely supersede local zoning and other land use controls, spring from the same source of power, and for many of the same reasons. State governments in the 1960s took back and exercised some of the police power over land that had been delegated to local governments in order to solve regional land use and management problems. However, regional controls tended to focus on a particular resource—a bay, a park, a wetland—rather than on statewide conservation and development problems. As in the statewide programs, the impetus for such controls often came from a real or perceived threat to a regional resource, often of crisis proportions. Among the more prominent examples: the Hackensack Meadowlands Development Commission, Adirondack Park Agency, and the New Jersey Pinelands.[8]

FEDERAL LAWS AFFECTING THE USE OF LAND

The "federalization" of some limited land use controls commenced with the panoply of national environmental and resource protection laws passed by Congress in the late 1960s and early 1970s. Broadly covering environmental impact analysis, clean air, clean water, coastal zone, and flood hazard protection, most of the laws required or encouraged a broad range of local plan and ordinance response, some of which are contained in preceding sections. The basis for this federal intrusion into state and local government affairs is not police power, which is the foundation of state and land use control, but rather spending power: with state acceptance of federal funds comes a host of federal conditions and rules, many related to environmental protection. Most experts agree there is no such thing as an inherent federal police power, when it comes to the use of land, upon which to base a federal system of land use control.[9]

Federal Clean Air Act
The primary purpose of the Clean Air Act is "to protect and enhance the quality of the nation's air resources so as to promote the public health and welfare, and the productive capacity of its population."[10] The federal government sets standards and identifies the critical air pollutants, in

order to meet clean air quality standards. However, it is up to the states—and ultimately local government—to devise a plan to meet the standards and therefore to maintain air quality. The principal vehicle for so doing is the State Implementation Plan, or SIP. The SIP, once approved, is designed to permit the meeting of primary ambient air quality standards as expeditiously as possible.

SIP requirements of attainment and maintenance of national air quality standards have a major impact on the location and direction of urban growth in such areas. The requirement of preventing significant deterioration has a significant impact on new development and growth in areas where air quality is still relatively good. Thus, these requirements amount to control of development and urban growth in both "clean" and "polluted" areas.

Federal Clean Water Act

The Clean Water Act has as its principal purpose the cleaning and maintenance of the nation's waters. It attacks the problem broadly by means of so-called structural and nonstructural techniques. The structural techniques pertain to the financing and construction of wastewater treatment plants and ancillary facilities. Nonstructural techniques pertain primarily to regulatory mechanisms, such as planning and land use controls. The purpose of both is to eliminate the discharge of pollutants into the nation's waterways.[11]

While the structural solutions have been vastly better funded, emphasis in the late 1970s moved to that which was *intended* to precede the construction of wastewater treatment facilities: the areawide waste treatment management, or "208" plans. The purpose of the 208 planning process is to abate water pollution by the management of water quality and land use in entire metropolitan regions. The required emphasis on land use controls in the plans is clearly set out in the Act. The 208 plans are required for any area identified by a state's governor as having "substantial water quality control problem . . . as a result of urban-industrial concentrations or other factors."[12] After drawing up the boundaries of such an area, the governor must then designate a single "representative organization including elected officials from local governments," which is "capable of developing effective area-wide waste treatment management plans for such area."[13]

Coastal Zone Management

The Federal Coastal Zone Management Act (CZMA)[14] of 1972 was passed during the heady days of national land use and environmental activism in response to the competing demands on the nation's coastal areas coupled with uneven state and local reaction. Congress discovered that the aforementioned demands (largely due to population growth and development) resulted in the destruction of marine resources, wildlife, open space, and other important ecological, cultural, historic, and aesthetic values. In response to these problems, Congress created a framework for the development and implementation of state-run coastal zone management programs. This framework—guidelines for the development and implementation of land and water use controls—is imposed if, but only if, states choose to accept federal assistance.

Regulations enacted pursuant to the CZMA specifically require the inland boundary of the coastal zone to be sufficiently precise that interested parties can determine whether their activities are subject to the management program, and define what constitutes permissible land and water access in the newly defined coastal zone. Regulations also set out the criteria for determining permissible uses subject to the management program.

Flood Hazard Protection

While several jurisdictions have enacted land use regulatory schemes for the purpose of reducing the loss to life and property resulting from floods, the real impetus for local regulation of flood-prone land came with the intrusion of the federal government in the mid-1970s, via the Federal Disaster Protection Act of 1973.[15] Its purpose is to discourage development— and in particular the building of structures—in flood-prone areas. The Act does so by making federal money available for federally subsidized flood insurance and relocation aid, and offering some procedural and substantive control over federal activities at or near flood-prone areas to those local communities that "choose" to participate in the federal flood management program. The price of that participation is local government enactment or promulgation of local land use development regulations that severely restrict the use of land in areas found to be flood-prone. In essence, these regulations must be designed in accordance with federal regulations promulgated pursuant to the Act, which restricts most structural development in floodplains to that which can be elevated above the highest recorded flood level or wave wash.[16]

Compulsory Purchase (Eminent Domain)

Generally, any unit of government in the United States—federal, state, or local—can use its sovereign powers to take private land use for public use. The same is true for quasi-governmental agencies and public corporations and utilities. The limits placed on the exercise of that power are defined in the statutes that created them.[17] The technical term most often used, "eminent domain," does not imply that a government's right to take such real estate interests is based on a preeminent sovereign title or prerogative;[18] rather, most authorities agree that it is based on the concept that the power is necessary to fulfill sovereign governmental functions in the interests of all the people who the government, as a general purpose government, represents.[19] The power is thus based not on ultimate ownership by the state, but on the exercise of its sovereign powers, vested in the legislature but exercised by the executive branch of the government.[20]

However, to say that eminent domain is a fundamental attribute of sovereignty clashes with the concept of individual rights, particularly those to private property: if government may take property for a public use, then the individual has no guarantee that private property is safe from confiscation. The U.S. solution to this dilemma was to adopt such a guarantee of private property rights in the Fifth Amendment to the United States Constitution, which provides that government shall not take private property except for a public use and upon payment of just compensation.[21] Thus, the U.S. Constitution limits the exercise of compulsory purchase by the federal government (public use and compensation), which is presumed to have such power (although never expressly granted) because it is a sovereign government. There is not much left in the public purpose clause after a series of significant decisions by the United States Supreme Court[22] (although many state courts have held condemnation invalid for lack of a statutory finding of public necessity for the contemplated project). Therefore, most disputes (and often litigation) over the exercise of eminent domain in the United States revolve around the issues of due process and just compensation. The process for compulsory purchase in the United States is typically governed by statute in each of the fifty states.

Compulsory Taking Process in Brief

Hawaii provides a typical example at Chapter 101 of the Hawaii Revised Statutes.[23] The opening section deals with acquisition of excess property, how money from the sale of such property is to be disposed of, and so forth. The Hawaii statute also permits taking lesser estates in land (leasehold, remainder, easement, etc.) than the "fee simple" interest (the largest interest in land that can be privately owned in the United States)[24] as well as the taking of improvements and fixtures on the land.[25] Still other sections grant the power of eminent domain to the unit of local government, the counties.[26] Such local government condemnations must be authorized by a resolution of the government body and published in a daily newspaper. The statute also specifically grants the power of eminent domain to public utilities (regulated corporations organized to provide public transportation and other public services like water and electricity).[27] Public utilities generally exercise such power for the purpose of acquiring rights of way through private property in order to carry out their quasi-public functions, on the theory that private property rights must give way to the public need for such services that the public utility has been organized to provide.

The largest part of the Hawaii statute deals with the method of acquiring private property through judicial action, which remains an important means by which government acquires property by compulsory purchase in the United States. The courts are the principal vehicle for such acquisitions, primarily because they usually determine the "just compensation" that state and federal constitutions require for compulsory takings.

In Hawaii, a non-negotiated condemnation action begins with the filing of a complaint (usually by the state attorney general on behalf of the interested state agency, or by a county on its behalf).[28] All parties who claim any interest in the real property to be condemned are issued a summons.[29] The complaint must state the use that the government proposes to make of the property, and a description of the property together with a map locating and describing it.[30] The circuit court (a court of first impression or trial court) has broad jurisdiction to determine any issue arising in the case, whether or not raised by the parties.[31] Generally the legal procedure is the same as any civil action in circuit court, except as noted below.[32] The government is subject to strict notice requirements to the landowner or owners,[33] and there are broad provisions allowing for additional parties to intervene.[34] Upon motion of the government, the court may put the government in possession of the property sought to be condemned at any time after the service of the summons at the commencement of the condemnation action. Once in possession, the government may "do work" on the property pursuant to the purpose for which it is condemning the property. However, it must deposit with the court an estimate of fair compensation first.[35]

Since compensation is the most important aspect of any condemnation action, much of the Hawaii statute is devoted to its assessment and computation. Generally, property is valued for the purposes of assessing compensation and damages (if any) at the date the summons is served on the property owner. Any subsequent change or improvement is irrelevant for compensation and damage purposes.[36] A lengthy section on assessment of compensation and damages[37] deals with the method of assessing compensation, particularly when only part of a parcel of land is condemned. For example, the statute provides not only for severance damages to the remaining land, but also for a set-off against the award of damages of any benefit or advantage to the landowner by reason of the condemnation and construction of a public facility by government. If the advantage outweighs the damage, then the landowner is entitled to nothing.

The rest of the statute deals with interest, taxes, and appeals. Consistent with the "quick-take" provision noted above, whereby the government can immediately take possession of the property sought to be condemned, the government may move the court for possession pending appeal of the circuit court decision (if any).[38] If the landowner claims (within ten days of summons) that the government is not taking its property for a public use, or that the proposed public use is not superior to the current use to which the land is being put, the landowner is entitled to an immediate trial on that issue alone. The owner may appeal the decision on that issue directly to the state supreme court "and the appeal shall be given precedence in the supreme court."[39]

EXAMPLES OF SPECIFIC POWERS OF EMINENT DOMAIN

The Hawaii statute on eminent domain grants the power to condemn to both Hawaii's counties and its public utilities. With scant modification, the counties, the utilities, and the agencies proceed under the procedures described above. In particular, state statutes creating and empowering special purpose state agencies so state in a paragraph reciting their power to exercise eminent domain:

1. The Hawaii Housing Authority

    The authority may acquire any real property, including fixtures and improvements, or interests therein, by the exercise of the power of eminent domain, which it deems necessary by the adoption of the resolution declaring that the acquisition of the property described therein is in the public interest and necessary for public use.[40]

2. The Airports Division of the Department of Transportation

. . . [T]he department may acquire property, real or personal, or any interest therein. . . . The department may acquire the rights and interests in airports owned or controlled by others, for the purpose of meeting a civilian need which is within the scope of its functions, even though it does not have the exclusive control and operation of such airports. The department may also acquire excess federal lands as permitted by federal law.[41]

3. The Hawaii Community Development Authority

The purpose of this chapter is to establish such a mechanism in the Hawaii community development authority . . . which shall determine community development programs and cooperate with private enterprise and the various components of federal, state, and county government in bringing plans to fruition.[42]

4. The Housing Finance & Development Authority

The corporation may acquire, by eminent domain, exchange or negotiation, land or property required within the foreseeable future for the purposes of this chapter. Whenever land within a completed or substantially complete and habitable dwelling or dwellings thereon is acquired by exchange or negotiation, the exchange value or purchase price for each such dwelling, including land, shall not exceed its appraised value.[43]

5. The Convention Center Authority

Upon the authority determining that a developer, acting in good faith, is unable to develop the convention center facility in cooperation with the holders of any interest in property in the convention center district, and upon making a finding that the acquisition of such property is necessary for its use for the purposes of this chapter, may acquire the property by condemnation pursuant to chapter 101, notwithstanding any contract to the contrary; provided, however, that the valuation of any such property acquired shall be done without regard to any increase or decrease in value of the property resulting from the application of this chapter.[44]

As is apparent from the language in these eminent domain paragraphs, the key is not so much the process, but the public purpose for which the state created each agency. That purpose is the principal limit upon the power of each agency to exercise eminent domain.

Public Utilities and Compulsory Land Acquisition

As briefly noted above, the power of eminent domain may be delegated to a public service corporation, or public utility, to enable it to acquire land for telecommunications, or for generating or transmitting light, gas, electricity, or other resource. A public utility is a company or corporation organized under the authority of a state to serve the public by supplying the people of a geographic district with services or commodities that, because of their nature, location, or manner of production and distribution, can be best produced and distributed by some organized form of enterprise operating under state control. The public utility then may acquire such private property as needed, subject to the procedural requirements of the state eminent domain statute. A local government may also acquire an existing public utility by eminent domain in order to operate the utility itself. The compensation and valuation rules for acquiring public utilities vary from the condemnation of other types of property.

Since public utilities are essentially private corporations granted special privileges (often the right to be free from competition in providing their service to a specific area of certification, and guaranteed minimum profit) and powers (compulsory purchase) on the ground of public convenience and necessity, state statutes carefully and precisely enumerate the powers, privileges, and their limitations. Otherwise, the exercise of compulsory purchase powers is similar to that carried out by general purpose governments and their agencies for public purposes and facilities. An exception is the "quick-take" procedure whereby a public utility is quickly vested with the right to occupy private property in order to avoid costly delay of a public project designed to provide a public service, which delay is therefore deemed to be contrary to the public interest.

Quick Takes

Under quick-take provisions, a condemning authority is permitted to take immediate possession and use of the property being condemned, thus avoiding project delays and the burden of interest payments. The process varies significantly from statutory compulsory purchase procedures. The condemnor is generally required to either pay a deposit to the property owner or deposit a payment or security with the court as a condition for possession. The deposit is not determinative of the final award, which is decided later, after the condemnor takes possession. The procedure also varies by state: in Arizona, the condemnor may apply for immediate possession, upon a deposit made or cash bond worth double the appraisal amount, including severance and direct damages; in New York, the condemnor must make a condemnation payment to the property owner or deposit such payment with the court prior to possession.[45] The federal condemnation statute is similar: no owner is required to surrender possession of his or her property unless the federal agency concerned pays a deposit with the court of no less than the property's fair market value. Additionally, after deposit is paid, title vests in the government; however, government does not obtain actual possession until the government obtains a judgment ordering surrender of the property.[46]

One question that frequently arises is who holds the interim right to service the areas at issue in the quick-take process.[47] In a recent Minnesota case, the court held that although general eminent domain process would allow the existing assigned service utility to continue to provide service unless it is shown to be "not in the public interest," in quick-take proceedings, the condemnor immediately obtains the right to service the newly condemned service area.

FEDERAL PRACTICE

There is a distinction between the process of compulsory purchase when exercised by agencies of the federal government (or a federally funded project) and agencies of the state government (including public utilities). Since 1971, land acquisition for most federal projects and programs is subject to the Uniform Relocation Assistance and Real Property Acquisition Policies Act of 1970.[48] The Act is designed to provide for fair and equitable treatment of persons whose property will be acquired or who will be displaced due to projects financed with federal funds. Since it covers many state and local government projects as well (because federal funds are often used to pay compensation to the landowner for the property interest taken for the government project), its negotiation provisions are illustrative of the place of negotiation in the compulsory purchase process.

Negotiation

Generally, federal (or federal aid) condemning agencies attempt to reach amicable agreements with a landowner whose land or interest in land the agency needs for a public project. The negotiation process starts with an appraisal of the value of the interest in property (easement, fee simple, part-parcel) to be acquired. Of course, before taking this step, the government agency will have developed a plan for the project and determined in advance what interests in private property the agency will need in order to accomplish its public purpose.

The appraiser will generally contact the property owner in order to inspect the property to be acquired. It is the appraiser's responsibility to determine the value of the property for purposes of acquisition. The property owner (and/or the owner's designated representative) is usually invited to accompany the appraiser as the inspection is made. The owner usually describes features the owner feels are unusual, and discloses whether there are tenants, other owners, or items of real or personal property belonging to other than the owner. The appraiser will, during the inspection, note the physical characteristics of the property, and review sales of comparable nearby property and any other elements that affect the value of the property. The appraiser cannot consider the effect of the contemplated public project on that value, however.

Based on the report of the appraiser, the condemning agency will determine the value of the property after a review appraiser examines the initial appraisal report to ensure all applicable standards are met. Among the factors in determining value are: the value of the land supported by confirmed sales of vacant comparable land; comparable sales of similar property; value estimated by a "cost approach" (replacement cost less deterioration, obsolescence); and value estimated by income approach (gross rent or income, vacancy or credit losses, remaining economic life, and capitalization rate). If there are tenants on the property, then the condemning agency must make arrangements with such tenants to acquire their interests in the property or their removal (if regarded as personal property under state law).

The agency then delivers a written offer of compensation to the landowner (by mail or in person) for the purchase of the property. The offer will typically contain the amount offered in just compensation; description and location of the property and the interest to be acquired; and identification of buildings and other improvements considered to be part of the interest in the property to be acquired. The landowner then has a "reasonable time" to consider the written offer, ask questions, request clarifications, and seek inclusion of relevant material that the owner feels has been omitted.

Acquisitions

If the owner reaches an agreement with the agency at this point, the owner signs a deed or similar instrument affirming that the owner and agency are agreed on the acquisition and sale of the subject property, the award of compensation, and any other conditions agreed upon (removal of personal property, time for vacating the premises, and so forth). If the agency and landowner cannot reach a settlement, then the agency will initiate condemnation proceedings in a court of law, as discussed below. In either event, the agency may not take possession of the property until it has paid the landowner the agreed compensation or deposited with a court an amount for the landowner's benefit at least equal to the agency's approved appraisal of the fair market value of the property, and given all occupants of the property at least ninety days' notice of the agency's intent to take possession and exclude occupants.

Procedural Rights Vested in Owner and Affected Parties

The principal rights held by an owner of real property about to be acquired by a governmental agency under the power of compulsory purchase are: compensation and due process. Both derive from the U.S. Constitution's Fifth and Fourteenth Amendments. Beyond these rights are rights, mainly procedural, conferred by statutes under which government agencies actually go about acquiring property by compulsory purchase. Once a compulsory purchase proceeding is contested, then the administrative process that attaches to such proceedings is usually guaranteed by both state and federal constitution and by state administrative procedure statutes. Among the procedural rights commonly held by owners of real property about to be condemned by a government agency are:

1. The right to notice. Actual notice is usually required with respect to affected landowners (those whose interest in property are being taken or damaged by the governmental action). Property owners with more generalized interests in the condemnation are often held to be entitled to some notice, usually by publication.[49]
2. Right to a hearing. If the matter is contested, then the right of the landowner is usually to a contested case hearing. This includes the right to call and cross-examine witnesses and to present other evidence. Intervention in such hearings to do the same things depends on the degree of interest in the proceedings that a potential intervener can show. The hearing may be before a court rather than an agency tribunal, depending upon the state statutory language setting out compulsory purchase procedures. From a constitutional

perspective, it is irrelevant what body actually provides the due process: court or agency.[50]

Thus, for example, the Santa Cruz Redevelopment Agency in California condemned an easement for public parking over a private parking area after negotiations with the landowner failed. The Agency had first given notice to the landowner, then held a hearing, then adopted a resolution of public necessity, then filed a complaint in eminent domain in court, all within a six-week period. The right to take was not decided by the trial court until two years later, however, only to be overturned by the California Court of Appeals three years later because the landowner's statutory right to raise certain objections at the trial had been violated.[51] In the course of its opinion, the court set out the statutory rights of objection that all landowners in California have in compulsory purchase cases.[52]

1. The government agency is not authorized by statute to exercise the power of eminent domain for the purpose stated in the complaint;
2. The state purpose is not a public use;
3. The agency does not intend to devote the property described in the complaint to the stated purpose;
4. There is no reasonable probability that the agency will devote the described property to the stated purpose within seven years, or within ten years where the property is taken pursuant to the Federal Highway Act of 1973, or such longer period as is reasonable;
5. The described property is not subject to the power of eminent domain for the stated purpose;
6. The described property is sought to be acquired pursuant to a statutory section on excess condemnation;
7. The described property is sought to be acquired pursuant to condemnation for a more necessary public use, but the defendant property owner has the right to continue the public use to which the property is appropriated, as a joint use; or
8. Any other ground provided by law.

PROBLEMS BETWEEN LANDOWNERS AND OFFICIALS IN THE ACQUISITION PROCESS

There are several problems that arise in the process of acquisition between landowners and condemning agency officials:

Condemnation of Blight

Sometimes a public project is planned in advance, so that land scheduled to be acquired actually loses value or becomes unmarketable. Some courts have determined that compensation must be paid for such blight as if the agency had acquired an option to purchase the property, in addition to the just compensation owed based on the pre-blight value of the property. Other courts have determined that such plans and their consequences are the price of planning in a free society.

Excess Condemnation

While public use and public purpose have largely been left to legislative determination without court interference, particularly following the U.S. Supreme Court's decision in *Hawaii Housing Authority v. Midkiff*,[53] nevertheless, there are some few limits on the quantum or extent of the interest in real property that a public agency may condemn for the purpose of constructing a public facility or other project. *City of Cincinnati v. Vester*[54] is frequently cited for the proposition that such supplemental condemnation is illegal. There, the Ohio state constitution specifically permitted not only excess condemnation, but later resale of the excess.[55] Cincinnati condemned three lots in toto, to widen a street, although it only needed a 25-foot strip from two of them. The owners alleged that this taking was not for a public purpose and was, therefore, not only a violation of the due process clause of the federal constitution, but also contrary to the requirement that a compulsory taking be for a public use under the Ohio constitution. The court propounded three theories upon which excess condemnation is generally permitted: the remnant theory, the protection theory, and the recoupment theory.

The court decided that the recoupment theory—the city would be able to dispose of part of the property not needed for street purposes at prices that would enable it to recoup much of the cost of the street construction—was the only ground on which the city had proceeded. After noting that some benefit must flow to the public and that public interest must be so paramount as to require the subject property for the public, the court held the taking (but not the constitutional provision upon which it was based) illegal: "we do not hold that the provision of the state Constitution might not be validly enforced in a proper case, but that as applied by the City in these cases violated the due process clause of the Constitution."[56] It is worth emphasizing that the major portion of the lots here involved were purchased for later resale at a profit rather than for any street-related or transportation-related purposes. The *Vestor* prohibition, then, is not against excess condemnation per se, but only that form of excess or supplemental condemnation, generally based upon either a constitutional or a statutory provision, have been upheld all over the country.

Indeed, there are often good reasons for a public agency to condemn more interests than are strictly needed for a particular public project. Generally called supplemental or excess condemnation,[57] the taking of such interests is likely to be upheld as a valid exercise of the power of eminent domain, provided there is adequate statutory authority and a plan sufficiently indicating the ultimate use of the property.[58] The term "excess condemnation" is not strictly accurate since it infers more property is being taken than can be justified for public use. If this were true, such a taking would be unconstitutional. The courts have dealt with such acquisition under four general headings:

1. *Essential to Operation of Facility.* Supplemental condemnation has been successful upon a showing that the purposes for which the land is acquired are reasonably essential to a successful operation of the facility.[59] "Reasonably essential" uses, which are not usually directly necessary for rapid transit development, for example, may include parking lots, stores, restaurants, hotels or other commercial facilities, or buffer landscaping that may help maintain property values in adjacent areas.

2. *Future Use and Disposition.* A number of cases recognize the validity of supplemental condemnation for future expansion. This approach allows the condemning authority to temporarily utilize the land to produce income, or to sell the land outright should it later prove to be surplus. As in other supplemental condemnation cases, a court must rely on constitutional provisions and statutes that describe in detail the power and duties of the public body involved.

3. *The Protective Theory.* A technique that justifies supplemental condemnation is known as the protective theory. For example, governmental land adjacent to a seaport facility could be sold under restrictions intended to preserve the facility, or at least to reduce any physical blight caused by such a facility.

4. *Remnant Theory.* Taking only the minimum land directly needed for the public project may leave many fragments of lots, the shape of which may render them separately valueless. A city or other condemning authority may wish to pay for the whole although it strictly needs only a part.[60] The basic advantage of such acquisitions is that the additional property

rights acquired can either be parceled together and sold for private development, used to enhance the attractiveness (and value) of surrounding areas, or, in the case of air rights, used for ancillary development such as hotel-office space located above the public facility.

Government Abandonment of Public Use

When the government agency no longer needs or uses the land or public facility that justified the compulsory purchase, there are strong policy reasons for it to return the land to private use. This problem or issue is generally dealt with by legislation. For example, when a state department of transportation decides to sell land it had acquired for an abandoned highway project, it first must offer to sell the land to the abutting landowner at a fair market price under New York highway statutes, even though the department could not be ordered to dispose of the property just because it is not being used for a highway.[61]

Severance, Partial Takings, and Compensation

When only part of a land parcel is taken by compulsory purchase, or when a project cuts off access to private property, problems arise. Generally, there is no compensation for loss of access to private property unless some part of that property is taken, in which case the loss of access is considered in the award of compensation. Much depends on the extent of the access lost, however. For example, a California court denied severance damages when government taking of a strip of landowner's land for a transportation project eliminated the owner's access to the southbound lanes of the abutting street, but left northbound access intact.[62] On the other hand, requiring a landowner to make lengthy and circuitous detours to his or her property because of the elevating of a highway sufficiently impairs access to require severance damages in Florida.[63]

Special Problems on Compensation for the Taking of Land

The valuation of real property for eminent domain purposes is often the most time-consuming and arcane part of condemning private property for public use. Entire treatise volumes deal with the subject in onerous detail.[64] As noted above, it is unconstitutional in the United States to take property by compulsory purchase without providing for compensation.

Who Is Entitled to Compensation

When a single entity holds title to real property in fee simple, there is little problem in ascertaining who is entitled to compensation. However, when property is owned severally or jointly, the co-owners or co-tenants are generally entitled to compensation proportionate to their shares or interests. The same is true with respect to lessors and lessees, mortgages and other lienholders and mortgagers, holders of licenses or easement, and the owner of the servient or dominant estate condemned. Difficult problems of apportioning an award can arise when the co-ownership is successive, and when condemned property is held by a tenant for life, with the estate to pass eventually to remaindermen or reversioners, and it becomes more complicated still if some of these future interests are contingent. Much depends upon the life expectancy of the life tenant, for example.

Similar problems of apportionment of compensation arise when leased property is condemned. The time remaining in the tenancy is often critical. Land leased for a long term (ninety-nine years) and condemned early in the term will, other things being equal, result in much of the award going to the tenant in possession rather than the landlord, whose right to the reversion is temporarily distant. However, one court has held that a subtenant, rather than a tenant, shares the condemnation award with the landlord when it is the subtenant who is in possession of the premises, and the tenant has removed all its fixtures prior to condemnation.[65]

More complicated still is apportioning an award of compensation between mortgager/borrower and mortgagee/lender on mortgaged property. Sometimes the apportionment will depend upon whether the state in which the condemnation takes place is a "lien" state (mortgagee has only a lien on the property against which the loan is made) or a "title" state (mortgagee holds title to the property), with the latter having greater rights to condemnation award proceeds in order to satisfy the debt of the mortgagor before the mortgagor/borrower is entitled to any part of the award. There is the position of other creditors of the borrower/landowner, who are also partially secured on (have liens on) the land condemned.

Lastly, there is the problem of apportioning such awards among landowners and those who have interests in the same land by way of easements, covenants running with the land, or licenses. While licensees rarely participate in such awards, most jurisdictions allow those whose rights of passage or use over the condemned land are terminated by the condemnation (and usually such rights are extinguished by the exercise of eminent domain) to share in the award to the owner of the land condemned.[66] The same is generally true with respect to options to purchase, which are not regarded as property rights enabling the holder to share in the condemnation award.[67] However, under appropriate circumstances, courts have held that a permit may be property for the purpose of sharing in a condemnation award, particularly one that has been "finally" granted, although not yet acted upon.[68]

Measure of Damages

Generally, the measure of damages in a compensation award is full compensation for the loss to the owner of the property taken, not the benefit or value to the government. When government takes only part of the land owned by a landowner, the value of the land taken and the decrease in value of the remaining land are included in the damage award. Particular problems arise when government takes only an interest in land, rather than a fee simple interest in a part of the property. For example, a highway authority may condemn only an easement for road purposes, leaving ownership of all other interests in the landowner. Government may also condemn a leasehold, leaving the owner with the reversion. Often excluded are such things as business goodwill, loss of future business, frustration of plans, and costs of removing buildings or fixtures, unless specifically provided for by statute.[69]

Damage to Business

As noted in the previous section, damage to a business caused by decreased access is generally not compensable unless the highway agency has condemned a part of the land on which the business damage occurs. Thus, a Louisiana court awarded the owner of a supermarket $5 million for the taking of a narrow strip from a 5-acre parcel, because the highway department also substituted highway access for frontage road access, causing a 50 percent drop in the supermarket's business.[70]

Valuation

The basis of valuing property interests taken by eminent domain for purposes of computing just compensation invariably begins with market value, often defined as fair cash value or fair market value. Courts generally consider three approaches to arrive at market value: market data or comparable sales, cost of construction or reproduction less depreciation, or capitalization of income. Which method is used and what factors to consider are generally within the discretion of the court.[71]

Highest and Best Use

The highest and best use of the property is often the measure of damages for compensation, and determining that use can be complex and time-consuming. Among the factors considered by the court are probability of a change in zoning[72] and geographical features of the property.[73]

Conclusion

Compulsory purchase and the regulation of land use in the United States is inextricably linked with the U.S. Constitution, in particular its Fifth Amendment, which governs the taking of property. Government may neither purchase nor regulate so as to take all economically beneficial use without paying compensation. State and federal statutes govern the process by which government may take land by compulsory purchase, but it is the courts that decide when a regulation goes "too far" and results in a taking of land by regulation. Statutes governing the physical taking of property require a variety of notices and hearings for the landowner, together with a judicial establishment of compensation if the government and landowner are unable to agree on what is "just." However, the Fifth Amendment's requirement that private property be taken only for public use has become something of a sham, particularly in federal court, where any colorable legislative declaration of public purpose will serve, so long as it is not an "impossibility," even if that purpose is ultimately never realized. The result is an abuse of the power of eminent domain at many levels of government, except only in a few states that apply a more strict public use test. The landowner has more protection from regulatory takings, so that if a land use control or plan has the effect of leaving the landowner without economically beneficial use, the property is considered taken, and government must either pay just compensation or lift the offending regulation. The United States is unique in this aspect of planning and takings law, which represents the care that the founders of the Republic took in 1789 to constitutionally protect its citizens from a potentially overbearing government like the one that its armies had so recently fought a revolutionary war to overthrow.

Notes

1. See, e.g., *Hunter v. City of Pittsburgh*, 207 U.S. 161 (1907).
2. See Bosselman and Callies, *The Quiet Revolution in Land Use Control* (Washington, D.C.: U.S. Government Printing Office, 1971).
3. Kelly, *Managing Community Growth: Policies, Techniques and Impacts* (Westport, Conn.: Praeger, 1993), 16–17.
4. Callies, "Impact Fees, Exactions and Paying for Growth in Hawaii,"

U. Haw. L. Rev. 11 (1989): 295; Blaesser and Kentopp, "Impact Fees: The Second Generation," *Wash. J. of Urb. & Contemp. L.* 38 (1990): 55; Juergensmeyer, *Funding Infrastructure: Paying the Costs of Growth Through Impact Fees and Other Land Regulation Charges,* Lincoln Institute of Land Policy Monograph 85-5, February 1985.

5. Bosselman and Stroud, "Mandatory Tithes: The Legality of Land Development Linkage," 9 *Nova L.J.* 9 (1985): 381, 397–399.

6. See Bosselman and Callies, *The Quiet Revolution in Land Use Control,* 1971; Healy and Rosenberg, *Land Use and the States* (Baltimore: Johns Hopkins University Press, 1979); Pelham, *State Land Use Planning and Regulation,* 1979; and DeGrove, *Land, Growth and Politics,* 1984.

7. For a general overview, in Japanese, see Callies, *Land Use Controls in the U.S.* (trans. by Makitaro Hotta), (Kyoto: Horitsu Bunku Sha, 1994). See also H.R.S. 205ff. See, for various analyses of the Land Use Law, Callies, *Preserving Paradise: Why Regulations Won't Work* (Honolulu: University of Hawaii Press, 1994); Callies, *Regulating Paradise: Land Use Controls in Hawaii* (Honolulu: University of Hawaii Press, 1984); Bosselman and Callies, *The Quiet Revolution in Land Use Control,* 1971, ch. 1; Mandelker, *Environmental and Land Use Controls Legislation* (New York: Bobbs-Merrill, 1976), ch. VII; Meyers, *Zoning Hawaii* (Washington, D.C.: Conservation Foundation, 1976); Callies, "Land Use Control in an Island State," *Third World Planning Review* 2 (1980); 187; Callies, "Land Use," *Univ. Haw. L. Rev.* 2 (1979): 167; Dinell, "Land Use Zoning in a Developing State," *Third World Planning Review* 2 (1980): 195; Mandelker and Kolis, "Whither Hawaii? Land Use Management in an Island State," *Univ. Haw. L. Rev.* 1 (1979): 48.

Fla. Stat. Ann. section 380.01ff.; see, for more detailed treatment of the ELMS Act, Healy and Rosenberg, *Land Use and the States,* ch. 5 (1979); Finnell, "Saving Paradise: the Florida Environmental Land and Water Management Act of 1972," *Urb. L. Ann.* (1973): 1035; D. O'Connell, "Growth Management in Florida: Will State and Local Governments Get Their Acts Together?," *Fla. Environmental and Urban Issues* 11 (April 1984); and DeGrove, *Land, Growth and Politics* (1984).

Vt. Stat. Ann. Tit. 10, section 6001ff. (Supp. 1977); for a more thorough discussion of the Vermont legislation, see Bosselman and Callies, *The Quiet Revolution in Land Use Control,* 1971, ch. 2; Healy and Rosenberg, *Land Use and the States,* 1979, ch. 3; Mandelker, *Environmental and Land Use Controls Legislation,* 1976, ch. 7; and Daniels and Lapping, "Has Vermont's Land Use Control Program Failed? Evaluating Act 250," *Journal of the American Planning Association* 50 (1984): 502.

Ch. 324 Oregon Laws 1969; see, for detailed analyses of the Oregon system, Knaap and Nelson, *The Regulated Landscape,* 1993; Leonard, *Managing Oregon's Growth: The Politics of Development Planning,* 1983;

Pelham, *State Land Use Planning and Regulation*, 1979; Morgan and Shonk-wiler, "State Land Use Planning in Oregon," *The Urban Lawyer* 11 (1979).

8. For discussions of these systems and the "takings" cases challenging them, see Bosselman and Callies, *The Quiet Revolution in Land Use Control*, 1971; DeGrove, *Land, Growth and Politics*, 1984; and Bosselman, Callies, and Banta, *The Taking Issue* (Washington, D.C.: U.S. Government Printing Office, 1973). See also Ch. 404 of the Laws of 1968, N.J. Stat., C.13:17-1ff.

Article 27, sections 800–810, McKinney's Revised Statutes of New York; "Adirondack State Park Residents Await Development Agency with Mixed Feelings," *New York Times*, August 24, 1971, 33; *The Future of Adirondack Park*, report of the Temporary Study Commission on the Future of the Adirondacks, submitted to the Governor of New York on December 15, 1970, 8–26.

N.J. Stat. Ch. 18A, Pinelands Protection, etc.; see, e.g., Goldshore, "Pinelands Regulation: Past, Present and Future," *N.J.L.J.* 104 (1979): 169; Note, "New Jersey's Pinelands Plan and the Taking Question," *Col. J. Env. L.* 7 (1982): 227.

9. Mandelker, *Environmental and Land Controls Legislation*, 1976, ch. 1; Bosselman, Feurer, and Callies, *EPA Authority Affecting Land Use*, NTIS, 1974.

10. Section 102(b)(1), Clean Air Act.

11. NRDC, *Land Use Control in the United States*, ch. 5; Bosselman, Feurer, and Callies, *EPA Authority Affecting Land Use*, (PB 235 351), (1974), ch. IV; Mandelker, *Environmental and Land Controls Legislation* (1976), 205ff.; Bosselman, Feurer, and Richter (New York: Practicing Law Institute, 1977) *Federal Land Use Regulations* (PLI 1977), 23ff.; Goldfarb, "Water Quality Mangement Planning: The Fate of 208," *Toledo L. Rev.* 9 (1976): 205; Marshall, Comment, "Sewers, Clean Water, and Planned Growth," Yale L. J. 86 (1977): 733; Rogers, *Environmental Law* (1977), ch. IV.

12. Clean Water Act, section 208(a)(1) and (2).

13. Id.

14. 16 U.S.C.A., section 1451ff.; for general description and comments, see, Chassis, "The Coastal Zone Management Act," *J.Am. Plan. Assoc.* 46 (April 1980): 145; Finnell, "Coastal Zone Management: An Introduction," *Am. Bar. Found. Res. J.* (1978): 153; Bosselman et al., *Federal Land Use Regulation*, ch. 5 (New York: Practicing Law Institute, 1977); NRDC, *Land Use Controls in the United States* (New York: The Dial Press, 1975), ch. 6; Mandelker, *Environmental and Land Use Control Legislation*, ch. 6 (1976).

15. 42 U.S.C.A. 4056ff.

16. See Plater, "The Takings Issue in a Natural Setting: Floodlines and the Police Power," *Tex. L. Rev.* 52 (1974): 201; Maloney and Dambly, "The National Flood Insurance Program: A Model Ordinance for Implementation

of Its Land Management Criteria," *Nat. Res. L.J.* 16 (1976): 665; Myers and Rubin, "Complying With the Flood Disaster Protection Act," *Real Estate L.J.* 7 (1978):114; Tierney, "The National Flood Insurance Program: Explanation and Legal Implications," *Urb. Lawyer* 8 (1976): 279; Marcus and Ambrams, "Flood Insurance and Floodplain Zoning as Compatible Components: A Multi-Alternative Approach to Flood Damage Reduction," *Nat. Res. Lawyer* 7 (1974): 581.

17. Dankert, ch. 11, Planning for Condemnation—the Condemnor's Problems, in *Institute on Planning, Zoning and Eminent Domain*, 1989, at section 11.03. See *Albert Hanson Lumber Co. v. U.S.*, 261 U.S. 581, 587 (1923), and *U.S. v. Carmack*, 329 U.S. 230, 241–242 (1946).

18. See Erasmus, *Eminent Domain Jurisprudence*, at 1-2 (ALI-ABA Course of Study, 1993).

19. *West River Bridge Co. v. Dix*, 47 U.S. 507 (1848).

20. 29A Corpus Juris Secundum 2.169.

21. United States Const., Amend. V.

22. *Hawaii Housing Authority v. Midkiff*, 467 U.S. 229 (1984).

23. HRS 101-2.

24. HRS 101-5.

25. HRS 101-13.

26. Ibid.

27. HRS 101-4.

28. HRS 101-15.

29. HRS 101-15.

30. HRS 101-16.

31. HRS 101-10.

32. HRS 101-11.

33. HRS 101-20.

34. HRS 101-21.

35. HRS 101-28.

36. HRS 101-24.

37. HRS 101-23.

38. HRS 202-32.

39. HRS 101-34.

40. HRS, section 356-18.

41. HRS, section 261-4(b).

42. HRS, section 206E-4(9).

43. HRS, section 201E-201(d).

44. HRS, section 206X-7.

45. See Searles et al., *The Law of Eminent Domain in the U.S.A.*, C975 ALI-ABA 333, 351 (1995).

46. Id. See Title III of the Federal Uniform Relocation Assistance and Real Property Acquisition Act of 1970.

47. *City of Rochester v. People's Cooperative Power Ass'n., Inc.,* 505 N.W.2d 621 (1993).

48. See Uniform Relocation Assistance and Real Property Acquisition Policies Act of 1970, URS, 42 U.S.C. section 4604.

49. See *In the Matter of the Decision of the State of South Dakota Water Management Board Approving Water Permit No. 1791-2,* 351 N.W.2d 119, 123 (1984).

50. Id. See also *Weiner v. State of Nebraska Department of Roads,* 137 N.W.2d 852 (1965).

51. *Santa Cruz County Redevelopment Agency v. Izant,* 43 Cal. Rptr. 2d 366 (1995).

52. Id.; see section 1250, 360.

53. 467 U.S. 229 (1984).

54. 33 F.2d 242 (6th Cir. 1929), aff'd on other grounds, 281 U.S. 439 (1930).

55. Id. at 243; Ohio Const. Art. 18, section 10.

56. *Vester,* 33 F.2d at 245.

57. Callies and Duerksen, "Value Capture as a Source of Funds to Finance Public Projects," *Urb. L. Ann.* 8 (1974); and Callies, Roberts, and Freilich, *Cases and Materials on Land Use* (St. Paul, Minn.: The West Group, 3rd ed., 1999).

58. Callies, Williams, and Sharpe, "Value Capture Policy," *Planning* 42 (October 1976): 22; 2A P. Nichols, *The Law of Eminent Domain,* section 7.516 (3rd rev. ed. 1976).

59. See Callies and Duerksen, 77–80.

60. See *Luby v. City of Dallas,* 396 S.W.2d 192 (Tex. Civ. App. 1965).

61. *Strong's Marine Centers, Inc. v. White,* 630 N.Y.S.2d 788 (1995). To the same effect: *Scoqlio v. County of Suffolk,* 651 N.E.2d 1249 (NY 1995).

62. *San Diego Metro. Trans. v. Price,* 44 Cal. Rptr. 2d 705 (1995).

63. *State D.O.T. v. Krieder,* 658 So.2d 548 (1995); see also *Jackson Gear Co. v. Commonwealth,* 657 A.2d 1370 (1995).

64. *Nichols on Eminent Domain,* vol. 4.

65. *DOT v. Western Inv. Co.,* 896 P.2d 3 (Or. App. 1995).

66. 11 McQuillin, *Municipal Corporations,* ch. 32 Eminent Domain, at sections 32.83–32.86.

67. *Pro-Eco v. Board of Comm'rs,* 57 F.3d 375 (1995).

68. *Village Pond Inc. v. Town of Darien,* 56 F.3d 375 (1995).

69. McQuillin, *Municipal Corporations,* sections 32.92–32.92c.

70. *DOT v. Schegemann,* 651 So.2d 1359 (1995).

71. McQuillin, *Municipal Corporations,* sections 32.92–32.92h.

72. *Gasparri v. DOT,* 655 A.2d 268 (1995).

73. *Village of Swanton v. 18.9 Acres,* 49 F.3d 893 (1995).

References

United States Constitution

Fred Bosselman, David Callies, and John Banta, *The Taking Issue*. Washington D.C.: U.S. Government Printing Office, 1973.

David L. Callies, "Regulatory Takings and the Supreme Court: How Perspectives on Property Rights Have Changed from *Penn Central* to *Dolan*, and What State and Federal Courts Are Doing About It," *Stetson L. Rev.* 28 (1999): 523

David L. Callies and J. David Breemer, "The Right to Exclude Others from Private Property: A Fundamental Constitutional Right," *Wash. U. J. Law & Policy* 3 (2000): 39

Steven J. Eagle, *Regulatory Takings*. Lexis Publishing, 2000.

James W. Ely, Jr., *The Guardian of Every Other Right: A Constitutional History of Property Rights*. New York: Oxford University Press, 2nd ed. 1998.

Richard A. Epstein, *Takings: Private Property and the Power of Eminent Domain*. Cambridge, Mass.: Harvard University Press, 1985.

Exactions, Impact Fees and Dedications: Shaping Land-Use Development and Funding Infrastructure in the Dolan *Era,* Robert H. Freilich and David W. Bushek eds., Chicago: ABA, 1995.

William A. Fischel, *Regulatory Takings: Law, Economics, and Politics*. Cambridge, Mass.: Harvard University Press, 1995.

Gideon, Kanner, *Just Compensation*. Calif.: Sherman Oaks (monthly).

Jan Laitos, *The Law of Property Rights Protection*. Gaithersburg: Aspen Law & Business, 1998.

Daniel R. Mandelker, "New Property Rights Under the Taking Clause," *Marq. L. Rev.* 81 (1997): 9

Robert Meltz, Dwight H. Merriam, and Richard M. Frank, *The Takings Issue* Washington, D.C.: Island Press, 1998.

Nichols, *The Law of Eminent Domain* (Kelly, ed.). New York: M. Benden, 1996.

Carol M. Rose, "Property As the Keystone Right?," *Notre Dame L. Rev.* 71 (1996): 329

Takings: Land-Development Conditions and Regulatory Takings after Dolan *and* Lucas, David L. Callies, ed., Chicago: American Bar Association, 1996.

List of Contributors

Zhan Xian Bin is a professor in the School of Law at Tsinghua University. Two of his recent books are *Encyclopedia of GATT and WTO* (1999) and *International Trade and International Taxation* (2000).

David L. Callies is Benjamin A. Kudo Professor of Law at the University of Hawai'i's William S. Richardson School of Law, where he teaches land use, state and local government, and real property. Among his books are (with Gordon Hylton, Daniel Mandelker and Paula Franzese) *Property and the Public Interest* (1999), *Preserving Paradise: Why Regulation Won't Work* (1994), *Regulating Paradise: Land Use Controls In Hawaii* (1984), and (with Robert Freilich and Tom Roberts) *Cases and Materials on Land Use* (3rd ed., 1999). His book, *Land Use Controls in the United States,* was recently published in Kyoto and Shanghai. He is co-editor (with Dan Tarlock) of the annual *Land Use & Environmental Law Review.*

Li-Fu Chen is associate professor, Department of Land Economics, National Chengchi University and a member of the committee on appropriation in Taiwan's Ministry of the Interior. He has published many articles on land use and compulsory purchase.

Anton Cooray is a professor at the City University of Hong Kong. He has published more than fifty books, book chapters, articles, and conference papers. His most recent publications are two monographs, one on town planning and the other on the environment. He is also the editor of the *Asia Pacific Law Review.*

Glenys Godlovitch teaches both law and philosophy at Lincoln University. She is a co-author and contributor to two texts on bioethics, law, and medicine, and is author of a number of journal articles on law and bioethics.

TSUYOSHI KOTAKA is professor of law on the Faculty of Law at Meijo University, where he teaches administrative law, and professor emeritus at Osaka City University. He has written extensively on administrative law and policy. His most significant works include *Law of Just Compensation* (2000), *Textbook on Administrative Law* (2nd ed., 2000), *Introduction to Land Acquisition and Just Compensation* (3rd ed., 2001), and *Commentary to Land Expropriation Law* (1980).

MURRAY RAFF is a senior lecturer in the Law School at Victoria University. His main fields are environmental law and property law. Among his many publications are articles on environmental impact assessment, the history of planning law, and environmental dimensions of the concept of property. His most recent work addresses the national competition policy review of the Environment Protection Act of 1970.

WILLIAM J. M. RICQUIER is a partner in the Singapore law firm of Tan Rajah & Cheah. His published work includes two editions of a book on land law in Singapore (*Land Law* [2nd ed., 1995]) and various articles on real estate law. He is a former senior lecturer in law, National University of Singapore.

EATHIPOL SRISAWALUCK is a faculty member of the Faculty of Law, and deputy director of the environmental and developmental law center, Chulalongkorn University. He specializes in agricultural law, natural law, and environmental law.

WON WOO SUH is professor emeritus at Seoul National University, visiting professor at Kitakyushu University (Japan), and past president of the East Asian Administrative Law Association. He is the author of *Treatise on Modern Administrative Law* (1983), *Seminar on Public Law* (1989), *Handbook on Public Land Law* (1989), and *Treatise on Administrative Law in the Age of Transition* (1996).

GRACE XAVIER teaches land law at the Faculty of Law, University of Malaya. Her areas of specialization are construction law and the law of arbitration. She has published articles on construction law and the law of arbitration, in both international and local journals. She has also published articles on land matters in local journals, in particular, on topics related to compulsory acquisition of land in Malaysia.

Index

Act on the Utilization and Management of the National Territory: Korea, 170, 176–178, 188
aesthetics: acceptance of, as legitimate zoning purpose, 14, 18
agricultural land, 1, 22, 29, 58, 308–309; compensation for, 80–83; loss of, 5, 10; preservation of, 314–317, 318; zone, 177–179, 289, 293

bad faith. *See mala fide*
Basco Enterprises Pte. Ltd. v. Soh Siang Wai, 269–270
bona fide, 213–214
Building Act: Korea, 14, 170, 171–172, 187, 191; restrictions, 179–180
Building Authority: Hong Kong, 11, 102–103
building regulations, 4, 11, 102–103, 147, 172, 239, 289, 313; building codes, 351–352
Buildings Ordinance: Hong Kong, 100, 103, 112 127

calculation of value, 7, 10, 12, 20–21, 43, 182–183, 296, 329–332 (*see also* compensation); appraiser, 362; comparable and similar property, 212–213; damages, 273, 358, 369; guidelines, 150–151; highest and best use, 43, 254, 369–370; low value, 339–340; market value, 43, 126, 131, 154–155, 182–183, 210–211, 273–274, 296, 363,

369; natural disaster, 273–274; potential development, 214–216; recent sales in vicinity, 216; willing vendor, 253–254. *See also bona fide; mala fides*
California, 24–25, 364
Clean Air Act: U.S., 353–354
Clean Water Act: U.S., 354
Coastal Zone Management Act: U.S., 354–355
colonial heritage, 5, 228–232
common law, 4, 6, 27, 28–29, 97–98, 232, 264
compensation, 6–7, 8–9, 14, 17, 22, 24, 76, 358 (*see also* regulatory taking; taking); agriculture, 156; appeal, 12, 16, 22, 44–45, 183–184, 216–217, 297, 333–334; appeal: absence of, 271, 342–343; apportionment, 367–369; based on use, 16; buildings, 85, 86, 120, 294, 296; business, 85, 156, 254, 273, 369; calculation of compensation date, 155, 182, 254; calculation of value (*see* separate entry); collective-owned land, 80, 90–91; cultural loss, 13; dams: hydroelectric power plants, 89–90; delayed payment, 340–341; disputes, 43–44; economic impact, 13; emotional loss, 10, 13, 44, 76; hearings, 254; historical loss, 13; illegal use of, 88; inappropriate, 272–273; infrastructure, 121–122; interested persons' claims, 270–271; land exchange, 16, 253;

379